The Tribal Imagination

THE TRIBAL IMAGINATION

Civilization and the Savage Mind

ROBIN FOX

Harvard University Press

Cambridge, Massachusetts, and London, England   2011

Library of Congress Cataloging-in-Publication Data

Fox, Robin, 1934–
The tribal imagination : civilization and the savage mind / Robin Fox.
   p.   cm.
Includes bibliographical references and index.
ISBN 978-0-674-05901-6 (alk. paper)
1. Tribes—Philosophy.   2. Civilization.   I. Title.
GN492.5.F69   2011
301—dc22   2010034146

To the memory of
Claude Lévi-Strauss
(1908–2009)
and
Ernest Gellner
(1925–1995)

Contents

Prologue: *The Miracle and the Drumbeats*　*1*

1　Time out of Mind
　Tribal Tempo and Civilized Temporality　*16*

2　The Human in Human Rights
　Tribal Needs and Civilized Ideals　*41*

3　The Kindness of Strangers
　Tribalism and the Trials of Democracy　*55*

4　Sects and Evolution
　Tribal Splits and Creedal Schisms　*83*

5　Which Ten Commandments?
　Tribal Taboo and Priestly Morality　*114*

6　Incest and In-Laws
　Tribal Norms and Civilized Narratives　*128*

7　Forbidden Partners
　Ancient Themes in Modern Literature　*165*

8　In the Company of Men
　Tribal Bonds in Warrior Epics　*196*

9   Playing by the Rules
Savage Rhythms and Civilized Rhymes   226

10   Seafood and Civilization
From Tribal to Complex Society   260

11   The Route to Civilization
From Tribal to Political Society   282

12   Open Societies and Closed Minds
Tribalism versus Civilization   319

13   The Old Adam and the Last Man
Taming the Savage Mind   341

Epilogue: *The Dream-Man*   359

Appendix: *Transitional Time at the Edge of Chaos*   363
Notes and References   369
Acknowledgments   405
Index   407

The Tribal Imagination

Prologue

The Miracle and the Drumbeats

THE BEST POETS go straight to the heart of things. C. Day Lewis celebrates the struggle between the demands of the unalterable past and those of the future yet to be created:

> In me two worlds at war
> Trample the patient flesh,
> This lighted ring of sense where clinch
> Heir and ancestor.

In the same spirit of confronting the power of the past on the present in the fabrication of the future, this book examines a fairly simple observation about mind and society. What we observe is that human nature is fundamentally tribal. The rules of chess are finite and simple, yet they can generate an infinite number of complex games. So consideration of this simple observation about human nature can lead us to anything in the human condition from nepotism to neuroanatomy to epic poetry to liberal democracy, and the subject of inquiry becomes coterminous with all human action. In this book we shall sample a few possible subjects, starting with a consideration of our parochial perception of time and how it adversely affects our notions of cause.

The original working title for this book was "The Miracle and the Drumbeats," and I have retained that theme while working on the variations. As with Day Lewis's protagonist, the past is eternally present in the fashioning of the future. The subtitle deliberately echoes Sigmund Freud's *Civilization and Its Discontents* and directly invokes Claude Lévi-Strauss's masterpiece *The Savage Mind*. The tempering of civilization by that savage mind is what this book is about, and the reason it is dedicated to Claude Lévi-Strauss, who taught us all about the Drumbeats and who, at one hundred grand years, sadly left us.

This book is also affectionately dedicated to the memory of Ernest Gellner, mentor, colleague, and friend. One great piece of luck in my life was to have him as a teacher of philosophy in my undergraduate years and thus receive an inoculation against relativism in all its forms. Gellner saved me from the spell of Wittgenstein; no good fairy ever put a kinder gift into an infant's cradle. It was Ernest who gave us the term "the Miracle" for the rise in northwestern Europe of capitalist industrial society and the changed meaning of our world—in *Plough, Sword and Book*. (Full references are in the Notes and References at the end of this book.) Some readers will hear in the title an echo of C. Wright Mills's *The Sociological Imagination*, which is fine.

A little background is in order to put these essays into context, both personal and professional. I have been intrigued by the rise and fall of civilizations since my schoolboy interest in Arnold Toynbee in post–World War II England, when we were desperate to know what went wrong, both with the war during which I grew up and the Great Depression into which I was born. Despite the euphoria of victory, there was an uneasy sense that something about civilization was fundamentally flawed. A secondhand copy of the abridged edition of *A Study of History* was the most thumbed and annotated tome in the small collection that my very small allowance permitted. This was augmented by Edward Gibbon's *Decline and Fall of the Roman Empire* (school library) and H. G. Wells's *The Outline of History* (a gift from my mother), and the game was afoot. What was civilization? Was its appearance inevitable? How had it arisen from the primitive tribal condition, and why did it seem so vulnerable and so inevitably to fail? Was civilization indeed an advanced stage that left the tribal behind, or was the tribal always with us in some form, beckoning us back? How far from the tribal state could we stray without going adrift and foundering? For Toynbee the threatening tribes on the fringes of civilization (the "external proletariat") were never so dangerous as the "failure of will" inside civilization itself.

Well-stocked public and college libraries sent me to Schopenhauer and Nietzsche, to Hegel and Marx (and more interestingly, Engels), to Schweitzer, Sartre, Freud, and Spengler, and produced a lot of information and even more puzzlement. This was all something of a strain for a young fellow whose main interests were politics, rugby, girls, and music—more or less in that order. Serious injuries took me out of sports, and opened a window of time for the pursuit of ideas. Had it not been for that you might be reading the memoirs of a sporting cabinet minister. Who knows? I was immensely fortunate to have found a sympathetic degree course in sociology at the London School of Economics in the early 1950s. We were encouraged to read the philosophers of history even though the prevailing empiricism did not hold their methods in high regard. I had to deal directly with Karl Popper and his criticisms of historicism. I was smitten with Popper and took his point, but still thought the questions could be asked in a way that was subject to falsification. Popper himself, as we shall see in Chapter 12, asked them in his own way, which became my way. My Marxist fellow-students impressed me with their diagnosis of our ills, but their solution I found repulsive.

Through comparative sociology I was led to Max Weber and Herbert Spencer, to Émile Durkheim and the developmental anthropologists, particularly E. B. Tylor and James Frazer. I was in fact specializing in social anthropology, but found to my disappointment that in the form of functionalism it had not only abandoned the questions that drew me to the study of the tribes, but it positively banned them. There was no point, I was told, in dealing with known error, however interesting it might be. So Freud and Jung were out too.

At Harvard in the late 1950s I found the questions still alive among the Americans (Sorokin, Kroeber, Steward, White). Freud was front and center, but mostly the clinical Freud, not the philosopher of history. In any case I got skillfully sidetracked to the Pueblos of the Southwest and sociocultural anthropology, and, to be fair, it has made me a decent living. But the questions still nagged. As I watched anthropology drift further and further away from them, I finally, in the London of the 1960s, discovered Darwin and the relevance of Darwinism to the questions. If nothing by Darwin is cited directly in this book, it is because everything in it is saturated with the Darwinian insight. It was meeting John Bowlby and Lionel Tiger that gave me the nudge that turned into a push that became a vocation. (See my *Participant Observer* for details.) Anthropologists, embarrassed by the laissez-faire capitalist propaganda of Social Darwinism (so-called) and by the ugly use of Darwinism in Germany and among advocates of racism generally, scooted in the other (ideologically safer) direction, energetically disavowing their own heritage and their purpose and status as a science.

But my curiosity was still there with Toynbee and Spengler and Spencer and Morgan, with Freud and Popper and all those for whom the question of the origin, nature, and viability of civilization was an issue that could not be avoided. I found through the amazing upsurge of developments in social biology and evolutionary science, combined with comparative ethnography (anthropology's precious archive of human social behavior in preliterate societies) a route back to the question of civilization and the savage mind. I have been exploring it ever since. What we have in this book, then, are a few more explorations in that same direction.

The problems of mind and society dealt with here are looked at from a broad point of view that is held in general, but not without a lot of dispute over details, by those of the Darwinian (or neo-Darwinian) persuasion. It has come to be known as the "novel environment hypothesis" (NEH). Organisms evolve adaptations to a particular environment. So what happens when that environment suddenly (in evolutionary terms) changes? Eventually the organisms either will evolve new adaptations or will die out. In the meantime they struggle to make the old adaptations work in the new environment for which they were not designed. What is hypothesized, then, by the NEH is that a lot of the behavior of a species can be understood as a result of the struggle between past adaptations and novel environments.

This position also embraces the idea of the "environment of evolutionary adaptedness" (EEA) to describe, in the case of *Homo sapiens,* the Paleolithic (the Old Stone Age): the period in which were formed the major adaptations that define us as a species. This period—geologically the Pleistocene—was not at all a fixed physical environment but one of extremes of "climate change" (that is what climate does—it changes), varying from extensive glaciation to intensive drought and everything in between. We are what Robert Ardrey called "the bad weather animal" *(African Genesis).* But the social environment was that of small bands of hunter-gatherers and at best small tribes, spread out over the landscape, coping with the bad weather and adapting physically, mentally, emotionally, and socially to the ever-changing conditions.

John Bowlby, the Darwinian psychoanalyst, originated the concept of the EEA in his *Attachment and Loss* (1969). While the details have been much debated, the general idea, which is all we need here, remains sound. It was Bowlby who at the Tavistock Institute in London personally introduced me to the notion of the evolution of behavior, and I can do no better than quote his own words. "What matters here is that, if man's behavioural equipment is indeed adapted to the primeval environment in which man once lived, it is only by reference to that environment that its structure can be understood." One way of estimating this primeval environment, in addition to using paleontology, primatology, genetics, and neurology, is to look at living examples of primeval societies, which is what anthropology was originally intended to do. If you want to understand the tribal imagination, look at the tribes. Chapters 11 and 12 will reexamine this issue.

Before Bowlby, the idea of the EEA had been there in the work of two other of my mentors. Julian Huxley in *Evolution: The Modern Synthesis* (1942) saw it in a negative light: as a matter of "whether some of his [man's] inherited impulses and his simpler irrational satisfactions may stand in the way of higher values and fuller enjoyment." David Hamburg similarly saw modern society as a major source of stress (on which he was the world's expert) and the diseases that followed from stress. He said: "An appreciation of the nature and magnitude of the recent changes in human environmental conditions may help the biological and behavioral sciences to understand the dislocations and difficulties of today's troubled human species" (in Washburn's *Social Life of Early Man*, 1962). What is now known as "evolutionary medicine" was born of this insight, as exemplified by Wenda Trevathan and her colleagues in their book of that name, and McGuire and Troisi in *Darwinian Psychiatry*.

While at Stanford in 1970, and when not marveling at the workings of the brain with Karl Pribram, I discussed with Hamburg the possible supportive role of some of these atavistic impulses: for kinship, for cooperation, for altruism. He saw the point, but still took a justifiably gloomy view of the prospects for our post-Miracle stressful society, particularly given our urge to blame others for our misfortunes (no other animal does that). He then went on to distinguish himself (Presidential Medal of Freedom) as a crusader for sanity in child development and international peace, which perhaps tells us something.

The question has recently been re-posed in cognitive terms as the problem of "the adapted mind." This is the mind that was adapted to the EEA, and developed quite specific "mental modules" to handle its exigencies, but that must now try to function in the novel environment. In the now-famous experiment described by Tooby and Cosmides, in *The Adapted Mind*, students who could not detect cheating when it was presented as an abstract problem could much more readily detect it when it was presented as a breach of a social contract, a breach of promise. This, the authors claim, is a result of the evolution of altruism and the problem of detecting cheaters and freeloaders.

The authors were concerned with the cognitive functions of the evolved brain, but the brain is also an organ of emotions. Think of our reaction when the corporate and banking executives, having failed us and caused a financial meltdown, took our hard-earned tax money to bail themselves out and used it to pay each other large bonuses. Corporations cheat all the time and we ignore it, but this was different: it was a sordid and egregious breach of a social contract; it was blatant freeloading, and our Paleolithic emotional brains responded with Stone Age fury. Unfortunately we were not allowed to try out Stone Age solutions.

As early as 1971 Antony Jay, taking off from the questions raised in his sparkling *Machiavelli and Management*, captured the spirit of it in the subtitle of his book *Corporation Man*: "*. . . Why His Ancient Tribal Impulses Dominate the Life of the Modern Corporation.*" Jay wrote perceptively of how these impulses both help and hinder the running of corporations. This balanced view was important because, as we saw with Huxley and Hamburg (and for that matter with Freud), it is too easy to view civilization as being entirely at war with the savage mind. Human societies, whatever their complexities, have to meet certain very basic human needs—the needs of the tribal mentality and metabolism—or they will not survive. So they cannot be totally at war with these needs, however much trouble they may have with them. This was brought home to me recently when watching James Cameron's film epic *Avatar,* which was a lengthy hymn to the virtues of tribalism and their opposition to the excesses of civilization. In *A New Great Reform Act* (2009) Jay makes his case for the serious reform of government, taking these same tribal needs and virtues into account.

Another bold pioneer, Desmond Morris (1969), called it the problem of the "human zoo," a phrase at once apt and deceptive because, unlike the animals, we built our own zoo: civilization. Unique among species, we created the novel environment, and the supernovel environment that followed on the Miracle, by ourselves and for ourselves. But we have not changed physically in any significant way since the end of the Paleolithic era in which we were formed. The tribal imagination then remains the default system: another way of framing the basic observation.

Lionel Tiger, my longtime associate and friend, has always understood the conflicts posed by the disjunction between our evolutionary heritage and our post-Miracle circumstances. In *The Manufacture of Evil* he looks at the role of religion in making the crucial transition from a world of kin to a world of strangers—a transition that is one of the persistent themes of this book. (See also his *Optimism: The Biology of Hope.*) He has been, of course, especially and famously concerned with the condition of men. Starting with *Men in Groups* and on through the alarmingly titled *The Decline of Males,* he has followed the fluctuating fortunes of human males. Their behavior having been honed by hunting, they must progress through a world where they can only hope for fragmentary analogs of their predatory predilections. We shall follow this further in Chapter 8, through what was perhaps the heyday of the male bond in the epics and sagas of Warrior Society. Tiger's work underscores my observation (in *The Search for Society*) that the purpose of the evolutionary agenda is not so much to explain what we do, as to explain what we do at our peril.

The prolific David Barash examined the conflict between rapid-change culture and slow-change genome in *The Hare and the Tortoise*. He has also called the persistence of the "tribal impulses" *The Whisperings Within*. Some of these Whisperings (our Drumbeats) come to us from deep levels of the brain, from the reptilian impulses of reproduction and basic survival. Others come from the mammalian novelty of emotions and from the primate development of binocular color vision, and still later from the hominid splitting of the functions of the brain between the two hemispheres: the most amazing evolutionary development since the origin of the brain itself. The tribal humans of the Old Stone Age brought all this baggage and more with them, and it was molded then into the behavioral and cognitive repertoire of modern humanity. But none of it was lost (Chapter 9). We do not lose anything in evolution, even if we do sometimes reduce it to a Whisper, or a very quiet Drumbeat.

A Digression on Politics. It is perhaps worth considering that while David Barash and I agree very broadly on this framework of interpretation, we disagree, amiably, on matters political. But then David Horowitz did denounce him as "one of the most dangerous 101 scientists in America." I suppose I have annoyed a lot of people in my time, but I really can't match that. There is, as far as I can see, no political consensus among those of us with an evolutionary orientation, despite the opinion of the academic Left, which would have us all be unreconstructed right-wing reactionaries. I don't personally know any evolutionary scientist of the extreme Right. In Europe the extreme Right *and* the extreme Left each embraced its own version of Darwinism, while in the United States both the religious Right and the academic Left are vocally *anti*-Darwin. Most evolutionists in fact seem to sit somewhere in the middle. Although I perhaps drift to the right of center, David Barash and my Rutgers colleague Robert Trivers, for example, are somewhere left of the Left. Bob's best friend, after all, was Huey Newton (see Chapter 8 of Trivers's *Natural Selection and Social Theory*).

Melvin J. Konner wrote my favorite study of the issue (the subtitle again tells the pessimistic side of the story): *The Tangled Wing: Biological Constraints on the Human Spirit*. Mel, a physician as well as an anthropologist, campaigns tirelessly and publicly for a single-payer national health system. The political ideas of Darwinians seem to derive from something other than evolutionary theory, which we variously mine in their support. In my own case, I have defended the rights of single mothers, nursing mothers, surrogate mothers (the "Baby M" case), and homosexuals. I have joined in the legal defense of Mormon polygamists up to the Supreme Court—in all these cases invoking evolutionary science in the arguments (see *Reproduction and Succession*). I opposed the Vietnam and Iraq wars (Chapter 3) but am skeptical about human rights as a basis for foreign policy (Chapter 2). I can't stand the sanctimony of political correctness.

I could go on with the list, but I doubt you would find any sinister consistency to it. I have engaged in both foxhunting and bullfighting, and I own a sporting-gun permit, but I was a founder of the National Faculty for McGovern, I support the U.S. Green Building Council, and I voted for Obama. Yet again I was once a member (albeit briefly and unwillingly) of what is now called a "designated terrorist organization" (see "The Man" in *Participant Observer*). I don't know where all this puts me on the political spectrum. I think of myself as a pragmatist or a skeptic, not an ideologue. However, this was true before I knew anything of evolution, but after I had read Bertrand Russell (*Sceptical Essays*).

I am suspicious of ideology, whichever direction it comes from. It degenerates too easily into the fanaticism that is the root of so many of our social ills. This would have made me a conservative with a very small "c" in the old language of politics. But the word has come to mean something different now, something Edmund Burke would not recognize, and I hesitate to use it. I have (at least in foreign affairs) been called a "realist," which I took to be a compliment but which, it seems, was meant as an insult. I have also been accused of being heterosexual, bourgeois, Eurocentric, and male. I admit to all four.

Continue. Mel Konner (along with Eaton and Shostak) wrote one of the best versions from the many out there about the influence of the deep past on the uncertain present: *The Paleolithic Prescription.* The authors, echoing Huxley and Hamburg, call the position they take "the discordance hypothesis," and they directly measure the effects that our massively self-changed (novel) environment has had on our Paleolithic-designed bodies and health. Much of this discordance is disastrous, and as we saw, Hamburg thought it was the basis of our modern stress diseases.

At the simple physical level, for example, we see large settled populations, after the agricultural revolution, being devastated by diseases, plagues, and epidemics unknown to nomadic hunters, and that were often derived from the very animals and birds that had been so patiently domesticated (William McNeill, *Plagues and Peoples*). Think of swine flu, bird flu, mad cow disease, *E. coli,* salmonella, anthrax, lactose intolerance, trichinosis, and smallpox, and especially plague: from the fleas that lived on the rats that fed on the grain that was stored in the granaries that the agricultural humans built.

In our hunter-gatherer existence, as another simple physical example, sweet things were difficult to find, so a craving for them was adaptive in making us search for sources of quick energy. But when we have an almost unlimited supply of sweets, the craving becomes a curse, and obesity—unknown to hunters—becomes a major disease. Also, it may be that cooked food gave us an advantage in allowing us to convert more energy, which we needed for an active nomadic life. But now the availability of large amounts of easily digested high-energy cooked food, when not balanced by constant exercise, again contributes to obesity—a point made by Richard Wrangham in his arresting *Catching Fire: How Cooking Made Us Human.*

There is a long list of such discordances that occur when the environment (in the broadest sense) changes markedly from the EEA. Consider: frequent childbirth and lengthy suckling meant few menstrual cycles for women in the tribal state. In modern society, however, relatively infrequent childbirth and short-term suckling, along with a precipitous drop in the age of menarche, have led to a radical increase in the number of cycles a woman experiences. Then think of the equally drastic reversal of this trend by the contraceptive pill, which in turn artificially suppresses those same menstrual cycles. Do we really know what we are doing here? Wenda Trevathan, in her insightful *Ancient Bodies, Modern Lives,* describes many such telling examples of civilized interference with a savage metabolism.

Yet without at least two health innovations—longer average life expectancy and wide-spectrum antibiotics—I would not be writing this. But are the doubling of life expectancy and the massacre of bacteria unqualifiedly beneficial things? In my own case I would have to say yes. But for mankind as a whole? Thus are the questions raised.

A Digression on Chronovores.   Increased longevity in the post-Miracle industrial societies is one of the many novelties we have imposed on our tribal selves, along with small families, nursing homes, and unemployment. In considering such things, the best of the science fiction writers are often ahead of the savants. My neologism in Chapter 1, "chronomyopia," was suggested by a similar coinage in Greg Bear's sharp-edged novel *Slant*. He describes a future dominated by conscious supercomputers, nanotech, deep-tissue psychotherapy, and diagnostic toilets (the 2060s—not so far off). It is a future in which people try to live as long as they can at whatever cost. In the end the state intervenes to stop the drive for extended life spans. The result is a class of old people on the edge of death who are having themselves kept alive, at their own expense, by "cryopreservation."

> They are the old and the sick and the law does not allow them to undergo any more medical intervention. They have had their chance at life, anything more and they are classified as greedy Chronovores, seekers after immortality, which is illegal everywhere but in quasi-independent Green Idaho, and impractical here.

In the course of the novel we find that things are in fact not what they seem to be, but to spell that out would be to give away the wicked plot. If readers think this is no more than sci-fi fantasy, let them look to the British National Health Service, which has formed the National Institute for Health and Clinical Excellence.It uses the acronym NICE—Orwell would have loved that. NICE has been tasked with establishing priorities for the expensive treatment of the old on a value-for-money (or cost-effective) basis. If the treatment is too expensive and you are going to die anyway, you may get classified as a greedy Chronovore and that will be it. (Since writing this I have watched the United States go through a period of hysterical paranoia about "death panels" and "pulling the plug on grandma." The Chronovores are panicking.)

Continue.   Lévi-Strauss in the preface to his masterpiece, *The Savage Mind,* gently informs the readers that while his book can stand on its own, it is nevertheless part of a series, and that those who had read at least his *Totemism* would be alive to the continuity and be at an advantage. The same is true here, but it would be cumbersome to recite all the publications that are a run-up to this book. Perhaps it is just worth noting that I have been wrestling with the Darwinian temporal perspective—with the vertical view of society and the eternal presence of the past—for exactly half a century. It was in 1960 that John Bowlby first talked to me about "the environment of adaptednes" and urged me to consider the relevance of "imprinting" to the mother-child bond, and the science of ethology in general. He liked a paper of mine that the Tavistock journal *Human Relations* had published on the psychological effectiveness of Pueblo Indian healing rituals. But he insisted I should try to understand the evolution of the human emotional system that these ceremonies were tapping into in order to be effective. Melvin Konner's recent magnum opus, *The Evolution of Childhood,* is an encyclopedic treatment of that emotional evolution on the fiftieth anniversaty of my fateful meeting.

A Digression on Epigenesis.   Despite the attractiveness and power of the evolutionary paradigm, many phenomena of society and culture are what the jargon calls "underdetermined" by the epigenetic rules of evolution and have to be understood in their own terms before we try to see the relevance of any evolutionary predispositions. Thus the fluctuations in literary representations of incest over the centuries that we shall ponder in Chapters 6 and 7 are purely cultural and historical variations. There is nothing in evolution that will tell us why the seventeenth century saw incest as horrific, the eighteenth as faintly comic, the nineteenth as dangerously romantic, and the twentieth as interesting but not much to make a fuss about. But an understanding of the evolution of incest inhibition and exogamy (marriage out) helps us to see what these historical variations are variations *on,* and thus to understand better how changing circumstances strain the limits of evolved emotional and cognitive adaptations. At least that is the hope; the readers must judge.

Continue.   Much of what follows in this book is about what Tiger and I, in *The Imperial Animal* (1970) called "behavioral gibberish." This results when you feed organisms information that does not accord with the "biogrammar"—the inherent rules for the acquisition of culture. We were obviously much influenced by Noam Chomsky (whose first-ever lectures I heard at MIT) to the point of proposing a "culture acquisition device" to embrace his "language acquisition device." Our rule was: garbage in: gibberish out. We looked at the "primate baseline" and its transformation by the "hunting transition" to what was the human default system of tribal society and mentality. Then we tried to see how the post-Miracle world was either in synch with or inimical to this default system. It is that simple and that complicated. Our epigraph from Jacques Monod's *Chance and Necessity*—"Every living being is also a fossil"—is at the very heart of it. We put it in French because Monod's book hadn't been translated when we were writing. This gained us no brownie points with the yahoos, of course, who saw it as up-front proof of our unregenerate elitism.

The studies that follow, in all their diversity, are continuations of this enterprise. They are a kaleidoscope of topics that may sometimes, on the surface, appear totally unrelated. But then the items in totemic classifications as described by Lévi-Strauss, or those in Francis Bacon's "Tables and Arrangements" (both in Chapter 1), look unrelated to us until we know the logic of the associations. Chapters 2 and 3 deal with topical events and issues with a degree of confidence that is perhaps not warranted, but that seemed to be called for by the press of life and its moral challenge. The reader will easily see where I was right and where I was wrong, and take comfort in Karl Popper's principle that we learn more from our errors than from our certainties (Chapter 12).

Some chapters deal with eternal problems like time, religion, incest, and sectarianism, some with current life and politics. Some deal with literature: drama, epic, verse, and novels—and with sex in literature (at least incest, but also sexual conflict). In this they have a lot in common with the work of the self-described school of "literary Darwinism." For example, see Joseph Carroll, *Evolution and Literary Theory,* or the poet Ted Hughes in his *Shakespeare and the Goddess of Complete Being.* Hughes looked for the sources of the bard's poetic vision in the calling of the tribal shaman and for the power of poetic metaphor in the bilateral functions of the cortex (Chapters 9 and 13). Some deal with history and archaeology, and some with the business of social and evolutionary analysis itself. The final chapter looks at the evolution of two persistent modes of thinking, feeling, and acting (what Ted Hughes calls "mythic" and "realistic") and how the interplay between them helps us decide whether history is indeed ending or just getting more interesting.

One theme that runs throughout—one major Drumbeat—is what we might call "the struggle between kin and strangers." This was Hobbes's true state of nature, and it is at least as pertinent to human history as the class struggle, as Lionel Tiger saw in *The Manufacture of Evil.* It involves one of the deepest Whispers, the most profound Drumbeats: what the sociobiologists have variously called "inclusive fitness" or "kin selection" and what was the founding matter of anthropology: kinship and marriage. Ed Wilson understood this completely in his use of my studies of exogamy (marriage out) in *Sociobiology,* his great synthesis of 1975.

"Who are kin and why are they kin?" and "What should we do about the others?" are the questions at the root of my lifelong interest in kinship and marriage. This issue of "kin versus strangers" is basic to all the discussions of the Miracle, in that modern society required a system of trust in which strangers (non-kin) could be dealt with under a rule of contract (Chapter 1). The theme is there in the question of human rights, and what right we have to vengeance and nepotistic assistance and the arrangement of our children's marriages (Chapter 2). It is there in the issue of tribalism and democracy in Iraq (and elsewhere), because tribesmen are kinsmen while citizens are strangers, to be neither trusted nor married (Chapter 3). It is there in the process of segmentation in society that is behind the formation of sects (Chapter 4). It is there in the Ten Commandments, with the dual injunctions for kin and neighbors, and it is the basis for the offense against Yahweh of marrying gentiles and the passage of Israel from kin-based tribes to a tribe-based nation (Chapter 5).

It was there in the epics of male bonding, in the battle between the male bond and the mating bond, and in the automatic alliance with the maternal uncle or the foster brother as opposed to the elaborate oaths, trials, and customs needed to bind strangers as if they were kin (Chapter 8). It was the guts of Morgan's vision of the vital transition in social evolution (Chapter 11), while Popper's Closed Society tried always to approximate a community of custom-bound kin rather than an association of free individuals (Chapter 12). Perhaps above all it is there in the tug-of-war between breeding with kin and breeding with strangers that is the essence of the incest taboo and its vicissitudes, especially the marriage of cousins (Chapters 6 and 7).

While I hope this material will be of interest to the relevant professionals, it is intended for a general audience. So I have eschewed the twin academic curses of nitpicking footnotes and padded bibliography. There are no footnotes as such. This means some ancillary material gets into the text, often in parentheses, but this is better than a constant shuffling between the text and the back of the book. Any book or article directly referred to in the chapters will be found in the Notes and References to each chapter, with an occasional hint at related material and matters of interest, and some digressionary discussion that, while germane to the issue, might have unduly cluttered the text. This makes for easier reading without sacrificing scholarly responsibility. I have in a few places, for convenience, used the convention of referring to a book by the author's name and the date of publication (for instance, Tiger 1969).

Another theme is the origins and rise of civilization and its transformations. I use "civilization" and "civilized" here in a value-neutral sense (as we say these days), except perhaps in Chapter 12 where an unfashionable prejudice shows through in favor of civilization. Civilization in the technical sense was in place once we had cities. We shall look at this in more detail in Chapter 10. When W. Lloyd Warner called his book on an Australian Aboriginal tribe *A Black Civilization,* he was technically incorrect, but he was playing on the two meanings of the word, the technical and the judgmental: the same contrast we shall see in the use of the word "culture" in Chapter 12. What we have since the Miracle is industrial capitalist civilization, again in a value-free sense: it is simply the latest stage of civilization that, for better or for worse, started in the first cities.

A Digression on Oxford.   My favorite story about Oxford involves an irredeemably judgmental use of the word "civilization." The time is World War I and militant ladies are roaming the streets of Oxford giving out white feathers of cowardice to young men of fighting age who are not at the front. (Yes, they did that.) They invade a college quad where a young don in cap and gown is walking across the lawn reading Virgil. Thrusting the white feathers at him, one of the ladies demands: "Young man, why are you not out there fighting for civilization?" Without hesitation and with devastatingly correct grammar he replies: "Madam, I *am* the civilization for which they are out there fighting."

Continue.   I also use, at least in Chapter 1, the word "savage" with an obvious irony; the same irony that is intended in Lévi-Strauss's punning use of *sauvage.* But in the body of the book I more usually say "tribal" and "the tribal mentality/imagination." This is not a technical use of "tribe." (In Chapter 12, we shall look at this again.) I mean it loosely to cover what used to be called "primitive" before we became more sensitive (and more sensible) and turned to "preliterate" or "nonliterate." It is therefore, in the nonjudgmental sense, precivilized, traditional society that characterized us for 99 percent of our existence.

   Also, I do not use "mind" or "mentality" or certainly "imagination" in any technical sense. The language of "mind" is a way of describing thinking and feeling and the inextricable connection between the two. As to the nature of mind, I am not convinced even by modern sophisticated dualism (even Popper's). Mind does not differ from brain; mind-speak is a way of talking about the activity of the brain. The brain itself (at least the neocortex) is amazingly malleable, and what we learn and remember and imagine can modify its structure, which is why we can produce complex civilizations in the first place. But the things learned and lodged in the brain are not heritable; we have to remake them and add to them in every generation to maintain the complexities of civilization. What is constant is the evolved neural-mental structure that is the default system. The brain may be a malleable organ, but if what is fed into it is garbage, then it becomes an organ of malleable garbage, and its output is behavioral gibberish. For the record, then, let us leave it at that, with me as a materialist and a monist, and mind still something of a mystery.

Speaking technically (again), for most of our hominid existence we lived in small bands, not in tribes conceived of as political entities; but I shall use "tribal" to cover them all, including chiefdoms. Tribal people as such continued to exist, and still exist, of course, in much of that "developing" world, but their societies are often much changed by prolonged contact with the first world. The tribalism I am interested in does not change; it exists in our heads, and we constantly reproduce it in our societies, whatever stage of development they have achieved. And whether we are looking at the individual or the collective mind, or at mentality or at society, we are still asking that nagging question about the Miracle and the Drumbeats. We are questioning our experimental status as a species, the experimental state of our global society, and the stubborn persistence of the savage mind in a world that thinks it has gone beyond it and can stay beyond it.

For C. Day Lewis, in his disturbingly accurate poem about our basic psychic struggle, "The men to come" would probably prevail over "The insolence of the dead"—but he knew the struggle would continue and be fierce: "The armies of the dead/Are trenched within my bones." He is Everyman who stands at "This moving point of dust/Where past and present meet" where he anticipates the relentless demands of the future: "And in my body rebel cells/Look forward to the fight."

> So heir and ancestor
> Pursue the inveterate feud,
> Making my senses' darkened fields
> A theater of war.

What follow here are one correspondent's dispatches from that battlefront, the crucible in which our imaginations are tempered.

CHAPTER ONE

Time out of Mind

Tribal Tempo and Civilized Temporality

I WAS GOING to start by quoting Johann Wolfgang von Goethe, who in his *Venetian Epigrams* says, *"O, wie beseliget uns Menschen ein falscher Begriff."* Wise friends told me it is not a good idea to start with an untranslated quote in a foreign language, but I like the gritty sound of Goethe, so there it is. What the old master is saying is that we—we humans—tend to be powerfully attracted to false concepts. We have a fatal attraction to wrong ideas. We are happiest when enthralled by delusion. So that is my cue to say that we humans of the modern age are trapped by our wrong perception of time.

Familiar Time

Our *chronomyopia*—our fixation on the present and familiar—leads us to overvalue the period of time we label "history" to the point of relegating more than 99 percent of human existence to "prehistory"—a mere run-up to the real thing. We casually refer to the beings inhabiting that huge percentage of time as "early man." It would be more logical to label hominids up to, say, the invention of tools, as "past man," those from thence until the Neolithic revolution as "present man," and ourselves as "late man." Whether there will be a "future man" remains an open question. The coming, significantly, of "post-historic man" has been forecast, and Francis Fukuyama, following Hegel, has announced *The End of History and the Last Man*, to quote his book title. (We shall return to the Last Man in the last chapter.) The "history" referred to is of course this blip at the end of human time—the last few thousand years of a very warm interglacial period, characterized by unusual population growth and frenetic socio-cultural activity in its later years. We shall never understand the significance of this blip until we understand that it is indeed a blip—a blink of the temporal eyelid—and not the Greenwich Mean Standard by which all human time must be judged.

It is not that we are incapable of taking the larger perspective—we are doing it right now—but that in the normal course of our affairs we have little incentive to do so: we may even have a disincentive to take the long view. Even those of us professionally concerned with vast stretches of time do not, in our ordinary lives, order our affairs with respect to epochs, or even generations. For most people, most of the time, a lifetime is a long time. We might take cognizance of the lifetimes of our children and grand-children, and operate some of our lives with reference to a generation or two of our ancestors, but that is the limit to our practical interest in temporal depth. Theoretically we can think of infinite stretches of time, but this ability has no practical applications. And our cognitive failings have an impact on our theories: only the historically recent seems to be of significance to us. We can accept, for example, that hominid history may stretch over 6 million years, but we seem to find it difficult to accept that the first 5.99 million of those years are far more important to an understanding of ourselves than are the last 10,000. To most of us, they are less important than the last 200! If, after Henry Ford, history is truly bunk, then what chance has prehistory?

Those who think as I do, often in despair, lament this chronomyopia as human fallibility: a sad failure of the imagination, or a perverse refusal to accept the obvious. But perhaps we should be more anthropological about it. It is, after all, something so universal, so deeply rooted in human thinking, that we have to ask ourselves why this is so. At a simple selectional level the answer is obvious: hominids developed consciousness, including consciousness of time, as a tool for survival. In an existence only one stage above the temporal consciousness of animals, and faced with the same survival problems, there would not only have been no value in a concentration on the very long term; there might even have been positive selection against it.

The temporal module that we evolved, then, while including the specifically human components of past, present, and future, had to be specialized in terms of *immediate* past and future. We often forget that languages are as concerned with the modalities of time, what grammarians call *aspect,* as with the tenses themselves: with *how* time is spent as opposed to the stages of its passage. But the "close-and-familiar" rule that applied, for example, to dealings with other humans, and resulted in kin, especially close kin, being preferred over strangers, must also have applied to time: close and familiar time is preferred over distant and strange. Otto Jesperson in *The Philosophy of Grammar* arranges time and tense in terms of this continuum of closeness and distance from the ever-shifting present (Figure 1.1).

It is perhaps necessary to keep repeating that we are certainly and obviously capable of contemplating vast epochs and even infinity. Originally we did this in myth, which has its own special place in the story of human survival. But only the odd shaman was allowed the luxury of *existing* in mythical time, with his spirit flights and journeys. And even he, in his daily practical life, had to be focused on the immediate, like his mundane and unshamanistic kin, or he would not have survived. What I am suggesting is that this survival-driven concentration on the immediate has had a continuing influence on our contemplation of the infinite. It is one reason we cannot learn from history; we cannot even think back to the last financial crisis and figure out that a boom will not last.

It shows itself in myth by the need to circumscribe time, to put it into some manageable imaginative constraints, starting with a definite, and not imaginatively too distant, point of creation. Even in the late seventeenth century it made perfectly good sense to sensible people to place the start of everything on the evening before the 23rd of October in 4004 BC. It still makes perfect sense to millions today. Eventually there came to be an idea of an ultimate end to time, some state of eternal stasis that would negate the agonies of time. But again this was reserved for mythical contemplation, and in life and thought the short view dominated.

Cyclical Time

Primitive time was annual, seasonal, lunar, diurnal, tidal, and metabolic; that is, it was inherently *cyclical*. The earliest known deliberate human engravings were records of the moon's phases (Marshack 1972).The pressure to categorize and then posit relationships between categories, including categories of time, is fundamentally social. It arises with the need

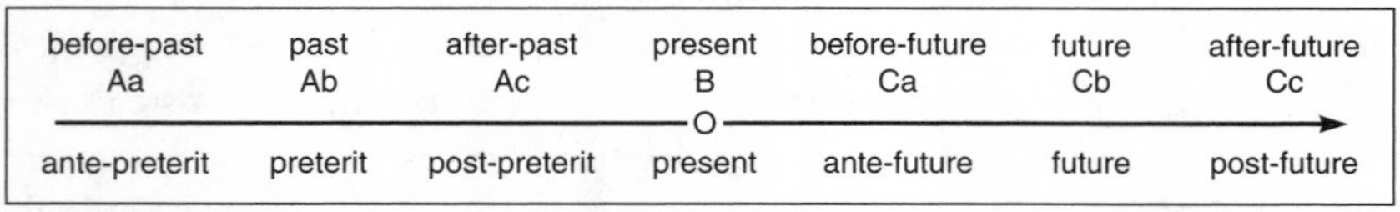

before-past	past	after-past	present	before-future	future	after-future
Aa	Ab	Ac	B	Ca	Cb	Cc
ante-preterit	preterit	post-preterit	present	ante-future	future	post-future

Figure 1.1   Time and tense

for social communication over and above the physical and the immediate—especially with the introduction of *time,* of referring to the past and the future, to things that have gone and are yet to come. This need to plan, to talk of the future in terms of the past, is the source of language itself. Melvin Konner in *The Evolution of Childhood* writes: "Human mental functions were formed in social contexts" and "Little understanding can be gained about the developing mind and brain without placing relationships at the center." Our mental categories of time would have evolved, then, in essentially *cyclical* structures of social relationships, and these would have been "at the center." Konner is thinking of fairly intimate relationships, but relationships of kinship could expand beyond the intimate even at the most primitive level of known human society. This requires a brief, not too technical, exploration.

Claude Lévi-Strauss, the founder of the philosophical-anthropological school of structuralism, distinguishes "cool" (ahistorical) social structures from "hot" (historical) social structures (in *The Scope of Anthropology*). Let us reserve hot and look at the characteristics of the most primitive cool structures. They are, he says, static and cyclical; life is eternal recurrence. Their views of time reflect this circumstance.

We are used to this eternal recurrence in the basic myths of the hunter-gatherers as described by Joseph Campbell, but it exists too in the most basic of kinship structures, and these kinship structures *were* the social systems of the early societies. They can look very complicated to us, but they are in fact literally "elementary," to use Lévi-Strauss's term *(structures élémentaires).* Let us try to get inside the heads of the users of one of these elementary systems and try to follow the naming and classifying of kin, for our ideas of time were forged in this context and it is crucial that we know them.

An obvious example is the feature of *alternating-generation* kinship terms. We are accustomed to think of our parental and grandparental relatives as receding from us in steps of "greatness": great-grandfather, then great-great-grandfather, and so on. Similarly, the descending generations are great-granddaughters, then great-great granddaughters, and so forth. With alternating terms it is very different. The generations are not seen as infinitely receding but as infinitely returning, re-cycling. Thus I would have a father and then a grandfather, but my grandfather's father would be "father" and his father would be "grandfather." In the descending generations I would have "son" but then his son (my grandson) would be "grandfather" and my great-grandson would be "son."

Pause. Let us try a simple diagram of this to make it visual so that we can grasp it as a whole, putting our right brain to work with, rather than against, our left. It is the *pattern* that matters. Figure 1.2 uses the standard symbols of F and M for father and mother, B and Z for brother and sister, S and D for son and daughter, and G for the prefix *grand-*; thus GF is "grandfather."

You are the center of your own universe of kin *(SELF)* and you are naming the relatives from whom you descend and who descend from you. I have put the grandparental terms also in bold so that their cycling through the generations is more obvious.

There are many other variations (all of these diagrams show simplified and idealized examples), and in classifying lines of collateral kin I can be even more thorough and have an endlessly repeating sequence of GF-F-GF-F-GF-F . . . But this schematic example will serve to illustrate that generations are seen as *infinitely repeating themselves*. I *(SELF)* call my great-grandparents by the terms for father and mother, then my great-great-grandparents by the same terms as my grandparents. In the generations following me, I call my grandchildren by the same terms as my grandparents and my great-grandchildren by the same terms as son and daughter, and so on.

And note that theoretically in such systems the terms go on to infinity: the great-great-great-grandfather would be "father" and his father would be "grandfather." Of course, such relatives will in fact be dead and may or may not be remembered as people; the future generations are yet unborn. But they are, in the native theory of kinship, logically present in the temporal scheme, if not physically known in actuality.

The details here matter less to our understanding than the obvious fact of the *cyclical* nature of the terms: the "eternal recurrence" concretely embedded in the classificatory scheme of kinship categories. We must make an imaginative leap out of our notions of what is normal or natural in classification and understand the absolute logic of calling a great-granddaughter

	Males		Females	
	GF		**GM**	great-great-grandparents
Ascending generations	F		M	great-grandparents
	GF		**GM**	grandparents
	F		M	parents
Own generation	**GF**/B	*SELF*	**GM**/Z	siblings and cousins
	S		D	children
	GF		**GM**	grandchildren
Descending generations	S		D	great-grandchildren
	GF		**GM**	great-great-grandchildren

Figure 1.2   Alternating generation terms

"daughter" or a great-grandmother "mother." If we can do so, we shall be close to an understanding of the nature of temporal thinking that was ours for that crucial "early" 99 percent of our existence.

You will have noticed that the terms for GM and GF appear in one's own generation along with brother (B) and sister (Z). Commonly in such systems, in your own generation, *unmarriageable* cousins are equated with siblings and *marriageable* cousins with grandparents (GF/GM), which fact would be puzzling were it not for the absolute logic of the alternating system. In this "the natives" prove to be much more logical than were the early anthropologists, who, taking these terms literally to be descriptions of biological relationships, concluded that "the natives" married their grandmothers! (More of this in Chapter 11.)

These systems of terms are not, we should note, abstractions by the anthropologist, but reflect the actual practices of the simplest systems of kin classification known to us: in particular those of the Australian Aborigines who were in place in Australia by at least 40,000 (and possibly as much as 60,000) years ago. (We shall meet them up close in Chapter 11.) Logically such systems could work with only four terms—grandparent, parent, sibling, and child—and an operator to indicate sex. If our perceptions of time arose in these social circumstances, it is not too difficult to see how they were constrained and cyclical; how, to follow Jesperson, the "before-past" constantly reoccurred in the "after-future."

Linear Time

With the Neolithic revolution and the advent of the domestication of plants and animals (starting perhaps 8,000–10,000 years ago), time became more linear; provision for the future had to be made, and the long-term lessons of the past remembered, by planting, irrigating, and herding societies. Thus time was seen, for the first time, as *linear and progressive:* it was going from somewhere to somewhere, like the rope in the rope trick that takes the climber into the clouds. Time was no longer eternally repeating itself. These were still very traditional societies; they were still "cool," and they did not envisage a cumulative change in their condition, which was seen as persisting. Time, however, was perceived as existing in an eternal stream more than as an eternal recurrence.

The difference might seem subtle, but it was in effect quite profound. Their time horizons had to expand, given the planning and organization that their new modes of subsistence required. This is reflected in the changes in those kinship systems that moved from *cyclical* to *linear,* from closed and self-contained to open and, theoretically, infinitely expansive.

Lineages and clans were seen as stretching forward and backward in a linear rather than a cyclical fashion. This was widely reflected in kinship classification, as is shown in Figure 1.3. The = sign represents marriage. The bracket over the terms means they refer to brothers and sisters. Remember that Z is "sister," so FZ is "father's sister."

Again: don't worry about the detail, first take in the *linear pattern* and its contrast with the former, alternating, pattern. *SELF* is you: so you must put yourself, if not in the shoes, still most certainly in the mind, of the user. You exist, in this example, in a matrilineal system where descent is reckoned in the female line: you get your lineage or clan from your mother. In the left-hand column you see the lineage of your mother's father, all called by the terms for "grandmother" and "grandfather" stretching infinitely both backward and forward in time in a perfectly linear fashion. Descent is through the women, all called GM—"grandmother"—while all the men married to the women of the lineage are called "grandfather" *regardless of generation*. In the alternating-generation system, generation is paramount; in the linear system, generation is overruled by lineality.

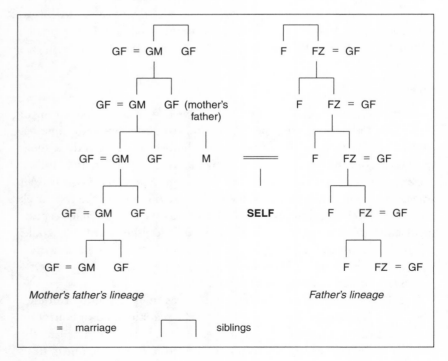

Figure 1.3   Lineal terms

In the right-hand example I see my father's (matrilineal) lineage doing the same thing, with everyone classified as "father" or "paternal aunt"—FZ (father's sister). All the men married to FZ are classified as GF "grandfather"— again *without regard to generation*. Such a system of terms is usually classed as "unilineal" because the users do see their relatives as a series of "lines"—through males or through females, stretching thus in time. (A minor caveat for the eagle-eyed professional: the father's mother would usually be called "grandmother." All of the other women of the lineage would be FZ—"paternal aunt"—as indicated.)

If you can pause on this and absorb for now the *general difference* between the *alternating* and *linear* conceptions of kin, then you will have stepped back in time. You will have experienced the first great episode in the evolution of perceptions of time unfolding in your own mind. And again the details matter less than that we understand the switch from the cycling of terms eternally over the generations to the existence of terms stretching as a "line" into the past and the future. But remember that the cyclical perception had been there since the origins of language itself. Linear time was an uneasy newcomer. (The transition between the two is dealt with in the Appendix.)

As to the models of alternating and linear systems we have looked at, there are numerous other combinations, and the reader can easily experiment with possible variations, or even consult my own and other analyses of them. But these models are enough to reinforce the basic point that with the advent of linearity in the agricultural and eventually literate societies of the Neolithic transition, a new view of social time entered human consciousness.

In the "alternating generation" societies there is rarely any concern with specific genealogy, for example. Ancestors become amalgamated as general "ancestor spirits" and are not remembered in any depth as individuals. In the linear societies, on the other hand, and in those that are nonlineal in terminology but that have accepted the linear view of social and genealogical time (Hawaiian and Maori, for example), depth of genealogy becomes overwhelmingly important, and the most significant measure of social status.

In traditional China and Polynesia, or today in Somalia, twenty to thirty generations of remembered ancestors were/are not uncommon (see Chapter 3 on Somalia), and the Chinese remembered and worshipped all their clan ancestors as individuals in ancestor temples. It was the Hebrew recording of the generations since Adam that enabled Archbishop Usher to calculate the date of creation (see Chapter 5 on Hebrew genealogy). But even though there is this crucial shifting to a lineally uniform body of kin, it is a static linearity. It is suited to static agricultural societies and cannot work with large, socially mobile populations.

Progressive Time

Our sense of social time has utterly changed even since what I have chosen to call the linear phase of time perception. Time for us is now, as Lévi-Strauss so aptly called it, *progressive and cumulative*. In the primitive state, thinking, couched in rudimentary language, was time-constrained. Enumeration, for example, was never well developed. Social time was, as we have seen, counted in generations, but these did not stretch through time, they constantly re-cycled themselves. When literacy and numeracy entered, consequent on the growth of trade and conquest in early empires (around 5,000 years before the present), vast distances of time, as in the Hindu and Maya compilations of the ages of existence, could be contemplated.

A glyph from Copan shows Maya gods bearing "bundles" of time, in one case calculated as $20 \times 20 \times 360 = 144,000$ days: about 400 years, a Maya *baktun*. The total time since the creation, represented by the totality of the number gods, was 1,405,800 days, or about 3,849 of our years (Aveni 2001). Significantly, Mayan kinship terms, as Fred Eggan discovered (though his discovery somehow got lost), seem to have made the same trek from alternating-generation to linear as on our model above. But even so, in this early stage of civilization the insistence on cyclical temporality still dominated. Vast ages rolled around repeating themselves. Jain theologians in India calculated cycles as long as 400 trillion oceans of years, an ocean being 100 million squared—and this is one cycle of many described by Joseph Campbell in *The Masks of God: Oriental Mythology*.

But even though early civilization found it hard to throw off the cyclical idea of time, the potential for a progressive view of time was now present in the linear model, and as civilization grew in extent, complexity, and numbers, so time became more and more progressive. Time future could build on time past; it could actually improve on it, not just endlessly repeat it. Time was no longer evenly spread out in the manner of unfolding generations, it rolled out in vast periods; it could actually speed up and change in quality.

Aided by improved technology, time began to be measured ever more accurately. Thus the "hot" societies described by Lévi-Strauss came about. It was not that cool societies never changed, but change was not of their essence. They could have continued cycling forever if not hit from the outside, as it were. Hot societies were of their very nature changing;

change was what they were *about*. They saw time past as simply a basis for hurrying into the future; novelty became virtuous, not suspect as it is in traditional societies.

The industrial revolution eventually drove such societies to an even faster pace, of course, but their view of temporality was lodged in the progressive linear view of time contained in the first temporal revolution. Apocalyptic religions looked essentially forward to vast changes rather than backward to eternal recurrence. The ladder of time was seen as leading upward to cataclysmic future events. Even if, in the religious view, these events were to mark the end of time, the secularization of this view was a basis for a future orientation in terms of cumulative progress that has marked the modern age.

Ending Time

However, in a cyclical recurrence of my own, I now come back to the original point. Even though our perceptions of time were thus revolutionized—from cool time to hot time—our basic thinking about time, the time we have in mind, was laid down in the cool, repetitive, cyclical age. Even in our theoretical thinking we still feel this constraint. Where is the social theory that confidently proclaims an indefinite series of social changes stretching into a limitless social future? Whether it is the currently unfashionable theories of Marxism—of the withering away of the state and the return of primitive communism—or the currently favored liberal-democratic view of the end of history, we still want to put a limit on time; we want to reach the equivalent of the coming of the kingdom of God on earth. We want to prevent time from simply proliferating unpredictably; we want it to stop somewhere.

Hegel's dialectic should theoretically have gone on indefinitely, but he had to stop it when Spirit found its Absolute Freedom in the Prussian state: an idea that has influenced the current end-of-history thinking. The great theoreticians of the historical period even tried to reintroduce cyclical time: Vico, Saint-Simon, Toynbee, Spengler, Danilevsky, Sorokin, who saw civilizations rising, flourishing, and falling on a predictable trajectory. Time may be, as the hymn says, "like an ever-rolling stream," but it rolls right round again, and you can indeed step into the same river twice. These thinkers have been infinitely more popular than those pragmatic historians like H. A. L. Fisher, who declared in his *History of Europe* that there are no patterns in history. Such randomness makes us nervous; patterns restore our confidence in the universe, much as conspiracy theories restore our faith in rationality.

Even Lévi-Strauss predicts that in a future of automation and infinite leisure, we shall take the heat out of our societies and return, in a renewed cool state, to playing with elaborate, "crystalline kinship systems," because these are our natural state of being. This is, at least to my kind of anthropologist, an appealing utopia, surprisingly like the glass bead game in Hermann Hesse's novel. But it is recognizably and firmly in the end-of-time tradition. So we want to circumscribe the future and discount the past. And as we started by observing, we refuse to take seriously the possibilities raised by our knowledge of the vast periods of time that went into our making. We are comfortable with "history" as we know it—essentially recorded history. If we expand this to include all of our relevant past, it overwhelms us with our insignificance and the precarious nature of the current experiment.

To Western thinkers since the Enlightenment, this past is mostly "nature"—a necessary but almost irrelevant prequel to "culture," whose advent was the beginning of all that is relevant. (I do not use the term "culture" very much. Through popular abuse and anthropological misuse it has lost any useful meaning and turned into a mere slogan. (More on this in Chapter 12.) This nature/culture distinction is yet another way of avoiding the implications of our evolution, which in turn reinforces our prejudice: time is indeed cumulative, progressive, and above all recent. We might indeed be the end products of its true immensity, stretching ultimately back to the big bang itself, because nothing new has come into the universe since then. (Cosmic novelty is the result of recombination from the basic hydrogen and helium, with a dash of lithium.) But to the chronomyopic, time past (before a certain recent time) is irrelevant. It is quantitatively long but qualitatively threadbare. It is not time that counts for very much. Thus the temporal prejudice in favor of familiar time, deriving from our original cyclical mentality, still effectively constrains us.

Our collective, social perception of time in fact jibes with psychological studies of individual time perception. William James in *The Principles of Psychology* wrote about the "specious present"—that short chunk of time (between three and five seconds) that is immediately sensible and dominant, like Jesperson's linguistic present. (We shall find it in the time constraints of the "neural line" in poetry in Chapter 9.) Also, the "speeding up" of time is what happens in the individual life history as we age. Two years to a fifty-year-old pass much more quickly than two years to a ten-year-old. Chronobiology also unveils how cyclical rhythms govern much of life—sleeping and waking, regulation of brain systems, menstruation, stock market prices, animal migration, and so on. There is a constant tug-of-war in the individual between the dominance of the present, based on biological rhythms, and the need to live in longer stretches of perceived time. This is exactly mirrored in our social perception of time with its overvaluation of the present.

Our leading contemporary philosopher of time, J. T. Fraser, argues that central to the concept of "the beautiful" (to say nothing of the good and the true) is the idea that it is something that stops time for us: it is literally timeless. It exists, as we like to say, outside of time; it is not for time but for eternity: *sub specie aeternitatis.* Time is decay, it is entropy, and we are unfortunately aware of this, and we want to resist it; we want time to be eternally present as it was in the primitive cyclical state.

David Hume saw the same thing was true with our perception of causality. It was something the mind intruded into the stream of events, and it was there because it had been necessary for our survival to think that way: to believe that there was not just a random stream of events, but that events had causes and effects. (See my "Prejudice and the Unfinished Mind" in *Challenge of Anthropology.*) There is a long list of such mental modules, but a hierarchy of preferences in temporal thinking, with the present at the top, continues to exert its influence despite our conscious knowledge of the reality of the evolutionary, phylogenetic timescale. Our basic notion of time fundamentally affects our notions of causality, which are short-term, contextual, ontogenetic, and historical. We are still the creatures of that tribal, familial, lunar, seasonal, generational, eternally recurrent social world that created the minds with which we think about, and create, our particular temporal reality.

Mary Douglas, just before her death, published the remarkable *Thinking in Circles* (2007), which analyzed the phenomenon of "ring composition." Many of the epics that seem so disorganized and episodic to us in fact conform to a pattern of narrative thinking that locates the meaning in the middle of the tale, works up to it, and then retraces its steps to end back at the beginning. She finds this in *Beowulf,* in Homer, in *Paradise Lost,* in the biblical Book of Numbers, in the *Aeneid,* and more recently in *Tristram Shandy.* This ring composition—ubiquitous in the ancient world—is known as "chiasmus" and most commonly arranges its episodes in the structural form AB C BA. The reader will remember Jesperson's diagram of time and tense (Figure 1.1) and will here again see an example of cyclical thinking in which the after-future returns to the before-past, as with generational kinship terms. Douglas wonders why modern and particularly Western readers and critics do not recognize such structures, and why they feel uncomfortable with them when they do. It could be that, trapped as we are in the imposed linear-cumulative view of time, we are decidedly uncomfortable when confronted with the aboriginal cycles in any form. Although we resist them, we are also drawn by their archaic power, drawn back to the cyclical thought-world of the tribe.

Beating Time

The progressive cumulative view of social time, which fights with our cyclical notions, in fact dominated the nineteenth century, from the Scottish Enlightenment of the eighteenth century, through the ambitious evolutionism of Spencer, Morgan, and the Social Darwinists, until the savagery of World War I destroyed all our certainties. These thinkers, while looking to what was known of the past, indeed while founding the disciplines that explored it, were largely concerned with it as the prelude to inevitable social progress and a utopian future. Time for them was, as we say, on our side. We looked to the past to see what of it still remained with us, in our psyches (religion) and our societies (monarchy), so that we would know what to get rid of.

One of the founders of anthropology, E. B. Tylor, in *Primitive Culture* (1871) was blunt about this. These relics of savagery were "survivals," and the business of the discipline was to identify them and set them up for eradication. His last words of his last volume: "It is a harsher, and at times more painful, office of ethnography to expose the remains of crude old culture which have passed into harmful superstition, and to mark these out for destruction . . . Thus, active at once in aiding progress and removing hindrance, the science of culture is essentially a reformer's science."

For Auguste Comte, another founder, the age of "positivism" would replace that of metaphysics; as for James Frazer, the age of science would replace that of religion. For Spencer, industrial (and peaceful) societies would replace military (and bellicose). Marx in turn announced that capitalism would be replaced by the classless communist society. In this he was influenced by Morgan, who at the end of *Ancient Society* predicted: "Democracy in government, brotherhood in society, equality in rights and privileges, and universal education, foreshadow the next higher plane of society to which experience, intelligence and knowledge are steadily tending." The list goes on. And throughout this intellectual turmoil the picture of "the savage"—the relic from time past surviving precariously into the present—was battered from several sides.

On the one hand, the Enlightenment looked to the future of man and rejected the savage past. We were rising from savagery and rejecting its heritage: the heritage of religion, magic, superstition, violence, and cruelty. The problem with modern society, in this view, was that we were not removing ourselves from savagery fast enough. The "survivals" were persistent. But it was only a matter of time and education and we would get rid of them. Maybe the last king would not be strangled in the guts of the last priest, as Voltaire hoped, but kings priests and all other survivals of the savage mentality would be at least phased out.

On the other hand, there was the tradition of Rousseau, which saw it the opposite way round. The savage was still in an Eden from which we had fallen. The corrupting influences in our oppressed lives were the forces of civilization itself, not the hangovers of savagery. What we must do is learn from the savages to return to the virtuous life in which all were free. Chateaubriand (as we shall see in Chapter 7) taught a whole generation of romantics to revere the virtues of the savage mind in *Atala*.

Marx in fact represented a version of this same thinking with his prediction of an eventual return to primitive communism. Thus he and Engels had a fascination with ethnography and with Morgan's declaration that future society would see "a revival, in a higher form, of the liberty, equality and fraternity of the ancient gentes." (More on this in Chapter 11.) But both views still envisaged an end to the cumulative time of the industrial capitalist present, whether it was achieved by stripping out the savage elements or by returning to them. There would be stasis and it would be good.

Neither side was neutral toward the savage: you were for him or against him. The argument still rages. The breakdown of faith in civilization that culminated in the resistance to the Vietnam War and the rise of the counterculture saw an upsurge in Rousseauism, and the virtues of the savage became a new orthodoxy (Chapter 12). It would be hard to get a hearing today in intellectual circles for any argument that said that the troubles of our civilization resulted from an inability to shake off our savage mentalities and instincts. Even so, while critics of industrial civilization might hold up the virtuous savage as a moral example, they still (being often Marxists themselves of a sort) look to a future in which we shall achieve a civilization embodying those virtues. They do not for a moment want to reverse time and retreat into the savage past. They want the savage virtues along with modern dentistry and birth control.

This orientation to the perfect future, on whatever model, is strangely pervasive. Time is flowing inexorably forward, and we are therefore bound to think of ends and goals for time, not of eternal recurrences. The recent rise in popularity of apocalyptic religions in the East and in the West is a measure of this, and looks fair to replacing the faltering Enlightenment project of rational progress. But the latter is still the dominant paradigm of industrial scientific society, and it still must believe, as did those founders, in the promise of a future perfectibility of man and society. This upward movement toward a peaceful, rational, scientific stasis, although assumed by those founders to be inevitable, would equally inevitably require effort, varying from mental hygiene to social revolution. But it would come.

This hope was based on a basic belief adopted by the empiricist philosophers in the seventeenth century and made the bedrock of progressive thinking ever after. This was the belief that the mind is a blank slate, and that we can therefore write on it whatever progressive and enlightened ideas we wish, and produce behavior to match. The *tabula rasa* view of the mind stems from the mind's own tendency to devalue long-term causation and to take short-term causal views. Cause must operate in time, and our minds therefore embrace relatively immediate causes more readily that distant ones. The negation of human nature by generations of social scientists and philosophers is one example of this deep-rooted bias in favor of short-term causality.

In this scheme, then, the residue of the past was irrelevant, there were no "innate ideas" that might stop us; there was no Old Adam or original sin. There was only the eradication of old shibboleths and the education of new generations in the liberal-democratic ideals of the Enlightenment. All that stopped us was bad thinking and bad institutions, and we could get rid of both through good education and either social revolution or social evolution, depending on the degree of urgency felt. There was deep revulsion at the idea that we might be stuck with some of the barriers to progress, that something in human nature was resistant to benign manipulation, that there even was a human nature at all.

This social evolutionary thinking, details of which will crop up repeatedly throughout this book, became tainted with the increasingly unpopular idea of "progress." To many in the generations after the war it could appear only as arrogant hubris. We could no longer feel comfortable placed on a ladder of progress leading inevitably upward to some kind of utopian future. Material progress could not be denied, but the idea of moral progress began to sound like a bad joke. Perhaps only American exceptionalism was itself an exception to this rule, and we shall look at that in Chapter 3. The cyclical theory of history began to be popular again. In general, relativism ruled, and Karl Popper (and George Orwell) taught us that all those confident predictions about the future were all too easily translated into excuses for manipulating the present.

But if prophecy was out, hindsight was still a great thing. Our social science fathers, when they were not confidently predicting a rosy future, had presented us with a really good idea. If we wanted at least to understand, if not to change, our difficult present, then we should try to understand how we got to it, and got to it over the long haul, not just through the brief time of recorded history. Daniel Smail, a medieval historian who discovered evolution, has taken his fellow historians to task for this failing in his perceptively titled *On Deep History and the Brain*. He finds the roots of their resistance to "deep history" in the lingering dominance of the biblical chronology in historical thinking, along with an obsession with written documents. This is true, but that very resistance itself is a symptom of the general chronomyopia that afflicts us all. Smail, however, fully understands that as a species we have been through a series of giant upheavals, physical, mental, and social, and they have left their mark on our bodies, our behavior, and especially the base of that behavior, our brains. Let us see what the marks are, with all the science at our disposal, and so see how they continue to affect us today.

Unlike our confident forebears, we must not seek assertively either to expunge the vices of the past or to restore its virtues, but instead must ask the question: *What can we in fact do, if anything, about the marks left by history and evolution?* Can we totally emancipate ourselves from them? Should we seek to reinvent them? Is the society we have invented for ourselves in any way compatible with them? Is the world indeed flat, or are there some very tribal bumps in it? In other words, we can try to learn the lessons of evolution, while remembering that evolution is simply history that lasts long enough for genetic changes to take place.

Recent Time

Most of the social scientists of the twentieth century were still caught in the chronomyopia of history and saw the only revolutions that mattered to be those within the historical period, and even within the emergence from the Middle Ages. It is not surprising. Overwhelmed by the drastic and even frantic and dangerous nature of the industrial age in which they found themselves, they concentrated on trying to understand what produced it: How had the modern capitalist industrial system originated, and why? It was what Ernest Gellner frankly called "the Miracle." Marxism said it was inevitable, produced by the dialectic of history. Spencer and his like saw it as the equally inevitable result of progress. But it was neither. It was a miracle in the sense that the origin of life was a miracle: there would have been no way to predict, before they happened, that some concatenation of circumstances would produce either.

Max Weber was the social science founder who put this question to the center of the debate. It still dominates, and rightly so. The concatenation of events that produced modern capitalism had been almost there in the preceding societies. He looked at Confucianism and Judaism, both of which had elements sympathetic to what he saw as the necessary element: an ascetic, this-worldly view of life. But they both lacked an essential element. It was not just the industrial revolution: China had advanced technology and industry and a highly literate bureaucratic elite. This elite however, under the Confucian ethic, was locked into total reverence for past authority: the ancestors. What was needed for the Miracle to happen was the appearance of a class with an ethic that would turn industry into a way of life, an end in itself, not just a source of plunder for the dominant class. It also needed a transformation of slaves, peasants, and serfs into mobile free labor that could respond to supply and demand. In terms that socialism was to make famous, it needed a bourgeoisie and a proletariat.

It needed, in Gellner's forthright terms, to be free of the rule of the thugs. It needed an individualistic, investing class, above all a self-disciplined class, which would view work as a vocation, and which would plough its wealth back into the industry from which it was derived: this was the essence of capitalism. Given this, populations could expand, vast numbers could be employed, wealth could be created, and a whole new species of problems presented in turn.

Weber found his new class in the post-Reformation Protestant merchant and manufacturing class: *The Protestant Ethic and the Spirit of Capitalism* (1904–1905) became the great founding work of historical sociology. The debate is energetically alive today, and it is one of the ideas and issues we must all try to assimilate. In northwestern Europe, particularly in the fertile ground of England and Holland, beginning in the fifteenth and sixteenth centuries, the Miracle happened that dwarfed all the previous upheavals and revolutions. Arnold Toynbee, uncle of the historian, had understood the peculiar position of England in his *Lectures on the Industrial Revolution* in 1884. He understood that such a revolution needed a "spirit" that was in favor of "improvement"—that favorite eighteenth-century concept. A totally new kind of society had to be invented that was willing to make quite radical breaks with the past. Time began to be measured ever more accurately and mechanically: it became "clockwork time," as Samuel Macey aptly names it in *The Patriarchs of Time*. Secular time was separated from sacred time, thus making the organization of work more efficient. Labor had to become ever more specialized, and the more specialized it became, the more interdependent society became. The teeming, tumultuous, frantic, complicatedly fragile world we live in and take for granted is its product.

We must tread a fine line here. While accepting the overwhelming reality of the Miracle, we must not make the mistake of ignoring the Drumbeats that resonate to the human nature molded by natural selection over millions of years of evolution. At the very least we must treat it as a hypothesis that the Drumbeats continue to sound, and that we must listen through all the bewildering noise of the unfolding Miracle. And we must treat as problematical the relevance of the Drumbeats to the success or failure of the Miracle. For this was not a divine act, it was a Miracle we made for ourselves, and it will stand or fall by our capacity to sustain it; and that capacity may in no small measure depend on the Drumbeats as much as it may be defeated by them.

Real Time

Our nature is certainly deeply influenced by the Miracle. But it is also the product of everything that got us to that point of transformation. And we do not shed the past as easily as the empiricists thought; we carry it with us. We must constantly remind ourselves that what we take for granted is so recent in time that we can hardly represent it on any meaningful graph. Whether it is the marvels of our science, the magnificence of our literature, our industrial urban societies, or our bloated populations and their easy mobility, they are all very recent phenomena, and as yet are still experimental phenomena. They have not been around long enough for us to know if they will succeed.

Consider a graph of evolutionary time that is relevant to us. The image of an hour-long film representing human life history has often been used, but the date of the beginning of the film has been repeatedly pushed further back. (Of course we should go back to the beginning of life on earth, or at least to the origins of sexual reproduction, or of the vertebrates, or of the land animals, or of the mammals, or of the primates, or the hominids . . .) The first signs of true humanity are perhaps the simple stone tools that my Rutgers colleague Jack Harris found along with hominid remains in Kenya and Ethiopia, remains from two and a half million years ago: the beginnings of the Paleolithic. If we represent this in an hour-long film, then rounding the numbers and avoiding spurious exactness, we can look at the *last minute* of the hour-long film. This would have started roughly 40,000 years ago, when our few, fully modern human ancestors of the late Pleistocene/Paleolithic were coping with a major ice age, the Würm Glaciation.

Thirty seconds ago came the cognitive revolution of the cave-painting Cro-Magnons in southeastern Europe. *Fifteen seconds ago,* at the beginning of our warm interglacial came the Neolithic revolution and the first domestication of animals and plants. *Seven seconds ago* came the first towns, *four seconds ago* the first states and writing, and hence civilization as we define it. *One-and-a-half seconds ago* the Roman Empire, the Han dynasty, and the Kushan empire in India, were at their height. At *eight-tenths of a second ago* the geographical discoveries and colonial conquests flick by, and finally, at *three-tenths of a second,* the industrial revolution nips by in a blink before the end. In fact if you did blink you would miss it. The rise in the world's population from a hundred million or so three seconds ago, to six and half billion at the end of the hour, would likewise only be visible only if you watched very diligently, because it happened in the last two-tenths of a second. Out of one hour, the world of the Miracle flashes by in a near-invisible blip at the end.

And this is if we choose that starting date. If we decide to make the film represent time since the appearance of the earliest definitive hominids, the Australopithecines, we must more or less halve those times. It is doubtful if we would even see the industrial age at the end. It would go by in less than one frame. Civilization in its broadest sense is, on our first timeline, four seconds at the end, and half that using the earlier date. We would just see it, but we could not take it in. We live in it and we cannot take it in.

We are that Paleolithic hunter, stranded at the end of a particularly warm interglacial that we are making even warmer. We are waiting for either another tropical period that will send jungles to the poles, or more logically another ice age that will send the polar ice (and it can return as easily as it goes) rapidly toward the equator. Both could happen; they have happened before, as have reversals of the earth's magnetic field, or massive meteor impacts, or equally massive volcanic upheavals, or slight wobbles in the earth's axis, or sudden flares of solar energy. They are part of that great cycle of time on which we are not even a blip. And we think we are writing the script.

Time Immemorial

The "savage" whom we either worship or disparage, but whom we in either case physically destroy in our rush to the finish line, has the last laugh. He is never expunged; he lives on in us. Lévi-Strauss teased his readers with a pun in the title of his most profound book, the book we know in English as *The Savage Mind*. The French title was *La Pensée Sauvage,* and the book jacket carried a picture of a wild pansy: *Viola tricolor.*

Pensée in French is both "pansy" and "thought," whereas *sauvage* can mean "savage" but also means "wild"—as opposed to domesticated, that is. The punning title then could perhaps be better rendered as "Wild Thought" or "Untamed Thinking." But the translators understood that this would make no sense to English readers, and rendered it as "The Savage Mind." The pun was intended to bring home the issue of the nature of "the mind of the savage." For the book was part of the great anthropologist's effort to dispel what he had previously called "The Archaic Illusion"— the notion that the minds of precivilized, prescientific, preliterate, preindustrial people had been (and still were, in those who survived) somehow fundamentally different from our own.

His compatriot Lucien Lévy-Bruhl had written of "pre-logical mentality"—of a mind lost in the wrong associations of magic and sorcery, steeped in "mystical participation" with nature, in which an objective scientific attitude is impossible. Sir James Frazer, however, had thought that magic was a kind of "pseudoscience" in that it accepted the idea of causality, but it got the causes and effects wrong: stabbing an enemy's footprint did not make him lame.

Lévi-Strauss demonstrates that the fundamentals of logical thinking were/are as present in the mind of the savage as in ourselves. Literacy and science of course make a huge difference, but they use the same mental material as the savage uses. In *Totemism* (*Le totémisme aujourd'hui*— another wordplay title) he examined the phenomenon of the naming of social groups, usually moieties and clans, after natural phenomena: snake, eagle, water, oak, crocodile, rabbit, emu, whale, raven, and so on. (Moieties are the two, usually intermarrying, halves of a tribe; clans are groups of kin related by descent from a putative common ancestor.) He showed this to be not a utilitarian or sociological phenomenon, but a subspecies of the process of "classification for its own sake" that characterized the mind, not just of the savage, but of humanity in general: the tendency to "order out the universe" as Tylor had put it. All living and inanimate things could, for example, be divided between two moieties of a tribe, as the people were. And there was logic behind the classifications; they were not arbitrary.

The actual series of classifications were peculiar to each society, as Durkheim and Mauss had shown in their classic *Primitive Classification*. But the tendency to classify and categorize in terms of correspondences was universal. It only looked like "mystical participation" because the elements were strange to us. Thus "water" and "land" animals might be distinguished, corresponding to two moieties (say Whale and Wolf), but birds would be distributed between these according to their—often strange to us—associations with water and land. We might make different associations, but the process is the same for us as for "the natives."

Thus the Zuni and Hopi (and other Pueblo Indians) line up everything in their natural and social universe according to the six cardinal directions (including up and down). For example, with the North, in conjunction with the West, are aligned the color: yellow, the animal: puma, the bird: oriole, the tree: Douglas fir, the bush: rabbit brush, the flower: mariposa lily, the corn: yellow corn, and the bean: French bean, and so on through the other five. Eventually everything can be theoretically mapped onto this grid. The setting up of categories and the assigning of items to these categories thus lies behind vast ethnobotanical and ethnozoological schemes that we find among the natives, and that can surpass our own in comprehensiveness, accuracy, and subtlety, down to the identification of genera, family, species, and subspecies.

Even if these classifications are in terms of "sensible properties," Lévi-Strauss says, there is nothing "prescientific" about them. "Any classification is better than chaos, and even a classification at the level of sensible properties is a step toward rational ordering." Nor is it "prelogical"—it involves a logic and *a science of the concrete* that is at the root of all science. And magic not only accepts the scientific principle of determinism—if it has a fault it is that it accepts it overly much. He invokes what he calls the "Neolithic Paradox" to make his point, which links it directly to our own.

"It was in Neolithic times that man's mastery of the great arts of civilization—of pottery, weaving, agriculture and the domestication of animals—became firmly established." These breakthroughs could not have been achieved except by "centuries of active and methodical observation, of bold hypotheses tested by means of endlessly rejected experiments." From a weed to a cultivatable crop; from a wild beast to a domesticated animal; from friable clay to watertight pottery; and so forth. How could all this have arisen from a savage mind hopelessly mired in prelogical magical thinking?

It could not. That mind had to be basically capable of all the functions of scientific logic to reach this point: the scientific logic had to be there. (We shall see it at work 5,000 years ago in northern Peru in Chapter 10.) In future centuries it would turn to experimental science for its own sake, but this was an extension—and a massively important extension—of what was there in the mind anyway.

Scientific Time

That second great breakthrough came in the sixteenth and seventeenth centuries and contributed, along with the Protestant ethic, to the reformulation of the world that was the Miracle. One thing Protestantism did, according to Weber, was to take the magic out of religion, thus making the transition to rationality in all things easier. But let us pause and look at someone who is credited, rightly, with first formulating the principles of the scientific method, Francis Bacon (1561–1626). Bacon was one of the shining group of humanists in England, including Erasmus, More, and Colet, who wanted to break with the deductive aridity of scholasticism and replace it with a science based on fact and experiment. The Greeks moved us to deduction and produced Aristotle, but thought got stuck there. We had to move from deduction to induction to produce science.

Karl Popper, when I was an undergraduate at the London School of Economics, had me read Bacon's *Novum Organum* (1620)—even though this was so I could see therein the weakness of "simple induction" and appreciate his own principle of "falsification" (more on this in Chapter 12). Bacon introduces his method of "bottom-up" thinking with the organization of facts into "tables and arrangements of instances." His most famous example is "instances agreeing in the form of heat." Put simply, he lists all the things he can think of that appear to generate heat. (I have simplified here.)

1. The rays of the sun.
2. The same reflected and condensed.
3. Ignited meteors.
4. Burning lightning.
5. Eruptions of flames from the cavities of mountains.
6. Flame of every kind.
7. Ignited solids.
8. Natural warm baths.
9. Heated liquids.
10. Warm vapors and smoke.
11. Damp hot weather.
12. Confined and subterranean air.
13. All shaggy substances, as wool, the skins of animals, the plumage of birds.
14. All bodies placed near fire.
15. Sparks arising from the violent percussion of flint and steel.
16. All bodies rubbed violently.
17. Green and moist vegetable matter.
18. Quicklime sprinkled with water.
19. Iron when first dissolved in acids.
20. Animals, particularly internally.
21. Horse dung, and animal excrement, when fresh.

22. Strong oil of sulphur when burning linen.
23. Oil of marjoram when burning the bony substance of the teeth.
24. Strong and well rectified spirits of wine.
25. Aromatic substances and warm plants.
26. Strong vinegar and all acids.
27. Severe and intense cold which produces a sensation of burning.
28. Other instances.

Bacon calls this a "table of existence and presence" and then proposes a corresponding table of absences—of instances where there is no heat present, which starts with the rays of the moon. A third table that shows degrees of heat is presented, and the experimental method can proceed by trying to discover the qualities of presence and absence and hence the "Form" or cause of heat. This would be present in all the examples in the first table, absent in all the second, and variable in the third.

But what is striking is that this first great demonstration of how to proceed in experimental science starts with a list that could have come from one of the grids of correspondence of a Zuni or a Fulani or an Australian Aborigine. It is basic analogical thinking. It could be a list of the items assigned to a "heat" (or sun) moiety as opposed to those of a "cold" (or moon). We would be asking ourselves: Why on earth do the savages consider "flint" and "wool" and "horse dung" and "marjoram" to be totems of the sun moiety?

I cannot resist using Bertrand Russell's example (in his *History of Western Philosophy*) of the basics of Bacon's thinking: "He valued his method as showing how to arrange the observational data upon which science might be based. We ought, he says, to be neither like the spiders, which spin things out of their own insides, nor like ants, which merely collect, but like bees which both collect and arrange." Bees have language and memories, like us, and put them to work in the same way. And they are an older and wiser species than we are. But then bees are not troubled by emotion. They respond but they do not, despite our anthropomorphizing, get angry. They collect and arrange, but they do not laugh, not even a little.

But for Bacon, collecting and arranging was the beginning of scientific wisdom, and the savage mind does both as an appetitive activity. It needs no utilitarian stimulus; it feeds on the diversity of things to order them. It did this to survive. Bacon's table is a Whitmanesque poem on the properties of heat; it is surprising and intensely imaginative, as is all good science. (It is fair to observe that the original was in very un-Whitmanesque Latin.) If there was ever a proof that the savage mind is always active, even at the birth of the modern inductive scientific method, it lies in Bacon's tables.

And it makes Lévi-Strauss's point and with it my own. The savage mind is the mind of mankind. It is a *"bricoleur"*—an odd-job man cobbling together the material of the senses. We have changed the content but not the structure of the mind. We are all filled with untamed, wonderfully imaginative and compulsively (ana)logical thought. And it is the thought that was born in the long journey through the ice and the drought, the forests and the savannas, and all those "selection pressures" that made it what it is. If there is a criticism of this picture of the savage mind, it is perhaps that it is too intellectual. All these categories have both an emotional and an evaluative component.

We shall look at these emotional factors, because they are part of the process of imagery and memory and the production of poetry, in Chapter 9. There was equally a selection for affective and affiliative states, as we shall explore with male bonding in Chapter 8, and incest avoidance (and attraction) in Chapter 6. And in all these cases we are asking that nagging question about the persistence of the Drumbeats and the problematical relationship of the world of the Miracle to them. Our thinking, our feeling, our associating, our exchanging, our valuing, our imagining were all created in a world we have only recently abandoned and transformed.

This is not a novel position, although the manner of treating it, and the subjects treated, in this book might be a bit unusual. With my episodic sense of time, I prefer to use a fugal theme-and-variations approach rather than the sonata structure that would be a continuous narrative. It is a fundamentally Darwinian position, but it perhaps owes as much to Freud's *Civilization and Its Discontents* as to anything sociobiological. Freud's title is misleadingly mistranslated; he called it *Das Unbehagen im der Kultur*—more like "Uneasiness in Culture." For Freud, savages, although less repressed than their civilized counterparts, were still the victims of the repression of libido and aggression on which all culture is founded.

But both Freud and Darwin proceed from the same premise: that we are not simply the imprint of our culture (whatever that is)—it is a two-way street, and we bring to it as much as we take from it. And for Freud the increase in social complexity that produced modern civilization did bring extra pressures—extra *Unbehagen*, what Popper, agreeing with Freud, called "the strain of civilization." (More in Chapter 12.)

For Freud all culture was based on self-control—what we in the days of advanced neuroscience have come to see as the increasing influence of neocortical control over the emotional brain, the limbic system, hence "delayed gratification" and more strategic timing in behavior generally.

Freud saw it as the increase of the power of the superego, the voice of conscience, of society, that resulted from aggression being turned ever more inward against the self (the ego) as more self-discipline was needed to meet the demands of civilization. For most people this could become too much. The strain of civilization could become more than we could bear. We long for release from overwhelming self-responsibility. We want to externalize the superego, to let someone, or some doctrine, become our conscience. It is another way of stopping time, of stopping the strain of time, of returning to the timelessness of the womb, or the tribe.

CHAPTER TWO

The Human in Human Rights

Tribal Needs and Civilized Ideals

WHENEVER WE make claims based on what is "human," we are treading on shaky ground. As our first chapter established, what we regard as human, and hence humane, may be so recent in our history that we have not even yet established its viability. There is a humanity that shapes our ends, perhaps, but it could be a humanity that is in deep conflict with what the Miracle established. Or it could not. Perhaps we are indeed acting out a basic nature that only a weight of tyranny keeps from flourishing. This was the view of the Enlightenment, and we are the heirs of its insistence on universal individual rights.

But at least we must treat with a decent skepticism the postulation of "rights" that are somehow reflections of a rights-loving nature. We must accept that the relationship between nature and rights is problematical. And given the perspective that has been established here, we must keep an ear open for the Drumbeats of that nature forged in the Paleolithic, the time of our making. The extension of rights to strangers was a slow and painful process, and however much we might feel in our civilized bones that it is both necessary and natural, our tribal selves tell us a different story.

What follows are some observations prompted by the free and easy use of the phrase "human rights" by politicians in the Clinton administration and their justification for armed intervention in defense of these same rights. Armed intervention is almost always undertaken for reason of power; "human rights" simply become a useful cover story for public relations purposes. If they were truly the cause, then why have we not intervened in Tibet, Burma, Congo, Saudi Arabia, Zimbabwe, Argentina, Cuba, Chechnya, Guatemala, Venezuela, Sudan, Iran, Pakistan, Egypt, Uzbekistan,

Syria, Rwanda, Algeria or even Gaza? We should start at the top of the list of offenders on the Human Rights Watch list and work down. Obviously we don't. But some of the rights-talk politicians obviously do sincerely think they have a monopoly on the use of the word "human" and that this is a legitimate basis for drastic action. That monopoly, from our particular point of view, we can evaluate and challenge.

The Human Factor

President Clinton and some of his entourage took to using the buzz phrase "human and political rights" to replace the simpler "human rights" of established piety. The new usage tended to be pronounced as a single word, much as Senator McCarthy spoke of "communist-atheist-homosexuals." A call to the White House press office produced no explanation of the coinage, but they assured me that "no policy change was implied." It's always nice to know that it's business as usual. One would like to think that some sense of the paradoxes and complications of the term "human rights" had come home to the administration, and that in consequence it was on its way to even more qualifications: perhaps "human, political, civil, economic, legal, cultural, national, sexual, and domestic rights."

This may be too much to hope for, but one gets the impression that the president meant to restrict "human" to "personal and family" and so needed to tack on "political" to cover all those "rights" that are to do with the wider society and participation in it. But what does this mean? That political rights are not human? That "human" has to do only with our persons and families? Whatever happened to "natural rights," which traditionally used to cover all of the above?

So much has now been written about "human rights" that, like President Clinton, we tend to lose our perspective and get confused. As with the classic issue of "natural rights" before it, the debate becomes so infused with passion that straight thinking is almost impossible. Argument about rights of one sort or another is both possible and desirable, particularly given the current penchant for using "human rights" as a basis for often quite brutal foreign policy decisions. But we have to recognize that putting "human" in front of "rights" when, for example, talking of the "human right" of people to free elections is simply to use a warm "hurrah" word as a rhetorical device.

In the same way, wars of political suppression become "humanitarian interventions," and anything we don't currently happen to like becomes "unnatural," even if it is something as basically human as the hunting of game animals or investment in multiple spouses. I think that the words "human" and "natural" both have a real content, and we can identify that content. But given the all-too-free use of these terms, perhaps we should ask ourselves what that content might be. The trouble is that we have used them as hurrah words for so long that we will balk at any result that is not consonant with our current enlightened prejudices. We want to get to define what is natural; we don't want nature to do it for us, for the result might not be pretty.

Thus if anyone were to make an argument, however logical, coherent, and backed by evidence, that there is no natural or human right to vote, for example, he would not be answered so much as ridiculed and condemned as reactionary and antihumanitarian. Yet a respectable argument could indeed be made that there is nothing in nature, or certainly in the nature of being human, that demands the right to vote as such. This is not so much a human or natural right as a right contingent on the fairly advanced economic and political development of certain civilizations. It is probably the sort of thing the president had in mind when he added political to human in the rights catalogue. The natural/human right might be phrased as "a right to a say in the affairs of one's group."

How such participation in group decision-making is to be ensured, however, is not defined by anything in nature or humanity. Voting becomes an issue only at a certain sophisticated level of political development. It may be possible to argue that at such a level everyone has a right to vote (although exceptions will rapidly be listed—children, lunatics, felons, peers, exiles, nonresidents, resident noncitizens, non-property-owners, unregistered persons, and so on), but such a right is scarcely natural or human. It is more properly cultural, or social and political, deriving from the nature of government so achieved rather than from facts of nature or humanity.

On the other hand, a proponent of kin-selection theory could make a very good argument that there is a natural and human right to revenge. Let us therefore play the devil's advocate and accept, for the sake of argument, the kin-selection or inclusive fitness position. Thus, if someone kills my nephew or grandson, he robs me of a proportion of my inclusive fitness: my own genes plus the replicas of those genes in relatives with whom I share a common ancestor. To redress this balance, it could be argued, I have the right to inflict a similar loss on him. That is, I should be allowed to deprive him of someone related to him by $r = .25$—the same degree of relationship as my murdered relative. This could be satisfied by killing two of his first cousins ($.125 + .125 = .25$), or any such combination that would level the balance sheet.

It is remarkable that many systems of vengeance in human society seem implicitly to observe the logic of inclusive fitness. They do not, for example, necessarily prescribe that I kill the person responsible: one of his kin or clan will do just as well. This system of vengeance is less efficient as a redress than a system whereby I would get to impregnate one of the perpetrator's females, thus forcing him to raise to viability a person carrying my own genes. Actually, in the example cited this would amount to overcompensation, because I would gain by .50 to a loss of .25. It would be more exact if my brother were allowed to make the impregnation, thus restoring the exact genetic balance.

Either method is of course impractical given intertribal or clan hostility, but note how ubiquitous is the practice of impregnating captive women or the women of defeated rivals. The advancing Russian forces in World War II made a massive effort to redress the imbalance caused by German depredations during operation Barbarossa. Russian genes are now being nurtured on a vast scale by the Federal Republic's economic and welfare systems. Serbian troops and militias raped Muslim and Croatian women, and then, to prevent abortions, kept them prisoner until they gave birth. They thus redressed the balance caused by these enemies in collaboration with the Nazi exterminators in occupied Yugoslavia during World War II.

I probably do not have the right to demand that any superordinate entity carry out this vengeance for me (although I may call on supernatural agencies, and will commonly use sorcery to harm an offender). In strict fitness theory I am bound to redress my own wrongs and either succeed or fail, thus determining my own ultimate fitness in terms of the genes that I, and those who have genes in common with me through descent, contribute to the pool. Perhaps the most basic claim we have against a collective entity, on this view, is that it leave us alone to settle our affairs.

It is generally observed, however, that as human societies evolve, many of the self-help functions are delegated to some superordinate authority. This is the essence of the social contract: for the sake of harmony within the group, certain basic rights to individual action are delegated to the group itself. Hence, compensation comes to substitute for vengeance. Again, this is often framed in reproductive terms: compensation for a murdered man is that which will enable his kin to raise another child to replace him.

In many systems before the advent of the monopolistic state, there was no question of personal retribution through the execution of the murderer. Just compensation ("blood money") that would enable the genetic replacement of the victim was considered sufficient. This can be seen as a humanitarian advance in human morals, or as a retrograde step depriving individuals of the right of vengeance, but either way there is no question that it preserved the idea of redressing the genetic imbalance caused by a human-activated death. The monopolistic state, however, declares that there is no individual right to vengeance, and reserves that right to itself. Thus the state exacts retributive justice, but leaves the kin of the victim without compensation, and the imbalance permanent. It is not clear how this is an improvement on the older systems of self-help or compensation.

The Woody Allen Question

It does however raise the interesting question: at a certain point of development in human social complexity, does the collectivity acquire "human rights" over against the individual? This is important because so much of the above-mentioned writing on human rights assumes them to be by definition *individual* rights. This often goes to the length of seeing no rights as inhering in any collectivity—except, perhaps, the family—and even as seeing the collectivity as the automatic enemy of human rights. Such rights are almost by definition rights *against* the state. But there have always been human collectivities; we are, as F. H. Bradley observed, following Darwin, following Aristotle, a rootedly social animal. In fact, Bradley argued, we could show that individuals did not exist: the social was real and the individual the abstraction. Take away from any so-called individual everything contributed to his nature and person by society (starting with the genetic contribution of his parents, grandparents, and so on), and what is left? Nothing. The whole idea of rights being peculiar to individuals becomes possible only with self-conscious creatures, of which humans are the only example.

What sense does it make to attribute individual rights to ants? Woody Allen's neurotic worker oppressed by the collective morality of the colony in *Antz* is funny only because it is impossible: an anthropomorphizing of the ant condition. But it is interesting because that is precisely what has happened in the human situation. A group-living mammal, living in socially complex colonies, like baboons or chimpanzees, suddenly, in evolutionary terms, became conscious of its own condition, probably by evolving powers of speech in which to talk about it. Baboons cannot have individual rights anymore than ants. They simply do what they have to do to be baboons and produce more baboons.

But once a primate is conscious of its condition, then it can start to ask the Woody Allen type of question: "Why must I always do the things the group wants to do? Why can't I decide for myself what is good for me?"

In this way it can formulate the notion first of "individuals" and then of certain things owing to individuals: just as the group has a "right" to a territory, so an individual has a "right" to . . . The answer is pretty much anything it can think up. Once started on this delusional pathway, there is ultimately no limit except the limits of imagination.

The individual "rights" that a primitive, self-conscious, but of necessity group-living primate would claim, would of course be based on its individual needs to feed and procreate successfully. But it is important to note that at this level the need to claim rights over against the demands of the group would not arise, because the group would be the individual's inclusive-kinship network. All individuals feed, struggle for dominance, mate, and raise young. In this process, the existence of the group is a necessity like the existence of natural resources. Individuals will make altruistic sacrifices for the group because it is essentially a group of kin, and thus represents the repository of their inclusive fitness. There is no way in which the small group of relatives could be seen as somehow having interests different from those of the individuals composing it. In Bradleyan terms, there could be no distinction between the society and the individual.

A Profoundly Unfair Process

But as levels of social complexity increased, after the Neolithic revolution, organisms would increasingly be dealing with (relative) genetic strangers who made demands on them in the name of social units whose genes were not identical by descent with theirs. It is at this stage that true conflict would occur, and that organisms would start to feel the need to assert their "rights"—that is, the things they needed to do in order to ensure their fitness: the means of reproduction.

In a strict sense this is the upper limit of the natural or human claims that an organism (read: individual) can have against any collectivity of genetic strangers. It is the area President Clinton seemed to have in mind with "human." It is a claim based on the functional necessities of reproductive competition. It cannot be a claim to reproduce successfully, only a claim to be allowed to compete for reproductive success. It is not a claim for fairness, something that Rawlsians would like to write into the "original situation." Natural selection is a profoundly unfair process; that is the point of it. Some start with a genetic advantage over others; all men are not created equal. But all have a right to play their hands to the best of their ability. The group has no obligation to level the playing field unnaturally, but it has an obligation to let the players play.

Thus we might say that the only basic human rights are those that allow individuals to compete in the reproductive struggle. These would be rights to access to potential mates, and the resources needed to acquire, hold, and breed with them, and to raise offspring so produced to viability. (This would underline the claim that rights to "equality" should be to equality of opportunity, not equality of outcome. The outcome has to be unequal, or natural selection would not take place.) Thus we could speak of a "human right to procreate," although I would prefer to state it as the "right to engage in reproductive competition." For it is important that we recognize these basic human rights not as claims to some kind of benevolence or handouts from the collectivity (even though we may decide such benevolence is due for other reasons). They are claims to be allowed to take part in the reproductive struggle. Insofar as we fail, we fail, and as long as we were not artificially restricted in our attempt, we have no cause for complaint.

To take a currently contentious issue: Is there a "human right" to free choice of marriage partner? (I am sure the president would have regarded this as a "human," not a "political," right.) To those of us reared in a relentlessly individualistic society, such a right seems obvious and basic. But it is so only in such a society. In a society where the clan or extended family is the basic unit—and note that this itself is the basic "human" unit—then it is equally obvious that such a choice is too important to be left to individual whim. What is at stake is the continuing reproductive success of a group of genetically closely related individuals. The parents of any potential couple carefully monitor the match in light of the probability of a successful reproductive outcome in all its ramifications. In so doing they are acting not only in protection of their own inclusive fitness, but also in terms of their greater experience and predictive ability, in protection of that of the young couple.

There is nothing either unnatural or inhuman here. On the contrary, our attitude of allowing whimsical affections and passions to decide the choice of partner, with the subsequent often awful consequences in divorce, stepparent abuse, one-parent family problems, and the like, can be seen as inhuman, unnatural, and reprehensible. But so high in our value system have we elevated individual choice as an absolute, that it appears to us simply "self-evident" that arranged marriages are unthinkable. It is an infringement of "human rights." It may be an infringement of something, and there may indeed be good moral arguments against it, but the "human rights" argument will not wash.

You might counter that I have just said that the group should not interfere with the right to compete for reproductive success. But in the case just cited it does not do so. Rather it seeks to *reinforce* the chances of individual reproductive success, and we could forcefully argue that it has the "human right" to do so. Societies with arranged marriages are easily outreproducing those with free choice, despite the access to better medical care, sanitation, nutrition, etc. in the latter. There is nothing in the "laws of nature" that says the kin group (the pool of genes related by descent) should not seek to enhance the reproductive success of its members. On the contrary, it should seek to do so, because individuals, given imagination, intelligence, and free will, and hence the capacity for delusion, as often as not act against their reproductive self-interest.

Thus non-kin collectivities, while certainly often acting against the interests of their members, will also often move in to prevent at least self-destructive behavior that might injure individual reproductive success: drug misuse, suicide, child abuse, infanticide, or abortion. More positively, they support those people whose behavior has reduced their chances of raising children to viability. Monastic institutions in the Middle Ages, while manned by celibate "brothers and sisters," were homes for a staggering number of otherwise doomed infants deposited by those unable to support them. Social welfare systems operate on the same principle: although we have no natural right to their assistance, they have a natural right to assist us. Here non-kin collectivities are taking over the functions that originated, and have their logic, in the kin group. If we support them and they support us, it is because of a natural extension of mutuality from the "original position" of kin support.

It is in the interest of a nation, for example, that it reproduce itself. Thus it tends, in its delusional-ideological system, to pass itself off as a super kin group. At the primitive level of evolving humanity (99 percent of our existence as a species) there was no need for such pretense. The kin group *was* the social collectivity. This is why I have argued above that at the most basic, and hence most "human," level, there would be no "rights" issue. In promoting the success of near kin we are promoting the success of our own genes (or more correctly, they are using us to promote their success).

Thus, still within the purview of basic kin-selection theory, we have another human right: the right to nepotistic assistance. We have the right both to assist close kin and to receive assistance from them in the pursuit of our own reproductive success. Until the advent of meritocratic bureaucracy, the world lived by this principle. It is what "kinship" is all about: all those gentes, clans, sibs, septs, moieties, phratries, lineages, houses, kindreds, and extended families. There is no human society that does not map out, often in alarming detail, its universe of kin, the better to calculate the degree and kind of help and obligation expected.

The term "nepotism," from the Latin *nepos* (grandson, sister's son), was first invented to describe the hypocritical (but most certainly "natural") tendency of prelates either to favor their nephews or to hide their illegitimate sons under the nepotic title. In another stunning reversal of natural values, we have now made it one of the worst crimes against "equality"—which it most assuredly is. This does not prevent us, though, at all levels of society up to the very top, from wallowing in the hypocrisy. The most basic feature of social evolution is not so easily defined away.

The point of the above examples is to make us wary of a free and easy use of the terms "human" and "natural." It is not to say that there are no other rights than those that exist in some guttural, shambling, scavenging state of protohuman existence. Of course there are. But it is to say that we should be more careful in the logical underpinning we choose to give to these rights, if for no other reason than that we do render the terms meaningless and empty and rob them even of rhetorical value. Also, as we have seen, human rights may be rights to all kinds of behaviors that our sophisticated and sensitive liberal natures may abhor. Hunting is a good example: England has decided to ban fox hunting on "humanitarian" grounds, which seem to have more to do with puritanical objections to the hunters' enjoyment than with the supposed suffering of the fox.

A very good case could be made, for example, that the "right to procreate" (which has now been established in U.S. common law—see *Reproduction and Succession*) includes the right to polygamy (polygyny and polyandry) for those who can afford it and want it. Why should the state—on grounds that are always fuzzy and derive largely from religious prejudice—limit the number of spouses? The overwhelming majority of human societies (approximately 85 percent) have allowed or enjoined it. Again the "advanced" societies have reversed this tendency, a tendency which is wholly "natural" in a reproductively competitive species of large land mammals with moderate sexual dimorphism and late-maturing young.

As with the Romans, the argument for monogamy is egalitarian. But as we have seen, nature is not egalitarian: if some succeed and some fail in the polygamy stakes, then the same is in fact true of monogamy, where some will always outbreed others. And yet again, the monogamous societies, while banning multiple marriages as "unnatural," hypocritically allow all kinds of multiple *mating*, serial monogamy being the most common example in modern Western society. Very often those things we have condemned as "unnatural" are things that we know will flourish if we leave them alone. For if something is natural, we have no need to buttress it with sanctions, it will take care of itself. (There are paradoxical counter-examples, as we shall see in Chapter 6. We condemn the practice of incest as unnatural, but it may in fact be more natural for us to avoid it.)

Nature's Neutrality

What then should we call these rights that are not basic, natural, or human, but that we "know" to be desirable? (Thus we may not know what human rights are, but we certainly know when we have lost them.) Surely, you ask, we should not give in to relativism and suggest that they are simply local preferences and have no universal validity? At least I hope you are asking that, because as we know that pernicious doctrine has achieved a sinister grip among the scribbling classes. It is perhaps strange that the relativist triumph should come at the same time as the pursuit of "human rights issues" has come to dominate international affairs and foreign policies.

The two trends are perhaps not unrelated. In a world of relativistic morals we would have no basis for attacking offenders against "rights" if these could be dismissed as mere cultural preferences. We therefore have to underpin certain rights as "human" to stress their universality. If they pertain to all humans—on what grounds is not always clear—then they are impervious to the relativist objection. What is truly strange is that a good many theory-befuddled academics and activists hold both views at the same time, lauding relativism in defense of "multicultural" agendas while denouncing, say, female circumcision as contrary to "universal human rights." Logic is usually the first fatality in ideological warfare.

These cherished rights enshrined in the U.S. Constitution, the Declaration of the Rights of Man, the United Nations Charter and Human Rights declaration, and all the treaties and commissions up to the Helsinki Accords and the establishment of the International Court with jurisdiction over Crimes Against Humanity, are highly evolved political and social rights that derive from the Western Enlightenment tradition with its basic values of equality and universalism. Many of them are peculiar to the Christian tradition. It is in their very nature that, despite their anchorage in attempts to establish rights based on "nature," they should in most cases either run counter to nature or concern things about which nature is strictly neutral. We have looked at some of the former. As examples of the latter we might suggest that "nature" gives us no clues about what form certain institutions might take, only about the rules of engagement, as it were. Thus we should be able to accrue resources so as to take part in the reproductive struggle.

But exactly how we should accrue those resources (whether they include that Enlightenment favorite, "property," for example) and to what lengths we should go to prevent others—our reproductive rivals—from accruing them, and to what extent we should assist our close kin by passing resources to them, on all these matters nature is silent. The winners will be rewarded, but they will be rewarded if they cheat as well as if they play fair. They will be rewarded if they kill and torture, if that is what gets more of their genes into the pool. They will be rewarded if they co-operate, if that is what gets it done. We can see that some behaviors will be self-defeating—too many cheaters will leave not enough suckers—and probably self-limiting as a strategy in the genetic long run. But in the short run a cheater can perfectly well manage a respectable score in the inclusive-fitness stakes. We still celebrate the con man and the huckster, and especially deride the cuckold. The law may take one view, but popular opinion is not fooled.

Inclusive-fitness theory is an effective way, but only one way, into the issue of what is basically human. I have taken it here simply as an example. Take another approach—say, the findings of psychology into the basic list of human motivations. Certainly we shall find some that suit our warm and compassionate version of "human," but there will be a list of others that that we would not want on any list of things to be fought for and protected and promoted. Take again those things we have in common with our nearest animal relatives, the chimpanzees, whose genetic material is 98 percent our own. There is the warm-and-fuzzy list all right, but there is also, as Jane Goodall discovered to her warmhearted horror, war-fare, genocide, hunting, cannibalism, homicide, female beating, infanti-cide, violence, domination . . . (see Wrangham and Peterson, *Demonic Males*).

Take, say, those features that have been found to be common to all hu-man societies by comparative ethnography. Once again, the list of saintly characteristics is overbalanced by the dark-side features that seem so ines-capably human. It is a pure act of judgment to say that the dark features, all of which can be shown to have contributed to survival, are to be re-garded as less "human" than the ones we have selected as worthy of pro-motion. And there will be yet others that have served their survival pur-poses and are regarded as benign by even a majority—and have been so regarded throughout history—that in our enlightened judgment must be read out of the list of the truly human.

Aspirations, Not Needs

So where are we left with our rights problem? Does it really matter if the term "human" is wrongly applied to rights? I think it does, because this is an area that is too important for us to indulge in systematic self-delusion. We are moving into a period when the pursuit of "human rights issues" is filling in the vacuum in foreign policy left by the disappearance of clear-cut "national interest" issues (for example, Robin Cook's much-touted "ethical foreign policy" for the United Kingdom). This has already been the excuse for us to break the rules of international behavior established in the "national interest" period, to bomb a sovereign nation (Yugoslavia) into submission, and kill at least 3,000 people.

It threatens to start another and more deadly war with China. It is moralistic, self-righteous, and aggressive. It is dangerous as well as hypocritical in its selective action. Yugoslavia was in the end massively bombed to preserve "the credibility of NATO." How useful, that "human rights" could be invoked as a cynical justification. (See also the human and national rights of Kuwaiti sheiks that were so gallantly protected in what otherwise might have seemed to be an old-fashioned war to protect our vital oil interests.) And given the moral state of our politicians, this is about all we can ever expect.

Robert Benchley was of the opinion that whenever a government began shouting "Spies!" it was inevitably trying to divert attention from its own shady business. Perhaps we can be forgiven for suspecting something of the sort when we hear politicians chanting the mantra of "human rights"—usually to cover some hypocritical, and inevitably blundering, manipulation of the United Nations by the powers in the Security Council. Given the inevitable skepticism about governmental honesty (or at least competence), we should at the very least insist on being clear about what we are doing and on what grounds we are doing it.

And I am saying that we should not do it on the grounds that what we are supporting or suppressing is in some sense essentially "human" when it is no such thing. A great deal of what is human is in fact what is at the root of what we are opposing, suppressing, killing, and destroying in the name of human rights. To achieve the kind of world envisioned in the treaties, charters, and commissions, we must indeed suppress and destroy—at the very least control—human nature. We are not acting for it, we are acting against it, or we are supplementing it in those cases where it gives us no guidance.

Human rights theorists are often quite honest about this. They disclaim any attempt to base these rights on human nature or human needs, and define them as "the best to which we can aspire" or as based on "a moral vision of a dignified human life" (Jack Donnelly, *Universal Human Rights in Theory and Practice*). This is fine, but it is not then plausible to claim at the same time that they are "based on the very fact of being human." They are not; they are based on the fact of individuals being trapped in oppressive collectivities. This is why they must, by definition, be individual rights.

There is nothing wrong with defining rights in terms of high human aspirations, but they will then require a very different justification from rights based on human needs. They involve, in effect, a purely teleological justification: human rights become the rights we need to *achieve* a certain desired end state of society, not rights deriving from the elusive state of true humanness.

Thus rights involving inclusive fitness are more likely to be respected currently in fundamentalist Islamic societies than in Western democracies. But societies based on Islamic law are usually the ones most offensive to human rights activists. It can be argued that human rights based on aspirations are no less human than those based on needs. True, but the problem is that we can aspire to virtually anything, and how do we choose between competing aspirations? Needs at least give us some criteria of arbitration, and very necessary ones, because many liberal-democratic-individualist aspirations—however laudable—have the quality we observed of running counter to basic needs and thus defeating their own objectives. Is there any point in aspiring to a state of affairs that is so inhuman it is unsustainable, however ethically laudable? The true hair-splitters will want to argue that such impossible aspiration, too, is very human, and so it is; we are nothing if not a paradoxical animal.

Human Rights and National Interest

One of the major paradoxes surrounding the human rights issue is that it became central to foreign policy as part of a deliberate strategy to protect the national interest. Human rights activists will not like this claim, of course. They prefer, as is their way, to think they are acting from nothing but the highest and purest moral considerations. But even they will admit that these explicit concerns—as opposed to a general U.S. urge to be the world's good guys—had a definite beginning in the Carter administration. They prefer, however, to forget that this stance was deliberately engineered by Daniel Patrick Moynihan to counter the hypocrisy of the third-world communist bloc. Moynihan, as ambassador to the United Nations, was tired of just sitting there and taking it when the bloc used anticapitalist moralizing as a basis for attacking the policy of the democracies at the behest of the Soviet Union.

So he developed the strategy of counterattacking (or even getting in the first punch) on the grounds of the abuse of "human rights" by these regimes. This brilliantly put the democracies onto the attack rather than having them constantly apologetic and on the defensive. It put the onus of explanation and justification on the totalitarian dictatorships and their bullyboy leaders. But it was not something that arose out of humanitarian concern for the benighted inhabitants of these third-world terror regimes; instead it arose out of the need to combat their belligerence in the United Nations, and hence to curtail the influence of our major competitor.

I am not saying that anything Senator Moynihan did could have been totally cynical, but he is quite clear about the development of this as a *strategy of foreign policy* first and foremost. It was in the defense of the national interest and in the interest of the Western alliance. As one strategy among many to promote our collective ends, it had its place. As an excuse for a foreign policy, given the huge amount of post–Cold War military hardware available, and the compelling urge presidents and premiers seem to have to use it, it deserves a close and skeptical scrutiny. This involves both a scrutiny of its practical dangers, best left to strategists, and of its theoretical underpinnings. With this latter enterprise, some otherwise useless academics can at least show that even if the emperor has new clothes, they are woven of dubious synthetic fibers.

CHAPTER THREE

The Kindness of Strangers

Tribalism and the Trials of Democracy

HE MISTAKE we make with the "human" in "human rights" is bound up with our insistence on "individual rights" as the only basis for a truly free and acceptable society. But this is one of those wholly new ideas in the world's history, dating in effect from about 450 BC in Athens, and having a shaky history since then. We in America have now moved from adopting it as the foundation of our own open society to wanting the world to adopt it in turn, on the basis that it is the natural state of humanity and that only wicked regimes prevent it from flourishing. But is this true? Or are we blinded by our own preferences?

The following ruminations were prompted by a particular event, the invasion of Iraq in 2002, and the subsequent events, and by reading two books, Fouad Ajami's *The Foreigner's Gift* and Philip Salzman's *Culture and Conflict in the Middle East*. So they return repeatedly to the particular problems of that most recent war of occupation, written in two stages: early in 2007 and then in 2009, with some final comments on the present state of affairs. But these ruminations on a particular case go the heart of the basic issue of the present book in that our leaders make claims about human nature and the natural state of human society as justifications for political action, and in this case armed intervention.

This is surely cause for a hard look at the claims, and an attempt at least to evaluate the assertion that they are based on what is "natural" for us and for those we insist on helping. To do this requires us to dig deeper into the machinations of politicians and local military strategies. It might require us to think the unthinkable: that our own version of rights and freedom is perhaps the artificial, not the natural, one. But we have had some practice in the last chapter, so here goes, starting with Samuel Huntington's acute observation in *The Clash of Civilizations* that "Western civilization is valuable, not because it is universal, but because it is unique."

Laocoön's Warning

Laocoön warned his fellow Trojans: "Do not trust the Greeks, even when they come with gifts." His warning went tragically unheeded, and they took in the wooden horse. Since then the course of history has been strewn with the corpses of ungrateful nations that, despite the misery stemming from their inability to manage their own affairs, bitterly resented and actively resisted the firm and forceful help of others. The stranger's gift of peace, order, and prosperity is less welcome to us than the death, chaos, and poverty that are our own doing, for they are our own, and that is what matters to us.

Like truculent adolescents, we do not want to be told how to do things or have them done for us. Gandhi said to Churchill, who sincerely thought India could not do without British help in its struggle to join the modern world: "You must let us make our own mistakes" (Hermann, *Gandhi and Churchill*). Once again we cannot learn from our own history. Think of how the invading Napoleonic armies were greeted as liberators by Enlightenment radicals in the European countries, as the bearers of the liberty, equality, and fraternity promised by the French Revolution. And let us remember how the people of those countries so decisively resisted, especially in Spain, and allied with the European monarchies to expel, often at bitter expense, the armies of reform and progress that their intellectuals had welcomed.

We will often take what we can use from what is offered, but we want, in the end, to do it ourselves: to manage our own lives, however badly. The main thing about the stranger, after all, is that he is strange. He is not like us; he will never understand us. Our greatest fear, perhaps because the possibility is often so seductive, is that we will become like him and lose our selves. The stranger's gift never comes without strings, and we do not want to be tied.

We of the post-Enlightenment Anglo-Saxon West are among the most earnest of the givers. We are not, like our medieval Catholic ancestors, really proponents of the Crusade and the holy war against the heathen. We are at heart Protestant missionaries. We want to bring the good news and the benefits of civilization to the benighted of the earth. And if they don't want it, then like good Protestant parents, and entirely for their own good of course, we must sternly make them accept it. Certainly we hoped to make good profits and attain political power in the process, but these were small prices that the benighted had to pay for the incomparable gifts we had to offer.

Critics of colonialism miss the point if all they see is the profits and the power. Our civilizing mission was, and still is, as dear to us as jihad is to Muslims. Even when it is not Protestantism per se that we are offering, it is the children of the Protestant ethic that we know as democracy, liberty, equality, and the free market. Our learned men tell us in fact that we are the foreordained bearers of a truth so fundamental that with its triumph history will come to an end, there being nothing left for mankind to achieve. If this is so, how can the benighted so stubbornly, and even violently, refuse our gift of a free leg up onto the stage of world history?

The continental Catholic colonial powers never paid more than lip service to the white man's burden, especially the Belgians (the French get a pass), but the British and later the Americans had it in spades. There is no question that we went into Iraq to defend our oil interests: that at least was the rational part. But the Holy Warriors of the White House saw a far greater opportunity. They could plant the banner of liberal democracy in the heartland of Arab totalitarianism, and thus change the world for the better.

To do this was to collaborate with the inevitable progress of mankind: a sure winner of a policy. We would simply give the inevitable progress a friendly shove in the right direction. The "Iraqi People" (much invoked) would dance in the streets, greet us as liberators, and gratefully accept our gift of free elections. How could they possibly prefer the savagery of Saddam and the hegemony of the brutes of Baath? Once rid of these monsters, the "Iraqi People"—like people everywhere, as "lovers of freedom" (Rumsfeld's mantra)—would set up a representative democracy modeled on our own. Ballot boxes and purple finger paint would be provided, political parties would be free to form, and the press would be unrestricted.

Once in place, this model democracy would stand as a rebuke and an example to the monstrous regimes in the Middle East, which would gradually succumb to the same happy fate. What is more, it would be an Arab democracy, thus saving the Arabs from the embarrassment of Israel being the only democratic state in the region. (Turkey might seem to be an exception, but the secular democratic state there is maintained—ironically—at the pleasure of the army.) Because democracies are inherently peaceful, the more of them in the region, the better, and the better for our "national security."

Above all, as the guarantors of this liberal democratic paradise, we would have a continuing benign influence in the area, which would, incidentally, protect our oil interests. To get the "American People"—inherently suspicious of foreign entanglements—to support this noble enterprise, it was necessary to scare them with Saddam's intentions and his putative weapons of mass destruction. After both the Gulf War and 9/11 this was not hard to do, particularly with the trusted figure of Colin Powell leading the chorus, and Saddam behaving for all the world as if he really did have the damn things.

Missionaries of Democracy

For the missionaries this was a chance too good to be missed. The "criminal enterprise," as Fouad Ajami calls Saddam's regime, was ripe for plucking. There was no way its army could stand up to the superior Western forces, and once the army was disbanded, the criminals tried, and "de-Baathification" completed, the grateful freed "People of Iraq" would take it from there. They would need help and firm guidance from the missionaries, of course. They would make mistakes, and there would be all the baggage of dictatorship to unpack. But it had been done in Japan and Germany with startling success, why not in Iraq? (Both totally misleading examples, as it happens.) To suggest otherwise was to suggest that the "Iraqi People" were somehow inherently incapable of "freedom and democracy." That was to be condescending and colonialist. Everyone everywhere wanted these benefits, and only wicked regimes prevented them from realizing these universal human goals, toward which, we must not forget, mankind was inevitably evolving anyway.

I am not caricaturing this position. Those who would see the ideology as a cynical cover for the Armaments Industry, Haliburton, and Big Oil interests are missing what is truly at issue here, and what is much more frightening. The colonial powers always look out for their economic and strategic (power) interests, of course; it would be foolish of them not to. But they have also always believed in the "civilizing mission" as just as important. This was partly justified by religion—bringing Christianity to the heathen—but was also seen as an end in itself: the production of an industrial, peaceful, democratic (sometimes socialist) world.

Herbert Spencer was the chief nineteenth-century apostle of this creed. As societies evolved from *military* to *industrial* institutions, so would peace and democracy spread around the globe. Free-trade advocates repeat it today: the more we are dependent on each other through trade, the less likely will we be to fight each other. Trade requires the rule of law, the rule of law promotes democracy, and democracies don't fight each other . . . We know the logic. It was the basis of Wilsonian internationalism: "Making the world safe for democracy." The White House Warriors were caught in this same chain of reasoning. President Bush's second inaugural spelled it out.

One British newspaper announced: "Bush Threatens World with Freedom." This is the fundamental belief of the missionaries. We have a precious gift that we can give the nations of the world, and whether they want it or not, we are going to give it to them. If they think they don't want it, then they must be reeducated, with force if necessary, to realize that they do. History is going to end in universal liberal democracy anyway, so they might as well learn to cooperate with the inevitable. Needless to say, the politicians are not consistent, and in the "national interest" are just as likely to prop up tyrannies as export democracy. But democratic idealism is still deep-rooted in American international thinking. It is the outward expression of American exceptionalism: we are the city set on a hill, the example to the world.

The problem for Euro-American liberal/radical critics of Bushism is that they really believe the same thing. It is no longer fashionable in progressive circles to think that some form of communism or socialism will be the inevitable end product, except among the few remaining Marxists in the universities. But some kind of democratic open society is seen as the only alternative for the decolonized peoples of the world. The critics find America imperfect in this regard, but they adhere as strongly to the ideal of liberal democracy as the most fervent neocon.

It is hard to find any serious postcolonialist who will agree that, having thrown off the imperial yoke, the ex-colonial peoples should be free to choose dictatorship, theocracy, tribalism, nepotism, clitoridectomy, or the rule of warlords. Respect for "indigenous cultures" goes only so far. The left-liberals assume as firmly as the Bushites that people everywhere really aspire to a state of liberal democratic polity where human rights and the rights of women will be assured, and tolerance and religious freedom will be institutionalized.

It is their constant embarrassment that this doesn't happen, and fifty years later the excuse that the failure lies in the pernicious aftereffects of colonialism is wearing thin; they do not really believe it themselves. (They have substituted, as villains, neocolonialism or neoliberalism or globalization or transnational corporations or . . .) But the alternative is hard to bear for the progressive mentality that assumes we can indeed write our own script and exclude all those factors of "human nature" that seem so stubbornly to resist our enlightened blandishments. The only allowable fact of "human nature" accepted by right, left, and center alike is the rather vague "love of freedom." This might well be true, but we all then eagerly assume that, given free choice, "they" will opt for a form of freedom we recognize and approve of, namely, one leading to the liberal democratic institutions we have fought so hard to develop, protect, and preserve.

Nature and History

Against this naive optimism of the missionaries of whatever stripe, we can set an opposing view that is historical and what we might call naturalistic. It sees that the institutions we so prize are not the *product of* a freedom-loving human nature but the result of many centuries of hard effort to *overcome* human nature. However desirable they may be, they are not natural to us. We maintain them with constant vigilance and the support of hard-won economic, political, legal, and social structures that give them a chance. These have taken literally thousands of years to put in place. In England universal suffrage had to wait until 1928, when women under thirty were finally included. In Switzerland this had to wait until 1971. In the United States it was only after the Voting Rights Act of 1965 that we could be said to have achieved, at least legally, true democracy, although the kind of democracy where 95 percent of incumbents are automatically returned as a result of gerrymandering (or, as we call it, "redistricting") perhaps requires its own special definition.

Again in England, it was not until 1688, after a bitter civil-religious war and a period of hard totalitarianism, that we were able to set up a system whereby political factions could compete for votes and, most amazingly, the losers would *voluntarily cede power*. This transformation took a long time and hard practice with many missteps. It was possible then under the umbrella of a constitutional monarchy, starting with William and Mary, and it should give pause for thought that the most stable democracies in the world are the constitutional monarchies: Britain, Holland, Sweden, Denmark, Norway, Belgium, and now Spain.

The monarch provides a focus of loyalty, legitimacy, and continuity that transcends the factions and enables them to take turns at governance without armed conflict. The United States also got its period of practice at democracy with its colonial assemblies, under the same umbrella, before it decided, perhaps rashly, to jettison it. They went instead for an elected, limited-term monarchy, where the high officers of state would not be elected by anyone but be appointed by the elected monarch. Under this presidential system, the head of state and commander in chief is in fact also a leader of a political party, and this gives rise to considerable ambivalence about loyalty to him, and is open to obvious abuse. Politicians in trouble can hide behind their sacrosanct role as commander in chief. But either system works well enough that the peaceful transfer of power can take place and does, sometimes even when the winner has in fact received fewer popular votes than the loser.

But far from being a fact of human nature, this voluntary ceding of power after elections, this basic feature of liberal democracy, actually flies in the face of nature. It is self-evidently absurd. Our political opponents are always disreputable, and their accession to power will be the ruin of the country. Listen to the rhetoric of campaigns: it almost amounts to criminal malfeasance to allow the opponents to take over. Yet that is what we do after a mere counting of heads: cede control to the villains and incompetents.

The cynic will say that the only reason we allow this to happen is because we know that in truth there is no real difference between political parties in these systems, and so we join in a conspiracy of the willing to take turn and turn about. Even so, this willingness that we take so for granted is an amazing and unusual and a fragile thing. Ajami quotes an Arab proverb, *min al-qasr ila al-qabr*: "from the palace to the grave." Once you have power, in the name of God and the good of the people, you keep it, and the voluntary relinquishment of power is simply seen as weakness or stupidity.

Even in the United States it is only fairly recently that we have given up the idea of elections as *total* spoil systems, except at the level of appointing unelected presidential (or gubernatorial) cronies to office. And our Western democracies still struggle with nepotism, corruption, and cronyism, whose energetic persistence should tell us something. (Look at Adam Bellow's excellent *In Praise of Nepotism* for examples.) How could we believe, then, that we could walk into a country like Iraq and do in a few months, or even a few years, or even several decades, what millennia had failed to evolve spontaneously? Because "the Iraqi People," like everyone else, "loved freedom"?

Ajami's book, subtle, intelligent, and moving as it is, makes almost painful reading. He is supportive of the removal of Saddam and the potential shake-up of the region as its bullyboy dictators quail at the sight of one of their number on trial (and now hanged) for sins that are commonplace among them. At the same time his intimate knowledge of the country and region shows how ill-equipped it is to face the task of governing itself according to the foreigner's model. He paints a vivid picture of the earnestness and sincerity of the attempt by American commanders, especially General Petraeus, to understand and help in "reconstruction." At the same time he sums up their situation as "bewilderment" in the face of the intransigence, as they see it, of the ungrateful natives. The old colonial administrators could have told him a few things about ungrateful natives.

For a start, there is no "Iraqi People." The phrase should be banned as misleading and purely rhetorical. Iraq as a "nation" (like the "nation" of Kuwait) was devised by the compasses and protractors of Gertrude Bell when the British and French divided up the Middle East in 1921. We know well enough the ethnic-religious division into Kurd, Sunni, and Shia. People who know very little else can rehearse that one (even if they do not really know the difference; the Kurds are Sunnis, after all). But what is not understood is that Iraq, like the other countries of the region, still stands at a level of social evolution where the family, clan, tribe, and sect command major allegiance. The idea of the individual autonomous voter, necessary and commonplace in our own systems, is relatively foreign.

Cousins and Strangers

I received a call in 2003 from a *New York Times* reporter, John Tierney, who was baffled by what he discovered in his Baghdad hotel. Each week there was a lavish wedding in the hotel dining room and ballroom. It looked very Western, until he discovered that the bride and groom were inevitably cousins, and more than that, they were mostly paternal parallel first cousins, as the jargon has it. In English: they were the children of two brothers, and if they were not that close, then the bride was usually from the same clan or tribe as the groom. Occasionally a woman from the mother's paternal clan was married, as in the case of Saddam Hussein. When questioned about this, the young people told the reporter, "Of course we marry a cousin. What would you have us do, marry a stranger? We cannot trust strangers."

One Iraqi informant explained to a colleague of mine that you must marry a cousin—best of all a *bint ami,* a daughter of your father's brother—because only members of your own lineage could be trusted to deliver a virgin. Strangers would cheat you on this. Your paternal uncles, you knew, would watch their daughters closely; anyone else's daughter was suspect. (France has recently been embroiled in a controversy over whether failure to disclose loss of virginity is a cause for annulment in Muslim marriages there.) Such a system of close-cousin marriage, the commonest form of preferred marriage in Arab society, literally keeps the marriage in the family. This goes to the heart of the matter. These groups are inward looking and suspicious of strangers. It is the "Mafia solution" to life: never go against the family. Trust is possible, ultimately, only between close relatives, and preferably those of the paternal clan.

It is hard to diagram systematic marriage with the father's brother's daughter (abbreviated FBD for convenience). Figure 3.1 attempts this. The man we have arbitrarily denoted our EGO (or reference point) can be seen to marry his FBD, and EGO's son in turn marries EGO's brother's daughter. But whom does EGO's brother (B) marry? The answer is that structurally he is the same as EGO, and he too would marry a daughter of their common father's brother. We shall see how basic this form of marriage is to Semitic society generally in Chapter 6 when looking at the descendants of Adam in *The Book of Jubilees*.

It probably originated in the desert-nomad stage of Semitic society when the patrilineal and patrilocal (descent through males, residence with

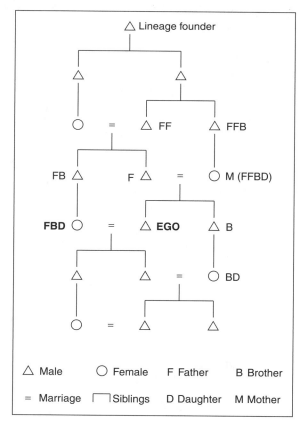

Figure 3.1   Father's brother's daughter marriage

the father) bands of Arab Bedouin wandered isolated in the desert, and when all other bands were potential enemies. They married within their own band, their own clan, their own tribe. Even among the settled Bedouin this was maintained, because it kept wealth and property inside the lineage. Outside were the unmarriageable strangers.

This "marriage in" is called *endogamy* and is contrasted with the more usual *exogamy*, or "marriage out" of the kinship group. Which cousin you choose matters in this contrast. Cross cousins, the children of opposite-sex siblings, when chosen as marriage partners, lead you to marry out of your clan or lineage, and this is the more usual form. Parallel cousins, the children of same-sex siblings, go the opposite way, and like the Arab example above, the marriage of the children of brothers must lead to marriage *within* the kin group. (Marriage between the children of sisters is very rare.) It can be a distinction without a difference, in that two groups could practice cross-cousin marriage with each other and still be bound in an endogamic relationship excluding outsiders, as in Figure 3.2. Here "sister exchange" in each generation results in consistent marriage with cross cousins. The triangles and circles here stand for "men of the group" and "women of the group," respectively.

We shall have occasion to look at this again when asking about the origins of the incest taboo in Chapter 7 and the Australian Aborigines in Chapter 11. For the moment it is enough to grasp that although these two groups are indeed locked together in marriage, there is the potential

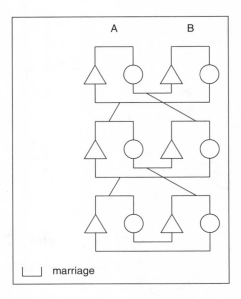

Figure 3.2   Cross-cousin marriage

to include an infinite number of other groups. If group A, a lineage or clan, can exchange cousins in this way with group B, it can do so with groups C, D, E . . . *n*. This is not so with parallel-cousin marriage; you are stuck with your own clan. For our present purposes the details of kinship and marriage systems can be left aside. (The keen can look them up in *Kinship and Marriage*.) It is enough to see that the form of marriage is an indication of the in-turned world of clan and tribe, where strangers are a dangerous option.

There is a telling scene in Mario Puzo's novel *The Godfather* that did not make it into the movie. Don Corleone's family are telling him of the brave deeds of his son, Michael, who has served honorably in the U.S. Army, risked his life, been wounded, and won medals in the service of his country. The old Don shakes his head in puzzlement and asks: "He does these things for strangers?"

The idea of voluntarily doing anything for strangers (non-kin) has to be worked at. It is another of those things we in Western democracies do every day without thought: it is "human nature" for us. We give large sums of our money to complete strangers, trusting that they will use it responsibly and for our benefit. Largely they do, as with banks and insurance companies and brokerages. When they do not (AIG, Enron, Madoff), our wrath is huge. We turn over other large sums to legally appointed strangers for purposes often unknown to us and for the benefit of complete and total strangers. This is taxation. It is everywhere hated, but absolutely necessary to run a complex society.

We trust strangers to do things absolutely essential to our lives and welfare. We take it for granted they will do them; they are "doing their jobs." But this is as foreign to much of the world as our odd acceptance of the relinquishment of power. And to that same world it borders on the immoral as well as the insane. In those places where the state cannot be trusted with the welfare of individuals, they turn to the older and wiser certainty of kinship, to the clan and the tribe.

Francis Fukuyama to his great credit understands this, and in his aptly named book *Trust*, he spells out how difficult it is for "low-trust" societies to develop the large corporations that are necessary for industrial capitalism. These societies—China, Korea, Italy (particularly southern Italy), and France are his examples—have great problems moving away from our Mafia solution, "trust only the family," to the essential "trust non-kin." Or even developing a legal system that enables them to have dependable contracts with non-kin. This includes a move to the use of monetary credit (Latin *creditum*, from *credo*, I believe), which is in itself a remarkable instance of trust and is why we call relations involving it "fiduciary": they are based on faith *(fides)*. Low-trust societies make the move, but have difficulty sustaining it and tend to depend on state support or even state ownership to create corporations. In their opposites, the "high-trust" societies—England, Germany, and Japan have managed to create systems in which strangers are trusted (enough)—non-kin relationships such as voluntary associations can flourish, and non-kin corporations can form with relative ease.

Alan Macfarlane in his *Making of the Modern World* has beautifully shown how this holds from way back in England, where all these elements of trust got a head start. England had a centralized legal system that valued individual rights, especially in property, and invented the legal instruments appropriately called "trusts" that again we take for granted today. This was the fertile ground that the Protestant ethic could work on. Japan is an interesting test case that Macfarlane looks at in detail, because it developed its high-trust, capitalist system without the intervention of Protestantism as such. It is easy to dismiss Japan as a copycat, but in fact the history of Japanese institutions reveals the functional equivalents of the "high-trust" European systems.

Strangers and Citizens

These thinkers illustrate a trend that has characterized the whole history of social science. This is a history of our concern with the massive transformation of society that was involved in the shift away from the kinship-dominated, religiously integrated, tight community. Spencer (*military* societies to *industrial* societies) we have mentioned, but the transition was central to the thinking of:

Ferdinand Tönnies: from *Gemeinschaft* (community) to *Gesellschaft* (association)

Henry Maine: from legal systems based on *status* to those based on *contract*

Emile Durkheim: from social solidarity that was *mechanical* to that which was *organic*

Robert Redfield: from the *folk* society to the *urban* society, from the *little* tradition to the *great*

Karl Marx: from *precapitalist* economies to *capitalist* economies

Lewis Henry Morgan: from *gentile* (clan) society to *political* society

Karl Popper: from *closed* (tribal) societies to *open* (democratic) societies

Louis Dumont: from *collectivist* societies to *individualist* societies

Talcott Parsons: from societies with *particularistic* values to those
with *universalistic* ones

Claude Lévi-Strauss: from *cool* (ahistorical) societies to *hot* (historical) societies

Karl Polanyi: from regulated *mercantile* society to self-regulating
market society

William Graham Sumner: from societies based on *folkways* to those
based on *mores*

and above all:

Max Weber: from societies with *traditional* forms of authority, to
those with *legal-rational* forms: with a big push from the Protestant
ethic. While all were ambivalent about what was lost and what was
gained by the transition, all agreed that it was inevitable, if often
savagely painful.

The whole of "development" sociology was about helping "the undeveloped world" (which later became "the third world") over the hump.
Weber most clearly saw that charismatic leadership ("rooted in biology")
was always there in the wings, ready to return us from the fragile rational-
legal and bureaucratic state to the more natural condition of traditional
authority and the patrimonial, status-governed, kinship-theocratic condition from which we emerged.

Only Tönnies perhaps saw that the tribal "community" was radically
natural: the default system of human social nature, and therefore the one
that was literally the most "attractive." If in the West it took us two millennia to emerge from this default system, and if we have only partly succeeded, and if our grip on liberal democracy is so fragile, why do we think
the Arabs can do it, or should want to do it, out of enlightened self-interest
more or less overnight (in historical terms)?

When it doesn't work, we are "bewildered." The hospitals in Baghdad
were up and running except that there was no electricity. And the main
reason was that as soon as copper wire was laid to connect them, the Iraqis
came out in the night and stole it. Copper brought a good price. When the
troops expostulated with those caught and tried to make them see that
their theft was against "the Iraqi People"—the indignant thieves demanded to know who these "Iraqi People" were who got between them
and the feeding of their starving families and relatives. They were not
responsible for some mythical Iraqi People, but for their kin: their cousins who were their spouses. The few ambulances in Baghdad cannot function properly to get the injured from bombings to the hospitals. The

armed clansmen of the injured commandeer the ambulances and turn out the unrelated wounded. Often firefights break out between armed groups competing for the ambulances.

Remember the graphic scene in *Lawrence of Arabia* where the tribal chief Aouda (Anthony Quinn) is told he should join in the attack on the Turks in Aqaba for the sake of "the Arabs." "Who are these Arabs?" he asks. He recites the tribes he knows, but demands to know what tribe is "the Arabs" that he should sacrifice for them. "The English" he understands as a tribe he can ally with against his enemies, including the Turks if it suits him. Thus some of the sheiks in Anbar province will ally with the Americans against al-Qaeda and its allies if it suits them. But their and Aouda's sole concern is with their tribal advantage. This was Aouda's highest moral imperative. And Aouda loved freedom above all other things.

If the tribal "imagination" we are dealing with is closer to the default system of human nature than is our cherished individualistic democracy, then we ignore its appeal at our peril. The marriage of close cousins may appear to us backward, unhygienic, or immoral, but it is the pattern that has dominated the world until fairly recently in historical terms. If we could get into God's memory, we would find that 90 percent of marriages have been with close cousins.

On a worldwide scale, most of these, however, have been "exogamic" in that they have been with cousins *out of* one's own clan. The Arab custom of marrying paternal parallel cousins as we have seen produces closed kinship groups that lack the wider social ties that are made possible by exogamic rules. As many as 50 percent of Iraqi marriages continue to be with close paternal cousins. The custom goes beyond the Arabs as such, and recently the British have had to try to come to terms with the preference of some immigrant Pakistani groups for such marriages, which are actually not forbidden in English law as they are in most American states.

Ajami describes the "small number of clans around Saddam Hussein, closed off from the rest of the country by intermarriage and inbreeding." At one time Saddam banned the use of tribal surnames. This might appear puzzling, but it was because most of his government was filled with his own tribe, and the surname *al-Tikriti* betrayed this too obviously. To be correct this was Saddam's tribal confederation or *qabila;* his tribe was the *Al-bu Nasir.* There are, we are told, some twenty-three or twenty-four "militias" in Baghdad. No one thinks to add "tribal" to militias.

Warfare continued in the supposedly "pacified" southern Basra province, which is overwhelmingly Shiite and so lacks the sectarian component. The fight there is for power between the Shia tribes (read: militias) and the criminal gangs formed around various clans. Again these will either use or attack the British troops as it suits them. The British have largely given up on certain tight tribal areas and concentrate on trying (unsuccessfully) to seal the border with Iran. They have now left and were congratulated by Washington on a mission completed. The al-Maliki government decided to move against the Basra "criminal gangs," and the result was a disaster until American air support blasted the tribes into submission—temporarily.

Hard-Won Democracy

In the West we had to move from tribalism, through city-states and small nations, through empire, feudalism, mercantile capitalism, and the industrial revolution to reach our present state of fragile open universalistic democracy (shrugging off communism and fascism along the way). Athens and Rome had a period of republicanism and democracy—at least voting and elections for free males—but this did not last and succumbed to autocracy and dictatorship with the growth of empire. The English were helped in the shedding of dominant kinship groups by the relative individualism of the Angles and Saxons, with their emphasis on the independent nuclear family. (See Alan Macfarlane's *The Origins of English Individualism*.) Christian monogamy and the banning of cousin marriages by the Catholic Church helped to break down extended kinship groups and encouraged even more individualism.

This breaking up of tight kin groups by expanding "prohibited degrees" (as far as third cousins) is perhaps not sufficiently appreciated. Think what it would have done to the Arab cousin-marriage system. In England the institution of primogeniture—inheritance by the eldest son—also helped prevent the dissipation of family fortunes produced by partible inheritance: division of the patrimony among all sons, common on the continent (and in China, but not Japan). It reduced the power of aristocratic clans by forcing the younger sons into the professions: the army, the law, and the church.

This move away from kinship and into the world of voluntary and non-kin organizations was in turn infused with the Protestant work and reinvestment ethic, and the Miracle happened. It did not happen all at once, but over several centuries of cumulative effort that fed on the new humanism and the growth of science and industry. As labor became ever more specialized and more mobile, family groups became ever less self-sufficient, and individuals became more and more dependent on strangers and on the institutions that made dependence on strangers possible: in particular, the rule of law and the enforcement of contracts.

And we had to do it by our own efforts, pull ourselves up by the social bootstraps, to make it stick. We have seen in Germany, in Italy, and in Spain how fragile this really is. Russia never did make it. France is always problematic. Latin America and the Balkans continue to be a mess. But in making this move we had to change the entire particularistic, communalistic, ritualistic, kin-dominated society that is natural to us, and we have to keep at it all the time. In Britain (and in northwestern Europe more generally) a noncorrupt civil service does seem to have been established, for example, but it perpetuates itself with exclusive schools, colleges, regiments, and clubs that protect the administrative class and make it self-perpetuating. Blatant nepotism in supposedly meritocratic governmental systems, however, is officially frowned on, and while members of the class may get a leg up, they still have to (as they had to in China) pass the necessary examinations. The effort is made.

In Africa, when a tribesman is elected to parliament, large numbers of his clan move to the capital expecting—indeed demanding as their moral right—positions, jobs, and handouts from their democratically elected relative. This what they understand democracy to be about, and it has a crushing effect on any attempt at rational, meritocratic government. Barack Obama in *The Audacity of Hope* tells of a visit he and his wife made to his relatives in Kenya. "Michelle saw how suffocating the demands of family ties and tribal loyalties could be, with distant cousins constantly asking for favors, uncles and aunts showing up unannounced." He will be lucky if they don't all decamp to Washington, D.C., in search of handouts and positions. We in the West had to turn "nepotism" and "corruption" from tribal virtues into criminal offenses, and we struggle with it. I live in New Jersey, and I stare into the pit.

Does this mean we should not make the attempt to encourage democracy elsewhere? Absolutely not. The best of the colonial regimes left a rough-hewn democracy as at least part of their legacy that was accepted and still more or less works in some places. India is a prime example. So are the West Indies. In Africa the nations of Ghana, Nigeria, Kenya, and South Africa have struggled yet somehow survive; but South Africa is in trouble, and Kenya had a recent unnerving slide into tribal violence—Kikuyu versus Luo, plus some forty other tribes. In all these cases there has had to be accommodation between the stubborn tendencies of our tribal human nature and the demands of unnatural democracy, but it seems marginally possible. In other countries it has totally fallen apart with the tribal, ethnic, and racial pressures winning hands down. You know the list.

The very diversity of India seems to help, in that the democratic parliament and the English language and court system (and perhaps cricket) are the only things that hold it together. Even so the political class in India is heavily criminalized, and the country with its caste system, and especially the underclass of "outcastes" that so troubled Gandhi, is scarcely a model of liberal democracy in most other ways. So what makes us think we can expect to transform Iraq and the so-called Iraqi People into clones of our democratic selves overnight, particularly as an unwelcome occupying force? Above all, what makes us think that our model is the appropriate one to be applied in blanket fashion anywhere in the world, no matter what the stage of social development?

We gave the Iraqis ballot boxes, and they voted almost entirely on tribal and sectarian lines: they voted as they were told to vote. We in the West have a sad tendency to confuse democracy with elections. Even rabid dictatorships hold elections. Ballot boxes in these countries mean very little. We counter that we favor "free" elections, but none of these elections are free in the sense in which we understand it, with individual autonomous voters exercising personal sovereignty at the ballot box. This has less to do with intimidation than with tribalism and sectarianism. For example, the Kurds vote as a bloc—or as two blocs along the lines of their own internal tribal divisions. They have a virtually independent state that we keep quiet about. It refuses to fly the Iraqi "national" flag and patrols its own borders with its own army. The Sunni tribes of Anbar also vote as a bloc, or withhold their vote as a bloc when ordered to boycott the elections. Now that they have decided to vote, they are organizing a plethora of parties on tribal lines, and organized as tribal coalitions, with the sheiks vying with each other for local power.

Meanwhile at least 2 million Iraqis are exiled in Jordan and Syria and are in the hopeless and dangerous state of refugees everywhere. Many cannot go back to their old homes because whole areas of Baghdad and other towns have in effect been ethnically cleansed by the sectarian militias, and physical barriers have been erected by the American forces to separate the warring factions, like the "Peace Line" in Belfast. The towns of Mosul and Kirkuk in the north are always on the brink of tribal and sectarian war. Christians have fled Mosul by the thousands, and the central government is afraid to try to hold provincial elections in Kirkuk because of the Kurd-Arab conflict over control of the town. We set up "national" police and a "national" army, and tribal and sectarian militias have infiltrated both. We set up a "unity government" that was inevitably

Shia dominated (or dominated by the al-Maliki Shia faction) and is riddled with corruption on an uncontrolled scale: the public feeding trough again.

Under Paul Bremer and the "provisional authority," Ajami reports, precious funds needed to equip and pay the troops and police simply disappeared. More than $9 billion is unaccounted for. Prime Minister Allawi admitted: "There was no auditing. Airplanes were flying in and the money out in suitcases." Once the "Iraqi People" were liberated, they looted everything in sight, and once there was a public purse in place, they looted that. They were providing for their families and clans with what was there. What is there is there to be exploited *now*. There is little sense of a national public good, no collective deferred gratification. The future is hypothetical. The parallel with New Orleans after Katrina is perhaps too obvious to draw.

Ajami would attribute this to the brutalizing (in the correct sense) of the people by the Baath regime. It is partly that; it is also inherent in the predemocratic condition of the state, which can hold together only through common national beliefs and rituals (which it does not have in this case) or by force, or both. The British in their brief tutelage of Mesopotamia stuck to indirect rule. They left the aristocracy and tribal leaders and the social hierarchy in place, together with the "old habits of ethnic and religious accommodation," which, Ajami declares, characterized their traditional dealings at their best.

The British, who also wanted the nation they cobbled together out of three provinces of the defeated Ottoman Empire to be a model for the region, gave it a more-or-less constitutional monarch from outside (Faisal the Hashemite) as a focus of loyalty. In 1958 his son and successor, and the royal family, were slaughtered, and the tribal thugs from Tikrit and Mosul took over. In all this the Shia resisted, revolted, and suffered massively, most recently when they were deserted by Bush senior and the allies after the Gulf War: a betrayal they have not forgotten and that echoes through all their dealings with the Americans. They have used the Americans to consolidate their new power and dominance over their Sunni rivals, and will keep enough of them there to be useful until they feel safe to try to rule alone.

Arab Attitudes

Ajami is at his best describing Arab attitudes, particularly those of the Shia. The great puzzlement of the U.S. liberators was why there was not immediate gratitude and total cooperation from the Shia. But Ajami insists that anti-Americanism will always trump gratitude. Thus the Shia Hezbollah in Lebanon supported Saddam against their sectarian brothers in Iraq, because he was anti-Israel/America. In general the Arabs supported the evil regime of Saddam, particularly in his war against "the Persians." That they could not deal with it themselves, and that the foreigners (read: Americans) had to come in to clear it out, only added to Arab "humiliation." This, along with "anger"—which seems to justify any excess—is their favorite word.

Thus the Shia in Lebanon originally welcomed the Israeli ouster of the tyrannical (Sunni) PLO, but soon turned on their liberators and Hezbollah was born. Wars of liberation have a short shelf life. There is a serious limitation to the gratitude of the liberated. The "freed" Shia in Iraq must avoid the taint of collaboration with the infidels to keep their credit with the other Arabs and Muslims generally. They can use the infidels to consolidate their new grip on power, but "there can be no Shia Trojan Horse for the Pax Americana." They will use us and lose us in their own time.

The complications are endless and ultimately absolutely frustrating. Ajami is excellent at describing the convolutions of Arab thinking and the despair it causes the strangers, who can only see it as "shiftiness" or "deception." Deception is synonymous with diplomacy for Arab and Persian alike. Confuse and deceive your enemy. This is the aim of the game. The Persians are playing it beautifully with their nuclear strategy, and we are shocked, shocked to find they have been "lying." The Sunni–Shia divide, we are painfully learning, goes deeper into Muslim history than the Catholic–Protestant in our own. When asked about the sectarian dispute, I usually reply: "Think Catholic versus Protestant during the Wars of Religion."

President Bush tells us that what we are *really* fighting are the "terrorists" in Iraq—specifically al-Qaeda. There were no al-Qaeda terrorists in Iraq, of course, before the invasion. If they are there now, it is because we gave them this golden opportunity. But are they there specifically to do harm to our way of life and our precious freedoms? Perhaps, but this is not their more immediate aim. They are there to kill "heretics"—the Shia, the allies of the hated Persians, the new upstarts who threaten the long-established Sunni dominance. If they can do damage to the Americans in the process, well and good, but their target really is the heretics.

Ajami explains that al-Qaeda (and letters in this vein to Osama bin Laden were intercepted) sees those Iraqis who cooperate as guiltier than the infidels: "This is why a sectarian war against the Shia *"rafida"* (refusers of islam) was the way out for the holy warriors." In "freeing the Iraqi People," what we did was effectively to free the Shia. In giving the Iraqis "free" elections, we put the Shia (or at least al-Maliki's faction) in power. In dethroning the Sunni, we started an insurgency. The insurgency gave cover to foreign terrorists—notably al-Qaeda. The anti-Shia violence of the terror squads gave rise to a sectarian war that may have gone into a retreat, but is still there in the hearts and minds of the people, and it will take very little to make it flare up again.

Bourgeois Democracy: Civil Society

Those who think there is any kind of straightforward answer by way of a "surge" in American forces, or a strengthening of the "national unity government," or a pouring in of more aid to alleviate unemployment, or any other "gifts," should read Ajami—not only *The Foreigner's Gift* but his other works, like *The Dream Palace of the Arabs* on the failure of pan-Arab Nationalism and Socialism. And they should do this particularly because Ajami remains sympathetic with the attempt to change the face of the area and produce something like a decent democracy there.

No one knows the Arab intellectuals better, or interprets their ambivalence and delusional natures with more skill. But like all the progressives of both right and left, Ajami sees the world in his own progressive image. He fails, as they do, to admit the power of the primordial attraction of the kin-based *Gemeinschaft,* and of charisma (the next man with a mustache) and of theocratic certainty, and of the grim stability these provide. The only reason our own numerous and stern religious fanatics do not force their own theocracy on us is because we do not let them—so far.

The old formula "no bourgeoisie, no democracy" still holds—noting that this is a necessary but not sufficient condition. This is why, if we wish to promote democracy, we should lose our obsession with promoting *elections* and promote those things we know nurture a strong middle class: the rule of law, education and literacy, and economic prosperity. Democracy may or may not follow, but if there is a middle class with a stake in its political future, it will have a better chance. What small commercial and professional middle class there was in Iraq, with its need for the rule of law to guarantee contracts, was destroyed by Saddam's "criminal enterprise." It is not something we can re-create with any amount of aid or surges, nor can we force it upon "the Iraqi People."

The bourgeoisification of tribal societies will in turn cause its own problems. For a time the more progressive members of the growing detribalized middle class in the cities will make democratic demands that are out of sync with the social and religious conservatism in the still-tribal areas of the country, including the city slums. This will be a cause of tension and violence. Something like this is true of all the Middle East, and explains a lot of what is happening in Iran. The various forces also have to be kept in balance. It is no use promoting advanced education if there are no positions for the educated to fill. Egypt and Pakistan have both produced an excess of lawyers who can find no work. A degree in law was seen as a sure path to government employment, and thousands of young men took it. Now, in Egypt, for example, most of the taxi drivers in Cairo have law degrees. What they need to be doing is promoting business enterprises, not waiting for government jobs. The mind-set, as we say, has to change, and policy with it.

The price of failure in Iraq, said President Bush, is too high. But what constitutes success? Perhaps the goals set, beyond the entirely worthy toppling of Saddam, were impossible to achieve in any kind of short run. The response has been to keep lowering the bar: now "security" is enough, and a pious hope that things will work out between the politicians. The administration may, by increased force and bribery (the Iraqi People understand both very well), patch up some kind of "order" for a while. But they cannot create the whole civil infrastructure and the sea change of values and attitudes that underpin a working liberal democracy. You have to create what theorists like Ernest Gellner call "civil society," defined as "a plurality of institutions both opposing and balancing the state, and in turn controlled and protected by the state": the society we took so long to create ourselves, and that we struggle so hard to maintain. Mere order, or lack of too much public violence, is not enough to produce civil society. Boots on the ground and bribes to the tribes can produce order, but they do not turn tribesmen into citizens.

Since the last passages were written (in early 2007), the "surge" has been put in place and 30,000 more troops have been added to the occupying forces. "Some kind of order," as I predicted, has been imposed by the mix of force and bribery. If that is what we want, then the surge "worked." But as even its most passionate advocates insist, there has to be a "political solution." This is a form of solution proposed, naturally, by politicians, who see the world as being of their making. As though the wheeling and dealing of corrupt politicians in Baghdad will somehow make for that crucial change in attitudes, values, and behavior that will produce the liberal-democratic state that we want to wish on the Iraqis.

The "order" that has been imposed results from things other than the increase of boots on the ground. Although that has been effective in dampening down violence in the cities, it only worked in conjunction with the revolt (or Awakening) of the Sunni tribes in Anbar province against the growing tyranny of al-Qaeda. The terrorists overplayed their hand and tried to impose their rule on the indigenous tribes. The tribes calculated that they had more to lose from al-Qaeda than from the Americans. The Americans under the clever General Petraeus seized the opportunity and offered to arm, subsidize, and even recruit the tribes. This worked, although the Shia government was apprehensive, because they understood, rightly, that the Americans were buying "peace" by supporting their natural enemies. In the end the Americans had to take over the payment system to the tribal forces they had "incorporated" into the national army and police force, because al-Maliki's government (the "national government") was unwilling to fork out the cash.

Petraeus had a short-term goal dictated by American political necessities. This combination of "force and bribery" succeeded in making for some kind of order in Anbar. We shall see what it will do for the long-term prospects for democracy in Iraq, given that it has in effect robustly boosted the tribal system that is inimical to such democracy. The American forces retired from the towns on June 29, 2009. The Iraqis celebrated this as a (government arranged) "National Sovereignty Day" with parades and celebrations. The joyful dancing in the streets finally occurred: so much for gratitude!

As of April 2010 when I write, in the presence of 160,000 American troops and 100,000 security forces recruited and trained by Americans, provincial and national elections have been held. It is not my wish to comment on details here. There is an air of unreality about all this "democratic" activity that goes on under the umbrella of an occupying force and a "security force" operating under its control. Who will control these "security forces" once the occupiers leave? Those who have wrested power will find it hard to give it up: "From the palace to the grave." The tribes will still be there. What indeed will happen when the American forces leave entirely (if they do) in 2011? Prediction is a tricky business. The imponderables are too great and depend a lot on events outside Iraq. But one alternative is not to keep more than 100,000 foreign troops there indefinitely. The Iraqi People, tribes and all, must figure this out for themselves.

Meanwhile we should not ignore the role of the most powerful Shia force, which had been responsible for a good part of the violence the surge was meant to halt. Muqtadar al-Sadr's Mehdi Army, a collection of Shia tribal militias and personal devotees, was ordered to cease fighting by its leader. He is so under the control of Iran that this had to be an Iranian decision. Perhaps the Iranians saw that their best strategy was not to continue the violence that they controlled, but to dampen it down and give the Americans no further excuse to stay. Those who see this as too Machiavellian to be true do not understand the Persians. Iran is the only real winner in this conflict, and will call the shots in the region for the foreseeable future, as long as it can survive its own internal conflicts. Iraq has been pacified and rendered up to Iranian influence by this war, and the Persians did not have to fire a shot.

Tribe and State

Reading Philip Salzman's timely but timeless book *Culture and Conflict in the Middle East* prompted me to add these reflections. He dedicates the book to my old teacher Ernest Gellner—one of this book's dedicatees, whose *Conditions of Liberty* has also been tenaciously influential. The balance between tribe and state, not just in Iraq but also throughout the region, from Morocco to Pakistan, defines the possibilities for democracy. The great virtue of this form of tribalism (the heir of the nomadic Bedouin tradition), after all, is that it protects the individual from the worst ravages of both neighbors and strangers. This includes the ravages of the predatory state organization that exists only for its own benefit and thrives on the plundering of its subjects.

The Arab philosopher Ibn Khaldûn (1332–1406) described the cycles of history in Arab society. Basically the society is tribal, with the tribes, mostly pastoral nomads but often a mix of herding, trading, and planting, existing in balanced competition against each other, raiding and feuding but not dominating. They exist in an uneasy relationship with the cities, which are based largely on trade and an inefficient bureaucracy headed by a ruler of one sort or another (emir, sultan, bey, sherif, and so on). From time to time a tribe or confederation of tribes with a charismatic leader sweeps in from the desert and takes over the cities with an Islamic reforming zeal. They rule for a while, but they eventually become decadent and tyrannical, corrupted by life in the city, and the cycle starts over again with a new tribal invasion.

There is always, then, a built-in, unavoidable antagonism between tribe and state. When states form, they can exist only by a mixture of bribery and force at worst and at best by tapping the support of the tribes in external wars, much as the British did with the Scottish clans, which they turned into regiments. The Jordanian and Saudi armies are formed from Bedouin tribesmen. States tend therefore to be autocratic and vicious in their suppression of the tribes, while the latter fight to protect their autonomy or to make the best deal they can, which is what has happened in Anbar.

When not concerned with avoiding or combating the rulers, the tribes are in a constant state of feuding with each other and raiding the towns and traders and the sedentary peasants who bear the brunt of attacks from both state exploitation and tribal predation. This was the historical condition of tribal autonomy. It is no less true today, although modern organization, technology, communications, and weaponry make the state a more formidable opponent of that autonomy, and cities have expanded in size and influence, siphoning off tribesmen. But as Salzman shows so thoroughly, the tribal system remains surprisingly intact, and the influence of its values is deep-rooted and pervasive, even in the towns. Educated bourgeois intellectuals, for example, are more likely to see their achievements as contributions to the honor of their lineages than to themselves as individuals. (See King and Stone, "Lineal Masculinity.")

While the tribe might stand united against states and other tribes, within the tribe there is constant feuding between the tribal segments. These range from tribal confederations down to clans, houses (lineages), and then extended families of five-generation depth that are the most immediate kin-based units (and that ideally marry within themselves, as in Figure 3.1).

Federation	*quabila*
Tribe	*'ashira*
Clan	*fukhdh*
House	*beit*
Family	*khams*

These exist in what Salzman calls "balanced opposition" to each other: a balance of power in which lower-level feuding groups can drop their differences and band together against like coalitions. The famous Arab proverb states something like "I against my brother; my brother and I against my cousins; my cousins and I and my brothers against the world." This is exactly what operates in the fluctuating alliances and coalitions in Anbar today.

This in its way—its competitive, violent, tribal way—is an egalitarian, freedom-loving, democratic method of dealing with the problem of order in society. To Aouda in *Lawrence of Arabia*, it was the essence of freedom. The freedom of the individual as we understand it, and which is the basis of our idea of civil society, makes no sense here. Freedom is indeed more than a word: it means profoundly different things to different societies. In the absence of a strong legitimate central authority with a monopoly of the use of force, this tribal system of segmentary opposition (as the anthropologists used to call it) is an effective form of political organization. But it is inimical to the idea of central control and particularly to the power of the state to settle disputes. Its very virtues at one level make it an enemy of centralized state control, however legitimate and benign.

The American army manual of counterinsurgency insists that the aim is always to "support the legitimate government." But that is the problem: for the tribes there is no legitimate government, there is only a compromise with those in power at the time. The tribesman wants to avoid the humiliating life of the peasant and his total submission, but his "freedom" is essentially a freedom to pursue the interest of his kin group, with violence if necessary, either for material gain or above all to protect the honor of the group. Vengeance is a high moral duty here; honor is a commodity more precious than gold. Aouda wanted gold from the British so he could gain honor by distributing it to his tribesmen. "I am a river to my people!" Men can increase the honor of the lineage through bravery, wealth or piety; women can lose it through sexual misconduct, meriting disgrace or even death as a consequence.

It is not our business to judge such a system; it was superbly adaptive in its historical context and formed the basis for the amazing expansion of Islam. It is our business to note that the kind of society we approve of and want them to adopt—our civil society—has had to make several huge shifts either upward or sideways, depending on your viewpoint, but huge shifts nevertheless. It had to surrender the power of revenge to the state, as we saw in Chapter 2. It had to agree to the voluntary relinquishment of power after elections. It had to institute and follow the rule of law, which is next to impossible in the tribal society because loyalty there is to the group, not to some abstract universal rules. "The ultimate goal," says Salzman, "is never following a rule, but winning, or at least not losing." This is certainly how we feel, and it explains the romanticizing of the Mafia, but it is not how we are allowed, or allow ourselves, to act anymore.

The shift we made, as it is now superfluous to insist, is to a precarious state of society that supports a liberal-democratic rule-of-law polity, but that carries within it a frightening tendency to lapse into the tribal state. This is a state with which at some deep level we are more comfortable, because it is more us. If we want "them" to adopt our system for all the good reasons put forward, we should bear this in mind and move with appropriate caution. And this is not to say that any one of these societies is "not ready for self-government," as critics have suggested. That is indeed colonialist and condescending and also stupid. They have been governing themselves in their own way for millennia, and the point of this essay is to suggest that we seek to understand that way, and its power and its continuing power in our own minds, before we try so arrogantly to replace it. To pose the issue as a simple conflict between good and evil, between freedom and tyranny, is both naive and irresponsible.

The White House children of the Protestant ethic should understand how hard won is the open society we live in, how much it is the work of centuries of struggle and suffering, how fragile it is, and how *we had to do it for ourselves.* Our fundamentalist Islamic opponents have on their side the atavistic attractions of the closed society, and we should take them at least as seriously as they take us, knowing how tempting those attractions can be. Before we try to make people over into our image, we should remember how unnervingly recent was our own makeover, and act with becoming humility, and never be surprised if our generosity is repulsed or ignored.

Everything about the antipathy of tribal to civil society said in this chapter applies in spades to Afghanistan, where we are about to repeat our mistakes. There again we should reduce our goals to the installation of a friendly regime and an accommodation with the "warlords" (read: tribal rulers) and the Taliban, and the tribes along the Pakistan border. We should have learned the lesson that we cannot impose liberal or representative democracy where it is not wanted and where ideas of freedom might even be antithetical. And this lesson applies across the board: a helping hand here and there may not be amiss, but we should always be prepared for the rejection of the foreigner's gift. No one who is in his heart a tribesman wants to depend on the kindness of strangers.

Afterwords

I told my Lebanese-American in-laws, who are Maronite Christians, that I was much impressed by a book written by one of their fellow Lebanese, Fouad Ajami. "Ajami?" they said, "Is he a Muslim? Where was he born?" In West Beirut, I told them, but he's really pretty secular. He's lived in the United States for many years; he's a professor at Johns Hopkins. "He's a Muslim," they said, and there was no more discussion. But they did make an interesting point about living in America and dealing with the non-Lebanese, nonfamilial world. So great, they said, is the feuding and backstabbing among some families of the Lebanese community, that it is often a wise choice, and a great relief, to deal in an impersonal way with the American stranger and his legally enforceable contracts.

Ayaan Hirsi Ali, on the first page of her startling book *Infidel,* tells of her childhood in Somalia. When people don't understand what I mean about tribalism and the tribal mentality, I have them read this book. She is writing from the tribal depths of the most tribal of tribal societies, Somalia. Her grandmother tells her as she makes her recite her lineage: "The names will make you strong. They are your bloodline. If you honor them they will keep you alive. If you dishonor them you will be forsaken. You will be nothing. You will lead a wretched life and die." Ayaan made the whole journey from this clan-ridden, totally kinship-based, tribal, feuding society to Western, open, liberal democracy on her own. She recapitulated the journey of the human race in her own person. No one has captured the reality of the shift better than she.

> Somali children must memorize their lineage: this is more important than almost anything. Whenever a young Somali meets a stranger, they ask each other, "Who are you?" They trace their separate ancestries until they find a common forefather.
>
> If you share a grandfather, perhaps even an eighth great-grandfather, with a Somali, the two of you are bound together as cousins. You are members of the great family that forms a clan. You offer each other food and hospitality. Although a child belongs to the clan of his father, it may be useful to remember your mother's bloodline, too, in case you travel and need a stranger's help.

The fear of the stranger runs deep. The answer is to establish kinship, to establish that the other person is not a stranger at all but in fact a relative. To overcome the fear of the stranger, to convert strangers into familiars, is perhaps the most important step to take in social evolution and perhaps the hardest. It is perhaps the loudest Drumbeat sounding from the depths of the tribal imagination.

The anthropologist Philip Salzman, our best commentator on the reality of tribalism in the Middle East, describes how he first went to Baluchistan in southwestern Iran in 1968 to study the pastoral tribes there.

> One of the first questions asked of me by the Baluch was how big my lineage was ... Perhaps the assumption of the Baluch was that, as I had bravely come so far from home to live intrepidly among strangers, and was obviously wealthy, having a new Land Rover, I must come from a large and powerful lineage. When I said that we had no lineages, the Baluch were incredulous. What did we do, they asked, when we were threatened, when we needed support? Why, we went to the police, I said. They laughed; they roared. Then they looked at me pityingly. Oh, no, no, no, they said; only your lineage mates will help you.

Don Corleone would have understood completely; he would have been able to handle Baluchistan. Ernest Gellner, in *Conditions of Liberty*, describes how in Morocco when political parties tried to recruit members among the tribes, they found they had do it by tribe or not at all. They could not recruit individuals. When a tribe decided to join a party, it solemnized the decision by sacrificing a bullock. Gellner thought that a good litmus test of civil society was that when you joined a political party, all your relatives did not have to sacrifice a bullock.

CHAPTER FOUR

Sects and Evolution

Tribal Splits and Creedal Schisms

OME YEARS AGO I went to a conference, in Ann Arbor, Michigan, of the Shakespeare-Oxford Society, because I am interested in the authorship question and one cannot get a sensible discussion of it in orthodox academic circles, where the issue is considered closed. I found that it was a joint meeting run with the Shakespeare Fellowship, a separate organization. As far as I could see, the aims and objects of the two societies were identical, and even the membership overlapped. But they had two councils and sets of officers, produced two newsletters, and had separate annual general meetings at the same conference. I could not get a coherent account of why there should be two societies except that at some time in the past there had been a personal dispute about something or other and some members had branched off and formed their own group. The two groups talked about joining up again, but it never happened and they continue that way to this day.

Some of the Drumbeats are so deep and so resonant that we fail to hear them at all. We are struck by the ethnographic dazzle of differences, for example, in religious and political sects, to the point that we cannot believe that a simple biological mechanism could lie behind the whole complicated cultural process. There are surely thousands or tens of thousands of reasons why sects form: look at the endless variety of ideologies they parade as justification for their differences. Or, as with our Shakespeare authorship groups, there are absolutely no ideological differences but they split anyway, often as a result of personal conflicts. (There were hints of a doctrinal difference, in that some of the dissidents favored the "Prince Tudor" theory—too long a story to tell here: see the Notes and References for this chapter.) Such surface accounts of sects, however, account for everything but *sectarianism itself*. Some of our intellectual fathers were very aware of this: that there was something common to all sect formation. Let us start with Karl Marx's colleague Friedrich Engels, who understood the idea of evolution much better than Marx himself. Engels was writing from the fractious heart of political sectarianism: nineteenth-century Socialism. He saw with startling insight that early Socialism and early Christianity were much more alike than they were different.

Christians and Socialists

Engels, writing in the German newspaper *Die Neue Zeit,* in 1894–1895, pointed out some parallels between the early history of Christianity and that of Socialism: both were movements of oppressed peoples, both offered salvation (Christianity in the next world, Socialism in this one), both were persecuted, but both were nevertheless successful. He explains, in a footnote, how different both these movements are from Islam. He echoes Ibn Khaldûn's theory of the oscillation between the purist "Bedouin" phases and the growth and corruption of towns, with the inevitable periodic clash of the two, the fundamentalists following a Mahdi or prophet who promises to restore the pure faith. (This is happening all over again today, but you don't hear Engels or Ibn Khaldûn quoted by the talking heads on television.)

Both Christianity and Socialism, however, he notes, also have their prophets: charismatic but often pretty unsavory characters, who attract followings and start sects. He quotes Ernst Renan (in his *Origines du Christianisme*) as saying, "If I wanted to give you an idea of the early Christian communities, I would tell you to look at a local section of the International Working Men's Association." Engels goes so far as to say that the sense of struggle against the whole world and the sureness of victory that characterized the early Christians, and is so lacking in their contemporaries, are best mirrored in today's Socialists. He was, of course, writing in 1894.

To make his point about prophets, he compares the careers of the early Christian Peregrinus Proteus (surely a fabricated name) and the Socialist "prophet Albrech" and his successor George Khulman from Holstein, known as "The Doctor." In the 1840s these two cunning miscreants plundered the coffers of the Swiss followers of Wietling while the latter was in prison, but had the undying loyalty of the communist communities, who revered the doctor's book *The New World: A Proclamation of the Kingdom of the Spirit on Earth*. Having fleeced the gullible Swiss, Khulman "disappeared." Quoting Lucian of Samosata ("the Voltaire of classical antiquity"), Engels describes how "Peregrinus Proteus" ("the wandering shape-changer"?) committed fornication and was condemned for strangling his father in Armenia. He survived the hanging and became the leader of the Christians of Asia Minor. When imprisoned he became a martyred hero, and at the same time a very wealthy man from Christian contributions. Later he was excommunicated, ostensibly for breaking dietary laws.

Engels, with his usual honesty, notes the variety of the gullible who were attracted to Socialism, a list remarkable for its contemporary relevance: "opponents of inoculation, supporters of abstemiousness, vegetarians, anti-vivisectionists, nature healers, free-community preachers whose communities have fallen to pieces, authors of new theories of the origins of the universe, unsuccessful or unfortunate investors, victims of real or imaginary injustice . . . honest fools and dishonest swindlers." The same was true of early Christianity, he observes. Some of the "great works" of the revered con man Peregrinus may well have found their way into the New Testament.

Mass movements, like Christianity and Socialism, says Engels, are bound to be confused at the beginning, not only because of the unformed nature of their beliefs, but because of the role prophets still play in them. "This confusion is to be seen in the formation of numerous sects which fight against one another with at least the same zeal as against the common external enemy." Engels had his own problems on this score with Marx, who was hypersensitive to dissension. While being supported by Engels's capitalistic industry, Marx spent a precious year of his life (1859–1860) writing his tract *Herr Vogt,* a violent and detailed attack on a potential rival. Engels pleaded with Marx to get on with his great theoretical contributions to Socialism (*Das Capital* was put on hold) and to "leave Herr Vogt to history." History has indeed rendered its verdict, and Herr Vogt would not be remembered at all except for Marx's denunciation (just as the early Christian sects are preserved only in the Church's denunciation of heresies). But the future of Socialism was less important to Marx than the countering of heresy and libel.

Thus sensitized to the power and inevitability of sectarianism (and fresh from the battle between "scientific" and "utopian" Socialism), Engels lists as the early Socialist sects "the Communists of the pre-1848 tradition, among whom again were various shades: Communists of Weitling's school and others of the regenerated Communist League, Proudhonists . . . Blanquists, the German Workers Party and the Bakuninist anarchists . . . to mention only the principal groups." Paralleling these in early Christianity, he cites those denounced in Revelation—the earliest insight into the true original Christian beliefs: "Nicolaitans of Ephesus and Pergamos; those that said they were Jews but were of the synagogues of Satan, in Smyrna and Philadelphia; the supporters of Balaam . . . those who said they were apostles but were not . . . and finally the supporters of the false prophetess Jezebel." It is supposed by Renan that these were gentile, Pauline sects and were anathema to the Jewish Jerusalem Christians, followers of James, the brother of Jesus, and the original Christian "orthodoxy."

These are the primitive divisions, it is true, but sectarianism did not lessen with the consolidation of Roman orthodoxy, as we shall see. The massive energy of the church fathers was largely directed against so-called heresies. Indeed, all we know of most heresies is what we learn from these diatribes against them. But they were numerous and dangerous enough to call forth these outpourings of official wrath. Even as Christianity became the official religion of the empire, most of North Africa was steeped in the numerous varieties of Gnosticism, and the whole north of Europe in versions of Arianism—more or less today's Unitarianism. Engels assumed that Socialism would ultimately be different: it would tend toward unity because of the new means of communication: "railways, telegraph, giant industrial cities, the press, organized people's assemblies." But in his own England, the tendency was inexorably toward fragmentation.

A few years earlier the staunch idealistic Socialist William Morris closely echoed Engels in his observations on English Socialism. I am not sure of the original, but Morris's words are quoted in William Gaunt, *The Pre-Raphaelite Dream.*

> Morris was faced with the curious fact that the simple thing is the last human beings arrive at; that the attainment of their avowed objects is the last thing many of them want; that the man in earnest to accomplish is an object of suspicion to those he works with. He gave an account of a meeting (in 1877) at Cleveland Hall, Cleveland Street, "a wretched place, once flash and now sordid, a miserable street," which illustrates the genius for complexity and frustration. It was the headquarters for the "orthodox Anarchists," most of the foreign speakers belonging to this persuasion; but a Collectivist also spoke, and one, at least, from the Autonomy section "who have some quarrel which I can't understand with the Cleveland Hall people." A Federation man spoke, though he was not a delegate; also Macdonald of the Socialist Union; the Fabians did not attend on the grounds that the war-scare (which was the subject of the meeting) was premature, "probably, in reality, because they did not want to be mixed up too much with the Anarchists." The "Krapotkine-Wilson crowd" also refused on the grounds that bourgeois peace *is* war. Here, then, were seven different factions who could neither combine nor agree.

Beer, in his magnificent but more or less forgotten two-volume *History of British Socialism,* notes that from the beginning there was a tendency to split, usually along radical versus gradualist lines. British Socialism was not originally Marxist at all, but arose out of its own Puritan and Leveler traditions, energized in the early nineteenth century by the Chartist movement and the early trade unions. Here again there was the seemingly inevitable gradualist versus radical split.

The followers of Robert Owen in the 1830s were gradualists who believed in Owen's Labor Exchanges and his Cooperative Societies, which together were going to transform English society. (They still exist. When I was a boy my mother was a staunch Tory, but a pragmatist who shopped at "The Co-op" to obtain the valued dividend.) Owen believed in education and cooperation, and founded his charmingly named "Association of the Intelligent and Well-disposed of the Industrious Classes for Removing Ignorance and Poverty." (Today we would have to give it a snappy acronym: AIWICRIP?) Opposed to Owen's utopianism, at least after 1832, was the trend known as Syndicalism. This shift of the unions toward radical political action was crystallized by Owen's major opponent, J. E. Smith, a weaver who became in turn a mystic, a theologian, and an Owenite. He broke with Owen and, influenced by St. Simon and Fourier, founded his own movement. He more or less originated the phrases of social democracy—"strikes," "general strikes," "bourgeoisie," "proletariat," "class warfare," and "class solidarity—that have become stock in trade, after the *Communist Manifesto.*

The shift was massively in Smith's favor, but then there was the inevitable split between the Social Democrats, who favored parliamentary action, and Smith and the Syndicalists, who believed in extra-parliamentary class warfare. Beer's history records the subsequent splits into the Democratic Federation, the Socialist League, the Social Democratic Federation, the Fabian Society, the Independent Labor Party, the Cooperative Party (the old Owenites), the Parliamentary Labor Party, the British Socialist Party, the National Socialist Party, the Socialist Labor Party, the Socialist Party of Great Britain (defectors from the SDF), the Socialist Sunday Schools, the National Guilds League (promoting Guild Socialism), and, of course the Communist Party of Great Britain, inevitably split between Stalinists and Trotskyites. Since Beer concluded his survey in 1921, we have seen Labor split between New Labor and the Liberal/Social Democrat Alliance (Liberal Democrats), with the various varieties of the extreme left wing always ready to go their own ways.

So Engels was perhaps too sanguine. Modern communications may in effect help the process of sectarian fragmentation rather than the opposite.

But if we face up to the persistent facts, we have to admit that the sectarian process, with its component of the charismatic prophet (and occasional Jezebel), seems to be endemic to all ideological organizations. It is so endemic that we scarcely think it worthy of analysis: it is simply the way the world works. But surely those of us of the evolutionary persuasion have learned that the obvious or self-evident about any species is what needs to be explained, and that only evolution can explain it. Here we have a classic case of features that are unquestionably cultural—ideology and charisma—but whose very existence seems to demand an explanation that goes beyond the cultural.

Max Weber certainly recognized this about charisma, to the embarrassment of his sociological successors. The concept of ideology owes its origins to the French *philosophes*, most probably Destutt de Tracy, and originally was used to bolster their empiricist theories of knowledge by which men's ideas were what caused action, and hence to change their ideas was to change their actions. But ideologies—that is, systems of ideas that impel action—are universal themselves, and therefore must, like the language and symbols in which they are couched, involve "an almost imperceptible transition to the biological"—as Weber said of charisma.

The only aspect of ideology that we are interested in here, however, is its relationship to its sister, charisma, and their seemingly inevitable relationship to sectarianism: the progressive fragmentation of ideologies into competing sets of ideas, and hence of the holders of these ideas into competing social groups. The ideas themselves may be arbitrarily cultural, but their continuous fragmentation seems to be, to quote Lionel Trilling's very apt book title *Beyond Culture*. Is there something in the nature of ideas that causes them always to produce their dialectical opposites, and then for these in turn to produce theirs, and so on in almost geometrical progression? Or are the ideological splits simply the surface manifestations of a tendency of groups of any kind to fragment and disperse?

Animal Dispersion

Why should living organisms disperse? This business of dispersion goes deep into the evolution of life. In *The Genius of the Beast*, Howard Bloom, finding his root example of the "evolutionary search engine," describes how bacteria come in two forms: those with stalks and those with propellers. The stalk bacteria form the basis of colonies and establish themselves. Some of their daughters (they reproduce asexually of course) are born with stalks and stay where they are, but others are born with those amazing propellers and strike out through the water to form new colonies elsewhere. The push toward dispersal here has solely to do with resources: the bacteria with propellers strike out to find new feeding grounds, and so-called higher organisms are no less driven by this need.

But once sexual reproduction came on the scene, they dispersed for another essential reason. As Norbert Bischof illustrated in his "Comparative Ethology of Incest Avoidance" in 1975, they disperse to avoid inbreeding, which they must do to preserve genetic variability, which is what sexual reproduction is all about in the first place. There is considerable dispute (summarized by Trivers in *Social Evolution*) about why sex replaced cloning as the successful reproductive mechanism, but the details of the dispute do not concern us. What follows from this innovation is what concerns us: the root of the tendency of all these organisms to disperse became, in addition to the search for resources, the conservation of the basic sexual reproductive mode itself. Too-close inbreeding defeats the object of breeding at all: the production of genetic variability for natural selection to work on.

Bischof lists the mechanisms that drive sexually reproducing mammals—primates in particular—out of the family group: abduction, repulsion, isolation, emancipation, threat, repulsion, and so on. The net result is not always perfect dispersion, but enough dispersion to ensure that inbreeding is minimized and variability is maximized. Patrick Bateson showed how even in sexually reproducing plants, dispersal mechanisms exist that force seeds and pollen out of their immediate circle of related plants, but land them in a circle of slightly less related plants: their cousins, in effect. This result, it seemed, could be generalized to all sexually reproducing species: breed out but not too far out, thus you maintain genetic variability, but you do not disperse your genes too widely and thus dilute them. It is a profound Drumbeat that will crop up again, particularly in Chapter 7. And we have already seen the Arab preference for close-cousin marriages.

Sewall Wright had already introduced the idea of genetic drift, in which small populations, as a result of dispersion, could be isolated and develop new genetic characteristics, and then spread these characters to other populations, thus speeding up the process of evolution. The key here, and the one least debated, is that the relevant populations must disperse members first to form the isolated groups, then further disperse some members to the other groups in order to spread their innovative gene combinations. Otherwise the innovating group could just die out and its new adaptations with it. This must have happened, in fact, numerous times, and those side branches of hominid evolution we see on the evolutionary trees represent such isolated and doomed populations. Dispersal then is vital to evolutionary change, both at the primary level of dispersal out of the immediate family and at the secondary level of dispersal of genes between populations.

But dispersal is rarely a random affair; animals don't just scatter. They not only disperse, but they do so in regular and predictable ways, as individuals, in families, in flocks, in territories, in migration routes, and so on. That they do so is obvious, but why should there be this form of order rather than a simple free-for-all? Various natural historians, mostly bird watchers like Lack, Howard, and Gilbert White, as well as animal watchers like Allee, had pondered the problem and seen that it was related to the exploitation of resources. But it was the demographer (and director of the London School of Economics) Sir Alexander Carr-Saunders who, looking at the issue of population control in primitive man in 1922, first formulated the "theory of the optimum number" *(The Population Problem: A Study in Human Evolution)*. There was a theoretical optimal balance between population size (biomass, as we would now say) and resources. What was amazing was how closely so-called primitive societies kept themselves to this optimum. If they became unbalanced, then measures were taken to reduce numbers—abortion, infanticide, and abstention being the most common, but "emigration" is in there too.

Carr-Saunders thought such population limitation was unique to man, and V. C. Wynne-Edwards's great contribution was to demonstrate that homeostatic population control is common to all social animals, down to the protozoa *(Animal Dispersion in Relation to Social Behaviour)*. This is achieved by "conventional competition," and I remember how, as a social scientist myself, and ex-student of Carr-Saunders, I was, as the English say, gobsmacked when I read Wynne-Edwards's definition of a society as "an organization capable of providing conventional competition." What that drew into the web!

Wynne-Edwards is in current disfavor because the dominant sect of the Human Behavior and Evolution movement, devoted as it is to the principle of individual selection, considers his notions of group selection heretical in evolutionary biology. He definitely vacillates between what we might call "group selection" and "the selection of groups"—we still seem to be confused by this—and William Hamilton, to the satisfaction of most biologists, elegantly disproved his theory that group selection accounted for sterile castes in insects. But if we look at the selection of groups, then we can see (as Darwin saw) that individual selection within a group can throw up social behaviors that produce a form of social organization that will be superior to that of other groups in that it promotes greater fitness in its members. (I explored this in an essay, "Self

Interest and Social Concern," in *Conjectures and Confrontations*.) There will thus be positive feedback between social organization and individual fitness, and such a group will expand at the expense of groups of conspecifics not so well endowed. The group properties could well be, for example, cooperation and communication, or even morality and religion, promoting more efficient conventional competition (or "ritualized aggression"), thus leading to a preservation of the optimum number.

Framed in this way, there is nothing about traits evolving for the sake of the group or anything such. A growing sect of theorists led and organized by David Sloan Wilson, and including Edward O. Wilson, the synthesizer of sociobiology, is beginning to see the differential selection of groups as central to the process of evolution. They call this multi-level selection (MLS) and basically argue that different kinds of selection—individual and group—operate at different levels, and that both have to be taken into account to understand, for example, the structure of insect societies (Wilson and Wilson, 2007, 2008). It is a sturdy paradigm that does not offend at all against the canons of maximization of individual fitness. But as a "middle-ground" theory it is not attractive to sectarians, and it has suffered howls of outrage from the kin-selection faithful.

Wynne-Edwards might have overemphasized the role of the group in selection, but his careful observations did show that there existed two basic dispersal mechanisms, over and above those communicative and competitive devices that cause dispersal within groups. These he called *irruption* and *emigration* (his chapter 20). Emigration has two functions: one is the "safety valve" function, which siphons off excess population, and the other is the "pioneering" function, which expands the range of the species and provides for gene exchange. Pioneering, he shows, is a property of expanding populations, especially in uncertain and variable conditions. Under truly erratic conditions, a group will export "pioneers" whenever there is a good season. The underlying principle here is that *groups cannot grow indefinitely large*. Dispersal is the law of life for all populations, the amount and kind of dispersal being determined by the principle of the optimum number.

Groups in which there had *not* evolved individuals with "dispersal traits" that would promote successful emigration would fail in adverse circumstances. Groups that simply "irrupt" (like lemmings or, at seasonal migration time, like wildebeest) are also always at risk; it is the *pioneers* who systematically carry their traits to other areas that succeed: those bacteria with the propellers. A group of Japanese macaques, observed over many years, was seen to have a hierarchical structure of ranked matrilines. When the group became too large for its territory, it split, with the lower groups in the hierarchy moving off to form their own unit. Over time all the males of group A moved to group B, and vice versa (see my *Red Lamp of Incest,* chapter 4). Thus fission and fusion ensured dispersal and genetic diversity.

A secondary issue is: Just who emigrates? Is it the successful animals or the marginal failures? It would seem that it might more regularly be the latter, because animals that succeed in breeding competition have no motive to leave: it was the lower-ranking macaques that moved. On the other hand, the more successful animals might prosper by leaving in adverse conditions. The "predatory expansion" that we shall meet in humans always would require successful males to lead it, but that is a fairly late development. Even so, another grim regularity seems to be the "'rule of tens"—I think first advanced by Williamson in his *Biological Invasions:* not more than 10 percent of invasive species get established, and only 10 percent of these become successful enough to dominate. Pioneering is always a risky business; the failure rate is massive.

As Carr-Saunders saw, primitive human groups can consciously regulate their numbers, but they are not free to buck the basic principle. Their conscious manipulation of it, however, is obviously a highly advantageous trait in itself. The remarkable progress of emigration out of Africa by our *Homo erectus* ancestors has been studied with this in mind. Before 1.8 million years ago, the dispersal rates of hominids matched those of the great apes; with *Homo erectus* things changed. Sophisticated modern analyses of the diffusion coefficient (D) in mammals, using such variables as the size of the area invaded (z), the time over which the invasion occurs (t), and the intrinsic natural rate of increase of the species (r), produce the formula:

$$D^{1/2} = z/(t)(2r^{1/2})$$

Comparing this coefficient for macaques, *Homo erectus,* and ancient hyaenids, Susan Anton and her colleagues find that it is much higher in the hominids than in the monkeys, but the hominids are comparable to the hunting and scavenging carnivores, if a bit slower. These acute analysts use this and other data to suggest why there was a virtual explosion of dispersion out of Africa, our larger-brained, tool-using, meat-eating ancestor following the also-dispersing herds of bovids as far as Southeast Asia and China. But what impresses me is that the hominids were bound by the rules of dispersal. They did not, with their increased brain size, and physical and cultural capacities, just disperse as they pleased or in patterns they made up from scratch. When groups became too large for the carrying capacity of the area they were in, the "pioneers" struck out, in predictable ways, for pastures new. At a predictable rate they colonized the available world.

Human Dispersion

With fully formed *Homo sapiens,* we find the same thing happening, although with those deliberate interferences and decisions Carr-Saunders noted. Groups do not grow indefinitely large. They constantly split up, and under predictable conditions they irrupt or emigrate. If the area is large enough to support them, they will simply split and divide there, dispersing within the area. In doing this they have an advantage over dispersing animals in that they can maintain relationships with the mother group and with each other by symbolic means. Among the Australian Aborigines, we can see how rules of preferential marriage bind dispersed groups, and how totemic relationships of clanship do the same thing. Thus, dispersed groups remain members of the same clan and marry members of related clans through such mechanisms as "sister exchange."

Napoleon Chagnon, in *Yanomamo: The Fierce People,* demonstrates just such a structure for the Yanomamo in the Amazon basin, the upper limit of local population being 150 individuals. The upper level of such integration in foraging conditions still seems to peak at about 2,500 for a tribe and perhaps 5,000 for the so-called linguistic tribe—those speaking the same language. Indeed, at this stage of social evolution, one of the prime functions of language (over and above sheer communication) was to define and maintain such group membership.

But just as inevitable as dialect drift was segmentation: the constant push to produce local units that were near-kin, usually within the second- or third-cousin range at most. If we want a "law," then, perhaps it could be this (other things being equal, of course):

The probability that any human group will fragment increases in proportion to the decrease in the average coefficient of relationship among its members.

Corollary: The groups produced by the fragmentation will have a higher average coefficient of relationship than the parent group.

In human terms, the less closely over time that the members of a group become related to each other, the more likely they are to split up. If the average degree of relationship falls below, say, $r = .015625$ (the relationship between fourth cousins), then a split is likely to occur, with more highly related people making up the smaller groups. This is the natural tendency; it cannot always be observed in modern conditions (where other things are not equal because free movement is often impossible) with predictable consequences. The more unrelated we become, the more we have to deal with "strangers" and all the threats and complexities this involves, as the Iraqis reminded us.

Robin Dunbar, in an elegant series of studies featuring precise correlations and the testing of alternative hypotheses (always welcome), has found a constant relationship between group size and the evolution of the neocortex in primates. The large size of the human neocortex poses a problem: it seems to be in excess of what is needed (as Alfred Russel Wallace first suggested). Dunbar's solution is that it evolved to deal with increasing group size, as did language itself. And what is the ideal group size that it deals with? The answer seems to be that the close personal group averages 12 individuals (Antony Jay proposed 10) and the manageable interactive group has an upper limit of 150 individuals.

This "rule of 150"—exemplified in Chagnon's Amazonian Indians— matches our rule of fission: groups much above that size will begin to dilute their coefficient of relationship and tend to split. Chagnon found this happened when a group reached about 300. With the advent of language, however, a mechanism arises for extending some recognition, as we have seen, to those who speak the same tongue, peaking at 5,000. The ideal human cooperative group, the tribe, therefore probably falls somewhere in between. Antony Jay puts the outer limit at somewhere between 400 and 700 people, this being the largest dense crowd that you can reach with an unaided human voice in the open air (Jay 1990). The manageable interactive group hovers on the 150 mark, as exemplified by Hutterite group fission, divisions of regular armies, and the number of academics in a discipline's subspecializations (more on this later).

The same fission will occur as groups become larger and more prosperous. Marshall Sahlins saw the segmentary lineage, that perfect model of human group fission, as an instrument of "predatory expansion." Usually acknowledging an eponymous human or divine ancestor (or a totemic counterpart), the lineage splits and divides in succeeding generations. Thus, when an overpopulated group irrupts and either moves into unpopulated areas or takes over an area from another population, then it can both move and split into manageable local groups and still keep an overall identity, by the process of lineage segmentation. The Bantu moving into the whole of sub-Saharan Africa, the Arabs moving across North Africa, or the Chinese moving into the southeastern provinces, all display this dual tendency. The groups would constantly split into small units of kin, but they would share the same name and ancestors, and indeed, could often trace relationships back more than twenty generations, like the Somalis. (The various forms of lineage segmentation are described in my *Kinship and Marriage,* chapter 8.)

The whole story of human expansion and the settlement of the continents could be seen as an extension of this model of continual segmentation, with the ethnic groups and their matched language families being the highest level of segmentation once the movements had occurred. Language groups did not always become nations, but they formed the basis of them in most cases (Switzerland being a remarkable exception). Even so, people recognize speakers of their language as in some sense "kin" in a way nonspeakers can never be. If you speak the same language, there is always the potential of forming an "imagined group" like a nation even when numbers go well beyond the limit of the "linguistic tribe." The world as a segmentary organization of peoples and languages is there in the work of the historical geneticists, as is brilliantly summed up in the diagram in Figure 4.1, adapted from Luca Cavalli-Sforza by Linda Stone and Paul Lurquin (2007). The human languages must, of course, also ultimately link back to a single source, but we may never be able to draw that tree.

The rules by which the fission and segmentation occur will, as cultural determinists are quick to point out, differ from culture to culture. Thus exactly who is counted as close kin, and when and how the splits will occur, will be determined by local cultural rules. But there are overpowering similarities. The predatory expansion model, common among pastoralists, is exclusively patrilineal (descent through males) and polygamous; matrilineal segmentation would just not work in these conditions, and monogamy would be less efficient. Horticulturalists, slowly expanding across empty territories in North America, could be matrilineal and monogamous. There are these constraints that overrule cultural determinism.

But what is most impressive is the *constant tendency to segment.* Cultural rules merely serve this tendency; they do not initiate it. And of course the driving force is mostly ecological, and it is the ecological contingencies that evolution is observing. Also, it is driven by the inner forces of kin selection and reciprocal altruism (see Trivers again), which demand workable, face-to-face kinship units: Dunbar's rule of 150. It also requires its own "pioneers"—leaders who will undertake a move and organize and sustain it. This is where it came from. What then happened when we developed large sedentary urban and peasant populations, and eventually industrial civilizations, where the division of labor and trading economies made non-kin and strangers an inevitable and constant part of our lives?

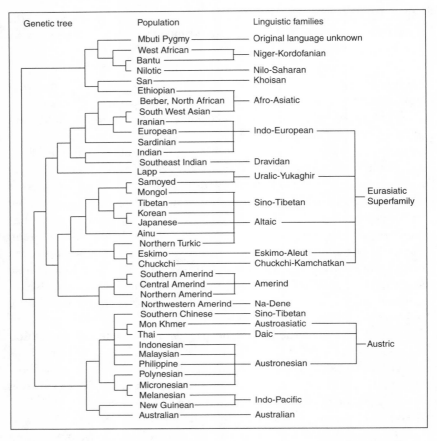

Figure 4.1 Human segmentation by population and language (after Cavalli-Sforza)

The advantages of the symbolic capacity, which could hold together the totemic bands and the segmentary lineages, would still be operative. Large ideological groups, often using the language of fictive kinship, could form. The earliest empires held together diverse ethnic groups with a common religion. But eventually religion broke free from its tribal and nationalistic roots, and transnational religious movements formed. These were truly ideological movements in the strict sense, usually offering some form of salvation from the misery of life that civilization had imposed on the masses of proletarians, slaves, and peasants. They were inevitably founded and developed by charismatic characters in the true, Weberian, sense: those who derived their authority from their own vision of divinity, not from any hereditary or legal status.

We must then ask ourselves: Why should not such groups simply persist? They are, after all, pure cultural inventions, so why should it not be possible for them simply to sustain themselves as unified movements? That they never do so is obvious, and we shall look at some examples. Some manage to maintain unity longer than others, but none of them are free from the segmentary process: as Engels observed, there are always sects and prophets. What seem from the outside to be small or imperceptible differences in ideas will rapidly form the basis of differentiation: what Freud called "the narcissism of small differences." Jonathan Swift, in *Gulliver's Travels,* describes the sectarian tendencies of the Lilliputians, whose Big Enders and Little Enders were willing to fight to the death over the correct end to crack a boiled egg. But he was wickedly and accurately satirizing the endless proliferation of sects in England at the time.

Human Sects

Edith Sitwell, in her charming history of Bath, lists, at the time of Jonathan Swift's sojourn there, just a few of the sects available, as detailed in John Ashton's *Social Life in the Reign of Queen Anne.* There were Antinomians, Hederingtonians, Theaurian Joanites, Seekers, Waiters, Reevists, Brownists, Baronists, Wilkinsonians, Familists, Ranters, Muggletonians, and the Countess of Huntingdon's Connexion. They are all now forgotten: the law of extinction seems to apply as ruthlessly to sects as it does to species. I believe a few members of Selena, Lady Huntingdon's sect, still practice their own form of strict Methodism, against whose puritanical precepts the great dandy Beau Nash carried on a gallant guerilla war. As with the contemporary United States and California, the most extreme of the sects drifted to the southwest of the country. Then some of them irrupted or emigrated, as the Pilgrim Fathers did to America, where they set up their own tyrannical theocracy in Massachusetts. Then they in turn split up, and the dissenters fled the new religious tyranny to found Rhode Island, the only colony where "religious freedom" had any true meaning.

But because this is dispersal in the arena of ideas, actual physical movement is less necessary, although it happens very frequently. What does inevitably happen is the driving down of the size of the group of believers to a level no greater than that of the linguistic tribe, and preferably the foraging band. Insofar, then, as the members needed to be together, before the advent of modern communications, sects tended to become localized. And note that the sects are usually named after their charismatic founders, mostly males, with a substantial female minority only in Christian

Europe and America. In the world of ideas, physical strength is not absolutely necessary to leadership, but males have been traditionally better at attention getting.

We are perhaps desensitized to the sectarian phenomenon because it is routine in Protestantism, the religion of the American majority and the one most significant in molding our society and values. So we must shock ourselves out of this familiarity and look at religions that we tend to see from the outside as being relatively monolithic.

Islam.   Our recent encounters with Islam have helped us to see that this is a sect-ridden religion, if not as insistently so as Protestantism. But from the very beginning there were fundamental divisions. This being Islam, we cannot so easily mark a division between "religious" and "political" sects: the political and religious community (the *umma*) is not distinguished as it is with Christianity. From the start, the two basic denominations were visible: Sunni divided from Shiite (AD 765) over the legitimacy of the succession to Mohammed. The Shiites themselves divide into the Seveners and the Twelvers, over the number of Imams they recognize in line of succession. Sunni Islam, the vast majority, itself split into numerous schools and sects. We are now aware that the Saudis (at least the ruling powers among them) are Wahhabis, being to Islam what the most extreme Puritans are to Christianity.

Through the celebrity status of various Aga Khans we know about the Ismaili sect, but perhaps few recognize them as the descendants of the Assassins *(hashishiyyin)*, whose leader, Haroun Al Rashid (The Old Man of the Mountains), invented the idea of suicide killing, with its sensuous rewards in paradise. (There is a school of thought that holds that the "72 virgins" reward stems from a mistranslation: it should be "72 raisins.") Four schools of jurisprudence, each with a charismatic founder, compete for allegiance: Hanbalites, Milikhites, Hanafites, and Shaffiites. The mystical wing is represented by the Sufis, with their own mystical sects, and various leaders founded the Qarmatians, the Murjites, the Mutazilah, Asharizm, Qadarites, and Kharajites, which latter means, perhaps redundantly, "seceders."

Some sects were local, as with the Sanusiyyah of Libya; some were avowedly radical, like the Futuwwah, a thirteenth-century urban youth league, perhaps the ultimate ancestor of the Taliban (which simply means "seminarians"). The Sulafiqqah was founded by Sayyid Qutb (who died only in 1966), the revered father of modern Islamic fundamentalism. The Sulafis represent that persistent tendency, noted by Ibn Khaldûn, to try to return Islam to its pure form, and which is at the root of current "Islamic terrorism." This reversion to purity was the aim of the Islamic Congress or Mujama, founded by Ahmed Yasin, in Gaza, and the Society of Muslim Brothers, founded by Hasan al-Banna, and the Ahmadiya, founded in 1889 in the Punjab. In America, Elijah Muhammed founded the Nation of Islam, from which a sect formed under Louis Farrakhan and of which there are now at least twelve significant subgroups, to say nothing of the Moorish Science Temple and the oddly named Five Percenters.

We could go on, for there are many more, but the point is made. It is interesting to look at the world's most thoroughly monotheistic religion to see that unity of belief in the one God and his prophet does nothing to prevent the sectarian tendency. And the sects are all derived, in Moslem countries and history, from male charismatic leaders, usually with a radical agenda to restore the purity of the religion. Osama bin Laden and Mullah Omar are thoroughly recognizable as members of this lineage.

Judaism.   That other rigid monotheism, Judaism, also lacking a central church, especially after the destruction of the Temple and the diaspora, is equally open to sectarian tendencies. Before the dispersion of the Jews, Pharisees, Sadducees, Essenes, Herodians, Samaritans, Ebonites, Nazarenes, Simonians, Cernintheians, Nicolaitans, and Zealots jostled for position. After the diaspora, Sephardic distinguished itself from Ashkenazi. In North America, Judaism split into Orthodox, Conservative, Reconstructionist, Humanist, and Reform, as well as Jewish Renewal and other smaller groups.

The ultra-orthodox wing, the Hassidim, is famous for its various sects formed by charismatic rabbis from Eastern Europe in the wake of terrible pogroms. Founded by the Ba'al Shem Tov (Lord of the Good Name) as a spiritual, even anti-intellectual, movement in the eighteenth century, it attracted the poorest and most illiterate of the Jews. Like later Pentecostal Christianity it was prone to runaway sectarianism, but because it had no fixed doctrines, these subsects were more like personal followings of the various local leaders than incipient denominations. They were often named after their places of origin in Eastern Europe: Kotzk, Sanz, Beiz, Satmar, Skvar. In New York there is a "New Square Hassidim," whose name is in fact an Anglicized version of "Skvar." The best-known current sects in New York are perhaps the Kabbalistic and extremist Lubavitch Hassidim, and the more quietistic Breslaver.

Hinduism.   But for a moment let us consider a radically different type of religion: polytheistic Hinduism. If strict monotheism curtails the development of sects, polytheism makes it ridiculously easy, because there are potentially at least as many sects as there are gods and there is no central church or doctrine to hold heresy in check.

But it is not that simple, because sects form in Hinduism that are not to do with individual gods. Any Hindu can devote himself to a particular god (my favorite is Ganesh, the elephant-headed deity) without starting a sect. But sometimes such extreme devotion does lead essentially to a sub-religion, and sometimes divergences of belief lead to genuine sectarian movements, which then crystallize into their own churches. Thus Vashnavism, centered on Vishnu or Hari, and which you used to encounter at most U.S. airports, itself divides into Shrisampradaya (devoted to Sita and Rama) and the Ayodha sect, whose violent opposition to a mosque on their holy site has caused thousands of deaths in western India. Shaktism, devoted to Shakti, espoused Tantrism, and Shaivism, the sect of Shiva, went its way. Most interesting perhaps is Jainism, the ultimate in nonviolent vegetarianism, broken into the Digambaras, or air-clothed ones, and the Shvetambaras, or white-clothed, on the issue of total nudity.

Even Yoga, which began, like Methodism, as a school of religious practice, soon developed its own four main schools: Jnana, Karma, Bhakti, and Raja, with the subschools of Kriya, Sdha, Tantra, and Kundalini. Any Yoga nut will tell you the differences in enthusiastic detail. There is of course Sikhism, founded by Guru Nanak, one of a line of gurus or swamis who found their own sects and receive the absolute devotion, and contributions, of their followers. Thus we have seen Maharishi Mahesh Yogi, Krishnamurti, Yogananda, and Swami Muktananda, and many, many more. With generations of Westerners eager for spiritual truth, this proliferation of Hindu sects has been a godsend, if one may say that.

Buddhism. The followers of Prince Siddhartha started as a sect of Hinduism: a kind of Hindu Protestantism. It rapidly split into Mahayana-Theravada (the Great Vehicle), Hinayana (the Lesser Vehicle), Madhyamika (the Middle Way), and Vajrayna (the Diamond Vehicle). As Buddhism, like Christianity, began its physical movement, sects sprang up to accommodate local beliefs and practices. In Tibet, Tantric Buddhism fragmented into four schools, Nyingma, Geluk, Sakya, and Kagyu, the latter having eight subschools of its own. A Yogic version emerged as Yogachara, and in China and Japan the Zen movement took over, then began its own rapid fragmentation. Jodo, the Pure Land, school competed with Jodo Shin, the True Pure Land School, itself divided into Otani and Haiganji. One could list more names—Jojitsu, Hosso, Ritsu, Shingon, Kusha, and so on, but the point is the same: ever further sectarian fragmentation.

Shinto. While in Japan we could note the thirteen official sects of Shinto, and the uncounted number of subsects, worshipping different mountains and practicing different forms of faith healing.

Taoism. Taoism comes up with the liveliest names for its sects, after having inevitably split between Tao-chia and Tao-chiao, and of course developing Neo-Taoism (hsuan-hsueh), it divided into three sects of "Church" Taoism. These were the Way of Right Unity, the Way of Supreme Peace, and the Third Way, which included the Five Pecks of Rice School, and the School of the Celestial Masters. At last count there were some eighty-six subsects of Taoism, including the Inner Gods of Hygiene School, the School of the Magic Jewel, the Inner Elixir School, and the School of Perfect Realization, northern and southern versions.

Whigs, Tories, and Pavlov

Before we get to the frenetically proliferating Protestant sects, let us pause to consider another major factor in the sectarian process. We have already noted that the commonest split is along conservative–radical lines. The Owenites, once established, became the status quo of the working-class movement and opposed the radical position of Smith and the Syndicalists. Out of the prosperous Muslim towns, a radical mullah or mahdi emerges from time to time to lead the revolt of the pure against the conservative establishment, and a new sect is formed. The prophet may well claim to be leading the flock back to the old and true ways—this is often the only source of his authority—but he is nevertheless the radical, in revolt against the establishment.

Thomas Jefferson, writing to John Adams about the rift between the Republicans and the Federalists, said: "The same political parties which now agitate the U.S. have existed thro' all time. And in fact the terms of whig and tory . . . belong to natural as well as to civil history. They denote the temper and constitution and mind of different individuals" (as quoted in Ellis's *Founding Brothers*).

Hans Eysenck in his *Psychology of Politics* explored this idea of the psychological basis of political divisions, and he deeply upset political opinion with his discoveries. (Tiger and I noted this in *The Imperial Animal,* but we didn't develop it further.) Eysenck was a strict behaviorist, but he recognized, as did his master Pavlov, that there was considerable variation in the "temper and constitution and mind" of different individuals, and that this affected profoundly the way they learned conditioned responses. Eysenck, doing attitude surveys of adherents of the British political parties—Conservative, Labour, Liberal, Fascist, and Communist—found a startling consistency that cut across party boundaries. Factor analysis showed there was another dimension than the conservative–radical, one that he labeled the "T Scale" after William James's "tough minded" versus "tender minded" distinction (and that correlated with Jung's extraversion–introversion continuum).

Thus extreme Fascists and extreme Communists, though widely separated on the conservative–radical scale, showed up in exactly the same place on the T Scale: obviously at the extreme tough-minded end, with the working-class members of both parties being the most extreme of all. Tough-minded Conservatives fell into the same quadrant as the Fascists, tough-minded Labour with the Communists. Liberals were always intermediate, and right- and left-wing parties had their tender-minded members, Labour having more than Conservatives. This, as you can imagine, pleased nobody, except perhaps the Liberals. But it is interesting to follow Eysenck's theoretical reasoning as to why this should be.

Pavlov had discovered that some dogs were much easier to condition than others. This led researchers to look for constitutional differences that matched the mental illnesses characterizing extrovert and introvert personalities. Simply put, extroverts had hysterical symptoms; introverts had anxiety disorders. These differences could be traced to differences in the speed of conditioning that was native to the individual's central nervous system. So hard-to-condition meant extrovert personality and tough-mindedness (and hysteria); easy-to-condition meant introvert and tender-minded (and anxiety—the guilt-ridden liberal?). Whatever the political philosophy or objective conditions of a group, said Eysenck, this basic personality division would always exist. Thus, regardless of the overt teaching people received from family, party, or society, there would always be those who took a tough line on discipline and the party line (the tough-minded) and those who resisted discipline and went their own way (the tender-minded).

So we see, in all sects there are those who, once the sect is established, regard it as a new orthodoxy to be rigidly followed and those who regard it as a base from which to branch out into something new. Perhaps the prophets, "pioneers," and innovators of all species are those who, in Pavlov's words, have "a preponderance of excitatory over inhibitory potential" and so form conditioned responses in a very stable manner. The new charismatic leader, depending on the nature of his promises, will attract either the tough-minded conformists or the tender-minded freethinkers; either way the group will split between them, and this will become one of the main energizers of sectarianism.

These personality differences (Jefferson's tories and whigs) are independent of the ideological content of the dispute. They are indifferent to belief. They will fasten on belief to work their own ends. We saw this initially in the split between Owen and Smith, but if we examine any ideological groups, we will see these personality types as divisive factors that are potentials for group fission.

Christian Sects

Catholics. So back to our sects, inevitably split along these lines, constantly budding and reforming. In their *Handbook of Denominations in the United States,* Mead and Hill list 157 sects or denominations. And this is a restricted number because they count the Roman Catholic Church as one. But as we have seen, from the first the history of the Church has been one of division and heresy, with the central church, based in Rome, trying with varying degrees of success to impose itself on the unruly congregation. Even the papacy itself became at one point divided, with one pope in Rome and another in Avignon, busily excommunicating each other and everyone else.

The gentile church initially broke free from the Jerusalem, Jewish church, under the leadership of Paul, whose excitatory potential certainly outweighed his inhibitory and led to the inclusion of gentiles who were not required to keep the food taboos or undergo circumcision. But the so-called heresies still flourished, and Marcionites (after Marcius) fought with Monatism (after Monatus—who extolled the virtues of radishes), and both fought with Monophysites, while the Copts and Arians went their own ways. Each of the heresies had its eponymous leader: Manicheism from Mani, Pelagianism from Pelagius, Bogomils from Bogomile, Waldensians from Waldo, and Jansenism from Jansen. The Church dealt with heresies either by trying to exterminate them, as it did successfully with the Albigensians, or even more successfully by simply incorporating them, as with the Franciscans. The Franciscans, of course, split on the death of their founder between the Conventuals and the Spirituals over the issue of the ownership of property versus absolute poverty (they will reappear in Chapter 13).

The founders of potential sects were made saints, and their followers became monastic orders: Benedictines from Benedict, Dominicans from Dominic, Augustinians from Augustine, Carthusians from Bruno, Trappists from de Ponce, Cistercians from de Molesme. The Jesuits, from Loyola, were perhaps the epitome of assimilation, while the Templars, from Bernard, became too much of a threat and were viciously attacked, surviving only surreptitiously. These are the main monastic bodies, but there are probably over a thousand such orders in the Catholic Church, many devoted to the cults of saints like their counterparts in India to the Hindu gods. Then there are numerous lay movements and orders, from Opus Dei on the extreme right, to the Knights of Columbus in the center, to Liberation Theology on the far left. We should not let devotion to the papacy blind us to the sectarian tendency in the Roman church.

Currently the Church is facing a schismatic movement in which Traditionalists, who object to the reforms of Vatican II, flock under the banner of Bishop Marcel Lefebvre, the French apostate. Thomas Franks, in his analysis of the chronically sectarian state of Kansas, describes the Catholic situation there:

> Where this craving for continuity and unity and orthodoxy has led, ironically, is to endless hairsplitting and quarreling and schism. The SSPX [Society of Saint Pius X], for its part, declares Vatican II heretical and denounces the vernacular mass, but remains nominally loyal to the Pope. (The Vatican regards the SSPX as schismatic.) This in turn strikes traditionalists as insufficiently traditional; you are either with the Vatican II organization (whatever it is) or with the true Catholic Church, they reason, and they have split off from the SSPX and formed factions like the Mount Saint Michael's Community or the Society of Saint Pius V [SSPV!]. At the end of this sectarian progression lies *sedevacantism,* the notion that thanks to the manifold heresies of the church since the sixties, there is no one occupying the papal throne.

The ultimate in Catholic schism in Kansas occurred when one David Bawden, dissatisfied with all of the above, called his own papal election (five people came) and had himself elected Pope Michael I. He wrote a book in 1990 about his own take on Catholic theology called *Will the Catholic Church Survive the Twentieth Century?*

The distinction Eysenck drew from Pavlov tells us that there is a strong personality difference between the prophet and what we should call the disciples. There is a disciple mentality that thrives on followership, and of course, in the nature of things, disciples will always be in the majority. The tough-minded have a passion for order, discipline, and dominance, and a rigidity that will not tolerate ambiguity. Sects demand both types: the hairy prophet who strides in from the wilderness with his staff proclaiming "Thus saith the Lord God of Israel . . ." and those who will follow him to the death in strict obedience. Then, in the nature of things, usually on his death but not always, there will arise new prophets attracting new followings of devoted disciples. Monty Python's *Life of Brian* ruthlessly satirized this tendency, as Spike Milligan led the followers of the unfortunate Brian into schism over the disposition of the master's sandal.

Protestants. The history of Protestantism is the history of such oscillations, without the umbrella of the papacy to provide a spurious sense of unity. Looking only at the 157 sects in Mean and Hill's list, we find that there is virtually no sect without subsects. Even the sedate Episcopalians have inherited their division into High Church, Low Church, and Moderates from their Anglican roots, and are about to split up on the issue of homosexual and female priests and bishops. The Baptists lead the way with 25, including the Landmark Baptists, the Free Will Baptists, and the Duck River and Kindred Association of Baptists. The Methodists follow with 13. The Church of God has 7, the Lutherans 9, the Mennonites 8, the Pentecostals 10, the Presbyterians 8, the Reformed (once the Dutch Reformed) a mere 6, and the hopefully named United Church of Christ has 9. Even the Quakers boast 3 (one, the Church of Universal Friends, has died out) and the seemingly monolithic Mormons, the Latter-day Saints, have 5.

And these are only the officially registered and recognized sects, as it were. The breakaway process is going on all the time. The Baptists, who were always split between the General (all souls saved) and the Particular (only elect souls saved), are at the moment going through another massive splitting process. This divides them all between Moderates, following the doctrine of the competency of the individual soul, and the Fundamentalists, stressing biblical inerrancy: a tender-minded versus tough-minded split if ever there was one, with Fundamentalism stemming from the charismatic W. A. Criswell. But this is just the end run of the almost manic potential of Protestantism for schism and sectarianism that is inherent in a doctrine the makes the individual soul sovereign before its God—Anabaptists, Husserites, Hutterites, Puritans, Calvinists, Moravians, Shakers and Jumpers, Pietists, and all the others we have mentioned, including the thousands, like those in Bath, that have passed away, some unnoticed even in their own time.

Sectarian Irruptions

One thing that cannot be explained by any general theory of sectarianism based on evolved traits of human nature is why in some cases the formation of sects seems relatively quiescent, while at other times sectarianism seems to explode. This seems to depend on cultural and historical factors that are not well understood. For example, the early part of the nineteenth century in western New York State saw a tremendous religious explosion, the results of which are still with us. Whitney Cross in *The Burned-over District* gives an excellent account of the fervor that was the "Second Great Awakening" from 1800 to 1850. From this we get the celibate and chaste Shakers, followers of Mother Ann Lee, who had to persist by recruitment from the outside, and did so in small numbers until very recently. They are remembered for their beautiful furniture and the hymn that Aaron Copland incorporated into *Appalachian Spring* ("Simple Gifts").

Most famous and most successful are the Mormons—the Church of Jesus Christ of Latter-day Saints, the followers of Joseph Smith. Their saga is well known, and they have kept themselves remarkably intact, but perhaps not so well known is the breakaway movement of Joseph's wife Emma, which exists as the Reorganized Mormons in Independence, Missouri. Although such subsects as the Bickertonites and the Strangites are recognized, there are numerous unrecognized and illegal fundamentalist polygamous sects in Utah and Arizona.

The modestly successful Christian Scientists, founded by Mary Baker Eddy, are still very much with us and have a worldwide following. Mrs. Eddy lived in constant fear of dissident followers who were attacking her with Malicious Animal Magnetism, and threw out those she suspected, but so far formal dissident sects have not materialized. Evangelism, on the other hand, founded by Charles Grandison Finney, onetime president of Oberlin College, has spawned a diverse movement that is the ancestor of Billy Graham and the revivalists generally, who often act as recruiters to any and all sects from among those they have saved.

We have already seen the ten sects of the Pentecostalists, who sprang from the same source but emphasized speaking in tongues and the like. They produced the Assemblies of God out of the Holiness movement of Charles Fox Parham, ultimately out of Methodism, and like the Baptists were subject to a black–white schism. The best-known modern representatives are the churches of Jimmy Swaggart, and Jim and Tammy Bakker, with their doctrines of worldly success and faith healing.

Less successful were the Perfectionists. Those who followed John Humphrey Noyes, founder of the Oneida community, aimed for perfection here on earth through the practice of "omnigamy"—the marriage of everyone to everyone else, and *coitus reservatus,* a kind of Western Tantrism. They did not survive. Neither did the Millerites, after William Miller, at least in their original form. This is not surprising, since Miller firmly predicted the end of the world on October 22, 1844. The failure of this prediction is known, with stunning understatement, as "The Great Disappointment." The survivors of Millerism became the Seventh-day Adventists, who have been revising the date ever since. One of their latter-day members became secretary of the environment under George Bush Sr., and announced that conservation was pointless because the world was about to end anyway (again). More constructive perhaps was Ellen Harmon White, who inspired the great Dr. Kellogg, another believer, to invent the cornflake.

The abolitionist movement, which was another outcome of the Great Awakening, was also inevitably driven to sectarian division. It split between William Garrison, editor of the *Liberator*, and Frederick Douglass, who edited the *North Star*. Likewise, the Anti-Slavery Society divided over the issue of the place of women. One possible generalization that arises from the history of sectarianism is that the less ideological the movement, the more likely it is to produce factions rather than sects. The line initially is perhaps hard to draw: sects often start as factions. But Tories seem prone to factionalism, while Socialists seem to spawn sects.

Why there are these periodic bursts of sectarian creativity is not clear. It is perhaps too easy to say they come at periods of great upheaval in society. The first Great Awakening came early in the eighteenth century, with the rapid expansion of the colonies. The second, as we have seen, came after the revolution and during the birth of the modern industrial state. There were others after the Civil War, and after World War II, particularly in the South, when extreme Fundamentalism crystallized and showed its teeth in Tennessee at the Scopes trial.

We might also say that we are currently living through another eruption, following World War II and the vast social changes we have all lived through. There has been a return to the traditional churches, but also a large and as yet not fully documented surge of "alternative" or New Age sects, which spread across the religious spectrum from ersatz Hinduism to pseudo-Celtic Witchcraft. They often sound suspiciously like the roll call of those Engels listed as devotees of early Socialism. It would make sense that times of stability favor stable denominations and times of upheaval promote a growth of sects. But this is something we must leave to the sociologists and historians.

If we move onto the world scale with Christianity, the result is even more alarming. If we look at the remarkable two-volume *World Christian Encyclopedia*, we find a count of 33,830 denominations. One of the largest categories of these is the "independents," which account for 386 million of the world's Protestants and ranks second to the Catholics. These are indigenous churches mostly in developing countries and include Brazil's Universal Church of the Kingdom of God, the Jesus Is Lord

Fellowship in the Philippines, and the Zion Christian Church in South Africa. Like all "Pentecostal" churches they are subject to constant fission, and the total number of subsects, changing as it does daily, is unknowable.

Academic Sects

We are concerned with the sectarian phenomenon itself, and it shows itself in all ideological movements, as Engels saw so clearly. He thought it occurred particularly in the early stages, before doctrines were settled and agreed on. Science is thus an interesting test case—by its very nature its doctrines are always open to question, and so it might be seen as always in an "early stage." But we know that this is not how it works, even if it is how, to good Poppereans, it should work. Since the publication of Thomas Kuhn's *The Structure of Scientific Revolutions,* we must view science as a series of lurches, from the establishment of periods of "normal science," when doctrines and practices are in place, through periods of revolution, when the established "paradigm" comes under attack, fails, and is eventually replaced.

Holders of scientific doctrines do not give them up easily in the face of contrary facts. Max Planck maintained that scientific theories never changed, it was just that their perpetrators eventually died out. There are always ways to maintain a paradigm in the face of contrary evidence, because many paradigms are more metaphysical than scientific and hence, as Popper showed, not open to direct refutation. There are, I think, still a lot of behaviorist psychologists, torturing and bribing their rats, convinced still that they have the ultimate paradigm of all behavior, including human.

What does happen in science, though, and especially in the soft sciences, is the proliferation of sects, almost always originating with a prophet, wielding his own form of charisma, the theory. Think of the sects of psychoanalysis that arose, many before the founder was dead. The true believers clustered around the daughter, Anna Freud, while Jungianism, Adlerism, and the schools of Klein, Fromm, Horney, and Sullivan went their own ways, each claiming to be the true successors. It sounds horribly like the list from eighteenth-century Bath.

Those of us who suffered through "personality psychology" in the 1950s remember at least Allport and attitude theory, Murray and personology, Lewin and field theory, and Sheldon and constitutional theory. Then there was factor analysis, gestalt theory, McDougall's hormic theory, role theory, and the theories of Tolman, Rogers, and Murphy (who perhaps invented the term "biosocial"). You might immediately object that these are not sects, they represent schools of scientific thought with bases in fact and experiment and so forth. But the religious would make the same objection: their movements represent serious theological differences based on experience, reason, and the like. The process of dispersion is indifferent to the truth, falsity, or even sanity of the sects.

Thus we should be interested in the commonalities that go beyond the ideological justifications for sectarianism. The process in both cases is the same. I could have chosen any behavioral science field. I am not picking on personality psychology. Hominid paleontology would have been better: every prophet with his own species. The American Association of Physical Anthropologists was driven to declare officially, "Read Our Lips: No New Taxa!" The process is something like this: There is an established doctrine, a prophet arises and challenges it, offering his own version, and a sect of disciples then gathers round the prophet, undergoes an often-painful initiation (the PhD degree), and persists until another of its number breaks off to form his own sect. The majority will always be followers; it takes a charismatic personality to strike out and establish a new "school."

The school is to the academy, what the sect is to religion. Functionally it is the same thing, and demands the same explanation. In the modern setting of science, with many large research universities, the opportunities for sect formation are almost too tempting. Potentially every department is its own sect, with tenure and grants and lavish resources to fund the prophet and his followers. And it is perhaps remarkable that despite the influx of women into the universities, almost all the prophets are still men.

A modern pioneer of ideological dispersal gets his PhD, moves to a new department, sets up his school with the proper flourish of ritual publications, and starts to attract disciples—graduate students—and to disperse them in turn. As Engels foretold, modern communication, now instant with e-mail, texting, and social networking sites, enables the disciples to stay in close touch despite physical dispersal, and this may well prolong the life of scientific sects. Or it may just facilitate greater segmentation; we shall have to see how this turns out. But there are several distinct requirements for the process. The prophet has to make certain promises, the main one being *novelty*. The old prophet could preach a return to ancient and pure ways, but his progressive counterpart has to declare something new. What use is there in science for anything old; it is ipso facto out of date, which is the worst of scientific sins. Try to get graduate students to read anything more than five years old. To do so gives them genuine physical pain.

Thus we find novelty paraded in book titles: *Evolution: The Modern Synthesis; Sociobiology: The New Synthesis; Evolutionary Psychology: The New Science of the Mind; Evolutionary Psychiatry: A New Beginning.* (Remember that these remarks were first addressed to a meeting of the Human Behavior and Evolution Society.) Very often this newness is simply a reinvention of the wheel, redefined by the prophets as a "circular motion-facilitation device" (or "standard social science model," or for that matter, "meme"). No matter: the claim must be made. The sectarians then go to work on the prophet's new list of normal science problems, reading only each other's publications and citing only each other, thus maintaining the purity of sect doctrine. The exception to the "nothing older than five years" rule is the ritual citation, in every paper, of the canonical works of the founders. That these citations are mostly ritual can be seen in the case of the original work of William Hamilton, where early on a mistake occurred in the cited pagination, and this has been faithfully repeated by the disciples down to the very present. Nevertheless, the names and works must be ritually intoned: In the name of Williams, and of Hamilton, and of Robert Trivers, Amen.

The prophet must also promise a relatively easy operational method that the more modestly endowed followers can pursue, to establish low-level but empirically sound (or at least repeatedly confirmed) findings, and hence reputations. Pavlov, Watson, and Skinner did this brilliantly for psychology. Malinowski did it for anthropology, and T. H. Marshall taught a generation of British sociologists how to correlate everything with social class. Perhaps the best example is still Murdock's cross-cultural method, which provided a lucky generation of anthropologists with an easy way to "test hypotheses" and hence generate theses with a minimum of imagination and effort. We are all, I think, aware of the facile operational practices in our own disciplines; we depend on them. I will forebear to mention the full list for our own sects and subsects, but I will admit I have already given up reading articles about some further item that can be correlated with fluctuating asymmetry.

The prophet also must provide a dense and impenetrable ritual language for the followers, in which they may couch their results and thus keep the unbelievers and uninitiated at bay. In the humanities this is *all* that the prophet needs to provide. A successful prophet must also give his sect a recognizable name, around which it can rally, as a clan round a totem. Often this will be the name of the founder, but in science the tradition of modesty usually means that officially the founder's name will be secondary. Officially, for example, the name is psychoanalysis, secondarily Freudianism. Jungianism is analytical psychology, and so on. Thus, while the official name may be inclusive fitness theory, I hear more and more of Hamiltonian analysis—except, of course, from the followers of Maynard Smith. Thus the original "ethology" was followed by "sociobiology" then "evolutionary psychology" and now "behavioral ecology"—there may be others.

Academic sects do not always fission on departmental lines, but may occur as interest groups within learned societies: the national societies are like the mother church, and they fragment while maintaining a surface unity, like the churches themselves. This often is informal and unrecognized, and can be deduced by the knowledgeable only from the way sessions and papers are organized, often to honor a prophet and promote his teachings, or by a candidate for prophethood to promote himself. And here we should perhaps add, in the ghastly modern fashion, "or herself," because in the soft sciences the number of prophetesses is on the rise, and we may yet see the advent of another Mother Ann or Mary Baker Eddy.

Margaret Mead was certainly a prototype prophetess, cloak, forked stick and all, striding through the annual meetings of the American Anthropological Association, trailed by her adoring band of female disciples like something out of *Patience*. But this was informal, however real: think of the heresy hunting and ideological frenzy that followed on Derek Freeman's questioning of her competence and doctrines. Annual meetings are interesting as a latter-day example of the primitive increase ceremony, which Durkheim saw as the essence of religion. The bands that had been scattered by the dispersion process came together annually to indulge in collective rituals of social solidarity, drink fermented liquor, trade goods and ideas, collect mates, and engage in orgiastic sex.

But at least, in the case of that same American Anthropological Association, one learned society has abandoned any pretension to unity and formalized at least forty sects, allowing them to become official subsects of the mother church, just like the medieval monastic orders. These are based on geography (Anthropology of Europe), ideology (Feminist Anthropology, Humanistic Anthropology), status (Association of Senior Anthropologists, Student Anthropology), subject matter (Medical Anthropology, Educational, Political, Legal, Biological, Nutritional), method (Visual Anthropology, Mathematical), academic status (Community Colleges), and on and on. There is a sadly named General Anthropology section, and a Cultural Anthropology section, and some members asked (irony of ironies) for a Scientific Anthropology section, but there were too few takers. The Californians have an Anthropology of Consciousness section, which studies, among other things, paranormal phenomena. They live in their closed intellectual groups, operating as mutual admiration societies, handing out their annual awards to each other.

We should look back here to Robin Dunbar's contention that sub-groups within disciplines tend to have about 200 members, which is what our neocortex can cognitively handle. The Anthropological Association has about 10,000 North American members. Divide this by forty official "interest groups" and you get an average membership of 250. Not everyone is a member of a subsect, and these often form from informal groups that eventually formalize their status, so the actual median number per subgroup is probably lower—closer to 225. But the correspondence in any case is remarkable. At least anthropology is honest and recognizes the situation. In other learned societies these groups can exist only informally, thus disguising the degree of fragmentation.

Again you might object that these are not sects in the religious sense but genuine interest groups, and again I will say this does not matter. Sects always claim to be genuine interest groups. If you really believed that Miller had demonstrated that the world was going to end in 1844, and that only his followers would be saved, you surely had a powerful interest in joining the Millerites. But the process is so remarkably similar in all these cases that we have to consider that something is going on that is not simply in the realm of the ideas themselves. They give the excuse, as it were, for the segmentation and dispersal process to take place as it does. It need not take place this way, with a charismatic figure banging together the symbolic petrol cans, like the chimpanzee Mike at Gombe, to divert the attention of some of the troop to him. It need not involve a dominance struggle between rival sects, blasting each other in publications and competing for grants and student recruits.

One could imagine a science fiction universe, perhaps the universe of Mr. Spock and the totally rational and logical Vulcans, in which the progress of ideas—religious, political, or scientific—took place within an orderly consensus, without the sectarian process happening at all. Some readers in the "hard sciences" have protested that these sciences are not sectarian and approach this rational model, but the history of those sciences is also riven with sectarianism (think of astronomy: steady state versus big bang). I readily admit that in principle the scientific method renders rational decisions possible, and they are arrived at: the resolution between cognitive and behavioral psychology, for example. We saw how in modern evolutionary biology the conflict between individual selectionists and group selectionists was not without its sectarian passions, even though in the end it will be productive and the evidence will indeed decide. I am reminded that the drive by the English Quaker astronomer Arthur Eddington to prove Einstein's general theory of relativity (by observing a total eclipse) was driven not so much by science as by the common ground of pacifism.

I think a process of scientific dispute without the sectarian elements would be unrecognizable to us. It would not be a human process; it would lack drama and motive force for us. The current dispute between the selectionists is dull compared with the days when the zealot Stephen Jay Gould and his sect of "Science for the People" led a noisy self-righteous crusade against the ungodliness of the neo-Darwinians. (Does anyone even remember what a "spandrel" is?) We want a rational resolution of the dispute about the origin of the universe, true, but we also want the soap opera of the bluff, blunt Englishman Hoyle versus the subtle French Jesuit Lemaître. True to Max Planck's dictum, the major proponents of the steady-state theory (Hoyle, Bondi, Gold) held rigidly to it until their deaths, despite the contrary evidence (accidentally discovered) of cosmic microwaves and the expanding universe. Remember that the phrase "big bang theory" started as a sectarian insult.

Because we are stuck with being human, we can look forward to an indefinite future in which the dispersal and migration of ideas will always piggyback on those deeper motives and processes we share with the migrating mammals. These Drumbeats are low and persistent, like the constant rumbles of a bullroarer in the background of an Aboriginal dance on that sea-girt continent the human migrants reached more than 40,000 years ago. These mammalian imperatives are the same motives and processes we share with our pioneering tribal ancestors who were always on the move and are still on the move in our tribal imaginations today.

CHAPTER FIVE

Which Ten Commandments?

Tribal Taboo and Priestly Morality

W HEN WE THINK of the move from tribe to civilization, it is usually the agricultural revolution of the Neolithic we think of. But across large areas of North Africa and the Middle East, the domestication of animals—cattle, sheep, goats, horses, and camels— had an independent life. Those were the lands of the pastoral nomads, wandering with their herds in the hills and deserts. Even in large areas of East Africa where they settled down, their economy was primarily pastoral, their lives dominated by the success of their cattle and by the incessant raiding of other herds that provided a rhythm to their lives.

These pastoral tribes, as we saw in Chapter 3, lived in an uneasy symbiosis with the cities and states through which they wandered. But many of them also settled down themselves and became city dwellers, some of them even becoming planters and traders. In many cases they simply conquered the settled agricultural city dwellers and blended with them into a city-state or eventually even a nation-state. Ibn Khaldûn saw how this produced tensions, how the tribal nomad in them was always fighting with the urban citizen, and how fragile was the veneer of civilization.

Tribe to Nation

One such people left an astonishing record of its own transformation from tribe to nation, even though it was a nation based on tribes. These were the Israelites, and the record is the Bible. The first five books of the Bible—the Torah or Pentateuch—record the struggle to move from a pastoral existence to that of city-based nation, eventually a kingdom and small empire. If it is not an actual history as we now understand it, it is the narrative of their past as they saw it and as it existed in their traditions. For our immediate purposes, we can use it as a lens through which to view the eternal struggle between the process of becoming civilized and the persistence of the savage mind: between taboo and ethics, between the establishment of Law and the Drumbeats of Custom. The Law that was being established in the teeth of Custom more than 3,000 years ago lives on with us in an almost alarming way. Another current dispute allows us an unusual entry into the process of becoming civilized.

The Edited Ten

The Supreme Court's decision on the display of the Ten Commandments on government property has pleased no one, and perhaps no one could be pleased. But at least we should settle on *which* Ten Commandments we should display if we are going to do it. Most people to whom I mention this, if they are not Old Testament scholars, are amazed or unbelieving. Of course, they say, there is only one set of Ten Commandments; we all know them by heart: they are the ones now in dispute. Not so. There are basically two sets of "Ten Commandments," and each is repeated twice. The set being popularized by proponents currently—the one appearing on courthouse walls and monuments—is in fact an edited and abridged version of what appears in the biblical texts of Exodus and Deuteronomy.

Some of the commandments are terse and to the point—"Thou shalt not kill"—but others have a lot of supporting matter that is left out in the popular versions. The current version achieved widespread popularity in this form when circulated by the Fraternal Order of Eagles, a national Christian and patriotic fraternity, to promote Cecil B. DeMille's film *The Ten Commandments*. Even some of the politicians proposing legislation for the public display of "the Ten Commandments" could not even name one of them, so I can take nothing for granted and will give one abbreviated version here (taken from the King James Version, which is the most familiar).

1. Thou shalt have no other gods before me.
2. Thou shalt not make unto thyself any graven image.
3. Thou shalt not take the name of the Lord thy God in vain.
4. Remember the Sabbath day to keep it holy.
5. Honour thy father and thy mother.
6. Thou shalt not kill.

7. Thou shalt not commit adultery.
8. Thou shalt not steal.
9. Thou shalt not bear false witness against thy neighbour.
10. Thou shalt not covet any thing that is thy neighbour's.

The original of this edited version (which follows St. Augustine rather than the Judaic version or that of Origen used in the Eastern Church) is only one of two found in the book of Exodus. It is described there (Exodus 20) as the set given to Moses on Mount Sinai, which he later destroyed in anger when he found the Israelites worshipping the golden calf. *It is not the set that God himself officially endorsed as "the Ten Commandments" and that he ordered to be put into the Ark of the Lord* (Exodus 40:20) and to be binding forever. This, the official or "ritualistic" set, as opposed to the preliminary version now circulating, was given to Moses when he went back to God and asked for a replacement for those he had broken.

The Moralistic Ten and the Tables of Stone

The first version found in Exodus, the one in contention, which scholars have deemed the "moralistic" version, suspiciously reappears later, pretty much intact, in Deuteronomy 5. This leads scholars to conclude that this priestly or moralistic version, composed sometime after the Israelites had conquered Canaan, was inserted into the Exodus story to give it more authenticity, as being more "ancient"—indeed, the first set of "commandments" delivered by God. But in the process of compilation (during or after the Babylonian captivity, ca. 586 BC) the second, or "ritualistic," version was left in. Less attention was paid to continuity in those days. This is one of many contradictions in the narrative, and would be of only antiquarian interest were it not such a live issue today. Those who take Exodus to be the revealed and inerrant word of God will have to suppose that God changed his mind rather drastically before giving Moses the second version. And if we are to take him at his word, then this was the official final version put into the ark, and the basis of the Law.

What was this definitive or "ritualistic" version? Anyone can read it in Exodus 34. It starts with God's familiar injunction to Moses to cut the two tablets of stone. We must pause on this injunction because, despite DeMille and Charlton Heston, it does *not* appear with the first, moralistic version in Exodus, but as an afterthought with it in later Deuteronomy. Let us, as they say, get this straight. In neither Exodus nor Deuteronomy does God either order Moses to hew tablets of stone or hew them himself, and then write the moralistic version on them, as portrayed in the movie and enshrined in popular imagination. In Exodus 20, God simply *speaks* the commandments.

It is not even clear who, if anyone, heard them. Moses is not with God at this point; he has "gone down" to the people. The people then witness "the thunderings and the lightnings and the noise of the trumpets, and the mountain smoking" and withdraw in fear, telling Moses to go to God. Moses does, and for ten more chapters—forty days and forty nights, he receives more than a hundred "commandments" from God. At 31:18 we are told: "And he gave unto Moses when he had made an end of communing with him on Mount Sinai, two tables of testimony, tables of stone, written with the finger of God."

Note that it nowhere says that what was written upon these tables (or tablets—translations differ) was the "Ten Commandments"—which as yet he had not called such. In fact, the logic of the statement is that *all* the "commandments" that God had given to Moses were on the tables of stone: more than a hundred. Three books later in Deuteronomy, where the author is recapping the events of Exodus, Moses reminds the people that he "stood between the Lord and you" so that only he heard the words—thus clarifying the puzzlement of the Exodus version. At least here we are clear that Moses did hear God. The moralistic ten then follow, slightly different but essentially the same, and then we are told: "these words the Lord spake unto all your assembly," which seems to contradict the idea (in both biblical accounts) that the people could not approach God but sent Moses to do it. However, after we're told that God has spoken to "the whole assembly," finally we get: "And he wrote them on two tables of stone and delivered them unto me" (Deuteronomy 5:22). We can see that this contradicts the Exodus account in that it has God delivering the two tablets of stone immediately after speaking the words, *not* six weeks and a hundred commandments later. One cannot envy the task of the priestly scribe who tried to reconcile these accounts, but even in the Deuteronomic version, there is no question of God delivering his commands one at a time, and inscribing them on the tablets of stone with his finger as he delivers them. That is pure DeMille.

The Ritualistic Ten

When it comes to the overlooked and ignored "ritualistic" Ten Commandments, however, the instruction to "hew two tablets of stone" is up front. "Hew thee two tablets of stone like unto the first" (Exodus 34:1) These were to replace the two that Moses broke in anger (Exodus 32:19).

We must then note carefully what God says: he says that he will write upon them *"the words that were on the first tables, which you broke."* God is quite explicit that this is an *exact replacement* of the original. God then speaks this authoritative version, and the episode ends (verse 28) with the words "and he wrote upon the tables the words of the covenant, the Ten Commandments." (Apparently it was Moses who in fact did the writing, despite God's original insistence.) This is the first time the words "the Ten Commandments" appear in Exodus, and it is with the ritualistic ten.

One problem with this "ritualistic" version is that the list is not quite as crisp as in the moralistic set; some "commandments" are run together. As in the moralistic version there is a lot of supporting matter, in this case largely to do with tearing down the shrines of the indigenous peoples and not playing the harlot with their gods, and such. But the following is a close enough summary, minus the lengthy commentary, of what should be on our public displays (King James Version):

1. Thou shalt worship no other god.
2. Thou shalt make thee no molten gods.
3. The feast of unleavened bread shalt thou keep.
4. Six days thou shalt work, but on the seventh day thou shalt rest.
5. Thou shalt observe the feast of weeks, of the first fruits of wheat harvest, and the feast of ingathering at the year's end.
6. Thrice in the year shall all your men children appear before the Lord God.
7. Thou shalt not offer the blood of my sacrifice with leaven.
8. The sacrifice of the feast of the Passover shall not be left until the morning.
9. The first of the first fruits of thy land thou shalt bring unto the house of the Lord.
10. Thou shalt not seethe a kid in his mother's milk.

The first, the second, and the fourth are recognizable, but the rest are often-obscure ritual prescriptions with nothing about murder, adultery, honoring parents, stealing, or any other moral or legal issues. Moses goes on to threaten with death anyone who breaks number four—working on Saturdays. Number six refers to "presentations at the temple" of all Israelite males. Christians will recognize that Jesus was so presented. Scholars bicker endlessly over numbers seven and eight, but obviously the presence of yeast in bread is a major concern. This is probably related to the issue of putrefaction, which is why the Passover feast should not be left overnight. Fermentation was probably seen as a kind of putrefaction—which it is—hence the banning of yeast.

God had in fact ordered the Israelites to eat unleavened bread at the Passover and to celebrate this forever (Exodus 13). He also told them to try to eat the entire Passover feast and to burn whatever was left the next day. These two "commandments" can be seen, then, as simply a continuing celebration of these pivotal events. But why the injunctions in the first place? Scholars believe all these prohibitions to be older than the actual Exodus story, going back, as we shall see, to tribal taboos. Commandments nine and ten, which run together in the text, are especially interesting in that they juxtapose a fundamental principle of agricultural ritual—the first-fruits ceremony—with a basic pastoral taboo on boiling an animal's milk.

The Book of the Covenant

What are we to make of this discrepancy? Since Goethe initially made the observation, in the eighteenth century, scholars have agreed that the "ritualistic" version is the older one. This conclusion is reinforced by the appearance of this same list of ordinances earlier in Exodus 23, the so-called Book of the Covenant—the result of Moses's forty-day sojourn with God on Sinai—wedged between the moralistic and ritualistic versions. Sir James Frazer paid particular attention to this set of laws in *Folklore in the Old Testament,* and I am indebted to his discussion.

They are not, in the context of the Book of the Covenant, explicitly called "the Ten Commandments." They appear in the more general list of laws, given to Moses on Sinai, concerning the treatment of slaves (especially daughters sold as such), oxen that gore (and should be stoned), and the price paid for violating an unbetrothed virgin (the amount of her bride-price), and so on. The list has some minor differences from the ritualistic ten: the reference in number eight is specifically to the *fat* of the feast, which emphasizes the putrefaction issue, and God lays claim to the sacrifice of the firstborn of every animal (and human—whatever that may mean). A version of this latter demand is in fact in the ritualistic ten: "All that openeth the matrix is mine. ("Matrix" is Latin for womb.) I see it as a subclause, although many commentators see it as an independent commandment (see Frazer for a discussion). But the list is essentially the same.

This Book of the Covenant is obviously one of the very oldest parts of Exodus: a list of Yahweh's ordinances, around which later writers wove the story of the invasion of Canaan. What is strange is that the eventual compiler of the book of Exodus makes so very explicit God's insistence that the second, "ritualistic" version of the commandments was *an exact replacement of the original.* The "original" ten must then have been the commandments in the Book of the Covenant. (This is my deduction, not Frazer's.) So we can only conclude that the original text of Exodus made *these* the writings on the tablets that Moses destroyed. As we have seen, the story has been unclear as to what exactly was written on the first tablets that Moses broke. Now we know: it was the ritualistic ten. The priestly scribes of Deuteronomy later inserted their moralistic version into Exodus without changing the plot to accommodate it, hence the glaring inconsistency.

A Kid in Its Mother's Milk

Can anthropology shed any light on this issue? Let us take the taboo on boiling milk, and specifically a kid in its mother's milk, perhaps the most obscure of them all. Sir James Frazer, in *Folklore in the Old Testament*, showed how the taboo was a fundamental proscription in pastoral (herding) societies in Africa. They also forbade boiling flesh in milk, and even more the boiling of the young of a milk-giving animal in its mother's milk. They basically did not like to mess with the milk at all, and refused to let it come into contact with water, vegetables, or iron, among other things.

The underlying principle for Frazer, which he introduced in *The Golden Bough*, was that of "sympathetic magic." Pastoral tribes from Mohammedans in Morocco, through the Maasai and Bahima (Banyankole) in East Africa, to the Herrero in the south, believed that by harming the milk you harmed the animal it came from. For pastoral tribes the possible destruction of the herds was obviously, and rightly, more important than mere moral peccadilloes like adultery or killing or stealing, which harmed humans but left the precious animals intact. This taboo was also, of course, the basis of Jewish dietary laws separating meat and dairy products.

If the ancestors of the Israelites were indeed a wandering, Bedouin-like, desert-dwelling pastoral people, then this joint commandment (commandments nine and ten) is an interesting commentary on their adaptation to a new agricultural life in Canaan. A great deal of Exodus can be read as just such a commentary: a kind of education of the Israelites in the problems, moral and ritualistic, that they must face in Canaan as farmers and city dwellers. Goats were the basic milk-giving animals of the desert nomads, hence the specifying of a kid. Frazer, as we saw, traces this to the pastoral taboo, but writers as varied as Maimonides *(The Guide of the Perplexed)* and W. Robertson Smith *(The Religion of the Semites)* have suggested that the prohibition was directed specifically against some ritual practice of the Canaanites, although they lacked any direct evidence for this.

However, some texts have been discovered more recently at Ugarit, the city-kingdom just north of Canaan, whose language and customs were common in the area. These suggest that the Canaanites and their neighbors did indeed "seethe a kid in milk." So Yahweh, the god of the Israelites, could have been reemphasizing that his people must be different and definitely observe the old pastoral taboo. The relevant lines (translated by Cyrus Gordon) in the Ugaritic story of "The Birth of the Seven Gods" are:

And the field is the field of the gods,
    The field of Asherah-and-Rahm.
By the fire, seven times the heroes
Cook a kid in milk
    A lamb in butter
And by the flame, seven times the offering.

To be fair we should note Gordon's caveat that while "milk" and "butter" are certain, "kid" and "lamb" are not. They could refer to mint or other herbs. But the passage remains tantalizingly suggestive.

Mary Douglas, in her discussion of the Abominations of Leviticus in *Purity and Danger*, looks at Maimonides' claim that what is abominated is that which is Canaanite. She uses specifically his example of the boiling of the kid in its dam's milk. This cannot be the *whole* reason for the taboos, she insists, because the Israelites in fact did adopt "heathen" practices, like sacrifice. She continues with her brilliant discussion of "wholeness" and of "abomination" being a fear of the anomalous—a challenge to the established categories. There is no doubt that as a psychocultural theory of avoidance this is right. But if the avoidance of heathen practices cannot wholly explain, for example, why pigs, camels, hares, and rock badgers are forbidden foods, it does not follow that such a motive was absent from Israelite thinking. On the contrary, they explicitly inveigh against the practices of the heathen and the worship of heathen gods.

Even Douglas cannot explain many of the "anomalous" categories, and it may be that the Israelites were struggling in their thinking between logical consistency, on the one hand, and avoiding heathen practices, on the other. She actually does not explain the matter of the kid and the milk and how this might be explained as an "anomaly," nor does she discuss Frazer's theory of it as a tribal taboo of the pastoralists. And she does argue that the prototypes of acceptable ("clean") animal foods are the herd animals of those same pastoralists; that is, cloven-footed beasts that chew the cud. This for her is what explains the anomaly of the "unclean" pig: cloven footed but not a ruminant. Disturbing the original categories may well produce the abominated anomalies: but the original categories themselves have to come from somewhere. Tribal taboos are surely one reasonable source for a tribal people such as the Hebrews.

Hebrews and Gentiles

The actual origin of the Hebrews again is disputed, but no one doubts, and their own traditions attest, that somewhere along the way most of them were of nomadic-pastoralist desert stock. The name *hebiru* or *khabiru* or *'apiru* is Akkadian, but crops up in Egyptian texts and means something like "wanderer" or even "outlaw." But before the origin of the Hebrews somewhere in the second millennium BC, the earliest Semitic-speaking peoples dispersed from North Africa (not Arabia, as was once thought). They emerged before the Sahara desert developed in a great drought, isolating the Berber in the west. During this time—up to 6000 BC, "they followed a pastoral and nomadic way of life throughout the period of the drought. They lived off herding and patch agriculture and occupied regions that were confined to the broad plains and steppe. Only gradually did they enter the more fertile areas of Palestine and Syria" (Thompson 1999).

A second great drought in about 2300 BC forced those who had developed settled agriculture to return to their traditional nomadic-pastoral way of life on the steppes, as did the "great Mycenaean drought" of 1300 BC, when the original Hebrews appeared. This ancient background as herding wanderers seems to have left its mark on the collective unconscious of the Semitic people, particularly the Arabs and the Jews. Even without the nomadic or transhumant component, the way of life in the area was always dependent as much on the herds as on the crops. The Semites were then in origin African pastoralists, and it should be no surprise that many of their magical beliefs share common features.

The "Hebrews"—wandering outlaws—sometime after 1500 BC moved into Palestine. According to the biblical tradition they came, with their herds, from Egypt, but there is no Egyptian record of such a people being there, in the otherwise overdocumented period of Ramses II. (Could this exodus, however, be a deeper remembrance of dispersion from a drought-ridden, but previously fertile, Sahara?) In late Bronze Age Palestine they gradually assimilated, and were assimilated by, local Canaanite farmers and traders, who were absorbed into the Hebraic "alliance." The anthropologist Frederick Barth notes that even today there is often a complex relationship of trade and kinship between city dwellers, farmers, and desert herdsmen, who may all be of the same "tribe." The tribe of Dan, for example, as Cyrus Gordon observes in *The Bible and the Ancient Near East,* was definitely a local group, absorbed physically and then ideologically by becoming one of the "children of Israel."

A good deal of the book of Genesis consists of this "construction of genealogy" to make up what Steven Grosby calls a "kinship nation." This is announced at the beginning of Exodus as the "twelve tribes" who were the "children" of Jacob/Israel. This was a slow process. But as is still the case in the Arab lands, there is a sense of the "purity" of the desert pastoral life, and a harking back to its values as the true ones. Thus Ibn Khaldûn, one of the great "fathers" of sociology, shows in *The Muqaddimah* (1377) how Islamic reformers always invoke this desert purity against the corruption of the urban Muslims. Khadafi rules Libya from a tent (at least symbolically), and in the Gulf States the remaining Bedouin herds and herdsmen have absolute right of way against the trucks and Mercedes of their modern contemporaries.

Something of this then may lie behind the constant harping in Exodus (and the rest of the Torah) on not falling into the ways of the Canaanites and the other heathen. While Mary Douglas may be right that all the abominations of Leviticus cannot be explained by this tension, a good deal of the rest of the Torah can. Thus, on the one hand, the Israelites were enjoined to avoid the ways of the Canaanites, and on the other hand, they were given lengthy instructions on how to outdo them in the splendor of the divine places and the raiment of the priests. Half the Book of the Covenant is concerned with this. These self-serving passages were undoubtedly written later by the priests themselves. But when it comes to morals and ritual, the stress is on the virtue of maintaining the purity of the tribal pastoral traditions in the face of an adoption of an agricultural way of life. This always includes the absolute devotion to Yahweh, initially not as an exclusive god, but as the tribal god of the Israelites who was "jealous" of his unique relationship with his people.

Thus the gods of Ugarit and Canaan were lustful and covetous: a good part of their epics concerns the petulant demands of their god Baal to have a palace built for himself as grand as those of his fellow gods. They were also bestial: Baal fathers seventy offspring from a heifer. They were incestuous: Baal marries his sister Anath. The priests of Baal imitated the god's bestiality in ritual, and the "temple prostitutes" were priestesses of Anath. These "heathen" fertility beliefs and practices, not uncommon in the early urban civilizations, are prominent as "abominations" in the Torah: "Whoever lies with a beast shall be put to death" (Exodus 22:19).

The tenth of the moralistic commandments, with its apparently curious ban on "covetousness" ("Thou shalt not *covet* thy neighbor's wife"—nor, for that matter, his female slaves), may very well be part of this "Don't be like the Canaanites or their gods" mantra that is so persistent.

But initially most of the differences that Exodus emphasized were ritual rather than moral, and God was insistent on this point: the ritual differences come first; the moralistic stuff can wait. What was owed to God was more important than what men owed to each other. Actually, Yahweh was just as insistent as Baal on having a "house" built for himself. (2 Samuel 7: 4–16: "Why have you not built me a house of cedar?") David was prevented from building it as a punishment, and Solomon finally obliged (1 Kings: 5–6).

Creation and Recreation

The curious theme of God having to redo an aspect of his work that failed, as with the two sets of Ten Commandments, is there in the Genesis stories of creation itself. The two versions are familiar enough. In the first (Genesis 1), after creating the material world, God creates man and woman (unnamed) and orders them to be fruitful and multiply. They evidently did not comply. Then in Genesis 2, in complete contradiction, it is stated that "there was no man to till the ground" and so God makes man (still unnamed) out of dust, and then makes woman from his rib, and puts them in Eden. Why the second version? A vast literature exists on this topic, but the story's parallel with the Ten Commandments story has not been much noticed: there is an original "creation" that does not work, and God then redoes the whole thing. Genesis 2 actually starts with the words: "Thus the heavens and the earth were finished, the whole host of them."

I am not a Hebrew scholar, but I have been told by those who are that the word translated as "finished" could mean "destroyed." (Cyrus Gordon thinks so.) Thus, to the writer, God found his first effort unsatisfactory, destroyed it, and started again. This time He did not make man and woman separate and equal, but made them part of each other so that they would yearn to become reunited as "one flesh." Was this because they had not fulfilled the original command to "be fruitful and multiply"? Thus God had to start over, with the spectacular results that follow in the Garden of Eden and great epic of Israel.

The disjunction between the creation accounts could be another editorial inconsistency in compiling different documents, or a cultic battle in which "Yahweh stories" replace those of the devotees of Elohim. We are familiar with all these arguments. But it could also be that this kind of "It didn't work so let's do it over again" plot was part of an ancient storytelling tradition of the kind Gordon finds in the texts from Ugarit. There are, of course, also two versions of the story of Noah and the flood, but these are not juxtaposed to each other as replacements or contradictions; they rather simply repeat each other in different words and images. But the theme of them is still that God botches the first job and has to redo it.

The story is not original to the Hebrews, but as the saga of Utnapishtim is found in the Gilgamesh epic of Sumer and Babylon. (The flood story is actually earlier than the epic and was incorporated into it.) Adherence to this old formula meant that the scribes who did the final edition of Exodus saw nothing strange in God's allowing his commandments to be destroyed and then later replaced. Nor were they too concerned with the particularities or inconsistencies that resulted from using this tension-building trope when they prepared their final version.

The fate of Israel itself can be seen as part of the same destroy-and-do-over trope. The Hebrew bible was, according to scholars of its composition, largely put together after the most traumatic event in their history, the Babylonian captivity (586 BC). The latent function of the narrative was to explain, and draw the moral from, this devastation of the Jewish nation. Thus the earlier part up to the end of 2 Chronicles is concerned to show how consistently the Israelites disobeyed God and went a-whoring after strange gods. Finally God had had enough, and he taught them the most terrible lesson of all by allowing the Assyrians to conquer them and then Nebuchadnezzar to destroy the temple and take them en masse into exile and slavery. The rest of the Old Testament is essentially about the establishment of the "New Israel" and the renewal of the covenant with God.

The New Testament itself can be seen as yet another version of this destroy-and-do-over theme. The New Israel had in turn failed, and the Romans, acting like the Babylonians as God's scourge, had again scattered the nation and destroyed the temple. The reasons for this went very deep. It was not just a matter, for the Christians, of the people's occasional backsliding, but of something fundamentally wrong with man. God's scheme to give man free will had resulted in continuing and ineradicable sinfulness. At some point, therefore, this phase of creation had to be destroyed, the mistake of free will rectified, and a New Heaven and a New Earth created in the Kingdom of God (2 Corinthians 5–17). Jesus, as represented by the authors of the gospels, seemed to think that his death would usher in this final destruction and re-creation.

Of course, it did not happen, so the genius Paul had to turn it into a Kingdom of the Spirit. This meant that the physical re-creation could be put off indefinitely, although a reminder of it concentrated the mind wonderfully. According to recent polls, at least 40 percent of Americans are "reasonably certain" it will happen in their lifetimes (20 percent are absolutely convinced). Be that as it may, we can simply note that the idea of God's (or the gods') dissatisfaction with a first attempt, and his (their) need to do it over again, runs deep in Near Eastern, and possibly universal, thinking. (For examples, see the Digression in the notes to this chapter.)

The Ten Today

But where does this leave the issue of *which* Ten Commandments we should regard as definitive? Proponents of the DeMille–Eagles–Deuter-onomy version will no doubt answer that, despite the contradictions, *this* is the version that has had the great influence on our lives and laws, and therefore this is the one that should be displayed in public places. Fine, but it seems they are willing to place the contingencies of history above the declared word of God in this instance. But they do have a point. The moralism of the second ten perhaps results from problems that were of accelerating importance to evolving urban societies with large popula-tions and more opportunity for crime. Adultery, killing, and stealing un-doubtedly loomed larger as behaviors to be controlled than did the keep-ing of yeast out of sacrifices. Parents were perhaps more in danger of neglect by their children and felt more in need of divine protection. The moralistic ten then accurately reflect the historical origins of the conflict between tribe and civilization, between taboo and law.

But the influence of the moralistic code on law itself has been greatly exaggerated. Only two of those commandments—the ones against killing (or "murder"; translators are divided) and stealing—are actually enforce-able by our current laws, and even then with numerous caveats. The mor-alistic version has been criticized to death, so we shall leave it. My con-cern has been with the ten that God authorized. The moralistic ten are, however, so enshrined in popular consciousness that the original version of this article—a short op-ed piece pointing out that the other ten actually existed—was refused by all editors on the grounds that it might "offend" the majority of their readers. The truth will always offend someone.

Most commentators seem to willfully avoid the issue, or just plain dis-semble. A recent serious and elaborately produced documentary on the History Channel was devoted to the history and interpretation of the Ten Commandments. It showed Moses breaking the first tablets, and then going up again to God to get the second set and putting them solemnly in the ark. But it *never says what was on the second set!* In fact it assumes, or does not question, that it was the same as was on the first. This is, as we have seen, in direct contradiction to the text of Exodus. A whole bevy of biblical "experts" participated in this charade.

The *New Oxford Annotated Bible,* to which, again, numerous experts contributed their wisdom, actually mentions that the list was different in the second case. But its commentary, by Judith E. Sanderson, disingenuously says: "The narrator here inserts a different version of the Ten Commandments, since the first version has already been recorded." And that is that! That this "different version" is the version put in the ark and approved by God, who insists it is exactly the same as the first, is not mentioned, so of course neither is its correspondence with the commandments in the Book of the Covenant. The "Ritual Decalogue" gets mentioned, but the blatant contradiction is again simply passed over.

Personally I think it would be just fine to display God's authorized Ten Commandments to remind us of the great relevance of religion in our contemporary lives. I would like to celebrate the first fruits of wheat gathering. I do the best I can with a neighborhood cookout when my five acres of corn are ripe. On Saturdays I watch college football: that's not work, so I should be safe. I don't have any male children, but if I did, getting them to Jerusalem three times a year might be difficult. But then I am not a Jew, so how does this apply to me or to any other gentiles? I love tortillas, which don't have a hint of yeast. It's hard to get kid these days, but if I do, I absolutely won't boil it in its mother's milk. Some things really are sacred.

CHAPTER SIX

Incest and In-Laws

Tribal Norms and Civilized Narratives

T HE DRUMS BEAT in closely related cross rhythms. Can the beat that produces our desire for vengeance and the favoring of kin be a variant of the beat that urges the marriage of close cousins, itself a cousin of the beat that drives us to sectarian fragmentation? And is there behind it all the oldest beat of all, the beat that warns us not to mate with those most readily available? If this is a truly ancient Drumbeat, what happens to it when the noise of civilization gains in crescendo? Let us ask our storytellers—our poets, dramatists, and novelists—because our storytellers know how to tap the tribal imagination; that is how they stay in business.

Genesis of the Taboo

But we cannot ask them without first knowing what we are asking about. Taboos on sexual relationship between close kin, between the members of the immediate family, were long thought to be a purely human invention. Animals, it was maintained, had no such inhibitions and mated incestuously. Thus the taboos on such animalistic behavior were thought to be the very foundation of human society; they were the ultimate Drumbeat of humanity, by which, in the immortal words of Lévi-Strauss, culture said "No!" to nature. Despite taking this momentous step, humans were thought to carry over into their humanness the even deeper Drumbeat of their animal desires.

The move from nature to culture represented by the imposition of the taboos was seen as precarious and counter to natural motives, which were ineradicable. In consequence, the taboos had to be stern and enforced by constant vigilance. In this traditional view, we all wanted to make love to our nearest kin, but once the momentous leap into culture had been taken, it would have been disastrous to go back into the maelstrom of incestuous animality. Our societies were built on the presumption of mating outside the family, it was the very definition of humanity itself, and so stern taboos, laws, and punishments were needed to keep incest at bay.

This was a plausible view because societies did almost universally ban sex and marriage within the immediate family, and punishments for breaches of this rule were often severe, including torture and death. In their mythologies, primitive tribes and ancient societies often portrayed incest, and the results of it were usually disastrous. There were exceptions to the rule (and we shall return to these), but they were almost always royal exceptions, and royal persons, as gods on earth, were allowed behavior that was not allowed to ordinary mortals. On the whole, then, it was agreed, there was a "grisly horror" of incest (Freud) that universally afflicted people and led them to impose and enforce the taboos, often extending them beyond the family to members of the clan, variously defined. Why, the question went, would we have such strong taboos if we did not have the strong desire in the first place?

Both popular opinion and the collective voice of the behavioral sciences echoed this orthodoxy. But there was always an undercurrent of skepticism. Why, the objectors asked in turn, do we seem, by and large, *not* to want to have sex with our closest relations? This would be the commonsense observation. Incest happens, but in proportion to non-incest, it does not happen very often. And most of this avoidance of incest does not seem to result from fear of punishment; there seems to be a genuine aversion to incest. This aversion seems to vary according to the relationship: strongest between mother and son, weakest between father and daughter, variable between brother and sister. But it is there, and usually only breaks down in unappetizing circumstances.

The orthodox view said that left to our own devices we would immediately resort to incest and so we have to be reined in by strong taboos and sanctions. To the question why we should not follow the desire to its logical conclusion, the orthodox had a string of often-contradictory answers. There would be a confusion of relationships; there would be bad genetic results; there would be conflict in the family; there would be too much attachment in the family; social bonds outside the family would not form; and so on. The skeptical view says that, on the contrary, left to our own devices we would probably mostly avoid incest spontaneously. The orthodox view asks why, then, if this is so, are there the universal strong taboos?

The skeptic answers that we often taboo things that we are averse to, not because we secretly want to do them, but because we disapprove of people doing things that are generally obnoxious to us. We strongly taboo murder, not because we are all given to implacable murderous impulses, but because we are averse to it, so that even if only a few people do it, it offends us. We do, however, understand the temptation to do it; we have all perhaps felt it momentarily. So the subject fascinates us and permeates our legends and stories from the beginning. Sex and violence, incest and murder—often linked in our fantasy productions—persist in our imaginative attempts to interpret ourselves to ourselves.

This has been one of the most interesting debates in the science of man (as we used to call it), and it is no secret that I have come down heavily on the side of the skeptics. I faced the united front of the great ones—Freud, Frazer, Lévi-Strauss—in supporting the views of Edward Westermarck, who basically said that close relationships in childhood led to the development of spontaneous aversion to sex in adulthood. Familiarity did not only breed contempt, it did not breed at all.

What led me to this were two observations. The first was the empirical observation that, in all the societies I looked at, this spontaneous aversion did seem to develop in varying degrees. It developed almost universally where children were reared together and allowed free physical interaction with each other: a situation that would have characterized the long period of our hominid development. The second was that the orthodox view might be totally wrong about what happened in "nature," because this view was based not on observations of nature but on suppositions about it. Again, in looking at animal behavior under natural conditions, indeed at the behavior of all sexually reproducing organisms, outbreeding seemed to be the rule and incest was rare. This was especially true in our primate relatives, and so by implication in our ancestors during the long haul through the savannas and the ice.

If, then, the avoidance of close inbreeding was the rule rather than the exception, the human incest taboo was, I argued, culture saying to nature not "No!" but rather "OK!" It was an amplification of the natural rather than an opposition to it. But how did this aversion come about? Was it instinctive? Were we born with such a natural aversion? This seemed impossible because we would not necessarily know who our relatives were. In any mammalian species a son knows its mother, and that seems to be the most universally avoided relationship. But it is a wise mammalian child that knows its own father, except in the relatively rare species that mate for life (and not even then). And brothers and sisters vary a lot in how they relate to each other. An anti-incest instinct does not seem probable. (Burt and Trivers, in *Genes in Conflict,* show that maternal and paternal genes within the same organism may be at odds about the desirability of different types of inbreeding.) But in all mammals there seem to be mechanisms that effect a dispersal of the members of the family so that the likelihood of their mating is reduced. Nature can implant a learning device as well as an instinct, and this has the adaptive advantage of flexibility, of varying responses to varying environments. It also can go wrong: it depends on the conditions of learning being met. This is the clue.

Why should this be? Is not the list of possible disasters proposed by the orthodox enough to explain why we avoid it? Not really. We have to go back to an even deeper Drumbeat to get this one, the Drumbeat we examined in Chapter 4 where we looked at the phenomenon of *dispersion* in animal and human life. We have to look to the origins of life as the emergence of self-replicating matter, and then to the crucial revolution that produced sex to replace cloning.

The origin of this sexual reproduction is still a mystery, but whatever the reason, this new form of reproduction won out over its rival (which is still around) by virtue of its ability to produce instant *genetic variability* for natural selection to work on. Close inbreeding results in a loss of such variability, hence mechanisms evolved to avoid it. At the same time, if breeding becomes too random, then any beneficial genes will be dissipated rather than concentrated and preserved. It is this loss of variation that seems to be at the heart of sexual strategies, not the bad genetic effects of close inbreeding. In small bands these effects would quickly be bred out, and even scattered bouts of outbreeding would reestablish a healthy stock.

So nature aims for a middle ground: organisms breed out to avoid losing variability, but not so far out that they dissipate genetic advantages. In human terms this means that the immediate family is taboo, but that marriage with cousins should be preferred. This is exactly what we find in human history until the dramatic growth and disruption of human populations upset the natural balance of the traditional society. Cousins would have been the most likely marriage partners in most traditional societies. There is evidence that people tend to choose mates who are genetically similar; cousins are ready-made candidates. As we saw with the Arabs and Iraq in Chapter 2, insistence on first-cousin marriage still persists in many societies. These two institutions, avoidance of incest and marriage of cousins, are at the heart of our humanity.

What are the human mechanisms that ensure the right result—from nature's point of view? Universally the suckled young male does not seem to want to mate with his mother, and in traditional society this would have been difficult anyway because she would usually be past breeding age when he became mature. The "suckling complex"—which itself has a strong hormonal link with sexuality (through the hormone oxytocin)—therefore seems to take care of the mother. Brothers and sisters are usually raised together, and this is what led Westermarck to think they develop an aversion they are not necessarily born with. In cases where they are allowed to play intimately together, before the age of six, they do seem to become actively averse to sex with each other at puberty.

This is well established now, with numerous documented examples. I called it (in 1962) "the Westermarck effect" to distinguish it from another pattern I called "the Freud effect." Here is my "law":

The intensity of heterosexual attraction between co-socialized children after puberty is inversely proportionate to the intensity of physical interaction between them before puberty.

When little siblings are left to their own devices (at least until age six), it appears they would act according to nature's script. We are still not sure what mechanism is involved in this "critical period"—whether it is aversive conditioning, negative imprinting, or a cognitive function—but it happens when the brain is maximally malleable, and it becomes fixed. It is important to note that the aversion they would develop was intended to be transient; it was meant to divert the siblings from each other briefly at puberty, long enough for them to mate elsewhere. But if, for example, they were kept around each other in relative isolation with no other sexual outlets, then the sexual imperative might well overcome the aversion.

In the cases that have been closely studied, varying from the Israeli kibbutzim and the Taiwanese, to the Trobriand Islanders and the Western Apache, there was a continuum. (For details, see my *Red Lamp of Incest.*) At one end were the freely romping siblings frolicking together; at the other end—the Freud end—were siblings raised together but not allowed physical contact. There were gradations between these two extremes, but at the Westermarck end the result seemed to be complete aversion, while at the Freud end it was the reverse. Despite the close rearing, the Freud-effect siblings were as sexual strangers to each other at puberty and needed strong taboos and punishments to keep desire in check.

It is a sad parody of human good intentions that incestuous desire in siblings can result from a quite conscious attempt to prevent it. With the Freud effect, culture saying "No!" to nature in fact had the paradoxical outcome of *promoting* strong incestuous desires. This is what Freud observed in his own Vienna, and he generalized his observations to mankind at large. For him the first line of human defense against the incestuous wishes was "repression": the desire was pushed into the subconscious and denied. It was dammed up, but the dam was always ready to burst. The result in either case was the same—no incest with siblings. The result was just achieved by different means: aversion and spontaneous avoidance, on the one hand, and repression plus strong taboos, on the other. In either case the siblings would not be attracted by incest, but attitudes to its occurrence would vary from relative indifference to superstitious horror, and all stations in between. The common denominator would be unease about the prospect of incest coupled with a fascination at the possibility of it.

Kindred and Affinity

There is a tendency to invoke "the incest taboo" as though it were a homogeneous phenomenon. But the three possibilities are quite different. With fathers and daughters there is less of a barrier; a daughter is a young fertile female, after all, and it does happen. This is fundamentally a power relationship, or has been in all traditional societies, and the most open to potential abuse. There is less opportunity for the spontaneous generation of avoidance here. But here we must look beyond the negative banning of sex and into the positive advantages of mating outside the family. This is the other side of the incest coin. The recognition of these benefits has a long history, and the word "exogamy" (marriage out) was coined to describe it.

In the prelanguage condition of our primate ancestors, when members of a group left it to mate elsewhere, they lost all contact with the home group. Among nonhuman primates it is the norm that either the males of a band or the females leave at puberty and mate elsewhere, so that was established. What our hominid ancestors seemed to add to the mix was continuing contact. I tried to express this in the formula: *while primates have kin, they do not have in-laws*. A father therefore in early human society had an interest in using his daughters and sisters—all the females he controlled—to forge alliances with other males in different groups: bands or clans. With the advent of hunting and language, all this was made possible, and the first human societies were formed. (For a brilliant extension of this idea, see Bernard Chapais, *Primeval Kinship*.)

The catch here is that incest avoidance and taboo were not the result of the advantages of marrying out, as most thinkers argued. The avoidance was there to start with, but avoidance alone resulted only in our running away from familial relatives and bumping into others (as it were). We must add to this negative impulse the positive advantages of continuing relationships between bands and clans. This gave the older males (the fathers) a stake in the mating fate of their daughters—of all the females of the band.

So fathers, and all the males, had to develop central nervous systems, based on the enlarging neocortex of the brain, that had the capacity to inhibit their immediate desires, let them practice long-term strategies, and, with the advent of language and naming, allow them to live according to rules of kinship and marriage. For this is what we now are talking about. Avoidance and mating are physical and behavioral responses; marriage is about rules. Injunctions about whom you could and could not marry, and what your obligations were to in-laws, were the earliest truly human rules: the rules of what the Anglican prayer book calls "kindred and affinity."

This introduced something that was definitely new in the world: not the avoidance of incest—that was there anyway—but the enduring relationship between natal kin separated by marriage but linked by kinship, by descent from a common ancestor: the prototype of this is the brother–sister relationship. Lévi-Strauss had spoken of an "atom of kinship," and this metaphor catches the spirit of it. The atom is in fact an atom of kinship *and* marriage. If we start with the basic group of the brothers and sisters, then to reach human status, after the advent of tools, hunting, language, and the sexual division of labor, we must add their spouses, as in Figure 6.1.

If the brother and sister cannot marry and breed, their children can, and in most preindustrial societies they were encouraged or enjoined to do so. If the children of the brother and sister marry, we have the basic first-cousin marriage pattern. If it is continued into subsequent generations, it becomes the "double cross-cousin marriage" rule that characterizes the most elementary systems of kinship and marriage, where a man marries a woman who is both his father's sister's daughter and his mother's broth-

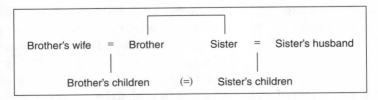

Figure 6.1   The kinship atom

er's daughter, as in Figure 6.2. Thus in future generations "brother's wife" and "sister's husband" will themselves be brother and sister.

Diagrams introduce momentary panic, but a moment's calm examination will see that this is as simple a system of systematic exchange between groups as can be manufactured. (We saw it in Chapter 3 with respect to *exogamy*.) It is best thought of as "sister exchange," and this is often how it is phrased: I give you my sister, you give me yours, and the succeeding generations will do the same thing. (We shall scrutinize this further in Chapter 11.) But what this basically human move does is set up a tension between the two bonds crucial to the human enterprise: that between the brother and sister, on the one hand, and between the brother and his wife, on the other: something that this simple primeval system beautifully illustrates. There is always a measure of conflict in these dual allegiances, in which a man must play the roles of brother and son (of kinsman), and those of husband and father; a woman must play the roles of sister and daughter (of kinswoman), and those of wife and mother.

We are caught in the continual conflict between the bonds that unite kin and the necessity of marriage outside the immediate bounds of kinship for

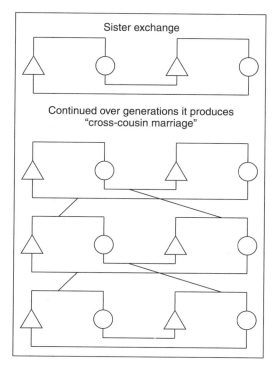

Figure 6.2   Sister exchange and cross-cousin marriage

reproduction. Cousin marriage was the widespread human solution. In fantasy and sometimes in fact, as with the royal rulers and nobility of Egypt, Persia, Hawaii, the Incas of Peru, and the Calusa Indians of Florida (we shall meet them in Chapter 10), we refuse the challenge and keep marriage in the nuclear family. But this is rare. More common is the systematic marriage with cousins, most commonly the children of brother and sister (as in Figure 6.2), but sometimes, as with the Arab peoples, with the children of brothers—as we saw in Iraq and will see again with the ancient Hebrews.

Stephen Faraone, a geneticist, pointed out to me that through marriage with the son of her father's brother, a woman ensures that her own sons have their father's X chromosome; it is the closest she can get, genetically, to mating with the father or brother. The marriage between the children of sisters, as I keep stressing, is most uncommon. The mother's sister is equated with the mother and often called "mother." Her children are like the mother's children (siblings) and treated as such. But the tug of war between kin and in-laws is always there; the mother-in-law joke *is* the oldest in the world.

There is also inherent here the relationship between a man and his sister's sons, which emerges as the *avunculate* with varying strength in many societies, and again competes with the bond of a man with his own sons. We shall find this a factor when looking at male bonding in Chapter 8. (And see my *Reproduction and Succession*.) In matrilineal societies (descent though females), there is often a denial of the husband's (that is, the brother-in-law's) part in procreation, and a reclaiming of the sister's sons at puberty, as with the Trobriand Islanders or the Tlingit of the Northwest Coast of America (Chapter 10).

The Atom and the Stories

Thus the simple kinship atom is packed with potential complexity—the quarks, leptons, and mesons of kinship and mating that produce the potential conflicts, and the strategies we develop to deal with them. Our prefrontal cortex evolved—rapidly, in evolutionary terms—as a response to the dynamics of self-control (delayed gratification) and out-marriage, so the memory of these things is deep in the structure of the brain itself *(The Red Lamp of Incest; The Search for Society)*. Because the putting together of this package is at the very heart of the transition to humanity, we can expect the tensions in it, and our fascination with it, to resonate in our imaginations and to be reflected in our stories and dramas about the basic strategies. It is often reflected there with an accuracy that has been overlooked, because no one was looking for it.

What follows in this and the next chapter is a survey of the literary imaginings of the incest issue from the earliest times in Egypt and Israel, up to our own times in the West. The rest of the world's literature demands a similar scrutiny, but we have to start somewhere. This can only be a sampling, and I dwell on some stories rather than others, either because they are so well known or because they are less well known, or they make a particular point, or because I like them a lot. Each telling reveals something more about how we portray and explain—or at the least display—our fascination with the incest stimulus, and the tug-of-war between the illegitimate family and the legitimate strangers as marriage partners. Some of them will be a surprise to the reader. Others of the stories have been retold hundreds of times and we think we know them; Camelot is perhaps the best example of a tale too often told, and Hamlet of one we know all too well. Here we must take a fresh look. What we think is comfortably familiar may turn out to look disquietingly different when put into this context of inquiry.

The stories and poems are thus a kind of cumulative analysis, with some often-surprising conclusions, like in the tale of the doomed children of the House of Atreus: What *was* the sin of Oedipus? What was the *real* conflict in Thebes? How do the descendants of Adam through Seth foretell the problem of democracy in Iraq and question the Westermarck effect? Does the story of Lot and his daughters reflect a demographic problem in evolution? Who takes the initiative in the incest stories of Ovid? What in the kinship atom was behind the linked fate of the Earnshaws and Lintons of Wuthering Heights, or the curious choreography of Compton-Burnett's siblings hovering on the edge of sister exchange? Even the eighteenth-century novel poses the problem of just how relaxed the attitude to incest could get before the gloomy intensity of Romanticism restored it to center stage in the theater of the passions.

Being literary these stories are the product of civilization, and civilization imposed all its new conditions on the animal evolved to live in the small nomadic band. In that band, incest would not have been such an issue. The basic mechanisms would have taken care of it: life expectancy was short; mothers would have been past childbearing once sons matured; daughters would have been married out at puberty or before; brothers and sisters would not have wanted to mate anyway. But with the settled life of agriculture and the growth of towns, the natural conditions were disrupted as often as not, and the rearing of children often departed markedly from what nature expected.

Written texts were produced by, or at least for, the literate upper classes, so we can expect them to reflect the conditions and obsessions of those classes. It is here that we get the most radical departures from the natural condition. Wet nurses rather than mothers suckled boys; even with suckling by the mother, the age at weaning became earlier and earlier; brothers and sisters were raised differently, without much physical contact; fathers often did not interact with daughters except formally. These were not good conditions for developing a natural aversion to incest; rather they were set to maximize a temptation to it. The literature reflects all this. In the fast-growing industrial nations, several unsettling changes occurred: the rise of the bourgeois nuclear family living in relative isolation, overcrowding in squalid conditions for the urban poor, longer life expectancies generally, and the progressive drop in the age of menarche in the towns (a drop of six months every twenty-five years). (See *The Red Lamp of Incest*.)

So incest has become more and more the object of fascination and speculation, and the subject of great literature. The incest is sometimes overt, sometimes accidental, sometimes suggested, sometimes symbolic, sometimes sacred, sometimes destructive, sometimes sordid, sometimes even comic, but endlessly fascinating to us, as it should be. We constantly reproduce that which produced us.

The Ancient World: Fathers, Brothers, Daughters

Isis and Osiris

The world of the ancient gods was rife with incest, if only because in the beginning they had only each other and they were all related. But many of the stories—after the primitive origin myths—concern the gods breaking out and breeding with, and even genuinely falling in love with, unrelated mortals. During the initial period when they were still concerned with themselves, however, incest was the rule rather than the exception. Because these were the fertility myths of the great agricultural religions, we must ponder the fact that they ascribed magical powers of resurrection and rebirth to the incestuous union.

The most touching of the myths from ancient Egypt concerned the devotion of Isis to her brother-husband, Osiris. This was a myth that resonated down the ages and established the theme of the devoted brother–sister pair whose divinity put them together and apart from the rest of mankind. The cult of Isis was one of the most popular in the ancient world, even well after the advent of Christianity. Indeed, Isis became a model for the portrayal of, and veneration of, the Virgin Mary. Isis too was the mother of a god—Horus, the god of light, her child by Osiris (but not through normal sex). Egyptian pharaohs, as we know, taking on the mantle of Osiris, married their sisters, thus constituting the best-known exception to the rule against sibling marriage.

For the Egyptians, as for the Greeks and Teutons, a series of sibling marriages characterized the early history of the gods. For the Greeks, Zeus married his sister Hera, and Ares, the god of war, had an incestuous-adulterous affair with his sister Aphrodite, who was married to Hephaestus, the smith god. For the Egyptians, Atum (Amen-Ra) the sun god created the first pair Shu and Tefnut from either his spittle or his sperm, and they in turn produced Geb and Nut (the earth and the heavens). Their union produced Isis and Osiris and the other married-sibling pair, Set and Nephthys. Anticipating the first family of Genesis, the brothers are rivals, but in this story the evil Set kills the good Osiris. Isis in the form of a hawk impregnates herself from the body of Osiris, hence the origin of Horus. After rescuing and protecting the body, it is discovered by Set and rendered into pieces and scattered. Isis searches for the parts and reassembles the body, except for the genitals. In language anticipating the Song of Songs she mourns for him:

> Come to thy sister, come to thy wife, to thy wife whose heart
>   stands still.
> I am thy sister by the same mother, thou shalt not be far from me.
> I am thy sister whom thou didst love on earth.
> Thou didst love none but me my brother, my brother!
>
> *(Adapted from Frazer, 1922)*

With the intercession of Ra, Osiris revives and becomes king of the underworld, ruler of the souls of the dead. In the resurrection of Osiris Egyptians saw, as Christians did later with the risen Christ, their hope for eternal life. And this was born of the love of the divine brother and sister. It is there also in what Paul Friedrich has called the suppressed mother–lover archetype, in the persons of Cybele and Attis, Ishtar and Tammuz, and Aphrodite/Astarte and Adonis.

The Taboo in Genesis: Lot and His Daughters (ca. 500 BC)

The first account of incest in the Bible itself is the story of Lot and his daughters in Genesis (15–21). Lot was Abram's brother's son (the patriarch was not known as Abraham until later), who went with him from Ur of the Chaldeans to find the promised land. Abram settled in Canaan with Sarai, his wife, who was his paternal half-sister, but Lot went to Sodom in the plains of Jordan, to avoid competition for resources with his uncle. God institutes a contract with Abraham (as he now is called) and demands that all the males be circumcised. He doesn't explain why. He (God) then decides to go undercover and investigate the "wickedness" of Sodom and Gomorrah, which he threatens to destroy. Abraham bargains with God, who eventually agrees that if there are ten just men in the city of Sodom, he will spare it. The Lord sends two angels in the guise of men to Sodom, and Lot invites them into his house. The Sodomite mob demands that they be sent out "so that we may know them."

And we too now know what the sin of the men of Sodom was. Lot offers his daughters to the mob, but they refuse to accept this bribe. Then the angels blind the leaders of the mob and they retreat. At the advice of the angels, Lot gathers his family and they leave the city for the protected city of Zoar, with strict orders not to look back. In an episode not often noticed, Lot tells his potential sons-in-law—"those who were betrothed to his daughters"—to leave before it is too late, but they laugh at him. God then destroys the cities of the plain. Thus the daughters' legitimate mates die with Sodom. Lot's wife, like Orpheus, does look back and is turned into a pillar of salt.

Lot does not feel safe in Zoar and goes with his daughters to the hills to live in a cave. The daughters panic because they think that there are no men left. It's not clear why they think this, since they have just come from Zoar, where there must have been men. Perhaps they were traumatized by the death of their fiancés in Sodom and didn't want to take chances. Zoar might be next. So the daughters gave Lot wine and made him drunk, and become pregnant by him.

The legend may reflect the memory of an evolutionary reality. Small bands must have often faced the problem of "breed in or die out." While outbreeding was preferable, it was not always possible. What if the legitimate mates died or were killed in disasters? The risks of inbreeding would have been outweighed by the needs of survival. In Lot's story, the sons-in-law (and Lot's wife) eliminated themselves, and the daughters took matters into their own hands. Lot's elder daughter gave birth to Moab, the ancestor of the Moabites. This included Ruth the Moabite, who in turn became an ancestor of King David and thus of Jesus. We shall find in Ovid this theme of incest giving rise to the savior and giver of life. Seventeenth-century Jewish heresies claimed that the Messiah must come from the worst stock if he is going to understand the true depths of sin from which he must save us. But having noted this and that the daughters here were the initiators, Lot being in his cups and not responsible, we shall move on to the less well known story of Tamar and Amnon.

The Old Testament: Tamar and Amnon

The children of David demonstrate the opposite possibility from that in the story of Isis and Osiris, and this duality will follow us throughout the inquiry. It is there in the basic tension between the brother–sister relationship and the needs of marriage. The consanguine relationship is somehow primary, the affinal relationship derivative. And yet the sibling bond is nonreproductive. There has to be compromise between the two demands if we are to be fruitful and multiply. But there is always the tendency to idealize the sibling bond and make it somehow self-sufficient, either with full-fledged incest or with the claiming of the sister's children by the brother, or at least a special relationship with them.

This tension is expressed, then, in the two extremes of the sibling incest story. The first one is where an ideal union is formed (or at least desired) that excludes outsiders and dodges the demands of exogamy, and the other where the relationship is one of unwanted sex, usually forced by the brother but sometimes initiated by the sister. In between is the situation where the two bonds are in a state of conflict and the sisters are pulled both ways: toward brothers and kin, and toward husband and in-laws.

Tamar is the full sister of Absalom and the half sister of Amnon, the sons of King David (2 Samuel 15–18). Amnon "falls in love with" his sister, although it cannot have been more than lust, because he treats her so badly. He enlists the help of a servant and pretends to be ill, asking the king to send the girl to him to bake cakes. Once she is there, he seizes and rapes her. He calls her "sister," which has a double meaning—it is the term of endearment for a lover in Hebrew poetry (see the Song of Solomon) and, interestingly, it was used as a general term for an available woman (matching "babe" and "doll") in American slang until recently.

Tamar in protesting says that Amnon need not force her because if he asks the king, "he will not withhold me from you." This is unlikely even as half sister, but half-sister marriage was not unknown in the ancient world; as we shall have occasion to note, it is the same genetic relationship as a first cousin, who is often the preferred marriage partner. Leviticus 18 specifically forbids marriage with a half sister, but Abraham had married his half sister, Sarah, and given rise to Isaac and Jacob and the chosen people. So, although Tamar might have been arguing to buy time, she had a good point; exceptions could be made. Jewish law stated that a man who raped a virgin should pay her bride-price and be required to marry her (Exodus 22:16, Deuteronomy 22:28), but it is not said how this would apply to incestuous rape.

Amnon, having been rebuffed, was "seized with a very great loathing" for Tamar, a loathing that was greater than his original lust. He ordered her away, and she protested that this was a crime greater than the rape itself. She flees to Absalom's house and hides there under his protection, since David refuses to punish his firstborn. After two years Absalom lures Amnon into a trap and has him killed. This was the beginning of the on-and-off feud between David and Absalom that ended in Absalom's death, with his long hair caught up in a tree, and David's great lament: "O my son Absalom, my son, my son Absalom! Would I had died instead of you, O Absalom, my son, my son!" (2 Samuel 18:33). This has ever since been the foundation of stories about fathers who could not bring themselves to punish their murderous sons (see the original black-and-white version of the movie *3:10 to Yuma*).

It all stemmed from Absalom's protection of Tamar and his revengeful pursuit of Amnon, which, incidentally, got rid of his rival elder brother, who stood between him and the throne. Given his subsequent history, we are free to doubt how much of Absalom's revenge was in his sister's interest rather than his own; I suspect the latter. But let us note for the record that Tamar here is the victim: there is nothing of Isis and Osiris and the sacredness of the brother–sister bond. It is a power rape pure and simple, although Tamar's reactions in trying to protect her interests in its wake are intriguing. The women in these stories, while distressed, still seek to survive and retain a shred of pragmatism in trying to make the best of it.

The Book of Jubilees (ca. 150 BC)

The creation story in Genesis left a number of questions unanswered, and various apocryphal books sought to provide the answers. Thus, in Genesis it says, "Cain knew his wife"—but who was she? There is no record of God creating any other humans after Adam and Eve, so logic says that she must have been his sister, a child like him of the first parents. Several traditions arose in Judaism about who she was and what really happened. The account in Genesis became canonical, but it was only one of several. These traditions were recorded and elaborated in *The Book of Jubilees,* written sometime in the second century before Christ, by a Pharisee who wanted to prove that the Messiah would come from the house of Judah.

Jubilees were divisions of time, based on the number seven; one jubilee is forty-nine years: seven times seven. In this version of the creation story, after the expulsion from Eden, Adam and Eve have the sons Cain, Abel, and Seth, and the daughters Awan and Azura. Cain marries Awan, and they have the son Enoch. Seth marries Azura and they have Enos. Cain, as we know, slew Abel because God preferred his sacrifices of meat to Cain's vegetarian version. Cain then is expelled, with the mark of God on his forehead to save him from human vengeance, and leaves to wander the earth; Seth becomes the heir of Adam. (This much the same cast of characters as in the Egyptian story, of course.)

This account is interesting to us because it insists on the logic of sibling marriage as the aboriginal form—just as in Egypt. What is more, in its chronicles of the descendants of Seth, who continue the line of Adam, it first follows that logic and has Enos marry his sister Noam. They in turn have three children, Barakiel, Kenan, and the girl Maaldeth. Kenan marries his sister Maaldeth, but after that the marriages take on a very interesting form. Genesis 5, where the lineage of Seth is first spelled out, simply says of the successive male heirs that "they had many sons and daughters." Similarly, in the Gospel of Luke where the genealogy of Jesus is given back to Adam (Luke 3:23), only the line of firstborn sons is given. *Jubilees* spells out how these in turn found marriage partners. Kenan's son Mahalelil marries the daughter of his paternal uncle Barakiel. The text spells this out, specifying explicitly that she is his "father's brother's daughter." This form of lineage endogamy then persists down the generations until Noah marries his paternal uncle's daughter Emzara and begets Ham, Shem, and Japheth, the ancestors of the modern races. Figure 6.3 shows how this works out.

You will be immediately struck by the similarity to Figure 3.1 in Chapter 3, showing the structure of paternal parallel-cousin marriage in Iraq and in the Arab world generally. And again the same principle applies: it is the way of keeping succession and inheritance in the paternal lineage: it is in that sense *endogamic*: marriage-in rather than marriage-out. (Cross-cousin marriage will always take you *out* of your lineal group.) It avoids marriage with the full sister (although the paternal half-sister can be allowed as an exception), but it does the next best thing in marrying the paternal first cousin.

For the author of *Jubilees* it is his way of asserting the purity of the lineage of Seth, which is part of his design. It shows how the line of succession was kept pure, but the observant reader will have spotted that it does not say whom the crucial father's brothers married. Whom did Barakiel

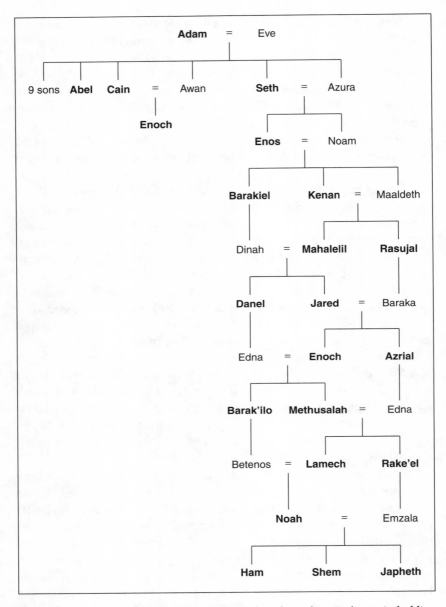

Figure 6.3 The descendants of Adam through Seth (males are shown in **bold**). The root *Barak* (male or female) means "blessed" or "fortunate."

marry, for example? If the rule were to be followed, he would have married the sister of his brother's wife Maaldeth. The author assumes we understand this; he is concerned with the line of immediate succession. This form of marriage avoids familial incest but keeps the marriage in the family (the lineage): one perfect solution, in fact, to nature's problem. If the brother and sister cannot have children, then the children of brothers can. (The children of sisters, as we have seen, almost never.)

It does, however, raise the issue of the Westermarck effect. Would not these paternal cousins have been reared together, and would not this dampen their ardor for each other? The answer seems to be that they would most probably have been raised in the same village or compound, sometimes in the same house, but not necessarily in close physical contact. Research on this by Alex Walter in Westermarck's own Morocco shows, in fact, that there does seem to be a dampening effect on sexual attraction, but that the parents welcome this. Marriage is not about sexual attraction, they hold; if the couple's familiarity leads to weak sexual passion, all the better, they can more readily concentrate on the real business of marriage. Also, it seems that childhood association works more negatively on girls than on boys. This may be because the "costs of inbreeding" are far higher for girls than boys, so their predisposition to avoid related males sexually may be more sensitive and intense. They will, however, have to have been raised with these males fairly intimately for the effect to take.

This form of marriage—with the father's brother's daughter—is allowed in Jewish law, and obviously the Pharisaic tradition that is enshrined in *Jubilees* endorses it fully. Marriage with the brother's daughter—structurally the same thing (either a man marries his paternal niece or he passes the privilege on to his son)—both was allowed and occurred. Even if the paternal first cousin was not available, biblical tradition endorses second- or third-cousin marriages of the same type. Isaac married Rebeka, who was his father's father's brother's son's daughter, while Jacob married Leah, and then Rachel, who were his father's father's brother's son's son's daughters. Keep the marriage in the patrilineal line: avoid marrying strangers, and totally avoid marrying gentiles. A lot of the Old Testament is about just this. Nehemiah's great contribution to the Israelites' rehabilitation after the captivity and exile was to prevent them from marrying strangers, thus regaining God's confidence. Fans of *Seinfeld* will remember that when in desperation George decides to start an affair with a cousin, it is his father's brother's daughter he picks, and he explicitly spells this out.

The Classical World: Patricide and Puberty

Sophocles, Oedipus Rex *(ca. 450 BC)*

The story of Oedipus is perhaps the best-known incest story in the world, and through Sigmund Freud the tragic hero's name has become the eponym for the desire of a son for his mother. We all know about the Oedipus complex. But some things need to be said. First, the incest was accidental: neither party sought it. Second, it is not clear that the crime of Oedipus was the incest at all. It was clearly very distressing to Oedipus and his mother Jocasta, but was it the crime that brought punishment to Thebes? We know the story. King Laius of Thebes is warned that he may die at the hands of his newborn son. So the boy is left out to die on a hillside, his feet bound or pierced (Oedipus means "swollen-foot"). He is rescued by shepherds and then adopted and reared by the king of Corinth as his own son.

Oedipus is never told of the adoption, so when he hears the prophecy that he will kill his father and sleep with his mother, he leaves Corinth and sets out into the world, where he quarrels with an old man at a place where three roads meet, and kills him. He solves the riddle of the Sphinx and thus frees Thebes from a plague. The city makes him king, and he marries the widowed queen, Jocasta. Eventually, however, Thebes is hit by an even worse plague, and the oracles declare that it can be lifted only if the killer of Laius is found and punished. With dramatic brilliance, Sophocles has Oedipus conduct his own inquiry that gradually, point by point, uncovers the facts and shows him as the killer of his father and the husband of his own mother, by whom he has had four children. At the news Jocasta hangs herself and Oedipus puts out his own eyes.

Oedipus does not "desire" his mother in this story. His marriage with her is a horrible accident. For Freud, of course, the story was a symbolic version of the truth: that all men desire their mothers and want to murder or at least replace their fathers. We can see from Oedipus's reaction that he is indeed riddled with guilt about what he has done. Freud would say that this is because he had these guilty feelings from the start. But while that is one reading of the story, it does not seem to me to be there in the original. It is clear from the outset, for example, that the cause of the plague is the anger of the gods—particularly Apollo—not at the incest, but *at the killing of Laius.* Creon, Jocasta's brother, brings the news of the oracle's demand. The oracle's message was simple:

> The man was killed,
> And thus the god's command is that we make
> The unknown killers subject to our laws.

It was absolutely the gravest sin for the Greeks to kill the father. This is the crime always stated as the cause and always listed first by Oedipus himself. That he then bred with his mother certainly compounded the crime; it doubled the offense against his father. But it was a kind of unfortunate by-product of the patricide, which was the true crime against nature and the gods that had to be punished. It was that crime that rendered the offender "unclean" and the city polluted. It did not matter that it was not intended: the taboo had been broken and the pollution followed automatically.

The play is consistent throughout on this. But there is no question that even if the incest was itself simply a compounding of the graver crime (a further offense against the father), it devastated the participants, and was meant to inspire horror in the Greek audience. Whether this was because they all harbored a secret desire, the reader can ponder. On my reading the Greeks were far more worried about patricidal designs by sons than about their possible incestuous longings.

Much of Freud's interpretation was suggested by Jocasta's remark (lines 980–983)—intended to comfort Oedipus—that many men dream of sleeping with their mothers and one should just ignore it and carry on. The ancients may well have interpreted this business of incest dreams differently from us. Herodotus tells of the traitor Hippias, who expected to become ruler of Athens on the coattails of the invading Persians, and who dreamed of sleeping with his mother. He took this as a positive sign: that he would take the place of his father; that is, regain his fatherland *(patris)*. Plutarch tells how Julius Caesar had the same dream before crossing the Rubicon and interpreted it the same way: that he would regain his own fatherland *(patria)*. Replacing the father was certainly there, but it was less to do with incest than with gaining (or regaining) the *patri*mony.

As the story continues to unfold in Sophocles' trilogy, it develops an interesting twist on the kinship atom. Creon is the brother of Jocasta who takes over from the banished Oedipus. He has always, as the brother-in-law of Laius, been a rival to his sister's mates, who turn out to be father and son. The enmity continues with his sister's children: Antigone, her sister Ismene, and two brothers. But the enmity had been there from the origin of the two lineages.

Figure 6.4 (from *Reproduction and Succession*) shows how the "house" of Cadmus and that of Echion of the Spartoi (born of the teeth of the

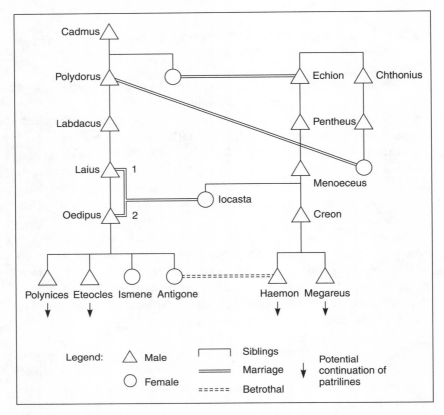

Figure 6.4 The two rival lineages in Thebes: of Cadmus and the Spartoi

dragon slain by Cadmus) had been rivals for control of Thebes and had used marriage in their struggle. Women pass back and forth between the two lines. At the end of Sophocles' *Antigone* the children are dead at Creon's hands, and he survives along with his son Haemon, who had been betrothed to Antigone (his father's sister's daughter). Creon, we might observe, is not only the brother-in law of Oedipus, but also his mother's brother. If we look at the whole trilogy, it is more about the battle between kin and in-laws, and in-laws who are kin, than about mother-son incest.

Publius Ovidius Naso, Metamorphoses *(ca. AD 7)*

In books IX and X of his *Metamorphoses,* written in the first decade of the Christian era, Ovid tells at length two stories of incestuous passion in which the women concerned were transformed into objects—one a fountain and the other a tree. In the original myths we just get the outline of the plot, but Ovid adds an in-depth, deeply empathic look at the psychology of the women involved, examining their deepest feelings in his exquisite Latin verse. This whole examination of literary incest began with my (still unfulfilled) ambition to do my own translation of Ovid, so perhaps the reader will bear with my few examples of the art.

The Story of Byblis.   The first story is that of Byblis and her brother Caunus, children of Miletus and grandchildren of Apollo, twins of surpassing beauty. At the onset of puberty Byblis finds herself in the grip of a genuine and unshakable sexual passion for her brother. This is not superficial lust but an all-consuming love that brings out some of Ovid's most feeling-laden poetry. Byblis is horrified by her feelings, but she cannot deny them. At first she is simply puzzled by the stirrings: *iam nomina sanguis odit*—now she hated the name "blood relative"; *Byblis iam mavult, quam se vocet ille sororem*—now she wanted him to call her Byblis rather than sister. But she has erotic dreams of him and cannot deny the reality of her ever-fiercer sentiments.

She goes through the stages of grief: bewilderment, denial, anger, bargaining—or rationalization—then resignation to her lot. She protests that the truth is the gods have their own sisters—*di nempe suas habuere sorores;* and that the Aeolidae fear not the bridal chambers of their sisters—*non . . . thalamos timuere sororum.* Then she makes the leap. What if he feels the same as she does? Perhaps she was suffering needlessly? Should she not at least give him the opportunity? She decides to write a letter. The process is agony for her, but she manages to put her thoughts down in some of Ovid's best verse. In my inadequate English paraphrase:

> You might have understood my wounded heart
> From my pale, shrunken face, my brimming eyes,
> My sighing without seeming cause, and if
> You had but noticed, all my frantic hugs
> And kisses that were more than sisterly.

(For the Latin originals, see the notes for this chapter.) She finally, with much emendation, gets it down on the "much corrected wax." But as she gives the tablets to the servant to deliver, she drops them. The omen terrifies her, but she goes ahead. Caunus is appalled and utterly rejects his sister. She in turn cannot dissemble or deny the reality of her passion. So

Caunus flees the country, and Byblis, granddaughter of the sun god, in desperate pursuit, finally falls exhausted and weeping on the hard ground, clutching the fallen leaves. The Naiads take pity on her and perform the metamorphosis.

> So Phoeban Byblis, drowned in her own tears,
> Became a fountain, which until this day,
> Insurgent from the holm oak's darkling roots,
> Among these valleys bears that lady's name.

As in primitive myth, love magic is born from primitive incest, so here sin is redeemed and turned into a creative force. The unnatural power of the forbidden is tapped and tamed. And although Ovid sets this as a cautionary tale, by his very eloquence he poses the question: How do we judge a feeling that is absolute and sincere, and in that sense innocent, but that is wholly unlawful, even sinful? Again also it raises the issue: If brothers and sisters on the whole don't seem to feel like this, what does the exception tell us? Perhaps only that it can sometimes happen, and that we have a guilty fascination with the possibility, or that this illustrates how fragile the mechanism is if the learning conditions for the aversion are not present.

Just out of interest: the story that follows this one is that of a forbidden love between two women, Iphis and Ianthe. By the intervention of Isis, Iphis is changed into a man, so the situation is saved. But again we have the portrayal by Ovid of a genuine emotion in conflict with law and morality. There is a lovely description of Isis, who is in a sense the goddess of forbidden loves and has compassion for those who overstep the limits.

The Story of Myrrha. Ovid's second incest story concerns another illicit passion, but this time of a daughter for her father. In the tale of Myrrha and Cinyras, Ovid retells the legend of the birth of Adonis from the viewpoint of his mother. Myrrha was a princess, the daughter of Cinyras, who was the son of Pygmalion and his statue, which came to life by the intervention of Venus/Aphrodite. Myrrha should be choosing from many suitors, but she conceives a passion for her father. She will not choose, and openly weeps when the suitors are paraded for her. Mistaking her tears for maidenly timidity, her father dries her cheeks and kisses her on the lips. This has decidedly the wrong effect.

> Myrrha was much too glad, and when he asked
> What sort of man she wanted, she replied,

"One just like you." He missed the irony
And praised her filial devotion. She,
Once the word was said, cast down her gaze,
In consciousness of all that was her crime.

Myrrha, in an orgy of self-justification, insists to herself that incest is
not unnatural, and cites goats and horses in her defense. Captive domestic animals are of course inbred to improve certain valued traits. They
have no choice; their wild cousins are the ones with the natural outbreeding mechanisms. Then in desperation she tries to hang herself, but she is
rescued by her doting nurse, who promises to help her. During the festival
of Ceres, when wives are absent at the ceremonies, the old crone takes the
princess in the dark to her father, having told him that a beautiful young
woman wants to sleep with him.

The begetter folds his flesh in sordid sheets,
And calms the cringing girl with soothing words.
So when by chance, appropriate to her age
He calls her "daughter"—"father" she replies,
That this might not become a nameless crime.

Ovid is so amazing. The final phrase converts what might just have
been pornography into a profound reflection on the naming of things and
what it does to the reality of them. Also note how Cinyras is first *genitor,*
which is the biological father: to stress that point. Myrrha, in response to
his inadvertent "daughter"—a term an older man might use to any young
girl—calls him *pater,* which is the legal father, and the term of address.
Ovid often plays with this distinction. (I was tempted to add to the force of
it by using "daddy"—but Latin has no such familiar diminutive, and it
would have been cheating.)

After several nights in the dark (the festival is ongoing) Cinyras finally
looks at his daughter's face by torchlight and freaks out in high Ovidian
style. She flees, like Byblis did, but in this case pregnant by her father-
lover, and again, in her extremity, kindly Naiads intervene and turn her
into the myrrh tree that bears her name. The baby still grows in its arboreal
womb, and finally bursts forth. It is, of course, Adonis, who is destined fa-
tally to attract the love of Venus and start the cycle of death and resurrection that underlies all ancient Near Eastern religion.

As with Byblis, Myrrha's sin finally creates something new in the world,
although it is an embalming perfume in this instance—a bitter perfume
much valued as a part of the journey to the underworld, and traditionally

one of the prophetic gifts the wise men brought to the Christ child. Sin and death remain paired (foreshadowing Milton), but in giving birth to Adonis the sad Myrrha is the founder of the great agricultural religions of death, resurrection, and life eternal.

There seems to be a different quality to the two stories in Ovid. The love of Byblis has a kind of innocent passion that makes her sympathetic and foreshadows the sibling love stories to come. Myrrha, on the other hand, seems purely lustful, and Ovid sees nothing redeeming about her desire. Byblis was just a pubescent girl in the first flush of attraction, which happened to fall on her brother. They were probably brought up in confined proximity at court, without physical interaction (boys and girls in Greece were educated separately). Myrrha was a marriageable girl with plenty of men and offers available. Her father was doing exactly what a good father should do (and what evolution has primed him to do) in trying to find a suitable husband for her. It is as if the brother is almost excusable, but the father is absolutely out of the question.

In both stories the initiator is the girl, like Lot's daughters. This is far from the "patriarchal" situation usually envisaged with dominant males sexually exploiting helpless females, as with Amnon and Tamar. The poet sees incest as a dangerous female impulse; the men are the horrified victims. Ovid is almost Wahhabist in his fear of female lust. But this is in line with the fact that in cases of consummated incest the female often is the initiator, and with the classical and ancient world's depiction of women (some women) as assertive, and as taking the initiative in matters sexual. The pursuit of the young Adonis by the older Venus was a best-selling story through the ages, as Shakespeare discovered to his profit in the sixteenth century and we rediscovered in the twentieth in the shape of *The Graduate* with Mrs. Robinson and Benjamin. Jonathan Bate in his *Shakespeare and Ovid* ingeniously tries to prove that the Bard reconstituted Ovid's tale to make Venus the mother of Adonis.

The Middle Ages: Volsungs and Camelot

The Volsunga Saga *(Tenth to Thirteenth Century)*

Sources. The saga of the Volsungs and Niblungs, while based on traditional tales of the Nordic gods, comes to us in traditional Icelandic verse, the *Elder Edda*, from the tenth century, and in a later prose version in the twelfth, anonymously compiled from older texts. William Morris and Eiríkr Magnússon did the first translation into English in 1888. But it is known to the world mostly through the German of Richard Wagner in his *Ring* cycle. We shall consider that briefly after looking at the original with its story of Sigmund and Signy, the fated twins.

Sigmund and Signy.   Sigi, the son of Odin, king of the gods, fights with his wife's brothers and is killed. Rerir, his son, takes revenge on his maternal kinsmen, but has no children himself until Odin and his wife Freyia take pity and send a magic apple to Rerir's wife, who eats it and conceives a son, Volsung, the eponymous hero of the story. He in turn marries and has twins, the boy Sigmund and the girl Signy—and ten other sons. (Figure 6.5 makes this easier to follow.) Signy is married most unwillingly but obediently to King Siggeir. At the feast a one-eyed man in a broad-brimmed hat appears and plants a sword in the oak tree that grows in the king's hall. The man is Odin in his usual human disguise, and he tells how only a great hero can draw the sword. Sigmund does just this, to the king's displeasure.

Siggeir treacherously kills Volsung and the ten sons, but Sigmund escapes and lives in the forest. Signy has two sons by Siggeir and sends them in turn to Sigmund to be tested and, when found wanting, to be killed. She then uses the services of a witch-wife to go disguised to Sigmund and conceives by him a son, Sinfjotli, who passes the tests and supports his father

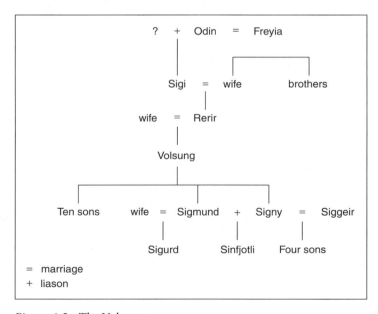

Figure 6.5   The Volsungs

against Siggeir. With Siggeir's house on fire and the king burning, Signy reveals to Sigmund her ruse, and that Sinfjotli is his son by her. "He is the son of both Volsung's son and Volsung's daughter, and for this and for naught else have I so wrought, that Siggeir might get his bane at last." Then she walks into the flames to die.

Sigurd and Brynhild.   Sigmund has other wives and other sons and daughters, including Sigurd (the origin of Siegfried), Helgi, and Swanhilda. He finally dies in battle when Odin shatters the sword Gram, and the story turns to the adventures of Sigurd and the Niblungs. Here Sigurd fatefully meets Brynhild (daughter of king Budull in this story) and eventually his (and her) demise. This next part of the story we shall meet in Chapter 8. For the moment let us pause and take stock before seeing what Wagner did with the tale.

The story starts with the rivalry between in-laws and proceeds to the conflict that arises from Signy's forced marriage, pitting Sigmund against Siggeir: brother versus brother-in-law. There is the strange episode where Signy sends her unwanted sons to be killed by her brother, thus nullifying her reproductive efforts with the stranger. (Two other of her sons are later also killed.) Then she uses the witch-wife trick to become pregnant by Sigmund, with deadly consequences for her husband, before immolating herself. This story is overtly about the conflict between the brother–sister bond and that of husband–wife, and also that between father and son and the maternal in-laws: no holds barred, no comment needed.

The Wagner Version.   We must take a leap into the future, since Richard Wagner's huge four-part operatic cycle *Der Ring des Nibelungen* stems from the 1870s. But Wagner saw to the heart of the plot, and even reinforced it, so we should consider his adaptation here. Using the saga of the Volsungs and the German medieval *Nibelungenlied,* he intensifies the basic conflicts in *Die Walküre (The Valkyrie)*—part two of the *Ring.* Odin becomes Wotan (Wodin), and Siegmund is directly his son by a mortal woman. Sieglinde is Siegmund's twin (Signy). They are separated in childhood, and Sieglinde is married to Hunding—a minor character in the *Eddas.* Siegmund, fleeing his enemies, seeks refuge in Hunding's house in the woods in which stands the great oak with the sword (now called Nothung). The twins gradually recognize each other and fall immediately in love. Siegmund draws the sword and they prepare to flee Hunding's wrath—into the forest.

Initially Wotan seeks to protect Siegmund and delegates the task to Brünnhilde, who here becomes his daughter (extramarital via Erda, the earth goddess) along with the other eight Valkyries, the guardians of the souls of dead warriors (see Figure 6.6). Then comes Wagner's most interesting innovation: Fricka, Wotan's wife and goddess of the marriage vows (which Wotan routinely breaks), insists in musical fury that the lovers be punished, not so much for the incest, which was common among the gods, but for the adulterous attack on marriage. (Note how this lines up with *Oedipus,* where it was not so much the incest as the patricide that was at issue.) This protector of the sanctity of marriage is something of a change from the Nordic original, who was more like Aphrodite in the bestowal of her favors. But the reformed goddess insists that Hunding must be allowed to kill Siegmund.

Reluctantly Wotan agrees and reverses his orders to Brünnhilde, who has difficulty obeying him. She cannot protect Siegmund, but with the help of the Valkyries she spirits the pregnant Sieglinde away—to the forest. Wotan shatters Siegmund's sword, and Hunding kills him. Then Wotan kills Hunding; he never told Fricka he wouldn't do that. As a punishment to his rebellious daughter, he puts her to sleep in a ring of fire for eternity. Eventually Sieglinde will give birth to the hero Siegfried (Sigurd), who will breach the ring of fire and fall in love (under a spell) with his aunt Brünnhilde. The deadly events will then surge on to *The Twilight of the Gods* and the destruction of Valhalla.

Wagner takes the fundamental conflict of the saga and violently underlines it. Fricka (Freyia/Frigg) is the spokeswoman for the sacredness of the marriage bond. Wotan and his daughter Brünnhilde defend their blood relatives, the incestuous siblings, and protect the child of sibling incest, Siegfried. (The relationship between father and daughter is, shall we say, very close. Fricka bitterly tells Wotan that the Valkyrie is *deines Wunsches Braut:* "your wished-for bride.") Thus the theme of incest versus in-laws (kinship-versus-alliance and siblingship-versus-marriage) is literally put

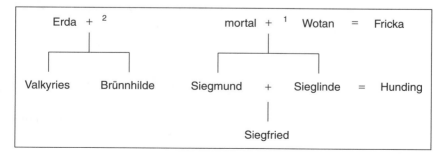

Figure 6.6 Wagner's version

center stage and played out for the grand drama it is. As we shall see, Wagner is in the forefront of the exaltation of the sibling bond that swept nineteenth-century fiction; but that is to jump ahead. Let us now turn to another medieval saga, that of Arthur, and the role of incest in the doom of another magical kingdom: Camelot.

Sir Thomas Malory, Le Morte D'Arthur *(1485)*

We shall save a detailed consideration of this other great (late) medieval epic until Chapter 8, when we will look at the male bonding of the Knights of the Round Table. It is enough here to note that an act of unknowing sibling incest between Arthur and his (half) sister Morgause (Morgawse), who is married to Lot, king of Orkney, begets Mordred, whose hatred of Arthur brings down Camelot in the end. Arthur was born of the rape of Igraine by his father Uther Pendragon. Morgause was Igraine's daughter, but Arthur did not know that. Merlin took Arthur at his birth and had him fostered until he could claim his throne by pulling the sword Excalibur from the stone (see Figure 6.7).

Mordred is balanced against Gawaine, who is his half brother by the same mother. Both are the sister's sons of Arthur; the legitimate one is good and loyal, whereas the child of incest is evil and destructive. Early in the story Merlin warns Arthur that a child born on May Day will destroy him. In an episode obviously echoing Herod and the Innocents, Arthur orders all the boys born on that day to be rounded up and set adrift on the ocean. Mordred is saved from the massacre and reared by foster parents. Perhaps his final killing of Arthur is a just retribution. Malory drew on many sources, and it was the French who seem to have introduced the incest theme. Mordred in other versions was the legitimate son of Lot and Arthur's sister (known then as Anna) and hence, as the grandson of Uther Pendragon, a legitimate claimant to the throne. Bernard Cornwell has revived this twist on the story in his stirring Arthurian series.

But once the incest theme was introduced, it took over the story and gave a motive to the fall of Camelot as secure as Wotan's evil dealings

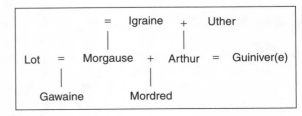

Figure 6.7 Kinship in Camelot

with Alberich did to the fall of Valhalla. This included an episode never reproduced in modern versions, where Mordred captures Guinevere and threatens to "marry" her: his father's wife. She escapes. (And as a footnote we may note the continuity of the magic sword stuck in the tree/ stone that only the hero could draw, and its subsequent shattering and reconstitution: obviously a deep theme in Indo-European myth. Freudians have a field day with the sword.)

Writers since have wrung every possible change on the Mordred incest theme. Arthur is sometimes seen as the rapist of his sister. Sometimes, as in John Boorman's film *Excalibur* (1981), where she is compounded with Morgan le Fay (Morgana), Igraine's other daughter, she is the guilty party, tricking Arthur into bed like the witch-wife and Sigmund. Sometimes Arthur tricks her into thinking he is her husband, or, as in the original, he seduces her without knowing the relationship. In *The Mists of Avalon* (1982), Marion Zimmer Bradley has the consanguine women of Camelot as priestesses of the Celtic mother goddess pitted against the in-marrying Guinevere and her Christian priests. Mordred is the product of a ritual sacred marriage between Morgaine (Morgan le Fay/Morgause) and Arthur, in which the siblings are initially unaware of their identities. In the book, they discover them by dawn's early light; in the film, they are masked and find out their relationship only later.

Throughout all these variations, one thing remains central: Mordred is a product of the brother–sister relationship. In this heavily Christianized story he cannot like Sinfjotli and Siegfried be a hero. But even the heroes were doomed, of course, and their societies with them. For Malory, the unheroic Mordred realizes the potential that cannot be realized, and hence he is an ambiguous and unclean thing. At a deeper level, like the heroes, he represents the eternal Drumbeat: the tug-of-war between the sibling bond and the affinal bond. It is the latter that should produce heirs, but Guinevere (like Fricka and Sarai) is barren; she cannot do the essential thing that the affinal bond is for. This is its fragility, and these legends show a constant anxiety about the barrenness of wives. Sisters represent perhaps the only viable alternative under some evolutionary circumstances, just as fathers had seemed to Lot's daughters (marry in or die out).

Mordred, as the sister's son by the brother, represents the challenge inherent in the basic tension from the kinship atom: he is the alternative claimant who is always in principle present but who cannot exist. Bradley understands this very well: once he does exist and makes his more fundamental but unallowable claim, then destruction must ensue. It is not, however, a matter of a patriarchal system beating out a matriarchal one. Even in matrilineal systems the sister's son must be the product of the marriage of the sister to someone other than the brother, and be claimed back by the brother in some manner. The Mordred theme is more profound than that: it is the symbolic representation of the struggle inherent in every kinship system: the sister must yield as genetrix to the wife.

The Renaissance: Hamlet, Whores, and Hellhounds

The medieval writers were only a half step away from the legends they were retelling and elaborating. The Elizabethan and Jacobean dramatists had moved further into domestic drama with characters more like living people than legendary heroes. They secularized the old Christian morality plays with their mixture of hellfire and buffoonery. But the incest theme still fascinated them, and they put their own creative gloss on it.

William Shakespeare, Hamlet *(1603)*

Hamlet and Oedipus have become complexly intertwined in the Western imagination because of the attention Freud and his disciple Ernest Jones *(Hamlet and Oedipus)* paid to it. Hamlet does not marry his mother, Gertrude, but the atmosphere of incestuous lust and accusation hangs heavily over the play. This is not all the playwright's invention; it is there in the old Danish legends that Saxo Grammaticus collected and Belleforest rendered into a French edition that was most probably the immediate source. We all know the story. Hamlet's father, the king of Denmark, has died, and his mother has married his father's brother Claudius, all too soon in Hamlet's opinion.

> Ere yet the salt of most unrighteous tears
> Had left the flushing in her gallèd eyes
> She married, O most wickedly to post
> With such dexterity to incestuous sheets!

The incest issue here is marriage with the dead brother's wife. This is what happened to Henry VIII, who was married to Katherine, the widow of his brother. When it didn't suit him, he quoted biblical authority that such a marriage was indeed incestuous (Leviticus 18:16). The trouble is that another biblical source quotes this marriage as not only legitimate but required (Deuteronomy 25:3–10). This is the law of the *levirate*, which is common in patrilineal pastoral societies: on a man's death his nearest agnatic kinsman (preferably his brother) should marry his widow. This was Ruth's claim on Boas, which her mother understood very well. One wonders whether Hamlet is going by one of the biblical laws here, or whether the accusation is more global and "incestuous" just means lustful or indecent behavior by his mother.

His father's ghost appears to Hamlet and says that Claudius murdered him and should be punished ("luxury" is lust):

> Let not the royal bed of Denmark be
> A couch for luxury and damnèd incest.

The whole play then evolves (it would take between four and five hours, if put on uncut) around Hamlet's failure to do just that: Laurence Olivier's "This is a play about a man who could not make up his mind." Actually he made up his mind right away—after hearing the ghost—that Claudius was guilty; he just failed to do anything about it except talk and pretend to be mad. The failure has been analyzed to death, but if we look closely at Hamlet's character, it seems he is of a basically narcissistic-histrionic nature and actually enjoys the agony of playing out the drama with him as the star. This explains the otherwise puzzling overlong play-within-the-play that serves only to prolong his inaction. He could have killed Claudius while he was praying, but makes the excuse that then the king's soul would go to heaven, so he must wait and catch him "in the pleasures of his incestuous bed."

The scene that most caught the attention of Freud and the Freudians is in act III, scene iv, where Hamlet launches a violent verbal attack on his mother. He is in fact instructed to see her in her "closet," which is to say her sitting room, where she would usually receive visitors, but no producer can resist setting it in her bedroom, with the large bed dominating the scene. In all the film versions—starting with Olivier—the scene is played out with energetic physicality on the bed (see Mel Gibson and Glenn Close).

In the play-it-in-the-bedroom versions, Hamlet orders the queen to "look thou upon this picture and on this" and then forcefully entangles their two lockets—hers with a picture of Claudius, his with a miniature of his dead father. If the meeting had been in her closet, then he would most likely have been simply pointing to two portraits on the wall. The old councilor Polonius is hiding behind the arras, and Hamlet stabs him through the tapestry. Having given this brutal shock to his mother's nervous system, he then berates her in an astonishing scene in which, psychologists are quick to note, the main point is not the murder as such but her sharing the bed of Claudius (on which she and Hamlet are tumbling, of course).

> Nay but to live
> In the rank sweat of an enseamèd bed,
> Stewed in corruption, honeying and making love
> Over the nasty sty!

His father's ghost, unseen to the queen, tells him not to harm her. But Hamlet continues his obsessive rant. Do not, he tells her,

> Let the bloat king tempt you again to bed,
> Pinch wanton on your cheek, call you his mouse,
> And let him, for a pair of reechy kisses
> Or paddling on your neck with his damned fingers
> Make you to ravel all this matter out.

For Freud and Jones the question of Hamlet's delay was answered by showing the prince's own guilt at his incestuous feelings. He in fact wanted to kill his father and possess his mother, and Claudius had therefore done only what Hamlet wanted to do. This drives Hamlet into what every producer and actor since has portrayed as an incest frenzy. Claudius becomes the father that Hamlet wanted to kill but now can't kill. In the same way that for Freud Oedipus was a disguised version of the real desires, so is Hamlet: only in Hamlet the disguise breaks down and we are shown the real feelings, even if we don't get the real incest.

For the Freudians, as we know, this is a universal feeling that humans are unwilling to accept, and so the playwrights, as custodians of the unconscious, have to do it for us. I think this is a wrong deduction. It depends a lot on Jocasta's reassuring remark to Oedipus that boys dream of sleeping with their mothers. But the incest of Oedipus was an accident, and Hamlet's was a case verging on pathology. Yet both testify that whatever our supposed deep and repressed motives, the prospect of incest still makes us fundamentally uneasy, and skilled playwrights can play on this unease. (It has even been argued, for example, that Lear's "love test" with his daughters is indicative of "repressed incest wishes," as is the obsessive love of Pericles for his daughter Marina.) There is no need to tell the rest of Hamlet's story. Hamlet's last words to Claudius before he finally kills him continue the accusation: "Thou incestuous, murderous, damned Dane." We know the story perhaps too well, and this much about it is included here for the record of our current inquiry.

John Ford, 'Tis Pity She's a Whore *(1633)*

In Ford's play the incest not only happens, it is the essence of the plot. Ford's contemporary, John Webster, had in a previous play, the bloody and magnificent *The Duchess of Malfi* (ca. 1614), used as his major villains Ferdinand, Duke of Calabria, and his brother the cardinal. One of their major assets was their sister, the duchess, who secretly marries a commoner, Antonio. Ferdinand pursues them and horribly torments and finally kills his sister. Webster means to leave us in no doubt that although the brothers are angry about her marrying beneath her and hurting them materially, Ferdinand's rage and cruelty stem from sexual jealousy pure and simple. We are to see nothing like it until Shelley's Count Cenci two hundred years later. But though there is incestuous lust here, there is no actual incest. Tourneur, Middleton, and Beaumont and Fletcher had used the incest theme, but treated it as the crime and sin they thought it was. Ford is different.

In Ford's play, the liaison of Giovanni and Annabella, a brother and a sister from a merchant family in Parma, Italy, is what the play is about. And it is not about lust and power, but about genuine love, which makes it all the more shocking. In the opening scene, Giovanni, returned from university, pleads for understanding from his confessor:

> Shall a peevish sound,
> A customary form, from man to man,
> Of brother and a sister, be a bar
> 'Twixt my perpetual happiness and me?
> Say that we had one father; say one womb-
> Curse to my joys!—gave both us life and birth;
> Are we not therefore to each other bound
> So much the more by nature? By the links
> Of blood, of reason? nay, if you will have't,
>
> Even of religion; to be ever one,
> One soul, one flesh, one love, one heart, one all?
> Shall, then, for that I am her brother born,
> My joys be ever banished from her bed?
>
> *(Act I, scene i)*

Friar Bonaventura's answer is an unequivocal yes. Go commit fornication if you must, he says, but with anyone but your sister.

It seems Giovanni has been away at university for some years since they were children together, and at first Annabella does not recognize him but sees this impossibly handsome young man and falls immediately in love. In a tender scene they declare themselves to each other and plight their troth:

> Giovanni.   . . . and by this kiss,—
> Once more, yet once more: now let us rise,—by this
> I would not change this minute for Elysium.
> What must we now do?
> Annabella.   What you will.
> Giovanni.   After so many tears as we have wept,
> Let's learn to court in smiles, to kiss and sleep.
>
> (Act I, scene iii)

Ford continues to paint his sibling lovers as genuine and innocent in contrast to the cynically corrupt ecclesiastical and political world around them. Of course, they cannot legally be married, and Annabella is forced to choose among her suitors, and once she knows she is pregnant she picks Soranzo, her father's favorite. Soranzo figures out she is not pregnant by him and reacts furiously, but she refuses to say who the father is. Soranzo finds out anyway, and invites Giovanni to a feast, to murder him. The sibling lovers meet privately for the last time, and he tells her it is better if they both die.

> Giovanni.   Kiss me. If ever aftertimes should hear
> Of our fast-knit affections, though perhaps
> The laws of conscience and of civil use
> May justly blame us, yet when they but know
> Our loves, that love will wipe away that rigour
> Which would in other incests be abhorred.
>
> (Act V, scene v)

In one of the goriest of all Jacobean tragic endings, Giovanni stabs Annabella and then, with her heart on a dagger, bursts into the feast and confronts Soranzo. As the bodies pile up, both are killed, and the inevitable cardinal confiscates all their goods for the Church. So the sibling bond here strikes out against the marriage tie represented by Florio (Annabella's father) and Soranzo. Despite the claim of the purity of their love, it cannot survive the onslaught of exogamous society, and death for all parties is the result.

John Milton, Paradise Lost (1667)

The Puritan poet John Milton wrote his majestic blank-verse parable *Paradise Lost* to "justify the ways of God to man" although he may have ended up, according to William Blake, being "of the Devil's party without knowing it." This was because of his sympathetic treatment of Satan as the great rebel against God's tyranny, something that the Romantics were to fasten onto with gusto. (Was it Cromwell versus Charles I?) His massive epic, however, was not intended to glorify Satan, and in showing the evil consequences of the Satanic rebellion he uses graphic and complicated incest imagery, which Blake caught so shockingly in his famous watercolor.

Satan on his way from hell to earth meets the figure of a beautiful woman who from the waist down was a foul and scaly serpent, while a cry of hell-hounds surrounded her waist. Satan then saw another figure, shadowy and vast with a crown and a spear (2:648–673). These were Sin and Death, and Sin explained how they came into being. She sprang from the head of Satan, like Athena from the head of Zeus. Satan was so enamored of her (that is, of himself) that he raped her, his daughter by male parthenogenesis. Sin continues her description of the childbirth from hell (I have modernized the spelling):

> Thine own begotten, breaking violent way,
> Tore through my entrails, that, with fear and pain
> Distorted, all my nether shape thus grew
> Transformd: but he my inbred enemy,
> Forth issud, brandishing his fateful dart,
> Made to destroy. I fled, and cried out *Death*;
> Hell trembld at the hideous Name, and sighed
> From all her Caves, and back resounded *Death*.
>
> *(2:780–788)*

So Death was born through the incestuous rape of Sin by Satan. But all was not over for the unfortunate Sin. Her son Death in turn raped her and produced the hideous hellhounds that surround her. Then they in turn eat their way back into the womb that bore them:

> hourly conceived
> And hourly born, with sorrow infinite
> To me: for when they list into the womb
> That bred them they return, and howl, and gnaw
> My bowels, their repast; then, bursting forth
> Afresh with conscious terrors vex me round.
>
> *(2:796–802)*

Comment is almost superfluous. Milton creates an anticreation in which incestuous rape "brought Death into the world and all our woes."

There were no female fallen angels; Satan had to create his own hell-bride from himself, as Eve had been created from Adam's rib. The children of Satan were Sin and Death, and they had nowhere to breed but with each other. The children of Adam were to be faced with the same problem, but their incest was productive: the Satanic family had nowhere to go but to itself, and then to the corruption of its Edenic rival.

Milton's epic was a kind of final statement of the Jacobean fixation on the horror of incest. It is hard to place in our ongoing inquiry because it was a parable, a fantasy, a massive return to mythology and the sublime landscape of myth. But we can see its continuity with *Whore* and *Hamlet:* incest was not to be taken lightly; its outcome was invariably bad or even terrible, however innocent the intention, as with Ford. But this was the outlook of the Puritans and reflected the horror of all things sexual that possessed them and that possesses them everywhere they crop up. In the next chapter we shall follow the continuing ups and downs of incest fascination in the post-Puritan period, and this will eventually lead us back to the conundrum of the cousins.

CHAPTER SEVEN

Forbidden Partners

Ancient Themes in Modern Literature

Sometimes the drums beat softly. Sometimes our faith in our ability to escape the beat (or at least more or less to ignore it) is high. The first part of the eighteenth century, with its elevation of Reason to the head of the list of the passions, did not abolish either the unease about, or the fascination with, incest, but it did produce its own attitude to it, which is instructive. This was the period where we in the West took a kind of cultural deep breath before the onslaught of the industrial revolution.

The Age of Reason

In England the Glorious Revolution of 1688 had established a constitutional monarchy. Bacon and Newton had established rational science. Hobbes, Locke, and Hume were to enthrone reason and empiricism. Mandeville and Pope were to preach that private interest promoted public good. Adam Smith was to show us how this worked and the wisdom of the invisible hand that worked it. William Petty thought that happiness was measurable and proceeded to measure it, encouraging Jefferson to enshrine "the pursuit of happiness" in his Declaration. There are many and all familiar examples of the belief that there was nothing we could not deal with pragmatically and sensibly. Men could be changed for the better by education. Because all knowledge came not from innate ideas but through the senses, all we had to do was to put good knowledge in, and good behavior would come out the other end. Thus said the philosophers; the writers and artists tended more to a cynical view of human nature. But no one got too excited or horrified about it. The Drumbeat of incest was there, but it was not savage in this reasonable world.

Daniel Defoe, Moll Flanders (1722)

Moll was born in Newgate Prison in London from a mother who escaped the gallows only because she was pregnant. The mother having been transported to the Americas, Moll grew up as an orphan and survived by her looks and her wits. She is an engaging character, a mixture of vamp and prude, who somehow maintains her dignity despite being used by men and ill-used by the world. *Moll Flanders* is the picaresque story of her adventures, which in fact set the pattern for the eighteenth-century novel. It was Winston Churchill's favorite reading, especially when he was ill.

About one-third of the way through she ends up in Virginia, having made a match with a man she likes and who likes her for herself. The man lives with his mother, who becomes a mother to Moll—she calls her "mother." Moll has three children—one dies—and seems set for a happy and settled family life. Then it begins to unravel. The mother starts to recount her life story, and with growing horror Moll realizes that this is her own mother and that she is married to her brother and the mother of his children.

We should note immediately that this is a half-sibling relationship. This will crop up often in the literature. It is also accidental. Moll and her brother/husband are only as related as first cousins. But this was not understood in pregenetic days, and Moll's horror and upset at her discovery are in the perception of the relationship, which is with a sibling and therefore unthinkable. That it was a genuine mistake does not mitigate things for her, but she is torn. To tell the truth would devastate their lives, but to keep silent seems a worse sin. In the end she reveals it to her mother, and they agree for a moment to keep silent, but it cannot last.

Moll pleads with her brother to let her go to England, but cannot explain why; he refuses; she refuses to sleep with him. In the end Moll cannot live with it and tells her brother all, after having him sign an agreement not to do anything impulsive or in anger, once told the secret of her behavior. After much confusion, they agree that she should go back to England, that it should be put about that she is dead so the brother could marry again, and that he would do what he could to support her.

Moll then resumes her life in England, but it deteriorates and she becomes a thief. However, Defoe engineers a resolution in the end. Moll escapes the gallows and goes back to America with a new husband. There

she meets her grown son, who is delighted to find her, effects reconciliation, and settles land and income on her from her now-dead mother's
estate. Once the aging and ailing brother is dead, they tell her husband
the whole story and he is "perfectly easy on the account." "For," said he,
"it was no fault of yours, nor of his; it was a mistake impossible to be
prevented."

This is the spirit of it entirely in Defoe's story. There is no illicit passion,
no submerged longings, no elevation of incest to a kind of sacred exception. It was an unpleasant mistake, which once found out caused anguish,
but which was resolved with Enlightenment rationalism and plain good
sense, and if not a happy ending, then at least, as they would have said, an
agreeable one.

Henry Fielding, Tom Jones (1749)

Tom is born under mysterious circumstances and is presumed to be the
child of Jenny Jones, a young woman with aspirations to learning, who
confesses to being the mother but refuses to name the father. Squire Allworthy, a widower in whose house the newborn Tom was discovered,
agrees to adopt and raise the boy. Jenny is sent away and not heard from,
and Tom grows up in the household with the squire's sister, Bridget—a
woman of virtuous disposition, and her son, Blifil, with whom he has an
adversarial relationship.

The novel follows the picaresque formula as Tom leaves home and has
a succession of adventures. He is pursued by his true love, Sophia, daughter of Allworthy's neighbor Squire Western. She is in turn pursued by
Allworthy and an angry husband, Fitzpatrick, and then again by Squire
Western in pursuit of his daughter. In the pivotal episode, Tom rescues a
Mrs. Waters from rape and robbery, and after a memorable meal (im-
mortalized by Albert Finney and Joyce Redman in the 1963 movie) he
beds her in the inn at Upton. After much bedroom-farce confusion and
hullabaloo, when the whole pack of pursuers descends on the inn, Tom
escapes and the mysterious Mrs. Waters goes off with Fitzpatrick.

The adventures proceed apace, and details do not concern us until
Tom, in London, lands in jail for fighting a duel with Fitzpatrick. He is
rescued by Mrs. Fitzpatrick, who turns out be Mrs. Waters. Tom's longtime friend Partridge (who had missed her at Upton) is appalled when he
recognizes her as none other than Jenny Jones.

> "Why then the Lord have mercy upon your soul, and forgive you," cried
> Partridge; "but as I stand here alive, you have been a bed with your own
> mother." (Bk. XVIII, chap. II)

Tom, reprobate that he may be, is understandably distraught. But all is resolved. Jenny reveals that she was part of a plot involving Bridget All-worthy, who was pregnant by a protégé of Squire Allworthy's, Summers. Jenny and her mother attended the secret birth, and Jenny passed off the baby as her own. So Tom is the squire's nephew, there was no incest, all are reconciled, Sophia forgives Tom, and all ends happily.

As with Moll Flanders and her brother, if this incest had happened, it would have been accidental. In Tom's case the near miss served to give him a scare and help him to reform. But in neither case are we anywhere near to Oedipus and Jocasta (also an accident). In the Age of Reason, the possibility or actuality of mother–son incest or sibling incest, while up-setting the participants, was not something desperate or terminal. In Tom's case it bordered on the comic. As long as it was not premeditated, it was an unfortunate accident you endured, dealt with, and moved on, the wiser for the experience. How things were to change.

The Romantics: Special Sisters, Ugly Father

By the last quarter of the eighteenth century, the Age of Reason had be-come the Age of Revolution. The Western world was about to lurch into another stage of its evolution that was led by geographical expansion, steam-driven industry, galloping science, and huge population growth. The optimists in politics and philosophy and poetry welcomed the changes, and saw the dawning of a new and glorious age of freedom. But the changes were feared and resisted by the humanistic pessimists who saw no possibility of good in them. Many hovered in between with a linger-ing faith in reason, but fearful of the growing collective brutality of so-ciety. The poets and novelists of the Romantic movement struck out for the individual. They put passion back in the forefront of imagination, and the dark passion and tormented guilt of the individual came to domi-nate, especially when that guilt and that passion were incestuous. Incest, from being a secret sin or an unfortunate accident, became a potent symbol for the rejection of society by the individual. (And other things as well: see the Digression on William Blake's *The Mental Traveller* in the notes.)

François-René de Chateaubriand, René *(1802)*

Some books capture entirely the spirit of the times, and Chateaubriand's *Atala* and *René* are aflame with the Romantic spirit of revolutionary and post-Rousseau Europe. The whole issue of the state of nature had been raised, the values of civilization called into question, and the virtues of the noble savage trumpeted. The old order—the *ancien régime*—was not inevitable but was rather a perversion of the natural state of man. But what was that natural state? Was it a state that permitted incest, as in the state of man after the fall? The French in particular looked to an idealized version of the American Indian as a model of the natural and good society. Chateaubriand, a nobleman and diplomat whose fortunes varied during the revolutionary and postrevolutionary periods, visited America in 1791. A product of the visit was the novels *Atala* and *René*, which featured the noblest of noble savages, Chactas.

René takes up where *Atala* leaves off, with Chactas becoming mentor to the young nobleman in the wilds of Louisiana. René spends most of his time in the forest in melancholy brooding over the event that drove him from Europe and that, he says, ought to be "buried in eternal oblivion." Finally with the help of the missionary Father Souel, Chactas persuades René to tell his tale.

His mother died giving birth to him. His father preferred his elder brother and had René reared away from the parental home. On visits to his father's estate, René came to be very fond of his older sister, Amélie, for they both had "a little sadness in the depths of our hearts, which we got from God or our mother." So like Giovanni and Annabella they were not reared in physical intimacy. This probably reflects the author's real relationship with his older sister, Lucile, in his lonely early life. Their father dies and Amélie contemplates becoming a nun, but René decides to travel and is miffed when Amélie seems relieved.

René describes what became the prototype for the Romantic grand tour, which does not help answer his longings or his *inquiétude*. He tries to find Amélie but she avoids him. He sinks deeper into melancholy—"alone upon the earth"—and writes her that he is contemplating suicide. She rushes to his side and restores him, and they restore their childhood happiness in each other. But Amélie is strangely anguished and begins to fade. Finally she departs, leaving him a sad letter urging him to marry and reaffirming her decision to take vows. René conjectures that she is in love with a man and dares not declare it. In a letter she disavows this, so René follows her to the convent, where she refuses to see him but invites him to the ceremony to play the paternal role of giving her away as a bride of Christ. He does so and hands the scissors to the priest to cut off her hair. She then must spend the night in a coffin in order to be symbolically reborn. As René kneels by the tomb, Amélie bursts out:

Dieu de miséricorde, fais que je ne me relève jamais de cette couche funèbre, et comble de tes biens un frère qui n'a point partagé ma criminelle passion!

> God of mercy, let me never rise
> From this funereal couch, and shower down
> Your blessings on a blameless brother who
> Has never shared my criminal desires!

René reaches down into the coffin, seizes his veiled sister in his arms, and cries out:

> Chaste épouse de Jésus-Christ, reçois mes derniers embrassments à travers les glaces du trépas et profondeurs de l'éternité, qui séparent déjà de ton frère!

> Chaste bride of Christ, receive my last embrace
> Across the cold indifference of death
> And through the vastness of eternity
> Which separate you always from your brother!

Forgive me for rendering Chateaubriand's high-Romantic prose as English blank verse; it just comes out that way to do it justice. René swoons and is borne away. Amélie is in a fever near to death. They both recover, she completes her vows, and after hanging around the monastery for a glimpse of her, he finally leaves for America to commune with the *heureux sauvages* untroubled by the *malaise* of civilized Europe.

As with Byblis, the sister here is the one who harbors the incestuous desire, but once this is revealed, in the operatic scene at the tomb, the brother understands that he shares the passion. (At least that's how I read it.) The scene is eerily reminiscent of Isis fluttering over the coffin of Osiris in order to become impregnated. There has never been anyone else in their lives. There is no marital bond to challenge them. René and Amélie set the tone for the Romantic-Victorian theme of the sibling pair as set apart from the world and somehow thus a symbol of purity in sharing a relationship that is forbidden to the world at large. Siblings are special. We have moved a huge step away from the accidental tumblings of Moll and Tom, or even the horror and tragedy of Tamar, Byblis, or Annabella. We are back indeed to Isis and Osiris, and Sigmund and Signy, and the mystical sacred marriage. For those who are as gods, the usual rules do not apply. But of course, Chateaubriand's siblings don't actually consummate their love. Byron took it that step further.

Lord Byron, Manfred *(1817)*; Cain *(1821)*

Manfred is the archetypal Romantic hero, and Byron was obviously trying to portray himself to some extent. Manfred wanders the earth, dissatisfied, tormented of spirit, haunted by a nameless crime that keeps him in a state of guilt and anguish. Romantic heroes had to break the bounds of normality, of social convention. René set the scene, and Byron was enormously influenced by him; every Romantic writer was influenced by him. Chateaubriand's sibling lovers were imaginary, even if based on his own feelings, but Byron had a real tempestuous affair with his half sister Augusta Leigh. We are back in half-sister territory again, and again it is not the genetic fractions that matter—a half sister is a first cousin—but the perception. Byron enjoyed being the model for his super-romantic heroes, and his affair with Augusta, which scandalized England (and titillated Europe), gave him a definite edge over the competition. We can't retell his life here, but his relationship with his sister, by whom he had a daughter, preceded his unhappy marriage to Anne Milbanke (the cousin of his mad mistress, Caroline Lamb). Their one daughter was called Augusta Ada. "Augusta" is obvious, if perhaps tactless, and "Ada" we shall meet later in Nabokov.

Manfred is described as a "dramatic poem" and has Count Manfred wandering the earth, like René, feeling alienated from ordinary mortals by a secret sin that cuts him off from normal men, and able to commune only with spirits (Destiny, Nemesis, and so on) He ends up in the Alps and confesses to the Witch of the Alps that despite his alienation, there was one he loved who was so like him she was his *anima*, his female self, and hence the only appropriate object of his narcissistic-Romantic affection:

> She was like me in lineaments—her eyes
> Her hair, her features, all, to the very tone
> Even of her voice, they said, were like to mine.
>
> *(Act II, scene iii)*

This beloved turns out to be Astarte. She is never named "sister" as such, but we are left in no doubt. "I loved her and destroyed her," he declaims. The spirits finally conjure up her ghost, and Manfred pleads with her for forgiveness in one of the great passages of high-Romantic poetry. This is the opening:

> Hear me, hear me—
> Astarte my beloved! Speak to me:
> I have so much endured—so much endure—
> Look on me! The grave hath not changed thee more
> Than I am changed for thee. Thou lovdst me

Too much, as I loved thee: we were not made
To torture thus each other, though it were
The deadliest sin to love as we have loved.

(Act II, scene iv)

The phantom speaks one sentence to tell him he will die on the morrow, then fades away. In case we are in any doubt as to the relationship, Byron inserts a scene in which Manfred's servant, Manuel, describes his master alone in the tower room one stormy night with the woman who was "The only thing he seemed to love/As he, indeed, by blood was bound to do, /The lady Astarte, his . . ." and here he is conveniently interrupted. In choosing the name "Astarte," of course, Byron deliberately harks back to the incestuous sacred marriage (between the goddess and her brother El) and hence a love between two beings more than mortal, who cannot find their equals outside each other. Byron undoubtedly means us to see the incest as a hideous crime—indeed, the most hideous possible—but in doing so he of necessity elevates the sibling relationship to the most special of special cases. If Manfred was to be tormented by agonizing guilt, he had to have committed the sin of sins.

Cain: A Mystery, another dramatic poem, was written just after *Manfred,* and is often cited as a vehicle for Byron to continue his theme of sibling exceptionalism. Like the author of *The Book of Jubilees,* Byron posits wives for Cain and Abel: Adah and Zillah. But while the sibling union might have drawn Byron to the story, it is not, as it is in *Manfred,* its essence. Cain is certainly a kind of Manfred, and in the most remarkable episode he journeys with Lucifer (who correctly denies any relationship with the serpent in Eden) through the Abyss of Space and into Hades, where he is given a vision of earth's history, including the dinosaurs: Byron had read Cuvier.

The central episode is the killing of Abel, who infuriates Cain with his piety and deference to God, who had treated them so unjustly. Cain is the rebel, and Adah's role is simply that of supportive wife. The main feature of their partnership is her gentle concern for Cain and their son, Enoch. This is contrasted with Eve's fury and her refusal to forgive her son. Nothing special can be made of the incestuous union, because there was no choice at the time and there were no others with which to compare them. Adah has one heart-wrenching outburst, echoing Giovanni's, where she complains that their children will not be able to marry each other: Lucifer has broken the news to her about God's institution of the incest taboo. She regrets this deeply—because of her love for Cain and her wish for her children to have the same happiness.

Oh, my God!
Shall they not love and bring forth things that love
Out of their love? have they not drawn their milk
Out of this bosom? was not he their father,
Born of the same sole womb, in the same hour
With me? did we not love each other? and
In multiplying our love multiply
Things that will love each other as we love
Them?

(Act I, scene i)

Adah did not know about the solution in *The Book of Jubilees:* marriage with the father's brother's children. It might have been some consolation to her. What the story of Cain did for Byron was let him write about the brother–sister liaison as something normal and natural. In a way, then, he is more shocking than he was in *Manfred,* where at least all concerned recognized it as a great sin with disastrous consequences; that was the point of it.

Percy Bysshe Shelley, The Cenci *and* The Revolt of Islam *(1818)*

Father–daughter incest is not prominent on the literary scene between Ovid's story of Cinyras and Myrrha at the start of the first Christian century and Shelley's *The Cenci* at the beginning of the Industrial Age, a thousand years later. The contrast between the two could not be greater. Cinyras cared for his daughter and tried to find her a suitor: the father's true role. His daughter spoiled the arrangement. Count Cenci refused to play the role and instead tried to seize his daughter for himself. Shelley found this actual story of incest and vengeance in a manuscript in Rome, and wove it into what some critics call the best English tragedy since Shakespeare, albeit one that's almost never performed. The very theme of Francesco Cenci's lust for his daughter Beatrice kept the play off the stage.

The likeness to Ford's play is striking, in that the "innocents"—Beatrice, her mother Lucretia, and her two brothers, Giacomo and Bernardo—are pitted not only against their tyrannical father but against the corrupt society of sixteenth-century Italy dominated by Pope Clement VIII. The pope and his minions refuse to help protect the family against the brutality of Count Cenci, even when he arranges the murder of two of his sons and rapes his daughter. The third major player is Orsino, often compared to Iago, a priest who also lusts after Beatrice and who incites her to plot the murder of her father when there seems no other recourse.

In an attempt to make the play palatable for the stage, Shelley never has Beatrice say outright "he raped me." But we are left in no doubt. In the scene just after the actual rape, straight out of an operatic "mad scene" (she sees her mother as the "madhouse nurse"), Beatrice lets fly:

> I thought I was that wretched Beatrice
> Men speak of, whom her father sometimes hales
> From hall to hall by the entangled hair;
> At others, pens up naked in damp cells
> Where scaly reptiles crawl, and starves her there,
> Till she will eat strange flesh . . .
> Horrible things have been in this wide world
> But never fancy imaged such a deed.
>
> *(Act III, scene i)*

This strongly echoes the Duchess (of Malfi) in the madhouse. Shelley paints Cenci as an unredeemable villain: a father from hell. There is no subtlety in his character, which, for Shelley, incarnates all the unrelenting evil of all kinds of tyrannous authority, which he spent his short life combating. Cenci does not just want to rape his daughter, he wants to degrade her into absolute subjection to his will. Her defiance of him, and her initial hopeless wish to reform him, make him wild with frustration:

> Might I not drag her by the golden hair?
> Stamp on her? Keep her sleepless till her brain
> Be over worn? Tame her with chains and famine?
> Less would suffice. Yet to leave undone
> What I most seek! No, 'tis her stubborn will
> Which by its own consent shall stoop so low
> As that which drags it down.
>
> *(Act IV, scene i)*

Here Cenci seems to foresee his own doom, because Beatrice does not take the high road. Far from turning the other cheek, she plots with Orsino to hire two men who hate her father to kill him in his bed. In a scene reminiscent of Macbeth, when they balk she takes up the dagger and threatens to do it herself. Finally they strangle the villain and throw him over the balcony to make it look like an accident. Then Beatrice makes her big mistake. She impulsively gives one of the killers a rich robe from her grandfather's closet. This leads to his apprehension, torture, and confession, which implicates the whole family and leads to their execution. Despite the horror of Cenci's crimes, the pope refuses to countenance patricide. Orsino skips town; Beatrice gives a touching last speech; the tragedy concludes.

For Shelley, of course, the story is all about patriarchal tyranny—literally so, even if he might perhaps have preferred Beatrice to show forgiveness. But for our purposes it is interesting in that it is the most overt text in English about the father–daughter case, in a literary world otherwise dominated by the brother–sister relationship. Shelley lays it out; this is all about power. He therefore underlines our point that the incest taboo is not homogeneous: the three cases are very different. Cenci, rather than nurturing his daughter and seeking for her a suitable mate, the true role of the father, seeks absolute power: the power of the old male over his sons, and sexual power over his daughter and wife. The other old males of the society tacitly support him. The pope tells Cardinal Camillo, who seeks to intercede for the victims turned murderers, that the old males must stick together against the young people generally. A husband cannot "rape" his wife, or even a father a daughter. Property is property.

In *The Revolt of Islam* (also 1818), Shelley picks up the incest theme again, this time with the more familiar brother–sister case, and perhaps with his own sister, Elizabeth, in mind. And here he runs counter to the Byronic guilt motif and puts forward what may be the first case for the brother–sister pair as a kind of ideal of purity: the natural unit for conducting the case against a corrupt society. It is as if Giovanni and Annabella rose up together to try to overthrow the corrupt Italian state. In the original version of this mini-epic, the incestuous union was overt: the pair was called Laon and Cythna, and this was the title of the piece, whose form was modeled on Spenser's *The Faerie Queene*. Again publishers panicked at the graphic descriptions of sibling lovemaking, and Shelley was forced to obscure the relationship.

What he seemed to want to convey was that his romantic siblings who set out to overthrow the tyranny of the sultan of Turkey were absolute equals. Somehow, a wife could not fill this bill as well as a sister. Between husband and wife there was always an implied subjection. They could work at being equal, but it was not in the nature—and certainly the legality—of the relationship. There was always a contract, an implied bargain, and always negotiations. This was not so with brother and sister. They could rise above this mercenary stuff, and their sexual union, far from being sinful, could be symbolic of absolute purity and disinterested love. They could opt out from the meretricious and sordid business surrounding marriage, family, in-laws, fortunes, dowries, settlements, inheritances, and the like that are the stuff of Jane Austen. They could be *sui generis,* and in that sense pure, and hence the vehicles for a revolution in the world's sensibilities. Unfortunately they lost their political revolution and were executed, but as always with Shelley, the ideal is the thing.

The Victorians: Soror Divina, Maritus Suspectus

The Victorians had a spate of stories that were not overtly about incestuous desires, and certainly not about consummated incest, but tales in which the brother and sister, or the supposed brother and sister, or the brother–sister surrogates, were, as we say, "wedded to each other." So close and attached were they, that one could not miss the point that they were meant more for each other than for their marriage partners. These stories put the "siblings versus spouses" issue to front and center. I will only summarize here, because most of the stories are well known and many commentators have trodden this same ground. One especially, James Twitchell, has gone into some detail over them, and I am so indebted to him that I have titled this chapter after the main title of his book *Forbidden Partners: The Incest Taboo in Modern Culture* (1987). Let us look at a few examples, not in Twitchell. (On Thomas Hardy's *Jude the Obscure,* see the Digression in the notes.)

Jane Austen, Mansfield Park *(1814)*

We must first take a step back, before the Victorians proper, to the transitional period of the Regency. Jane Austen might seem an unlikely candidate, but her novels were the great ethnographies of family relationships and the marriage market at the beginning of the nineteenth century. In at least one, *Mansfield Park,* she deals pointedly with the sibling–spouse conflict that we have seen at the heart of the kinship atom. Fanny Price's mother was one of three sisters in a good family. She had made a bad marriage—for love—and ended up destitute with nine children. Her two sisters, who had made good marriages, decided that Fanny, aged nine, should go to live with one of them—Mrs. Bertram—and her family at Mansfield Park. Sir Thomas Bertram has misgivings, he thinks "of his two sons, of cousins in love"—but his wife's sister, Mrs. Norris, tells him, in a stunning anticipation of Westermarck:

> You are thinking of your sons—but do you not know that of all things upon earth that is the least likely to happen; brought up as they would be like brothers and sisters? It is morally impossible. I never knew of an instance of it. It is, in fact, the only sure way of providing against the connection. Sup-

pose her a pretty girl, and seen by Tom or Edmund for the first time seven years hence, and I dare say there would be mischief . . . But breed her up with them from this time, and suppose her even to have the beauty of an angel, and she will never be more to either than a sister. (Vol. 1, chap. 1)

It is not to work out quite so neatly. Fanny is, after all, nine years old, and was not in close physical contact with the boys before the crucial age of six. Timid and lonely, Fanny is befriended by her older cousin, Edmund Bertram, her mother's sister's son. They grow very fond of each other and live happily like brother and sister, as Mrs. Norris predicted. But as in all Austen novels, the plot must turn on who gets to marry whom to the best advantage. Fanny, has, as they say, no fortune, and young men were expected to marry to advance the family's fortune and social standing.

Jane then delivers us a perfect couple, Henry and Mary Crawford, brother and sister, worldly and wealthy, and uncommonly devoted to each other. The two sibling pairs get along well, and Henry falls in love with Fanny, and Edmund with Mary. It seems a match (or two matches) made in heaven, because Mary brings wealth to Mansfield Park and the penniless Fanny gets a charming and well-heeled husband, something she could not have expected. But Fanny's hopeless love for Edmund dooms the affair and leads to her incomprehensible (to her family) refusal of the eligible Henry. Jane plays out the agony exquisitely for 473 pages, until it is resolved and finally Edmund decides of Fanny that "her warm and sisterly regard for him would be foundation enough for wedded love."

Fanny and Edmund are not exactly brother and sister, but they are as closely related as half siblings, and a great deal of the novel is devoted to showing them as a happy sibling pair. That the breakup of this idyllic couple should be effected by another sibling pair was a masterstroke of plotting. The passion of the surrogate sister for her brother is pitted against the advantages of out-marriage and results in one of the few happy endings to these stories. It is perhaps worth noting that the happy couple are the children of two sisters (in the jargon, matrilateral parallel first cousins). This is, as we have already seen, very rare. Sisters are universally identified with each other, and in most kinship terminologies are equated: so mother and mother's sister are both "mother." These cousins are ideologically the children of the same mother, and are rarely preferred marriage partners. Jane knew exactly how to go against the pattern.

Emily Brontë, Wuthering Heights (1847)

Jane Austen hovered between eighteenth-century rationalism and self-interest and the new Romanticism with its dark heroes either plagued by incestuous guilt or glorifying their sibling love. The Brontë sisters did not like Jane much, and rather than making fun of the Gothic style, as Jane did in *Northanger Abbey,* they adopted it with gusto. Critics have seen more than overtones of a father–daughter passion in Jane Eyre and Mr. Rochester, but the more obvious case is Emily's Heathcliff and Cathy in *Wuthering Heights.* I was born where the Brontës lived, and lived where they were born, so I feel very close to them and the atmosphere of their novels. The two children are never overtly stated to be siblings, but, as the plot goes, Mr. Earnshaw, the master of the Heights, returns on a stormy night on the moors from a visit to Liverpool with a young, dark-haired, gypsy-looking boy under his coat.

The boy seems to have a deep attachment to him. Earnshaw says he found him in the street and took pity on him, but that doesn't seem plausible, and we are obviously supposed to understand that he is an illegitimate son. He is called Heathcliff (significantly, after a son who died in childhood) and grows up in the family in an ambiguous position, but develops a deep and passionate mutual attachment to Cathy, and a deep hatred of her brother, Hindley. Inevitably, as Cathy becomes marriageable, the old issue arises: How will she choose? Despite her almost visceral attachment—"I am Heathcliff"—she is drawn to the good life offered by Edgar Linton at bright and lively Thrushcross Grange, the absolute symbolic opposite of the wild and gloomy Heights. Cathy's temptation is too much for Heathcliff, who runs away, and the marriage takes place.

The whole story is too complicated to tell, and is well enough known. Suffice it that Heathcliff returns several years later, wealthy and a gentleman, to wreak his vengeance. He marries and degrades Edgar's sister Isabella—they have a son, Linton—and ruins Hindley. Cathy is pregnant with young Catherine when she takes ill and lies near death. In one of the most famous scenes in English literature, Heathcliff invades her room, takes her in his arms, covers her with "frantic caresses," and upbraids her for her desertion of him.

In the William Wyler movie of 1939 (Laurence Olivier and Merle Oberon) they got just about everything wrong, but they got the emotions right, and it is still the best version, despite the dreadful ending. No producer from then until now can resist putting Heathcliff and Cathy's last meeting at her bedside, and having her die in Heathcliff's arms. In fact, during their last meeting she was sitting in a chair, and she dies later in childbirth with neither Heathcliff nor Edgar present: more tragic in its way but not as cinematographic. Heathcliff's reaction to her death is in the best tradition of High Gothic:

And I pray one prayer—I repeat it till my tongue stiffens—Catherine Earn-shaw, may you not rest as long as I am living: you said I killed you—haunt me, then! The murdered do haunt their murderers, I believe. I know that ghosts have wandered the earth. Be with me always—take any form—drive me mad! Only *do* not leave me in this abyss, where I cannot find you! Oh, God! It is unutterable! I *cannot* live without my life! I *cannot* live without my soul! (Chap. 16)

Heathcliff bribes the sexton to put his grave next to Cathy's and, on his interment, to break open the adjacent walls of the coffins so that the bodies can mingle in death as they could not in life. But as in the tragedies of Shakespeare, everything has to be tidied up at the end; the world has to go on. Emily reunites the torn families in the end with the marriage of young Cathy successively to Linton (a marriage forced by Heathcliff), who dies, and then to Hindley's son Hareton, whom she loves. The symmetry of the result is remarkable and was pointed out in a brilliant essay, "The Structure of Wuthering Heights," published originally in 1924 by one C. P. S. No one seems to know who this author was—the paper was read to the Heretics Club at Cambridge, but the insight was keenly anthropological. I simplify in Figure 7.1.

Again we have two pairs of siblings (with Heathcliff as the dark and anomalous member) both united and divided by marriage. The sibling passion of Cathy and Heathcliff, which is one of the truly grand romantic passions, battles with the necessities of marriage. But if the siblings are denied their consummation (until their corpses rot together), their children are allowed to fulfill it. Hareton marries his father's sister's daughter, while Linton marries his mother's brother's daughter, the prototypical cross cousins, who are of course, under sister-exchange, the same person (Figure 7.1). Emily's solution is staggering. I refer you back to the initial discussion of the kinship atom. The atom here is sundered and then united; the basic human paradox is propounded and then solved. If we are in awe of Emily, it is with good reason, but not a reason we always appreciate.

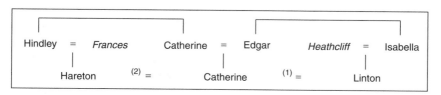

Figure 7.1   The structure of *Wuthering Heights*

George Eliot, The Mill on the Floss *(1860)*

In what is perhaps the best description ever of a childhood sibling relationship, Tom and Maggie Tulliver grow up in their idyllic home in the
mill on the River Floss. They are passionately close, even in their (often
fierce) quarrels, and seem to be inseparable. Included in the relationship
is Philip Wakem, a hunchback boy, whom Maggie sees as a brother; she
also wishes he were her brother. As they grow older, their father loses the
mill in a dispute with Philip's father, and then dies, leaving them in precarious circumstances. Maggie and Philip move from a sibling to a tenta-
tive romantic relationship, which is squashed by Tom.

Relief for Maggie comes from her cousin (her mother's sister's daughter)
Lucy, and Lucy's suitor Stephen Guest, a friend of Philip's, who is a shal-
low dandy but has an undoubted sexual attraction for Maggie. Maggie
becomes increasingly attracted to Stephen, with the obvious complications.
In the end they elope together, but Maggie regrets this and returns in isolation and disgrace. She reconciles with Lucy and Philip; Stephen flees the
area. The novel comes to an abrupt end when the river floods, and in a
melodramatically memorable scene, the estranged Tom and his sister are
reunited in a death by drowning.

> "It is coming, Maggie!" Tom said in a deep, hoarse voice, loosing the oars,
> and clasping her.
> The next moment the boat was not seen upon the water—and the huge
> mass was hurrying on in hideous triumph.
> But soon the keel of the boat reappeared, a black speck on the golden
> water.
> The boat reappeared but brother and sister had gone down in an embrace
> never to be parted—living through again in one supreme moment, the days
> when they had clasped their little hands in love, and roamed the daisied
> fields together.

Critics have disliked two things about the novel: the ending, which appears contrived, and the attraction that the superficial fop Stephen has
for the sensitive and intelligent Maggie. But we can see here a detailed
and brilliant rendering of the conflicts in the atom. The ideal pair is of
course Maggie and Tom. They are the brother and sister whose relationship
is perfect in its love and innocence: but this cannot be perpetuated into
sexual adulthood. They are René and Amélie, or Manfred and Astarte, or
Laon and Cythna. But they live in the real world of rural England, not the
world of Romantic imagination; they can neither consummate their love
nor go off on a world tour to avoid it. They must look outside this bond for
marriage partners.

Tom solves the problem by not marrying, and he is violently set against Philip for Maggie. Ostensibly this has to do with Philip's father, but it is clearly due to Tom's extreme possessiveness. She, while deeply attached to the brotherly Philip (a legitimate substitute for Tom?), is attracted to the marriageable stranger Stephen, who offers her the good life. It was Catherine's dilemma with Edgar, and even as Heathcliff and Cathy could be truly united only in death and sleep together in the quiet earth, so it is with Tom and Maggie and their orgasmic union in the unstoppable and unforgiving river (of life?). If the siblings cannot make the move outside themselves, it is the only solution.

The nineteenth century was remarkable for its obsession with the sibling relationship, and its extensions and surrogates which, many critics have pointed out, reflected the real-life obsessions of the authors: Chateaubriand and Lucile, Byron and Augusta, Shelley and Elizabeth, Emily and Branwell, Charles and Mary Lamb, William and Mary Wordsworth (see the glowing declarations in *Tintern Abbey*), George Eliot (as Mary Evans) and Isaac. We must not forget Poe and his marriage to a fourteen-year-old paternal first cousin raised in the same household, Virginia Clemm. Both Shelley and Leigh Hunt, the guru of the young Romantics, had more than friendly relationships with their sisters-in-law.

Fathers and daughters were in there too. Twitchell lays out in persuasive detail a number of Gothic novels, including the arch-Gothic *Castle of Otranto* (1765) by Horace Walpole, that seem to contain implicit warnings, to adolescent girls in particular, about the dangers of too-passionate an attachment to family members. Mary Shelley, in a novel, *Matilda*, never published in her lifetime, portrays a father obsessively in love with his daughter, which is perhaps a reflection of her own relationship with William Godwin. We know that adolescent girls are attracted to older men with power and resources, but be warned, these novels seem to say, certain of these older men are much too dangerous: stay away.

Bram Stoker, Dracula *(1897)*

The vampire count seems to be a particular kind of surrogate father to be avoided at all costs. He is the evil father who takes blood and offers a living death. He battles with Van Helsing, the good father who gives blood, and with the help of the young men tries to protect the possibility of normal marriage. Stoker strongly suggests that the "victims" of Dracula, Mina and Lucy, in fact collaborate with the elegant monster. Their fascination with him is in fact a kind of invitation. Without their participation he cannot have his way. Here we are back to Myrrha rather than Beatrice, and the ambiguity in the father–daughter relationship.

The female vampire, or Lamia, might seem to represent an evil mother figure. She is older than her victim and initiates him into manhood in a bloody rite. Bram Stoker's Lamias are unforgettable, and Dracula diverts them from young Harker with a squealing animal to satisfy their lusts. Evil mothers they may be, but in tribal societies it was often the duty of older women to initiate boys into sex or even become their first wives. Mary Shelley's *Frankenstein* (1818) is more complicated, but Victor Frankenstein's monster promises to be with him on his wedding night, and comes through by killing the bride, Victor's cousin-sister Elizabeth, thus preventing the consummation. "Elizabeth" was, we remember, the name of Shelley's sister, and he had a heavy hand in the novel's composition.

The theme is still alive and well today. But in such great vampire success stories as *Buffy the Vampire Slayer, Interview with the Vampire,* and the recent *Twilight* series, there has been a conscious attempt to make the vampire look younger and more attractive: less like a father and perhaps more like an older brother. But there is no avoiding the fact that to be a vampire he must be very dead—or very undead, which is worse. He is still very much the forbidden partner, however attractive he may be to the young woman at risk.

Oscar Wilde, Salomé *(1893)*

No one seems to consider Oscar Wilde's play *Salomé* relevant to the incest issue, but Herod's lust for his stepdaughter, to whom he gives the head of the prophet Jokanaan (John the Baptist) in return for the striptease Dance of the Seven Veils, is not even a thinly disguised incest lust. "I will not have her dance while you look at her in that fashion," says Herod's wife Herodias. "What is it to you how pale she is . . . You must not look at her." Herodias is the widow of Herod's brother, and foul play is suspected in his death. Every producer (and Richard Strauss, in his smack-in-the-face opera) leaves us in no doubt that Herod's lust goes somewhere beyond the normal. To be fair, so does Salomé's lust for Jokanaan; the play is about a clash of abnormalities. The prophet rejects her lustful advances just as she rejects those of her uncle/stepfather.

Most so-called father–daughter incest turns out to be an abuse of stepdaughters, so Herod may be far more typical than, for example, Count Cenci. However, there is in his case an interesting twist: because Herod was Salomé's father's brother, in Jewish law he had a right to marry her; she was in this sense a lawful potential spouse (polygamy was also allowed). Remember that the right of a man to his father's brother's daughter was an inheritance of the right of a man to his brother's daughter. We are back to the nagging persistence of marriage with the paternal cousin and its implications. John the Baptist's obsessive complaint against Herodias is her "incest" in marrying her brother's husband (and incidentally murdering that husband). So here again we have the conflict of laws in biblical tradition that we saw in *Hamlet,* between the duty of a man to marry his dead brother's widow (the levirate) and the condemnation of this marriage as incest. Like Henry VIII, the interested party can cherry-pick this one.

From our perspective, Herod can be seen as killing Salomé in revenge for her obsessively preferring the stranger to him, the legitimate kinsman. This is pure Wilde, of course. In Mark's story (6:14–29), Salomé—whose name comes not from Mark but from Josephus—is simply the passive tool of her manipulative mother. In Wilde's story she ends up, briefly, with only the dead stranger's head: "I will kiss your lips Jokanaan." Wilde's play is, probably consciously, the mirror image of Racine's *Phèdre,* where the heroine's passion for her stepson Hypolite also brings universal destruction. Byron also had tackled the case of a woman's fatal sexual attraction to her stepson in *Parsinia,* not one of his best or best-known poems. But let us move on into the twentieth century, where a more relaxed atmosphere prevailed. The unease and fascination are constant; the strategies for dealing with them, both in practice and in imagination, vary with the times.

The Moderns: Just Doing It

The twentieth century continued the nineteenth's fascination with incest as a plot device, particularly with the brother–sister theme. Germany seems to have been rife with such plots, which owe their origin to Goethe's *Wilhelm Meisters Lehrjahre* (1795), which contained, among other things, the first serious discussion of Hamlet's motives for delay. But this *bildungsroman* (coming-of-age novel) had its heroine, Mignon, be the result of a liaison between the monk/harpist and a girl who turns out to be his sister—the accident again. German literature in the first half of the twentieth century was, to quote an excellent commentator, Barton Johnson, "awash with sibling incest." Nabokov found it a "fashionable theme" and eventually turned to it himself.

Edgar Allen Poe, The Fall of the House of Usher *(1839)*

In America the theme seems to have almost exhausted itself; in the obsessive brother in Poe's story we find decided overtones of Ferdinand in Webster's *The Duchess of Malfi*. Note the narrator's comment that

> the stem of the Usher race, all time-honored as it was, had put forward at no period, any enduring branch; in other words, that the entire family lay in the direct line of descent, and had always, with very trifling and very temporary variation, so lain.

The name had been transmitted intact, so this must mean that the Usher heir had always married a close paternal cousin. There was, Poe says, "a deficiency of collateral issue"—all those who married could trace a direct relationship back to a common Usher ancestor. Ushers had always married Ushers, and the two nervously debilitated siblings were the result. The incest is never openly stated, but they had lived in isolation for "decades" and were both approaching death. Every schoolchild knows the story, and the gruesome ending where the sister Madeline returns from the crypt where brother Roderick had interred her before she was fully dead, and where her bloodied walking corpse falls on him and he dies in her embrace. It is like a sanguinary Gothic parody of the "clean" death of Tom and Maggie in *The Mill on the Floss*.

The film version by Roger Corman (with Vincent Price) misinterprets virtually every element of the original story except the atmosphere. In the most egregious departure, Corman has the named visitor (anonymous in the story) answering not the call for help of Roderick Usher, his former friend, but that of Madeline, his clandestine fiancée! This departure at least recognized that the plot needed a conflict between the closed brother–sister bond and the potential bond of husband and wife, to be accepted by a cinema audience. The original was more horrific in its claustrophobia; the movie was more human with its conflict. Melville had an overt half-sibling relationship in *Pierre: Or the Ambiguities* (1852), and Hawthorne played with the theme in *Alice Doane's Appeal* (published anonymously in 1835, then ignored by the author).

The English had long since dropped the remorse and guilt over sibling incest and reverted to a civilized acceptance when it was an accident and a shrug when it was not. Perhaps the post-Victorian, more-aristocratic English had less of a horror of inbreeding, which after all was what they were about with both offspring and horses. "Line-breeding" of horses is in fact "cousin breeding" in order to "fix" *desirable* traits, my daughter Kate, who breeds champion Arabians, tells me. The Ushers could, like the Ptolemies, have produced outstanding descendants: it depends on the original stock.

In one of the first, loosely described "existentialist" postwar novels, Iris Murdock used brother–sister incest essentially to comic effect. *A Severed Head* (1961) is the story of the decline and fall of Edward Lynch-Gibbon, whose wife, Antonia, goes off with his therapist, Palmer. Edward then is attracted to Palmer's sister, Honor Klein (an anthropologist), only to find she is having an affair with her brother. This is deliberate incest, but it is not marriage: the siblings might have sex, but they do not take it further than that. Agatha Christie could not resist the theme, and in the posthumous *Sleeping Murder* (1976—the year of her death) she has a lustful brother murder his sister after he is rebuffed by her. She rather gives the plot away early on when her heroine goes to a performance of *The Duchess of Malfi* and sees the duchess strangled on stage by orders of her brother, and hears his chilling line: "Cover her face, mine eyes dazzle, she died young."

William Golding, The Scorpion God *(1972)*

William Golding, the greatest of fabulists, best known for *Lord of the Flies*, nicely turns the issue on its head in a tale set in a petty kingdom in predynastic Egypt. The princess Pretty Flower shocks the priests and the court by her lack of attraction to her brother (who in turn does not like "bouncing up and down" on her). Also shocking is her resistance to her "lawful desire for her father." She compounds her sin by being attracted to the Liar, who tells obscene tales of foreigners who would rather marry strangers than their own family members (echoes of Iraq). In a scene like a strange parody of Giovanni and the friar, the Egyptian priest (the Head Man) hears Pretty Flower's confession concerning her liaison with the Liar:

> "How did you justify yourself to yourself?"
> "I pretended to myself that he was my brother."
> "Knowing all the time that he was—a stranger, as in the fantasies of white men?"
> Her voice came muffled through her palms.
> "My brother by the God is only eleven years old. And the fact that the Liar was—what you said—*can* I tell you?"
> "Be brave."
> "It put a keener edge on my love."
> "Poor child! Poor twisted soul!"

"What will happen to me. What *can* happen to me? I have shattered the laws of nature."

"At least you are being honest."

The priest laments that with such sinful and unorthodox ideas abroad, is it any wonder that floods ravage the land, thus demonstrating the anger of the gods. He tries to console Pretty Flower:

> In all of us there is a deep, unspoken, a morbid desire to make love with a, a—you understand what I mean. Not related to you by blood. An outlander with his own fantasies. Don't you see what these fantasies are? They are a desperate attempt to get rid of his own corrupt desires, to act them out in imagination; because—by the laws of nature—they cannot be externalized. Do you suppose, my dear, there are real places where people marry across the natural borders of consanguinity?

We might answer with an unequivocal yes, and remind the Head Man that even in Egypt incestuous marriage was reserved for the royal families as an exception. Except that the work of the late Keith Hopkins showed that sibling marriages were common among the Egyptian nobility and the nonaristocratic but wealthy classes that imitated them. What is more, even the Roman colonists who moved to Egypt after Caesar's conquest joined in the practice, presumably to give themselves legitimacy with the locals.

Thus Golding's idea that with the Egyptians, because familial in-marriage had been defined and sanctified as normal, exogamy would appear unnatural and sinful, may be uncannily near the truth. Whatever sexual possibility is defined as forbidden can become tempting, and that usually is incest. Golding's impish inversion makes the point better than all the pontificating of the anthropologists.

Ivy Compton-Burnett, Brothers and Sisters *(1950)*

The reclusive spinster Ivy Compton-Burnett returned with comic wit to the central theme, as found in Jane Austen, of the conflict between brother–sister affection and the needs of marriage. She does this by introducing six pairs of siblings who meet in the restricted atmosphere of a small English country town in the indefinite Edwardian period that is always her setting. The central pair is Andrew and Dinah Stace, although they have a younger brother, Robin, who acts as a kind of cynical chorus to the events. The siblings are part of a closed world in the home of their parents, Christian and Sophia. The relationship twists are hard to follow in prose. Figure 7.2 should help keep the record straight, even if it gives away a crucial twist of the plot.

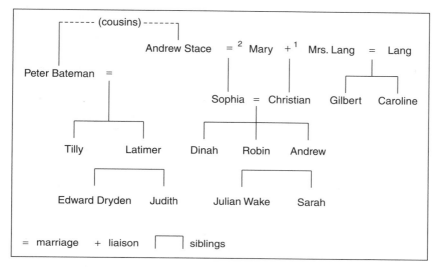

Figure 7.2   The Stace family

They have a pair of poor-relation cousins (the exact relationship is not defined), Tilly and Latimer. The latter cling to hopes of marriage with their better-off cousins that remain unfulfilled. Christian, the father of Andrew and Dinah, was an orphan, adopted at age ten and reared by old Andrew Stace with his daughter Sophia, essentially as brother and sister. The two become inseparable and want to marry. Old Andrew adamantly refuses permission, and writes a letter, which he locks in a drawer, but he dies before revealing its contents. It remains there for years, during which Christian and Sophia do marry and have the children described.

Three other sibling pairs are introduced: Edward and Judith Dryden—he is the rector of the parish; Julian, a barrister, and Sarah Wakes; and Caroline and Gilbert Lang. The latter have moved to the town with their elderly French mother, who had them late in life. Julian and Sarah also would like to marry the Stace siblings, but as a first move outside themselves, Andrew and Dinah become engaged to Caroline and Gilbert Lang. The various siblings think only in terms of a "double marriage" that will ensure they do not need to break up. Then the shoe drops. The letter in the drawer is discovered, and it turns out that Christian is old Andrew's natural son and hence the half brother of Sophia (this makes them the sixth pair of siblings). On finding this out Christian has a heart attack and dies.

Sophia and the children take the news stoically. But at the same time Mrs. Lang, after looking at some family photos, tells Christian that she is his mother, but she will not reveal who the father is. Still, because Gilbert and Caroline are "by blood, half uncle and aunt" to the Staces, that engagement is called off. Andrew and Dinah then become engaged to Edward and Judith. Figure 7.2 shows the relationships to this point, but has to reveal the next twist that, of course, the mysterious father is old Andrew Stace who had an affair with Mrs. Lang when she was a young French maid. At this, Edward and Judith drop out of the picture. Julian then proposes to Dinah but is turned down, so tries Caroline, who seems to accept, and it is suggested that Sarah will accept Gilbert. As a side plot, Tilly accepts a marriage proposal from a local merchant on condition that he will in turn take on Latimer as an apprentice.

Ivy has her characters behave in an almost casual fashion about all the twists and turns. Sophia dramatizes, but stoically accepts. It is treated as a series of twists of fate about which not much can be done, and so long as the siblings remain bonded and together, it can be tolerated. Marriage is essentially secondary, a necessity that has to be addressed, with, as we saw, the double marriage with another sibling pair being the only acceptable solution. This would involve classic "sister exchange," of course (see Figure 6.1 in Chapter 6), which we have canvassed as the most elementary form of marriage exchange. (Judith does seem to marry a stranger in the end, but it is not clear what Edward will do.) The key pair of Andrew and Dinah, who feel that the incest of their parents only makes them emotionally closer, will join the young Robin in London, and life will continue uninterrupted by connubial exigencies.

Ivy's exquisite creations, written almost entirely in dialogue, read more like leisurely Chekhovian dramas than novels. The BBC found them perfect as broadcast plays, needing to change very little. She is perhaps the most critically underrated English novelist of the twentieth century, although her books were popular. Critics found them too removed from "real life." Yet Ivy grew up in a family with a tyrannical mother and twelve siblings and half siblings, where all seven girls did not marry and two even committed joint suicide. She was very close with two of her brothers, like Dinah in the story, and both died (one at the Somme) (Sprigge 1973). This was all real enough. But we do not need much further analysis to see that she has produced a sophisticated parody of the basic situation and its inherent sister exchange, where the sibling pairs try to look outside themselves, but not with much enthusiasm. Almost any other sibling pair will do as marriage partners, so long as the childhood sibling bond remains intact.

Vladimir Nabokov, Ada, or Ardor: A Family Chronicle *(1969)*

Nabokov had played with the incest theme in his wildly successful *Lolita* (1955), with Humbert Humbert as the lustful stepfather. *Ada* is much more subtle, a kind of grand climax to the sibling-incest motif that started in earnest with the Romantics but had much older roots, as we have seen. "Adah" was the name of Cain's wife in Byron's poem (and of Byron's clever daughter named after her and his half-sister, Augusta), and the reference is deliberate. In the novel Nabokov is at his elusive, allusive, and enigmatic best—or worst, depending on your point of view. The allusions, direct and indirect, to stories of sibling incest are numerous. Ada says, for example, "I'm Fanny Price, actually." And there is a discussion of Chateaubriand's *René* and incest, where the placing of the word *"donc"* is crucial.

Here we are concerned only with the genealogical plot. The genealogy of the Zemski-Veen families is so difficult that Nabokov puts it right up front in a family tree, but typically he makes this only an approximation of the truth—that is, insofar as we can ascertain the truth (or are meant to). At the heart of the plot is a pair of supposed first cousins, Van and Ada. Van's father, Demon, and his first cousin Dan, married twin sisters, Marina and Aqua, who were their second cousins. Figure 7.3 is my pared-down summary of Nabokov's "official" version of the relationships.

Note that Daniel is the son of Ardelion, and that Marina and Aqua are sisters. When Ada is twelve and Van fourteen they begin an idyllic sexual relationship, elaborately described, only to discover that Demon, through an affair with Marina, is in fact Ada's father, and that Marina is also Van's mother, and hence they are full brother and sister. Some early critics missed this and had them half siblings, but despite the enigmas of the plot, it seems they are the Full Monty. (I confess that I too missed this on first reading of the opaque discussion on flowers in chapter 3.) Lucette turns out to be their half sister and intrudes on the affair with her love for Van.

In an excellent article already referred to, Barton Johnson makes a valiant attempt to look at all the generations and see how Nabokov intended us to see the truth. He produces his own version of the genealogy, but he too has a problem getting the relationships straight on a diagram, although he gets them right in the text. My own attempt to capture the elusive true picture is in Figure 7.4.

In this interpretation of Nabokov's hints and innuendoes, Dedalus and Dolly produced Aqua, Demon, and Marina, while Demon and Marina,

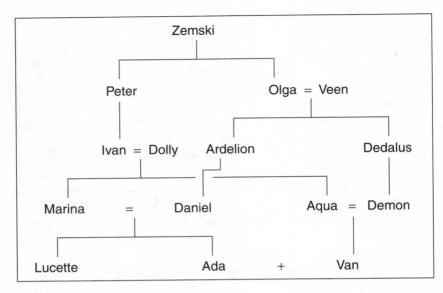

Figure 7.3 The Zemskis: official version

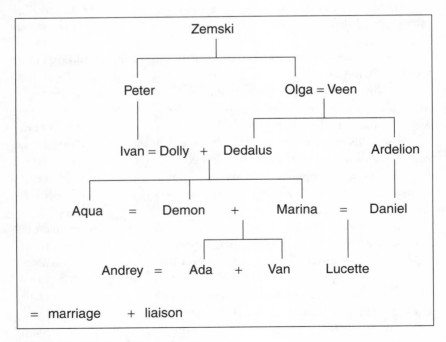

Figure 7.4 The Zemskis: real version

as we have seen, produced Van and Ada. So the sibling incest went back a generation, and our pair reproduced the sins of the father's in their own lives (and, pushing it back, maybe even the sins of their grandparents). This totally closed sibling–cousin world (which, incidentally, exists in a parallel universe to Earth) was invaded by Ada's marriage to Andrey and was ended by her return to Van, who, as a psychologist dealing in illusions, occupies a whole section of the book with his treatise on time. The closed family finally closes down completely with the sterile union of Ada and Van in old age. It could not break out from itself, and died out.

Strangers and Brothers

Strangers and Brothers was, as I remember, a novel (one of many) by Charles Snow about the narrow society of an Oxford college, but it serves nicely as a reminder of the Iraqis, in Chapter 2, who were appalled at the idea of marriage to a stranger. For most of our history as a species this would not have been an issue; we married cousins because that was who was available. Even so, we married cousins who took us out of our immediate family, and for natural selection that was good enough, even ideal. But as our populations increased and our range of ties grew wider, we had to deal with strangers as in-laws, and it was always difficult.

In myth and legend, where we tap the bandwidth of the tribal imagination, we try to turn back in on ourselves, never without problems and rarely with happy endings. The Romantics—Shelley, Chateaubriand, Byron, even Poe—kept their siblings in a cocoon without outside ties (for better or for worse). But Ovid, Ford, Fielding, Austen, Brontë, Wagner, Eliot, Hardy, Compton-Burnett, Nabokov, and the authors of *The Book of Jubilees* and *The Volsunga Saga,* knew that this was impossible, however desirable, and that cousins and strangers had to come into the picture as marriage partners.

Sometimes this ended badly, as with Ford and Eliot, sometimes happily as with Austen's Fanny and Tom, and with the perfect cousin-marriage reconciliation that ends the sibling agony of *Wuthering Heights.* Nabokov's Ada makes a halfhearted stab at out-marriage, but that collapses, and the end, if not bad, is bleak and not fruitful. *The Book of Jubilees* found the perfect solution to Cain's problem in marriage with the father's brother's daughter, which Arab societies still see as the ideal way to keep marriage in the (patriarchal) family.

The formula in reality is always a move outward:

siblings → cousins → strangers

The strangers are genetic strangers; they may be familiar people, of course. In some small-scale societies there are technically no strangers; everyone is kin, however distant. The categories can be broken down and recombined:

(siblings + parallel cousins) → (cross-cousins + strangers)

or, where half-sibling marriage was allowed (as in Athens and Sparta):

(full siblings) → (half siblings → cousins → strangers)

although the restriction against maternal half-siblings is usually stricter than against paternal.

Or it can be, as in Europe under Catholic marriage laws, where up to third cousins were banned:

(siblings + cousins) → strangers

and so on. This banning of cousins in marriage is an often-overlooked crucial factor in the modernizing of Europe and the development of individualism, as we saw in Chapter 2. Actually the category of parallel cousin itself can be broken down, as in the Arab case where patrilateral parallel cousins (father's brother's children) must be distinguished from matrilateral (mother's sister's children):

(siblings + matrilateral parallel-cousins) →
     patrilateral parallel-cousins →
          strangers

and of course there are strangers and strangers, but that we know. Readers can perhaps try breaking down that category for themselves (related strangers versus unrelated strangers, strangers who share a language or religion versus those who don't, and so on).

In the small bands and tribes in which we evolved, the formula would take care of itself: we would avoid siblings and forge alliances with cousins. In the more complex societies that followed, there was more and more intrusion into the formula, often producing the reverse of its effect in magnifying the sexual attraction of near kin rather than dampening it. And complexity meant that the trend toward dealing with strangers as a natural part of life, rather than as an occasional emergency, moved inexorably forward. In our literature and legend we constantly explore the possibilities and boundaries inherent in the initial position: this is part of the purpose of legend and literature, and they rarely let us down.

The nonsibling possibilities are less in evidence. Although father–daughter incest is probably the most common, it is not the most explored in high literature. Pornography has a field day with it, and it dominated the High Gothic (roughly 1750–1830). But in most fiction the father's role was to try to control the *marriages* of his daughters, usually standing in the way of their free choice of husband. See Jane for the definitive studies. Among serious authors, when real father–daughter incest is dealt with, it is either, as in Ovid's case, the result of a daughter's desire not to look further, or as in Shelley's *The Cenci,* the consequence of a power-mad father's lust for dominance over his rebellious family.

Cinyras was doing his best as a father and was tricked, but with Cenci there was clearly not a nonsexual, protective father–daughter relationship, geared, as it should be, to the eventual out-marriage of the daughter. Yet most fathers and daughters do indeed develop a loving and mutually supportive bond, although this is something that feminists seem strangely unwilling to accept at face value. (Perhaps "first-wave" feminism was, among other things, the residue of poor father–daughter relationships. Think of the vicious attacks on "daddy's girls.") The majority of "father–daughter incest" today (insofar as reliable statistics are possible) seems in fact to be "father and stepdaughter incest," in line with findings about the dangers of step relationships generally (Daly and Wilson 1996, 1997). The substitute father usually has not known the girl as a baby and infant, when the caring bond develops. In her *Father–Daughter Incest*—regarded as the definitive study—Judith Herman recognizes the distinction but lumps both categories together when citing incidences, which is confusing to say the least.

As to mothers and sons, that becomes the least interesting case: Hamlet was pathological; Tom Jones had a near accident; Oedipus too was not deliberate, but Jocasta had not suckled him anyway. Neither had Mrs. Waters suckled Tom Jones. The suckling relationship, which nature assumes as part of the normal environment of development, seems to rule out the mother–son possibility. Except, of course, that it is not universal: in upper-class families in Europe, for example, wet nurses were nearly always employed. Gertrude would not have suckled Hamlet.

After cheap glass and rubber became available in the nineteenth century, and once baby formula was perfected, bottle-feeding became popular: very much so in the 1930s. The basic pattern established in the Paleolithic band was again disturbed, although bottle-feeding by the mother herself might not be too far removed from the real thing, and it still might work as a bonding mechanism to some extent. Because of her mother's illness and hospitalization, I bottle-fed my middle daughter, Ellie, in her early weeks, and I can attest to the almost frightening power of the bonding involved: something that men rarely experience. (See my *Participant Observer.*)

The pattern was disturbed even further in the 1960s by the oral contraceptive pill, which upset all the established rules of mating behavior. Some have argued that the pill makes incest taboos redundant because there would be no deleterious genetic consequences. But it was not bad genetic consequences that were responsible for the taboo in the first place. Somehow the pattern seems to be holding, and there is no rush to dismantle the taboos, although there have been legal challenges to them in Sweden and Germany. But there has been a change of circumstances that demands its own literary genius to catch the essence. Perhaps as the complexity of modern life grows more and more intolerable, and the demands of the strangers too unbearable, some new Shelley will find the idea of the closed family both attractive and viable, and create a Nabokov lineage that succeeds and flourishes: or not.

The theme is irresistible: Frank Herbert in his colossal *Dune* (1965) has his victorious interplanetary hero, Paul Atreides, marry his sister for dynastic reasons, and Salman Rushdie ends *The Enchantress of Florence* (2008) with a father–daughter twist. A Nazi brother–sister liaison adds to the horrors of Jonathan Littel's numbing holocaust novel *The Kindly Ones.* It is also there in Andrew Lloyd Webber's musical version of Gaston Leroux's *The Phantom of the Opera,* if you want to look for it, and for that matter look at the plots of our enormously successful TV soap operas. The latest episodes of the *Inspector Lewis* series on PBS *Masterpiece Theater* had a liaison between a woman and her foster son (whom she killed), with an important clue from *Oedipus Rex,* and a case of full-blown brother–sister incest (twins) with stillbirths, madness, murder, and suicide.

If one is simply looking for incidences—for examples of the use of the incest theme—they are numerous. Looking only at my own reading of contemporary authors, in addition to those mentioned in this chapter already, I find it there in Anthony Burgess, John Irving, John Barthes, Ian McEwan, Robinson Jeffers, Doris Lessing, V. C. Andrews, Toni Morrison, William Faulkner, A. S. Byatt, Gabriel Garcia Marquez, Stephen King, Martin Amis, Robert Heinlein, Anaïs Nin, Joyce Carol Oates, Anne Rice . . .

It is not the most popular plot; male adultery and female infidelity take pride of place (the eternal triangle). The storytellers recognize the centrality of the invention of marriage and the vulnerability of that institution. That lives with us all, all the time; incest lurks in the background. But incest is, as all producers know, a powerful draw. We continue to dance to the rhythms of this primeval Drumbeat: of the conflict between kindred and affinity, between incest and in-laws, between siblings and strangers. If there are indeed only seven basic plots, then this is surely one of them.

CHAPTER EIGHT

In the Company of Men

Tribal Bonds in Warrior Epics

FROM GILGAMESH and Enkidu, through David and Jonathan, up to Holmes and Watson, the three sergeants in *Gunga Din*, Aubrey and Maturin, or Butch and Sundance, the Drumbeat of the male bond has been celebrated in literature, song, and drama. The combative male group from Jason and the Argonauts through the Knights of the Round Table, Robin Hood and his Merry Men, D'Artagnan and the Three Musketeers, to the Seven Samurai/Magnificent Seven exercises a constant fascination. This holds whether the male group is noble in its purpose, like Hawkeye and his Mohicans, or downright nasty (but ultimately redeemable), like the Dirty Dozen. The Western outlaw band (the James Gang, the Daltons) draws us as surely as the Pre-Raphaelite Brotherhood or the Twelve Apostles. There is a continuing appetite for World War II "buddy" movies *(Saving Private Ryan, Band of Brothers)*, where men die for each other as surely as Romeo died for Juliet in the world's most famous heterosexual tragedy. Even there Romeo's death could be seen as having less to do with Juliet than with his devotion to Mercutio.

In a simpler age, when we still wore our real emotions on our sleeves, we could sing "I miss my buddy, my buddy misses me" and "Those wedding bells are breaking up that old gang of mine" without politically correct blushes. Perhaps Professor Higgins and Colonel Pickering, and Albert Doolittle and his mates, were the last great flourish of unashamed male bonding, quivering openly before the insidious female threat that demanded respectability, responsibility, and marriage. "Let a Woman in Your Life" and "I'm Getting Married in the Morning" were the last hymns to male exclusivity and female exclusion before the unisex revolution drove these arcane sentiments underground. To be fair, however, the postrevolutionary *Midnight Cowboy* returned unabashedly to the theme: however unlikely and unheroic the bonded male pair in question, this was a story of love and loyalty between men, with women purely peripheral to the bond; they were linked to it only through paid sex.

Hunters and Fathers

The theory of male bonding as a special instance of bonding in general was first formulated by Lionel Tiger, in his *Men in Groups,* in 1968. Tiger saw intense emotional attachment between males as having its roots in the prehuman group-living primates, but coming to full flower in hominid evolution (in the EEA—environment of evolutionary adaptedness—of the Upper Paleolithic, when modern humans were formed) with the development of hunting and warfare. Males hunting or fighting together had to develop a special kind of trust that went beyond simple friendship as might be expressed in grooming or proximity. This kind of dependence involved, firstly, a selection among young males for those with the right qualities (for males will differ in their bonding capacities), and led to elaborate recruitment systems of trial and initiation. The second element was "female exclusion," in which the heterosexual bond was ritually downgraded (as at "stag parties" today) and exclusive male groups were formed, with their secret ceremonies, oaths, and sanctions.

The heterosexual bond was necessary for reproduction but was seen also as inimical to the male bond, necessary for predation and protection. There was in consequence a constant tension between the demands of the reproductive bond and those of the male bond, a tension as demanding in its way as the conflict between the sibling bond and the spousal bond that we examined in Chapter 7. Men would be ambivalent about the heterosexual bond insofar as it threatened the male association; women would find the demands of the male group equally threatening to the needs of the family.

This whole evolutionary scenario later came to be seen in light of the differential reproductive strategies of males and females, and hominid males and females in particular. In the prehunting stage of hominid development, males had not been responsible for provisioning females and young. Male chimpanzees occasionally hunt, but the meat is not part of the steady food supply. They do, however, form cooperative male bands, which operate exclusive of females for a good part of the year and which carry out lethal raids on other such bands.

With the transition to hunting/scavenging, and the incorporation of meat into the regular diet, the evolving hominid infant, with its ever-increasing demands for fuel for its growing brain, required what Robert Trivers, in 1972, came to call a "high male parental investment." This mitigated the totally selfish behavior of the males and required them to divert energy and resources to the women and children. It would always be in the female's interest to garner male support for herself and her offspring. This would be largely in the form of high-energy protein from meat—the females provided the bulk of the carbohydrate themselves. The males would still be inclined to promiscuity, or at least polygamous mating, to maximize their own reproductive success.

Male and female reproductive strategies were thus always asymmetrical, and this asymmetry was, if anything, intensified during the course of hominid development. Looked at from the point of view of "survival of the group," of course, both male protection and provision, and female reproduction and nurturing of infants, were equally required. But from the perspective of individual reproductive success, these two forms of bonding would be at odds. It could be argued that the most successful males would be those that balanced male bonding, for the protection and provisioning of the whole group, with the particular care and provisioning of their own mates and young. The alternative strategy of random promiscuity would probably have less chance of success unless it was totally concealed: something not easy in a small hunting group.

Nineteenth-century anthropology suggested the alternative of "group marriage" in which mates were held in common. While theoretically possible, this has not been found to occur in actuality, and arose from a misunderstanding of cousin-marriage rules and kinship terms, as we shall see in Chapter 11. Even in societies where the ideology of procreation excludes the father as progenitor of his children, individual rights to mates are recognized, and these include rights of sexual access. Regardless of the theory of procreation, sexual jealousy appears to be universal, although there are exceptions for ritual orgies and wife lending. With the latter, however, the males are still in control of sexual access. (See my *Red Lamp of Incest* for details.)

The strength of the Tiger-Trivers thesis is that it forces us to recognize the male–male bond as equal to, and in many ways inimical to, the male–female bond, serving its own important evolutionary functions. We can expect, therefore, that once symbolic capacity was developed, this emotionally charged relationship would receive attention in ritual, art, music, and story. In the same way that sexual competition between dominant and subordinate males for fertile females would dominate the earliest narratives (Fox 1997), so we would expect to find the male–male bond and its vicissitudes as a theme around which oral narratives, and then written epics, arranged themselves.

Our analysis of some classic literary epics, then, will involve a simple switch of focus in which the male bond is put to the forefront of the narrative and the rest of the action is seen as affecting the bond, for better or for worse. In particular, it requires us to examine afresh the role of the females in the plot to see to what extent their actions affect the creation and stability of the bond, and often its dissolution.

We should always remember that the making of epic narrative was itself a male activity, and thus should indeed reflect basic male concerns. I do not therefore intend to argue that male–female relationships must always, in reality, take exactly the form we find in the epics; fortunately this is not the case. But it might be instructive to look at these powerful writers as narrators of a particularly intense version of the universal theme.

As with the cases of literary incest, this will involve us in a creative retelling of the stories. With the *Iliad,* for example, we must put Briseis back into the prominence she deserves; in *Beowulf* we must reassess the role of Grendel's mother; in the *Morte D'Arthur* we must get beyond the miasma of the romantic triangle; in the saga of the Volsungs we must face up to male failure. Throughout we must look again at the roles of males and females in the light of their contrasting mating and parenting strategies: in a world dominated by warriors and the warrior ethos, how did the women protect their interests?

I have been generous in my examples of the poetry itself, because that is why we are looking at literature in the first place. What makes great poetry, gripping stories, and high drama? Beyond the magic of their words is their resonance with our deepest human feelings. We dance and sing to the Whispers and the Drumbeats. Let us listen to them.

The Story of Gilgamesh

The earliest known written epic is the Babylonian story of Gilgamesh. Gilgamesh was ruler of the Sumerian city of Uruk around 2700 BC. In Assyro-Babylonian society he was worshipped as a god and celebrated in verse, which was standardized by 1300 BC. The most readable modern verse translation is by David Ferry, who uses the Babylonian text dating from the seventh century BC, but I will use my own here—derived from various sources, including translations of the Akkadian and Old Babylonian versions. All poetic "translations" are of course inventive reworkings of the often-fragmentary or obscure originals.

The Goddess Aruru, at the request of the gods, created the wild man Enkidu as the double of Gilgamesh. He was to be a counterweight to the growing power of Gilgamesh, which was threatening to the gods. Enkidu ran wild and Gilgamesh went after him, accompanied by a "temple prostitute" called Shamhat, who was to tame the wild man: to "show him the things a woman knows how to do," as Ferry puts it. Enkidu lost his wildness; the beasts fled from him. Gilgamesh has a dream about struggling with a meteorite, and his mother, Rimat-Ninsu, interprets it. The meteorite of the dream is in fact the perfect companion (Tablet I):

> He is the meteorite, the strongest man
> in all the land who comes to save his friend.
> Give him your love; embrace him as a wife;
> his strength is yours and it will never fail.

Shamhat, usually described as a "temple prostitute," is actually a priestess of the goddess Ishtar. These priestesses, representing the goddess, had intercourse with men who gave gifts to the temple, much as happened in ancient Judaic and Canaanite ritual, and still happens in parts of southern India, where the practice is known as *devadasi* (Singh 1997). Shamhat divides her clothes to dress Enkidu "as a bridegroom." Meanwhile Gilgamesh, as king, is asserting his right over a new bride. This enrages Enkidu, who challenges him. They fight, but neither can prevail. Gilgamesh's mother intercedes with the god Shamash, and hearing her pleas, Enkidu breaks off the fight and weeps. He and Gilgamesh grasp each other's hands and swear eternal friendship. Ninsun, Gilgamesh's mother, adopts Enkidu as her own son (Tablet III):

> Enkidu, I did not give you life
> but now before these priestesses I vow
> to take you as my own, and Gilgamesh
> shall be your brother.

Gilgamesh and Enkidu then take on the great demon Huwaw or Humbaba and defeat him. After this victory the goddess Ishtar falls in love with Gilgamesh, pleads for his semen, and offers him "riches beyond the telling." Gilgamesh repulses Ishtar, claiming that her lovers, like Tammuz, all came to a bad end. Ishtar then begs her father, Anu, to give her the Bull of Heaven to attack Gilgamesh. But Gilgamesh and Enkidu together kill the bull and tear out its heart. Enkidu rages against Ishtar, and the gods decide that Enkidu must die. He falls sick and dies, and Gilgamesh mourns movingly and elaborately over more than seventy lines (Tablet VIII):

> When the beating heart was still at last,
> he took a veil and covered his friend's face
> as if it were a bride's. He hovered like
> an eagle over him, then paced about:
> a frantic lioness that lost her cubs.
> Gilgamesh cut his own tangled locks
> and heaped them on the ground.

We are reminded of Isis in the form of a hawk hovering over the body of Osiris, and we shall see Achilles pacing frantically and tearing out his hair in grief. Gilgamesh in his misery tries even to become Enkidu (Tablet VIII):

> I made the happy wretched over you
> and when you died I let the filthy hair
> grow matted on my skin. A lion's mane
> I wore and wandered through the wilderness.

The rest of the epic deals with Gilgamesh's quest for immortality, and his search for Utnapishtim, the earliest Noah-like flood survivor, who holds the secret.

There is no question that the world's first great written epic poem is a long hymn to the bond between the two heroes. Looked at from this angle, the roles of the women can be seen as either promoting or undermining the male bond. The goddess Aruru creates the bond by creating the heroes in the first place. The temple priestess/prostitute, Shamhat, is crucial in taming Enkidu and then introducing him to Gilgamesh. Gilgamesh's mother then adopts Enkidu, thus further cementing the bond, whose stability she predicted. With regard to the bond, then, these can be termed *enabling* females. The goddess Ishtar, on the other hand, by her desire for Gilgamesh, threatens the bond, and after Enkidu has raged at her, destroys it. She then is, for the bond, a *disabling* female.

Many of the basic themes of the bond between men and the varying roles of the women are then established in this powerful poem. We shall forego further discussion of them here, and pick them up as we proceed through the later epics.

Táin Bó Cualinge

Sources.   The *Táin Bó Cualinge* (The Cattle Raid of Cooley) refers to events that, by tradition, happened in Ireland around the time of Christ, at the height of barbaric Iron Age society. The language of the mixed verse-prose epic is that of eighth-century Irish Gaelic, but the completion of the stories dates to the twelfth-century *Lebor na hUidre* (Book of the Dun Cow). In the fourteenth century a version was written known as *The Yellow Book of Lecan*. Both versions, compiled in monasteries, show heavy Christian interpolations from the monkish authors, but the essence of the pagan story comes through clearly. The whole "Ulster Cycle" can be found in Cross and Slover's *Ancient Irish Tales*.

The Bond of Fostering.   The cattle raid in question was instigated by Queen Medh (Maeve) of Connaught, to capture the brown bull owned by Dáire, one of the chieftains of Ulster. The army of Ulster is immobilized by a spell, and the hero Cúchulainn has to meet the invaders alone. He delays them by challenging their best warriors to single combat, which they cannot refuse, but always lose. The bulk of the story concerns these combats and battles, but the central event is the combat of Cúchulainn and Ferdia. This is particularly poignant because they had been lifelong friends, fostered together as children with Scáthach, an Amazon queen who taught them the arts of war, and who is thus the *enabling* female of the story. Cúchulainn frequently refers to them as "Scáthac's foster-sons." Fostering was a sacred duty in ancient Ireland, and the bond of foster brothers was likewise sacralized. This theme is going to recur in the other epics.

The Plotting of Medh.   The bond is, however, threatened by the manipulations of Medh, whom commentators have treated either as completely mythological or as representative of the high status of women in Celtic society, and north European society generally, at this time. Determined to sabotage Cúchulainn, she decides to suborn the loyalty of Ferdia. She thus becomes the major *disabling* female of the story. She tempts Ferdia with an offering remarkably like that of Ishtar to Gilgamesh, including "a chariot worth three-times seven bondmaids," a tax break for his kith and kin, fine jewelry, and her daughter, Finnabair, for wife.

Finnabair has already been provocatively dangled before him as bait; Medh then adds, "and my own friendly thighs on top of that if need be." She offered the same prize to Dáire in return for the bull. The Irish did not have ruling queens, so Medh's queenship was, according to

Thomas Kinsella, a mistake of the scribes—she was in fact the goddess of Tara. The parallel with Ishtar probably reflects a theme deep in Indo-European-Semitic myth. But in both cases the purpose of the fertility goddess, as is appropriate, is to disrupt the male bond with heterosexual temptations.

At first Ferdia is not tempted, but Medh appeals to his pride through a false statement impugning his honor, attributed to Cúchulainn. Ferdia ("the fiery") is quick-tempered and agrees to the fight, but demands six hostages to make sure she keeps her word. In a touching commentary on male honor, Fergus, the Ulster hero who had defected to Medh, feels compelled, at risk of his own life, to warn his friend Cúchulainn.

The Fight at the Ford.   We thus move to the tragic single combat. During the fight, both heroes have antiphonal verse debates with their charioteers, reflecting the same dialogue Krishna has with Arjuna in the Bhagavad-Gita. This bond with the wise charioteer is a kind of grace note on the theme. The two combatants engage in a lot of prefight banter, and while Ferdia, perhaps a little guilty, is truculent, Cúchulainn often laments the breaking of the bond and invokes their common fosterage. In Thomas Kinsella's elegantly minimal translation:

> While we stayed with Scáthac
> we went as one
> with a common courage
> into the fight.
> My bosom friend
> and heart's blood,
> dear above all.
> I am going to miss you.

He chides Ferdia for imagining that Finnabair will ever be his. Medh has used the same trick on fifty men before, he says. He is particularly bitter that Ferdia should let a woman come between them.

> If they had offered her to me,
> if I were the one Medh smiled at,
> I wouldn't think to do you harm
> or touch the least part of your flesh.

"We made one bed and slept one sleep," he says. They alternately fight and banter, and Cúchulainn returns again and again to the theme.

Now I know it was your doom
when a woman sent you here
to fight against your foster brother.

Yours is the blame for what must come,
Son of Damán mac Dáiru
—coming, at a woman's word,
to cross swords with your foster brother.

The Death of Ferdia.   The combat is described in heroic detail, but finally, by using the superweapon, the *gae bolga* (a kind of sling thrown with the foot), Cúchulainn mortally wounds Ferdia. He carries the body from the ford where the fight took place, and faints beside it. Loeg, his charioteer, rouses him, and the victor breaks into a series of laments (interspersed with prose conversations) that match in emotion and beauty those of Gilgamesh for Enkidu.

When we were with Scáthac
learning victory overseas,
it seemed our friendship would remain
unbroken till the day of doom.

I loved the noble way you blushed,
and loved your fine form.
I loved your blue clear eye,
your way of speech, your skillfulness.

He returns again to his main complaint:

Medh's daughter Finnabair
whatever beauty she may have,
was an empty offering,
a string to hold the sand, Ferdia.

He remembers his dead friend tenderly:

Your curled yellow hair
like a great lovely jewel
the soft leaf-shaped belt
that you wore at your waist.

You have fallen to the Hound,
I cry for it, little calf.

Cúchulainn is the Hound: his name means "The Hound of Colin." They cut the *gae bolga* from Ferdia's body, and Cúchulainn ends in a fury of grief with the same two lines repeated in each stanza, hammered away in the Old Irish: "*Cluchi cach gaine cach/go roich Ferdiadh issin n-ath.*"

> It was all play, all sport,
> Until Ferdia came to the ford.

Thus we can see that the heart of this great epic is another hymn to the male bond, and the most obvious of the complaints against the disabling role of the female. Heterosexuality is seen largely as a threat to the sacred bond, or, insofar as the heroes have their heterosexual partners, subordinate to it. Cúchulainn's sexual escapades are little above rape, and rarely rise above friendly teasing. In the whole of "The Wooing of Emer," where Cúchulainn gains his bride, there is no love poetry remotely matching his threnody for Ferdia.

Beowulf

Beowulf is a seventh- to tenth-century Anglo-Saxon poem, written in England, but about events taking place in Denmark and southern Sweden. More so than the *Táin* it is filled with Christian interpolations, but they do nothing to hide the intensely pagan nature of the values and mores of the warrior age. The hero, Beowulf, a prince of the Swedish Geats, heeds a call for help from the Danes, who are beset by a monster, Grendel. Beowulf sets sail with a picked band of followers for the land of the "Spear-Danes" and the hall Heorot, home of the Danish king Hrothgar. Here they await the attack of Grendel.

The foremost male bond of the poem is that between Beowulf and Hrothgar. The bond between Beowulf and his band is certainly there and very real, in the tradition of Jason and his Argonauts. But the specific bond is that between the hero and the king—foreshadowing Launcelot and Arthur. We are introduced early (line 612) to Hrothgar's queen, Wealhtheow, who takes mead round to all the warriors. She is especially gracious to Beowulf, who makes a "formal boast" to protect her people.

Grendel attacks, there is a huge fight, and Beowulf tears off the monster's arm. Grendel retreats to his lake home to die, and Hrothgar sings the praises of Beowulf, adopting him as his son "in his heart." The queen praises Beowulf and stresses how she trusts him to be "strong and kind" to her sons. Wealhtheow does not figure prominently in the poem, but she does fill the role of *enabling* female in her endorsement of Beowulf. She can be seen as being balanced against the next major player to appear. The night after the fight, Grendel's mother, bent on revenge, attacks Heorot and carries off one of Hrothgar's warriors. Beowulf dives to the bottom of the mere and overcomes Grendel's mother in a furious fight. He brings back her head to Heorot, where there is much mutual praising as the Geats prepare to depart. At one point Hrothgar is overcome with emotion. From Francis Gummere's consciously archaic translation—in *Epic and Saga*—which keeps to the alliterative spirit of the original:

> Then kissed the king of kin renowned,
> Scyldings' chieftain, that choicest thane,
> and fell on his neck. Fast flowed the tears
> of the hoary headed. Heavy with winters,
> he had chances twain, but he clung to this—
> that each should look on the other again
> and hear him in hall. Was this hero so dear to him,
> his breast's wild billows he banned in vain;
> safe in his soul a secret longing,
> locked in his mind, for that lovèd man
> burned in his blood.

Beowulf returns home, where he succeeds to the throne of the Geats. A dragon ravages the country, and again he leads a band to fight it. This time, however, they desert him, except for Wiglaf, who rebukes the others and tells them they must defend their prince. Wiglaf and Beowulf slay the dragon together, but Beowulf is mortally wounded. The shirkers, ashamed, come back and find Wiglaf supporting the dying hero, like Bedivere with Arthur.

> Wearied he sat
> At his sovran's shoulder, shieldsman good,
> to wake him with water.

The episode ends with:

> There Wiglaf sitteth,
> Weohstan's bairn, by Beowulf's side,
> the living earl by the other dead,
> and heavy of heart a head-watch keeps
> o'er friend and foe.

This great poem of warrior virtues shows again the male bond as central. Beowulf and Hrothgar dominate the body of the text, and the hero and Wyglaf end the tale. We have already noted Wealhtheow as the rather shadowy enabling female, but the critic might hold that there is no balancing disabling female who threatens the bond. But this would be to miss the point that Beowulf comes nearest to death not from the male monster Grendel but from Grendel's unnamed *mother*.

Yet again, there have been numerous interpretations of her symbolic value: psychoanalysts have a fine old time with her, and structuralists see her, like Enkidu, as Nature as opposed to the heroes' Culture. But from our perspective she is a female, like Ishtar and Medb, of superhuman powers, who is the most direct threat to the male heroes. It is surely not insignificant that she is a mother, and is out to protect the mother–child bond, the aim and object of the heterosexual bond, from the depredations of the rival male bond.

The disabling female need not always be so monstrously threatening. She can threaten more by simply diverting a hero from his primary allegiance by her feminine attraction. We shall look now at examples of where this passive attractiveness is fatal to the bond between heroes.

The *Iliad*

Achilles and Patroclus.   The *Iliad* is attributed to the blind poet Homer, and although written in about 750–725 BC, it concerns an earlier, Mycenaean society of the Greek Bronze Age. All the great epics are retrospective; it is only recently that epics in verse and prose, like those of Frederick Turner or Frank Herbert, have looked to the future. The preeminent male bond in Homer's story is that between the Greek heroes Achilles and Patroclus. Indeed, we can see that this bond and its vicissitudes are what the story is *about*. The plot is too well known to need much recitation. Menelaus's wife Helen elopes with Paris and is taken to Troy on the coast of what is now Turkey. The Greek principalities combine to attack Troy, and the poem covers an episode at the end of the ten-year siege

Agamemnon, as high king and commander in chief of the Greeks, has appropriated Briseis, a captive girl belonging to Achilles, the greatest of the Greek warriors, who then refuses to fight against the Trojans. Patroclus, Achilles' constant companion, prevails on him to lend his armor and chariot so that the Trojans might mistake Patroclus for his friend. Thus Patroclus hopes to aid the Greeks, who are losing badly and are driven back on their ships. Hector, the Trojan hero, kills Patroclus, then Achilles in turn kills Hector and mutilates his body in fury. Achilles in turn is killed, but his death is not reported until the later *Odyssey*.

Helen and Briseis.   Our interest is in the nature of the bond between the two heroes, and their women. Helen could be seen as a disabling female, except that she does not directly affect any particular male bond. She is, however, ultimately the "cause" of the terrible conflict—or at least the Greeks' excuse for it. Briseis, on the other hand, while completely passive, is the direct cause of the breach between Agamemnon and Achilles, and thus sets in motion the death of the heroes. The disabling female does not have actually to attack the bond to threaten it. Her role is often merely to act as a serious distraction: she is the agent of the heterosexual bond in its constant battle for attention with the male bond.

As with the earlier epics, the gods and goddesses (or as in *Beowulf,* the monsters) play their part. Thus Hera, the queen of the gods, is instrumental in aiding the heroes, while Thetis, Achilles' goddess mother, is strictly enabling. In one of the most memorable episodes in the poem, she commissions new armor for her son from Hephaestus, the blacksmith of the gods.

Who Was Patroclus?   Achilles, then, is a semi-divine Greek prince, the leader of the Myrmidons. But who is Patroclus? He is described as the "dear companion" of Achilles. They were raised together in the house of Patroclus's father, Menoetius. Patroclus is in fact the "older brother" of the pair. They were thus, like Cúchulainn and Ferdia, virtual foster brothers. He seems always to be there with Achilles in any crisis. He is there during the quarrel with Agamemnon, and it is he whom Achilles asks to handle the delicate matter of handing Briseis over to the heralds. Achilles addresses him on this occasion, and often later, as *diogenes Patroklus.* Fagles gives this simply as "Prince," while Fitzgerald has "my Lord." The Loeb Classical edition (Murray) has "sprung from Zeus." The last is the most literally correct, although it could be "god-born," that is, "divine." He has other epithets, including *megathumon* (great-hearted) and *isotheos* (godlike man), but the point is that he is never seen as anything less than the equal of his companion Achilles.

When the delegation from Agamemnon visits Achilles, Patroclus is again always with him. All others, including servants, are excluded. Together the two cook for and serve the ambassadors, and Patroclus appears "like a god in the firelight" (Fitzgerald). In a defining episode, for him, Patroclus, carrying a message from Nestor to his friend, meets the wounded Eurypylus, who bemoans at length the condition of the Greeks and asks how Achilles can ignore their plight. Patroclus (again called *diogenes*) helps Eurypylus, then goes on to rebuke Achilles savagely, and essentially as an equal (these are my own translations):

> Who was your father, you who have no pity?
> No, not the master horseman Peleus;
> nor was your mother Thetis. The gray sea
> spawned you on the cliffs, inflexible man.

The Grief of Achilles.   Achilles accepts the rebuke and gives his armor to his friend, with strict instructions not to pursue the Trojans once the Greek ships are safe. Once Patroclus is gone, Achilles prays long and hard to Zeus to keep him safe. Zeus is torn. Then Patroclus kills the high god's favorite, Sarpedon, and Zeus allows Apollo, patron of the Trojans, to aid Hector and the Trojans in killing Patroclus. Nestor brings the news, and Achilles is distraught:

> A black grief struck Achilles; with both hands
> he poured the dust and dark ash on his head,
> defiling his fresh tunic and fair face.
> The mightiest of the mighty, in the dirt
> outstretched upon the ground, tore at his hair.

Briseis and Patroclus's Ghost.   Thetis persuades Achilles to reconcile with Agamemnon, and Briseis is returned. She sees Patroclus's body and is deeply moved. She recounts how, when she was captured, Patroclus protected her and agreed to arrange her marriage to Achilles. She is wracked with grief for him. Nothing, however, compares with the grief of Achilles. After he has his revenge on Hector, and Hector's corpse, Achilles holds funeral games for his friend as for a king. The ghost of Patroclus visits him, prophesies Achilles' death beneath the walls of Troy, and asks that they be buried together in the same barrow. Achilles begs the vanishing shade to stay and weep with him, but he arranges the burial as requested. He causes a great funeral pyre to be built, and sacrifices twelve noble Trojan captives on it to appease his friend's shade.

> Achilles, like a father robbed by death
> of his own new-wed son, wailed for his friend.
> He burned the bones, and paced with heavy tread
> and ceaseless groans around the funeral pyre.

Achilles has not killed his friend as Cúchulainn did Ferdia, but he was responsible for his death. He sent Patroclus to die in his place and so must die in recompense. So let us move on to a truly Christian version of the theme, but still in a warrior setting full of pagan overtones and derivations.

Le Morte D'Arthur

Sources. We have already met Malory in Chapter 6 with the story of Mordred. Here we must put that substory into the context of the plot involving the Knights of the Round Table and the fall of Camelot. Sir Thomas Malory's *Le Morte D'Arthur* (published by Caxton in 1485—*Morte Darthur* in the original) is the best known of the medieval romances, and was indeed a mélange of material from the French romance writers, recreated by Malory. The material circulated freely among medieval authors. Geoffrey of Monmouth took generously from the Welsh *Mabinogion* (with its tales of "Gwenhwyvar") for his *Historia Regnum Britanniae,* which in turn was used by the French, who in turn supplied the basis for Malory's exquisite recreation. Our own age remembers it best for the themes of the Holy Grail, particularly as in Wagner's *Parsifal,* and more popularly for the love triangle of Arthur-Launcelot-Guinever (or Guinevere, as she is now rendered), with the Lerner and Loew *Camelot* as perhaps its best vernacular rendition.

The Real Triangle and Morgause. We, however, must look at another triangle: that of Arthur-Gawaine-Launcelot, in the setting of the quintessential male band: the Knights of the Round Table. In the modern retellings Gawaine tends to get lost, or even become a villain, yet he is from the start Arthur's most constant companion, and is with him to the end. He is, of course, Arthur's nephew, the son of Arthur's sister Morgause, Queen of Orkney, and King Lot. By an irony that haunts the tale, Arthur slept with Morgause without knowing she was his sister, thus begetting Mordred. The same woman gave birth both to Arthur's boon companion, his most loyal friend, and to Gawaine's half brother, who is to bring about Arthur's ruin, and who is Arthur's son. The cast is large and sometimes hard to follow. I will reproduce the genealogy of Arthur's kindred here, adding a few new characters to help keep it straight (Figure 8.1).

Morgause, except in some modern feminist versions, also tends to get lost in the retellings. But she is crucial: she is at once enabling in supplying nephews who aid Arthur, and at the same time ultimately disabling in supplying both a nephew/son who is Arthur's nemesis, and another

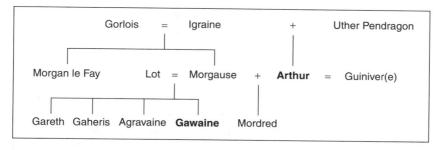

Figure 8.1 The kin of Arthur

nephew, Agravaine, who aids and abets Mordred in his plotting. Indeed, insofar as Gawaine's intransigence toward Launcelot prolongs the civil war and prevents reconciliation between the parties, the sons of Morgause can be seen as centrally effective in the doom of Camelot. (In the end she is killed by her son Gaheris when caught *in flagrante* with her lover.) Add that Gawaine's ultimate hatred of Launcelot stems from the latter's unwitting killing of two other brothers, sons of Morgause (Gareth and Gaheris) when rescuing Guinever. Morgause herself actively pursues a hatred of Arthur, as does his other half sister, Morgan le Fay, who at various points in the plot betrays almost everyone.

Which Way the Women?   The women mostly, wittingly or unwittingly, serve to disable the bonds between the knights. The Lady Ettarde betrays Gawaine and Pelleas, who had "plighted their troth" to each other. Pelleas leaves her for Nimue, the Lady of the Lake (Launcelot's foster mother), who had previously been the cause of Merlin's desertion of Arthur, which ended with Merlin being tricked and imprisoned in a rock. But in "The Book of Sir Gareth," Dames Linet and Lyones are both directly enabling, succoring Gareth and helping to establish him as one of the knightly company. Linet prevents Gareth and Gawaine from unwittingly killing each other. These women stand in sharp contrast to Morgan and Morgause. Others, like Elaine and Guinever, do not actively seek to disrupt the male bonds but because of their drawing power become the cause of the dissolution. One way or another the band of knights, bonded through battle and ritual, is threatened by either female attractiveness or female manipulation.

Launcelot, Tristram, and Marke.   Though Gawaine dominates the early books, later he is replaced by Launcelot du Lake, who becomes the focus of male and female attraction. Launcelot gains the undying loyalty of the band, and is especially close to both Arthur and Gawaine. He pledges devotion to Guinever, but then so have all the knights, and it is not at this point an obvious problem, but part of the chivalric devotion to the married "lady."

The relationships become dense and complicated, particularly with the advent of Tristram (Wagner's Tristan), and we must forgo the details. Let us simply note that relations between Tristram, his maternal uncle King Marke, and Launcelot and Galahad, are destroyed by Tristram's love of Marke's wife, and leave it there as a reprise of the theme of the disabling woman. In my version of the opera this would have its own leitmotif.

Morgan Strikes Again.   Later, when Tristram returns, there is a reconciliation and Tristram is finally made a knight of the Round Table. But in his triumph there is another foreshadowing of disaster when Morgan le Fay, in one of her ongoing plots, gives him a shield with a painted device that is intended to reveal to Arthur the liaison between Launcelot and Guinever. She then combines with Marke to send letters to Arthur with the same accusations. The plot fails but the accusations fester.

Women and Madness.   The general theme so far is that the knights recruit new members to the band, usually through a fight or a trial of adventures. They swear eternal loyalty and watch each other's back, but at some point a woman actively or passively breaks up the bond, and there is disaster for the male group. Thus both Tristram and Launcelot are driven mad by their conflicts over women. Tristram wanders in the woods, and the other knights go after him to bring him back to sanity. The conflict between Guinever and Elaine (Elaine, the mother of Galahad—see Figure 8.2) drives Launcelot into the same predicament until the knights rescue him. The guys are relentless in their efforts to save one another from the results of breakdowns induced by heterosexual feelings, which predicament is beautifully parodied in *Monty Python and the Holy Grail.*

Percivale and the Grail.   The episode of *The Book of Galahad* is very much a father–son story, in which Galahad and Launcelot fight each other without knowing they are father and son, like Sohrab and Rustum. Percivale (Parsifal) is harder to place in the story. He is very much a loner on his Grail quest. His parents are not named; in the legends he is "The Son of the Widow"—a title familiar to all Freemasons. His mother saves his life by taking him into the forest (like Sieglinde). A clue to his identity lies in the fact that his unnamed sister is the bearer of the Holy Grail, an office that is reserved for a member of the Grail family. So their mother could have been the sister of the Fisher King, the keeper of the Grail (Pelles in Malory) who had no children of his own. This would be another example of the sacred bond with the maternal uncle, and would mean that Percivale could be Galahad's maternal cousin as well as Launcelot's in-law. All the legends see Percivale as a member of the Grail family without spelling out the details, which I attempt to do in Figure 8.2.

The Vision and the Quest. After the vision of the Grail and Arthur's pledge to search for the holy vessel, the knights go off on their almost wholly individual quests. It is as if the Christian idea of individual salvation is inimical to the pagan ideal of the male bond. Even so, Percivale and Bors are with Galahad at his achievement of the Grail. Galahad and Percivale die, and Launcelot receives Bors (who is his paternal cousin—Figure 8.2) into eternal brotherhood. Equally, Launcelot and Gareth (Figure 8.1) are firm in their loyalty to each other; Gareth saves Launcelot's life, and Launcelot makes Gareth a knight. Thus Malory carefully sets up the male alliances that are to be sundered.

Arthur, Launcelot, and Guinever. The ingenious Malory has carefully held the issue of Guinever and Launcelot in suspense since, several books ago, Marke and Morgan sent their accusatory letters. Now it all starts to come apart when the news is out. The nephews of Arthur divide over the issue. Agravaine and Mordred are for action against the lovers, while Gawaine and Gareth swear loyalty to Launcelot, who saved their lives, and, they point out, the lives of the plotters. Heedless, Agravaine and Mordred persuade Arthur to agree to trap Launcelot into going to the

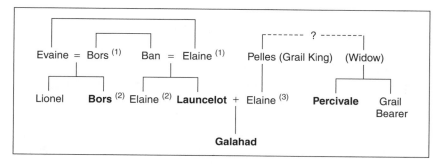

Figure 8.2   The kin of Launcelot. Nimue (The Lady of the Lake) was Launcelot's foster mother. Elaine was the name of Launcelot's mother, sister, and wife (at least the woman who ravished him to produce Galahad) and also of the Lady (of Shallot) who died for love of him.

queen's chamber, and there they surprise him. While making his escape, Launcelot kills Agravaine and twelve knights.

Arthur demands Guinever's death by fire, for treason. Gawaine, still bound in friendship to Launcelot at this point, pleads the innocence of the lovers and refuses to be Guinever's executioner. His brothers Gaheris and Gareth submit to Arthur's command but refuse to bear arms at the execution (as do many other knights). Launcelot with his partisans rides to Guinever's rescue and, without recognizing them, kills the unarmed Gareth and Gaheris. Launcelot takes Guinever to his castle of Joyous Gard.

The Final Battle.   The band of knights is thoroughly severed now, between Arthur and Gawaine and their supporters on the one side, and Launcelot with his cousins Bors and Lionel and their kin on the other (Figure 8.2). The killing of his brothers has rendered Gawaine cold with fury against Launcelot. Launcelot is devastated that he has killed Gareth in particular, and protests his innocence of intent, but to no avail. Arthur wavers and is always ready to find some compromise, but Gawaine is adamant. In the battle, Bors wounds Arthur, but Launcelot will not let his cousin kill the king.

Arthur weeps with misery that he must fight Launcelot. At the pope's intervention (not usually mentioned in modern versions), Launcelot gives up Guinever, but at Gawaine's insistence the war continues. The loyalists leave off fighting Launcelot to take on the traitor Mordred, who has imprisoned the queen and threatened to "marry" her. In this battle, Gawaine himself is mortally wounded. Arthur holds his dying friend and laments:

> Alas, my sister's son, here now thou liest, the man in the world that I loved the most; and now is my joy gone. For now, my nephew, Sir Gawaine, I will discover me unto your person: in Sir Launcelot and you I most had my joy and mine affiance, and now I have lost my joy of you both, wherefore all my earthly joy is gone from me.

The Death of Arthur and Gawaine.   Gawaine on his deathbed writes an eloquent letter of reconciliation to Launcelot, taking upon himself the blame for prolonging the conflict and begging Launcelot, "for all the love that ever was between us," to come over and help Arthur against Mordred. In particular he asks his friend to visit his tomb and pray for him. Launcelot does these things, and he and Guinever, in contrition, become hermits. But he is too late to stop Mordred and Arthur from killing each other. In the boat with three queens, including his now-mourning sister Morgan le Fay, and with Nimue, the Lady of Lake, Arthur is borne away to the Isle of Avalon. Thus in the end the women are there to tend to the man they harmed so much, and to bear him away from Camelot and his knights forever.

Chivalry and the Love Interest.   We still see Malory through the spectacles of Romanticism, and see the main issue as the "love interest"—with all the stuff about chivalry and knights and adventures and quests and battles as somehow secondary. But if we shake off this miasma and take a fresh look, what we see as central are the chivalry and the deep emotional and even spiritual bonds between the knights. The love interest is intrusive and destructive of this sacred bond. It is not clear that Arthur loves Guinever nearly as much as he loves Gawaine and Launcelot. He would have burned Guinever (and certainly without any trial) for causing the destruction of the Round Table, but he could not kill Launcelot, and Launcelot could not kill him. Arthur–Gawaine–Launcelot is the bonded triad around which the story moves, and the destruction of this basic male bond by the power of heterosexual attraction is the heart of the tragedy.

Chanson de Roland

Sources.   The continental romances (France, Spain, Portugal, Italy, and Germany) from the twelfth to the sixteenth century, some preceding and some deriving from Malory, are replete with the same themes. Most are totally forgotten now, even though *Amadis de Gaul* was wildly popular: the "James Bond" series of its time. (Some fifty *Amadis* novels were written, according to the commentator Hope Moncrief.) It is enshrined in *Don Quixote* as the exemplary romance, taken as his chivalric model by the Don. In its first English translation, by Anthony Munday (1590–1595), it influenced Shakespeare, Sidney, and many other writers.

In the translation by the poet Robert Southey, this story, probably Portuguese in origin, became popular in early nineteenth-century England. Amadis has the classical retinue of foster brothers and long-lost brothers, the romantic attachment, Oriana, the fantastic adventures in which disabling females seduce the favorite brother Galaor, and an enabling female, Urganda the Unknown, who seems modeled on the Lady of the Lake.

Roland and Charlemagne.   But the best-known romance is certainly the *Chanson de Roland,* and again the theme is the friendship unto death of Roland and Oliver. Roland probably was a historical warrior in the retinue of Charlemagne. He is mentioned briefly in a history as "Hruodlandus," and his death at Roncesvaux in AD 778 is noted. He was killed by Basques, not Saracens as in the *Chanson,* and Basque ballads sung to this day celebrate his death as the "the darling of king Karloman" (Charlemagne's brother). In the romances he is, as we have come to expect, the son of Charlemagne's sister.

Some sources hint that like Mordred he was the product of incest. There are many versions of his youth, told in *Chansons de Geste* other than *Roland* (summarized in Hope Moncrieff), but all agree that Bertha, the sister, was estranged from her brother (because of the incest?) and that Roland had to win his way back into his uncle's favor. Like Cúchulainn he has a precocious childhood, then performs mighty deeds to impress his uncle, and is returned to favor.

Roland, Oliver, and Ganelon.   He meets Oliver in the traditional way, through combat. Oliver's uncle, Duke Girard, is in contention with the emperor, and they agree to fight by champions. Charlemagne nominates Roland, who has fallen in love with Oliver's sister, Alda. They fight until exhausted, then they embrace and swear undying friendship. The quarrel between their uncles is made up and Roland marries Alda, who was much mentioned between them during the fight. Because love of her has softened Roland's heart toward his opponent, she can be seen as the *enabling* female in the relationship.

The pair has, however, made a great enemy in Ganelon, Roland's stepfather (Figure 8.3). He is the Mordred of the tale, and works for everyone's destruction. He was at the time the most hated figure in Europe for his treachery, more hated than Judas. Dante places him in the lowest depths of the inferno. Just how his relationship to Bertha, Roland's mother, makes him hate his stepson so is not explained. But in the end his treachery brings about their death in the famous episode of the Pass of Roncevaux/Roncesvalles.

Ganelon's Treachery.   Charlemagne is withdrawing from his war with the Moors in Spain because the Saracen king Marsilius had promised

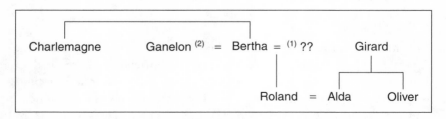

Figure 8.3   The kin of Roland

submission. Ganelon is chosen as ambassador to the Saracens to negotiate the terms of the peace. The choice was made at Roland's mocking suggestion, because, he says, Ganelon is "prudent and a man of peace." Ganelon enters into a conspiracy with Marsilius to ambush the rearguard, urging that by eliminating Roland he will reduce Charlemagne's power to wage war. Back at the emperor's camp Ganelon reports that Marsilius is to be trusted, and urges that Roland (and hence Oliver) be given the place of honor in charge of the rearguard, with the flower of French chivalry.

The Death of Roland and Oliver. Caught in the ambush, outnumbered twenty to one, they fight to the death. Oliver begs Roland to sound his horn to summon the main army, but Roland is too proud. Oliver, like Patroclus with Achilles, hotly rebukes him for sacrificing so many to his pride; Roland relents and, when it is too late, finally sounds it, "not for succor, but for vengeance." Charles hears the horn, but Ganelon insists that Roland is hunting. Finally they go back to the pass and find Roland, Oliver, and all the French knights dead, including the warrior-cleric, Archbishop Turpin.

The Grief of the Heroes. In the manner of the great epics, the heroes are dramatic in their grief for the loss of a "companion." In the poignant lines of the original (Bédier's edition):

> Rollant li ber a pluret, sil duleset;
> Jamais en tere n'orrez plus dolent hume.

"The brave Roland wept and lamented; never has the world known a more sorrowful man." In what is perhaps the best English translation, Dorothy L. Sayers renders Roland's grief:

> Sir, my companion, woe worth your valiant might!
> Long years and days have we lived side by side,
> Ne'er didst thou wrong me nor suffer wrong of mine.
> Now thou art dead I grieve to be alive.

Charlemagne's grief is even more ecstatic. He swoons and falls, weeps and tears out his white hair:

> All my life in sorrow I must reign,
> Nor any day cease grieving and complaint.

It is, I think, not an entirely subjective sensation that the vowel-rhymes of the original, so well rendered into English here, give a constantly melancholy, echoing feel to the verse. After much fighting and talking, the Saracens are defeated and destroyed, and Ganelon is torn apart by four wild horses. All France mourns the two heroes, and at the news of their death, Alda herself drops dead. In other versions, like Guinever she becomes a nun. There is no directly *disabling* female in the story, but the evil Ganelon comes into it through his relationship to Roland's mother, who thus passively introduces the traitor and may be reckoned disabling on that account.

Foster Brothers and Companions.   In her incisive commentary, Sayers offers us a picture of "nurture and companionage" in the poem. The first we have already come across in the fostering of Achilles and Patroclus, and Cúchullain and Ferdia. Boys thus fostered together became "companions." This relationship was very strong, overshadowing blood relationship. The Twelve Peers who accompanied Roland and Oliver and died with them, she notes, are always given in pairs: Gerin and Gerier, Ives and Ivor, Orthon and Berenger, and so on. "Intimacy and friendly rivalry," she says, prevailed through life, and, as the poem's great moments show, led to massive grief after death: grief of one companion for another, and of the foster father for them both.

The Volsunga Saga

The Failed Bond.   We looked at the earliest part of *The Volsunga Saga* in Chapter 6 with regard to the incestuous relationship of Sigmund and Signy/Sieglinde. In this section, in the interests of fairness, I am taking up the story where we left off, because it turns into an epic about a male-bonding disaster. It is thus a test case: *Why does the male bonding fail?* All the epics celebrate the individual deeds of the heroes, but some, like the Nordic tales of the Volsungs and Niblungs, stand out in their individualism. They also, like the Irish epics and unlike the Greek, have strong, even dominant, female characters.

The twelfth-century saga of the Volsungs, in both its prose and its verse versions (the *Eddas*), is usually taken to be "about" the hero Sigurd (Wagner's Siegfried). Yet perhaps it could more easily be seen to be the story of his second wife, Gudrun, and her fatal relationships with her mother, Grimhild, and the warrior maiden Brynhild (Figure 8.4). As in all the epics, there is no female bonding in evidence. The women are either passively attached to their males or fiendishly plotting against each other

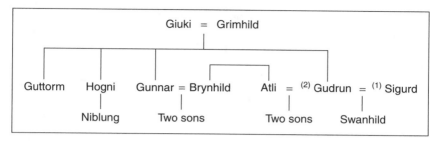

Figure 8.4   The Giukings, or Niblungs

to destroy them. Thus the story of the Volsungs is "about" male bonding that never gets off the ground. Let us see why.

Sigurd and Brynhild.   Sigurd, the son of Sigmund, has his whole future told to him by his mother's brother Grifir. Fortunately the author does not tell us what this is, although throughout the tale various people, usually the wives, foretell the future, which is, of course, fixed by fate. Sigurd forms an early alliance with Regin the smith. But Regin is using Sigurd to kill his brother Fafnir, who had been turned into a dragon to guard a treasure horde. After killing Fafnir, Sigurd kills Regin. He then braves the Ring of Fire to find Brynhild, who gives him a love potion and they swear eternal love. The poet of the *Edda* gives the women by far the best verse, as when Brynhild sings to Sigurd of the power of words, of runes—sea-runes, ale-runes, help-runes, bough-runes, thought-runes.

Sigurd and the Niblungs.   The plot thickens as Sigurd finds his way to the Giukings (or Niblungs). King Giuki and Queen Grimhild have three sons, Gunnar, Hogni, and Guttorm, and a daughter, Gudrun (Figure 8.4). As the poet puts it:

> Sigurd of yore,
> Sought the dwelling of Giuki,
> As he fared, the young Volsung,
> After fight won;
> Troth he took,
> From the two brethren;
> Oath swore they betwixt them,
> Those bold ones of deed.

Note that the oath was sworn with only two of the brothers, Gunnar and Hogni; Guttorm must have been thought too young. Grimhild wants to have Sigurd for her daughter, Gudrun, so she gives him yet another potion, which makes him forget Brynhild, and the two are married. Then, true to his oath, Sigurd sets out to help his blood brother, Gunnar, find a bride, who is of course Brynhild. Using his magic helmet Sigurd takes the form of Gunnar, rides through the fire, and wins Brynhild, who has sworn to marry the man that did so. Thus is the recipe for disaster set, for once Brynhild and Gunnar are married, in true soap opera fashion, Sigurd's memory returns.

The Murder of Sigurd.   Gudrun is disturbed by Sigurd's love for Brynhild and reveals to her the truth about her wooing. Brynhild is furious and distraught. She wants revenge, and persuades Gunnar to break his oath and, with Hogni, kill Sigurd.

But the henpecked brothers find a way out: Guttorm has not sworn the oath, so he can creep up in the night and kill Sigurd, who in turn kills him before dying. The first "Lay of Gudrun"—her lamentation over the body of Sigurd, is interesting in that her female relatives gather to give her support and rebuke Brynhild, who, at the top of her voice, commits suicide, foretelling the rest of the tale with her dying words. She demands to be burnt on a pyre with Sigurd, which is done.

There Sigurd's story ends. His promising bond with the Giukings is brought to nothing by the machinations of Grimhild and the fury of Brynhild. But Grimhild is not done. She engineers the marriage of Gudrun to Brynhild's brother Atli, who covets Fafnir's horde of gold. Atli tricks Gudrun's brothers to come to his hall, and after a furious fight captures and kills them horribly: Hogni's heart is torn out while he lives, and Gunnar is fed to snakes, in the original "worm-hole." Gudrun smuggles a harp to him, and playing it with his toes, he charms all the snakes but the fatal one.

Gudrun's Revenge.   Gudrun fights along with her brothers, but cannot save them, and vows vengeance on Atli. She has two sons by him, whom she kills and, Medea-like, feeds to him. Along with Hogni's son Niblung she kills Atli. Her story ends the book, as with the sons of a third marriage she avenges the death of Swanhild, her daughter with Sigurd (named after her paternal aunt) who was trampled to death by horses. Finally Odin, who had started the saga, ends it by ordering the death of the last of the Giukings.

Which Way the Women?   These are the barest bones of the plot of this primeval soap opera. Wagner makes up his own version for the rest of the Ring—*The Twilight of the Gods*—but he does not change the fundamentals as regards the male bonding. We can see that the themes we have been exploring are all there. Sigurd tries to form a "normal" male bond with the Giuking brothers. They swear their oaths and go through the by-now familiar routines. But the women sabotage the bond. Grimhild and Brynhild are the archetypes of disabling females.

The mother seeks to advance the reproductive interests of her daughter, and Brynhild is thwarted in pursuit of her own. Gudrun, on the other hand, even though manipulated by her mother, is loyal to Sigurd, and even to her treacherous brothers, and is effective in organizing her kinsmen for revenge against Atli and the killers of Sigurd's daughter. Gudrun sacrifices her own reproductive interests by killing her sons by Atli. In however convoluted a way—and this is a splendidly convoluted plot—the valiant Gudrun has to be counted an enabling female, and her selfless devotion contrasts dramatically with Brynhild's egregious self-concern.

A Test Case.   For enthusiasts of male bonding, this is a disappointing saga, but it is an interesting test case for our hypothesis. The great lays of lamentation, the fine poetry (like the Hell Ride of Brynhild), the massive grief and furious verse of deprivation belong to the women. The men, though brave warriors, are dim and malleable. Gunnar and Hogni die bravely, but their spineless treason to their blood brother, at a woman's instigation, leaves the male bond in tatters. *The bonding of the males is always threatened by the competing interests of the females:* the females as lovers, wives, and mothers. It is to these two sides of the equation that we must now turn.

Male Sympathies: Female Strategies

If Tiger is correct about the adaptational significance of the male bond, we are dealing with something other than just male friendship. For what is being argued is that the strength of feeling men have for each other is the equivalent in intensity and specificity of the sexual feeling men have for women, or the feelings parents have for their children. That is to say, this *menschkeit*, these "male sympathies" as we used to say in college brochures, are a genuine, specific human need. What we see in the epics and romances is that in a warrior society these emotions will be particularly favored and reinforced, because of the warrior's crucial need for dependable male support. It is literally a matter of life and death: males who bond will have allies they can trust; it is that simple.

What comes out from these examples above perhaps anything else is this intensity of emotional attachment, and the terrible grief engendered by the death of a companion. The cultural situations are completely different from Sumer to Camelot, but they have this desperate and passionate sense of loss in common. Helen Fisher (2004) describes the chemistry of rejected love, or the loss of a loved one, as an upsurge of dopamine and norepinephrine (and a drop in serotonin) driven by the caudate nucleus of the brain, leading to (in succession) protest, separation anxiety, abandonment rage, and finally resignation and despair. She is writing of heterosexual love, but it could just as well describe the emotions of our heroes when they suffer the loss of a companion.

This raises the question of whether the male bond in these cases involves physical homosexuality. The answer is that it may or may not. There can certainly be literary versions of the bond that sound very much like homoerotic passion. Who could doubt that this was the case with, for example, Antonio and Sebastian in *Twelfth Night*, or the other Antonio and Bassanio in *The Merchant of Venice* (Hamill 2005). This, though, runs along with heterosexual attachments. Certainly there was physical sexuality between males in classical Greece and Rome, with the qualification, noted by Paul Veyne (1982), that the passive position in the partnership could be assumed only by an inferior. We are well aware that in Greece, marriage, while a duty and even a pleasure, often took second place to the physical love between men.

But Socrates and his friends in the *Symposium*, taking the middle ground, poked fun equally at men who were totally uxorious and those who were preoccupied solely with boys. In some cases the erotic bond between males was indeed used to strengthen the warrior group, as with the famous and formidable "Sacred Band" of Thebes: 300 paired lovers sworn to defend each other to the death. Homoerotic attachment certainly was there, but it was rarely dichotomized as it is today between "gay" and "straight"—with "bisexual" to account for those who can't be so pigeonholed. Homosexuality in Western history was seen more as a mode of experience than as a type of personality (it was what you *did*, not what you *were*), and everyone was capable of it. The legal punishments were not for homosexuality but for homosexual *acts* (sodomy). In the end we cannot *reduce* the male bonding of warrior companions to homosexual attraction.

Something else, something even more basic than physical homosexuality, is involved. This is perhaps only doubtful to those who have not served actively in wars and been through repeated battle experiences. The depth of emotional attachment between men of the same platoon or company who have shared terrifying experiences and risked their lives for each other is real and always moving. It may not these days be expressed in powerful epic verse—it probably never was, this was the contribution of the poets. But no one who has witnessed the reunion of those baptized together in fierce battle, or seen the tears shed over fallen comrades, can doubt that this is one of the most powerful emotional bonds known to us.

There is certainly no evidence in the text of the *Iliad* that Achilles and Patroclus were lovers. There does not seem to be any suggestion that Malory meant us to see the Arthurian knights as homosexual. Indeed, a major part of their problem was the strength of their *heterosexual* attachments, which were fatal to the male group, as was also the case with the Volsungs, where the male bond completely succumbed to the interests and passions of the women. Those contemporary critics who see all literary instances of male affection for males as proof of "repressed homosexuality" have the same problem as other conspiracy theorists: their hypothesis is invulnerable to disproof; we have no way of knowing if they are wrong. The safer view surely is that the male bond could *involve* sex, but it was not *about* sex, as the bond with the female was. Without sex between male and female there could be no reproduction, but the male group reproduces first by recruitment (knighthood is a kind of cloning)— only secondarily by sex.

Sons, for example, are rare in these stories. Galahad is an interesting exception, but even there, Launcelot's bonds with Arthur, Tristram, Gareth, and Gawaine are stronger than his bond with his son. The typical relationship between males of different generations is between a man and his foster father, and a man and his mother's brother—who can be one and the same. A son, particularly one like Mordred who can pass as a maternal nephew, is a dubious blessing. Foster brothers often are preferred to real brothers, and most often the bonds are between two strangers who fight and then embrace each other for life. Someone you have tested is a known quantity.

Insofar as this classical bonding binds males who are not related, it cannot be explained by inclusive fitness theory alone. This would handle the maternal uncle, perhaps, but not the "companions." It is rather perhaps an elementary instance of what Trivers in 1971 called "reciprocal altruism," in which genetic strangers are assimilated to kinship roles, typically through the device of fostering. Fostering might seem at first to pose the same problem as sterile castes in insects. Why should anyone invest in someone else's genes? It works, however, as long as everyone does it: I raise your sons; you raise mine.

The other great theme in the epics and romances is the subordinate but often fatal role of the female, and the strife between the needs of the hetero-sexual bond and the male–male bond. The women, as we have seen, play either beneficial roles, like Shamhat, Ninsun, Wealhtheow, Thetis, and Gu-drun, passively destructive roles like Helen, Briseis, or Guinever, or posi-tively disabling roles like Ishtar, Medh, Morgan le Fay, Grimhild, Brynhild, and Grendel's mother. The women's complex qualities and characters are certainly not exhausted by the distinctions that lie along the enabling–disabling continuum. But we are looking rather narrowly at their function vis-à-vis the male bond. For the epic poets, the women revolve around the male bond and make sense to the structure of the epic only if we see them as creating situations that affect the bond for good or evil.

In contrast to the men, the women in the epics do not bond with each other. On the contrary, they are either passively attached to a male or, more usually, locked in conflict over a male, or seeking to advance the interests of their offspring at the expense of males. It is not that women cannot appear as towering figures in these stories; they do so, in all their wonder, from Ishtar, through Medh, to Brynhild. But they do not appear as female bands, and they do not form female-bonded groups. The earls' wives who gather to support Gudrun and rebuke Brynhild are the near-est thing we get, however transient, to an active female group. In Wag-ner's version the Valkyrie are kind of a bonded female group, but they are totally subservient to Wotan, and when they do disobey him it is to pro-tect the mother–child unit of Sieglinde and her unborn baby, Siegfried. If the men in these epics fear the women, it is as they love them: as indi-viduals, not as cabals or as female conspiracies.

The need for males to bond may be part of the hard wiring of behav-ior, but this should not be confused with "determinative." Only the need is programmed; the form that the bonding will take will vary with the external circumstances, as is the case with the heterosexual bond, and as is indeed the case with all genotypes in nature: the phenotype is always problematical. This is where the literary interest lies: in the twists and turns of strategy that the characters display in trying to meet the need in their peculiar local circumstances. Thus the need for males to bond with each other as strongly as they bond with females, if not more so, is clearly most obvious in warrior societies, like those of the epics. But is it simply an artifact of those societies, disappearing under conditions of trade and peace? Would the literature of less warlike soci-eties reflect the same themes? I think the answer is that it does, but of course the emphases and outcomes will be different. This is the subject of another investigation.

I have committed myself to the view that the bond, being a genuine need, will persist. Although the details may differ, it will continue to find its place, often through comedy and gentle satire (see the contemporary sitcom *Two and a Half Men*) in the literature and drama of societies far removed from the warrior ideal. And even in these increasingly androgynous societies, the warrior virtues, and the male bonding that goes with them, often continue to get a lively representation in literature and the arts, the popular media, and even (or especially) in sports. It is at the heart of the success of the *Godfather* novels and movies, where women appear only as subordinated wives, rebellious sisters, mistresses, and whores.

It is part of the enormous appeal of Patrick O'Brian's *Master and Commander* series. It received eloquent treatment in the superb but under-appreciated remake of the bible of aristocratic male honor, *The Four Feathers*, where the men's duty and attachment to each other, even unto death, far outweigh their attachment to the undoubtedly attractive female. She is in fact, as we might expect, a major cause of conflict to the male group. In *The Man Who Would Be King*, Sean Connery and Michael Caine gave perhaps the most perfect rendition of the theme, through Kipling's story of two ordinary British soldiers, bonded through Freemasonry and vaunting ambition. To reinforce the bond, they foreswear women until such time as they conquer a trans-Himalayan nation, only to have the desire for a woman (a passively disabling woman) bring them down and lose them their hard-won kingdom.

The current fuss over Mary Magdalene and her true role in the life of Christ, inspired by *The Da Vinci Code*, misses the point that whatever her marital status, in the plot of the epics that are the gospels, she was a source of disruption to the male band of the Apostles. *Jesus Christ Superstar* portrayed this very well. The reader will no doubt be thinking of many other examples, including two remarkable recent films, Richard Attenborough's *Closing the Ring*, in which an enabling female bonds the men even beyond death, and Anders Thomas Jensen's *Flickering Lights*, in which a disabling female threatens but fails to break the bond between four Danish childhood friends.

A safe evolutionary prediction would be this: *Although social conditions may cause the male bond to be muted, they will never extinguish it.* As the current saying goes: "It's a guy thing."

CHAPTER NINE

Playing by the Rules

Savage Rhythms and Civilized Rhymes

W E NEVER LOSE anything in evolution. In its saga of growth and control, the brain continually added new structures and incorporated and reconnected the old: all those that had helped it adapt as a sea creature, an amphibian, a reptile, a mammal, a primate, an ape, a hominid, and then, and for now, a human being.

Stemming from the Brain

The brain began as an organizing blob on the front end of sea creatures with primitive central nervous systems. With the earliest reptiles its most simple elements, the *brain stem (pons, medulla)* and *cerebellum,* which remain essential to our functioning, were in place. Without them we could neither breathe nor move, and certainly not move in a coordinated way. Even with the transition to the mammals, the *olfactory bulb* and the sense of smell remained central. The old mammalian brain—the *limbic system*—connected up the major equipment of the *hypothalamus* and *thalamus* (for basic bodily functions) with the *amygdala* for emotions and the *hippocampus* for memory. The neurochemicals serotonin and dopamine were produced by a reward system, the *nucleus accumbens,* both to calm the organism and bring it pleasure in performance.

This was the old cortex (the paleomammalian brain), and it worked for 62 million years or so; it is the basis of our appetites and pleasures. Then one group of tree-living mammals, having developed grasping hands and binocular color vision (and a diminution of the sense of smell), began to spend more time on the ground. These were the apes, and they had a rudimentary new cortex—a *neocortex,* that took some control of the old and reorganized it yet again. The brain's two hemispheres (left and right) began to take on different functions, and the *corpus callosum* that connected them grew thicker to make sure they still acted in concert. Then some of the tree-livers took to the ground permanently, stood upright, and walked on two legs. Within 1.5 million years their brains tripled in size and complexity, mainly in the frontal lobes. This process was by evolutionary standards very rapid, and the result is still problematical.

The new brain with its expanded *prefrontal cortex* could plan for the future and take greater control of the mammalian emotions of these apes-becoming-men. But the old brain walked with them through the long Pleistocene drought, and it kept the new brain company, sometimes in subjection but mostly in partnership, and sometimes in revolt. Paul MacLean taught us to think of it as "the triune brain"—the new cortex enfolding the old mammalian cortex in turn enfolding the reptilian (Figure 9.1). Without the emotions of the old mammalian brain we are nothing; we have no motives; nothing moves us.

But life could have become stuck at this point without the advent of what we like to call an "emergent property"—or perhaps just another miracle. The made-over apes began to speak, to turn images into words, to communicate about things that were not immediately present. And

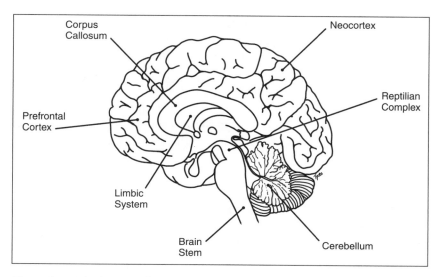

Figure 9.1   The brain so far (illustration by Joan Tycko)

this involved not just the specialized speech areas that developed in the left side of the new brain, but the whole ancient organ in a new concert. When we speak words, our whole brain resonates down to the most ancient and uncomprehending reptilian base. Some forms of speech, and particularly speech that was rhythmical and musical, and in fact easily turned into song, dug the deepest. Keep the brain in mind; we shall return to it.

Death, Breath, and Swinburne

I recently published a Shakespearean sonnet ("Life Is Too Short") with a terminal couplet rhyming "death" and "breath." For the sake of illustration I will give it all here.

> When we were young and all the world was green,
> We used to tell each other "Life's too short"—
> To justify our sins. We didn't mean
> It literally of course. Now we are caught
> In its stark literalness, and so we know
> (We wheezing, balding ones way past our prime,
> Whose memories melt away like last year's snow)
> The humorless reality of time:
> Of time foreshortened, of the loss of friends,
> Of old ambitions unfulfillable.
> We curse the destiny that shapes our ends,
> And 'til recorded time's last syllable
>> Confront, with shaking limbs and labored breath,
>> The loss of beauty and the fear of death.

The first line echoes Dylan Thomas; the seventh, François Villon; the eleventh and twelfth, Shakespeare; but the couplet at the end was suggested by none of these. Only once in the 154 sonnets (in Sonnet 99) does Shakespeare rhyme these two words. But there is of course always:

> Come away, come away, death,
> And in sad cypress let me be laid;
>> Fly away, fly away, breath;
> I am slain by a fair cruel maid.
> (Twelfth Night, Act II, scene iv)

Because we build our verses always, like Troy, on the remains of previous constructions, I was sure that I was echoing someone, and it must have been someone I knew and liked, of course. The rhyme is perhaps obvious, and often enough used; there are not many alternatives in English. But the poet who came through with the greatest insistence was the eccentric high Victorian, Algernon Charles Swinburne (1837–1909).

The aristocrat Swinburne shocked and titillated the prudish public of his day with his atheism, his republicanism, his sensuality, and his taste for flagellation developed as a schoolboy at Eton. Although not much read today, he was the most popular poet of his times and was considered one of the greatest verse technicians in English. The lines that leaped into my head were from a chorus in his verse-drama *Atalanta in Calydon*—surely one of the toughest statements of antifaith in any language:

> Because thy name is life and our name death;
> Because thou art cruel and men are piteous,
>   And our hands labour and thine hand scattereth;
> Lo, with hearts rent and knees made tremulous,
>   Lo with ephemeral lips and casual breath,
> At least we witness of thee ere we die
> That these things are not otherwise but thus;
>   That each man in his heart sigheth and saith,
>   That all men even as I,
> All we are against thee, against thee, O God most high.

Swinburne was not really an atheist. He believed in God, but he thought God was a terrorist: a genocidal torturer and killer of innocent civilians, and therefore morally inferior to his creation. God for Swinburne was a sadist. His gift of consciousness was a clever torment, for it meant the consciousness of death. Or at least that was the way Swinburne posed his atheism. He was the natural and very conscious heir of Shelley.

Swinburne was lucky to be writing in a poetic form that allowed, even demanded, the archaic verb forms "scattereth" and "saith" (pronounced "seth"); it doubled his chances of finding a rhyme for either "death" or "breath." Thus a little earlier in *Atalanta:*

> For now we know not of them; but one saith
>   The gods are gracious, praising God; and one
> When hast thou seen? Or hast thou felt his breath
>   Touch, nor consume thine eyelids as the sun,
> Nor fill thee to the lips with fiery death?

But most frequently he linked the one directly with the other—still earlier in *Atalanta:*

> And stir with soft imperishable breath
> The bubbling bitterness of life and death

These two lines stir those of us (how many?) who love and admire Swinburne, and to the others represent all they dislike about him. We can purr all we like about the alliteration and assonance in that first line and the brilliance of "bubbling bitterness" in the second, but when we add that this is the poet railing against the "high gods" and their sadistic toying with our intimations of mortality, we lose the *New Yorker* readership for good and all. Life and death and everything that rhymes and resonates with them are no longer suitable subjects for poetry. A sensitive reaction to one's own dysfunctional family relationships expressed in irregular lines of prose, on the other hand, is going to get editorial approval, and reader satisfaction.

Swinburne's most famous use of the rhyme is surely the lines from his "Hymn to Persephone." Speaking through a Roman pagan who has just heard Constantine's proclamation of the Christian faith as the official religion of Rome (AD 314), he declares his love of the usurped goddess and prophesies the end of the new faith in turn. The lines that shocked his contemporaries were:

> Thou hast conquered, O pale Gallilean; the world has grown grey
>   from thy breath.
> We have drunken of thing Lethean, and fed on the fullness of
>   death.
> Laurel is green for a season, and love is sweet for a day;
> But love grows bitter with treason, and laurel outlives not May.

I was at a dinner recently with a number of longtime *New Yorker* readers who thoroughly approved of the magazine's poetry selections. I did a little experiment. I recited the first Swinburne lines I quoted here (from *Atalanta*) and then asked any of them to recite as many lines from any poem in the *New Yorker* that they remembered. Not one of them could do it. I then asked them to recite anything they remembered, and they all had a bit of Poe, or Longfellow, or even W. H. Auden they could come up with. They didn't think it proved anything. "Memorability" said one disdainful lady critic, "is no longer a category that applies to poetry." How true.

Swinburne was not hampered by these advanced sensitivities and so could take on life, death and breath without embarrassment. I was first of all curious about just how often he had in fact done this in his huge output. The thin-paper two-volume copy of his collected works that I carry with me, not counting the index and frontmatter, runs to 1,278 pages. Someone must have done a count of lines: I estimate about 30 per page, which would give us roughly 38,350. Then came the pleasurable task of reading through to see how many times the rhyme was used (including the alternatives ending in -eth and the like).

I must admit up front that not all of Swinburne is pleasurable reading over the long haul. You have to be a real devotee (and I am) to plough diligently line-by-line through the "Memorial Verses on the Death of William Bell Scott" or the republican ramblings of "Ode on a Proclamation of the French Republic." But Swinburne shirked neither politics nor perversion, and verse was his medium. Because he could do anything he liked with verse, his "Heptalogia," where he pokes parodic fun at the poetic greats, including Browning, Tennyson, and Rossetti, is hilarious. But he is at his obvious best in the epic Arthurian company of "Tristram of Lyonesse" and "The Tale of Balen" and the Greeks in the aforementioned *Atalanta in Calydon* and *Erechtheus*—his true republican drama.

Anyway, reading patiently through, I culled 175 examples of the "death" rhyme. This count is a bit on the low side. As I read through I simply stuck a shred of paper in each page where the rhyme occurred, then flicked back through to count. Each shred marked a double page, of course, and sometimes there was more than one rhyme on the facing pages that I might have missed. I would go back through and double check, but that is perhaps a needless accuracy. But as an example of multiple uses of the rhyme in one poem we can look at the remarkable "double sestina" of "The Complaint of Lisa" (after Boccaccio's *Decameron*, x, 7). Here the same rhyme set is used over twelve 12-line stanzas and one 6-line epigraph, according to the strict rule of the double sestina (I don't remember seeing another example), which varies the rhyme placement in each stanza. It opens:

> There is no woman living that draws breath
> So sad as I, though all things sadden her.
> There is not one upon life's weary way
> Who is weary as I am weary of all but death.

The lady critic (she taught "creative writing" at one of those gray-zone colleges on the fringe of the Ivies) thought this last line a very bad line even in its own terms; it didn't scan as an iambic pentameter, for one thing. I pointed out that it is a common enough prosodic device to use dactyls to drag out a line for effect. Swinburne was aiming to show us Lisa's utter weariness and in fact did it to perfection. The critic felt Swinburne would have benefited from her creative writing class. We moved on. The final six-line stanza in which Lisa addresses her song itself:

> Song, speak to me who am dumb as are the dead;
> From my sad bed of tears I send forth thee,
> To fly all day from sun's birth to sun's death
> Down the sun's way after the flying sun,
> For love of her that gave thee wings and breath,
> Ere day be done, to seek the sunflower.

The sunflower has itself appeared in each stanza as regularly as death. But this gives us 13 such rhymes in one poem. I don't think we'll be far off to add another, say, 5 for the ones I missed, and count 180 such rhymes in total. This gives us a "death" rhyme, mostly with "breath" but also using "saith" and "altereth/transformeth/sickeneth/quickeneth" and other such archaisms. I get the feeling, and I will check this out, that the archaic verbs were used more in the Arthurian poetry than the rest, which makes sense; it sounds more medieval.

But our count reveals an average of a "death" rhyme every seven pages. If we go by lines, the 180 will have to be at least doubled, because of course a rhyme always involves at least two lines, often three or more (as with "The Complaint of Lisa"). Again let us estimate 400 for convenience. This gives us a "death" rhyme every 96 lines: 1.043 percent.

The reader might object that there is nothing unusual about this, given the lack of alternatives. So as a kind of control I picked at random from my shelf of poets the collected poems of John Donne (the Nonesuch edition). One would not perhaps expect the rhyme to crop up much in his love poems or satires, epistles, and epithalamions. You do not celebrate someone's marriage by reminding him of death. But then there is "The Anatomy of the World" and the "The Progresse of the Soul"—toward eternity—and the "Elegies" and "Divine Poems," including the famous "Death Be Not Proud," to which we shall return in the epilogue to this chapter. Surely the rhyme, if commonplace, should be used in these? It actually on my count occurs only three times in the whole body of Donne's verse. It is the more effective for being rare. In "Elegy IV: The Perfume" Donne describes being caught out in an affair by the father of the girl, who smells her perfume on him. He curses all perfume:

Base excrement of earth, which dost confound
Sense, from distinguishing the sick from sound;
By thee the seely Amorous sucks his death
By drawing in a leprous harlot's breath.

This was probably written during a time of plague (1590s) when perfume was used to cover up the smell of sickness. "Seely"—originally meaning "fortunate" or "happy" (as in Scilly Isles)—is modern "silly" but it could mean something like "naively foolish," as it seems to in this case *(OED)*.

In my edition, Donne has 234 pages of poetry, so his "death" rhyme would occur only once in eighty pages: a ratio of 1:80 compared with Swinburne's 1:7—more than ten times less. If we count Donne's lines at about 30 per page, he has roughly 10,700 lines. The "death" rhymes then come out at 0.056 percent of lines. The difference with Swinburne's 1.041 percent would satisfy any statistician as significant. The use of the "death" rhyme in Swinburne is then demonstrably deliberate, and might even seem excessive.

O Death! Making It Personal

Swinburne, like Webster, was much obsessed by death, and he too saw the skull beneath the skin. (See Phillip Henderson's *Swinburne* for the life of the poet.) One way to deal with death is to personify it, and he does this often, "O Death" being not uncommon. Perhaps the most moving example is in one of his later poems when he was contemplating his own demise, in the marvelous sequence "Dirae": the sonnet "Intercession," where the poet pleads with Death for a little more time. Even here, unlike our sensitive contemporaries, Swinburne unburdens himself through consideration of a persona: a gladiator. He prefixes his poem with the gladiatorial salutation: *"Ave Caesar Imperatur, moriturum te saluto."* Ah! But note how he changes it from the plural *(morituri salutant)* to the singular: changes from the collective to the individual. Swinburne never misses a trick.

It is worth quoting the sonnet in full, because my belief in the greatness of Swinburne, warts and all, stands or falls by it: if I am wrong about this, then I am totally wrong. Critics and commentators have not paid it much attention. If you can finish it without tears, then there is not the soul of poetry in you.

O Death, a little more, and then the worm;
  A little longer, O Death, a little yet,

Before the grave gape and the grave-worm fret;
Before the sanguine-spotted hand infirm
Be rottenness, and that foul brain, the germ
  Of all ill things and thoughts, be stopped and set;
  A little while, O Death, ere he forget,
A small space more of life, a little term;
A little longer ere he and thou be met,
  Ere in that hand that fed thee to thy mind
The poison-cup of life be overset;
  A little respite of disastrous breath,
  Till the soul lift up her lost eyes, and find
    Nor God nor help nor hope, but thee, O Death.

I would have pointed out to the creative-writing critic that Swinburne knew exactly when to use monosyllables, as in the last two lines, to soul-wearying effect, just as he knew how to break the strict iambic meter with "longer" to stress the word. I would have pointed out the metrical beauty of the last two lines, where the stress in the penultimate line falls irregularly on "soul" and "lost eyes" and then returns to crushing regularity in the final line, with the repetition of "nor" and the meeting with Death.

I could have, but she would certainly have doubted his "sincerity" or "authenticity" or both. "Poetry," she avowed, "has long-since freed itself from these contrivances." So it has. "It is the poetry of ordinary language." So it is. Useless then to point to his brilliance in the rhyming of six words with "yet" (including the eerie "grave-worm" fretting—consider the meanings of "fret" here) and four with "worm" before letting "mind" and "find" and of course "Death" and "breath" finish his rhyme-work. (This is not an exact Petrarchan sonnet; Swinburne extends the rhyme *-et* from the octave into the sestina.)

He could have used one of his favorite trilogies of rhyme, "fire/pyre/desire" to get the death job done. If rhyme were of no consequence to meaning, what difference would it make? But this alternative trilogy would have suggested a death ending in a Viking blaze of glory. Instead he chooses the crucial "worm" and the consequent "infirm," and so on, and hence the totally Poe-like anticipation of sordid bodily decay in the grave, which cannot possibly be heroic: a perfect example of the marriage of rhyme-sense and meaning that is central to the sonnet's heart cry, and to my argument.

Would the critic have noticed, I wonder, the stunning use of the subjunctive mood? This is not the poem of a Welshman raging against the dying of the light. Swinburne is an aristocrat facing death. His is a poem (in one sentence, which allows no letup of tension) that is a plea to Death for a stay of execution: a huge "What if?" (Remember Macbeth's "If it were done when 'tis done, then 'twere well / It were done quickly.") It is absolutely right, then, that its verbs be in the mood of the hypothetical future: the "might be." This use of the subjunctive enables the poet to rhyme "mind" with "find"—which would not have worked with the indicative "finds."

This is a poem of a man who has no comfort in the afterlife, who sees death steadily and sees it plain, who speaks without sentimentality of the decay of his living body and culpable brain, yet who with absolute humanness pleads for "A little respite of disastrous breath." If this is not one of the great sonnets in the English language, then I am at a loss to know what greatness is. Perhaps you have to be over seventy ("Old men, grey borderers on the march of death") to appreciate the emotion fully and pass the tear test, but anyone can appreciate the skill.

And it pushes to the forefront what I am struggling to say in this essay. The modern critic would see Swinburne's repeated use of the "death"/"breath" rhymes as artificial and constrictive and above all repetitive: "Hallmark Card versification," as my lady critic called it. To her, Swinburne stuck "death" and "breath" at the end of lines and then made up something to go in front of them: pretty much as bad lyric writers use "moon" and "June." Well, at his worst he was guilty of something like that, I admit: over 38,000 lines you are going to flag sometimes. And let us not forget he was writing volumes of (unpublished) flagellation verse, which must have stretched his imagination to the limits. Edith Sitwell, who loved Swinburne and produced one of the best anthology/criticisms, nevertheless was appalled by:

If you loved me ever so little,
  I could bear the bonds that gall,
I could dream the bonds were brittle;
  You do not love me at all.

"Deeply unfortunate," says Dame Edith, which is perhaps too kind. Hallmark usually does better. W. S. Gilbert in *Patience* pokes gentle fun at the Swinburne mannerisms:

Oh! to be wafted away,
From this black Aceldama of sorrow,
Where the dust of an earthy today
Is the earth of a dusty tomorrow.

(Aceldama was the Potters Field, for the burial of strangers, purchased by Judas's thirty pieces of silver.) But at his best he was dazzling. Back to *Atalanta* and the anger at God, and the breath/death theme:

> Thou hast kissed us, and hast smitten; thou hast laid
> Upon us with thy left hand life, and said,
> Live: and again thou hast said, Yield up your breath,
> And with thy right hand laid upon us death.

Notice that God's left hand gives life—as if to say he didn't really mean it: it was a sinister gesture, a cruel joke. His right hand, the hand of his so-called justice, deals the blow he meant for us all along. The anthropologist Robert Hertz in his study of universal symbolism, *Death and the Right Hand,* didn't read Swinburne, but he would have seen the point. And see the use of enjambment: it stops us in our tracks after "Live" and then God addresses us not with the familiar "thy" but with the plural and formal "your." These things were never accidental in Swinburne in top form; it was never a matter of what to shove in there before the inevitable rhyme. In one of the sexiest poems ever written he hits it again, and again the gladiatorial theme: the Empress Faustina adored gladiators:

> She loved the games men play with death,
>   Where death must win;
> As though the slain man's blood and breath
>   Revived Faustine.

This is the vampirical Faustine whom, in the epigraph to the poem, the gladiators salute in the correct Latin plural. Swinburne had this in mind when he used the singular in the death sonnet. And I can't resist the stanza that has my postadolescent female students shrieking with excitement to this day (the shadows of Baudelaire and de Sade hang heavily over Swinburne's verse):

> What adders came to shed their coats?
>   What coiled obscene
> Small serpents with soft stretching throats
>   Caressed Faustine?

Swinburne and his aesthetic friends suitably shocked their prudish (if prurient) Victorian audience, as they intended to do. This was "The Fleshly School of Poetry" after all. How can you beat his line from "Tristram"—

"And their four lips became one burning mouth." For what it's worth to students of "gender," the young ladies adore "Faustine" while the young gentlemen don't get it—as a rule. (See the Digressions on Dame Edith and Edna Millay in the notes.) But there is absolutely no question here of rhyme driving meaning as it would in comic-doggerel verse. Someone as absolutely in command of rhyme as Swinburne was never at a loss. But it goes deeper than this.

The Neural Line

The great classical Indo-European poetry in Greek and Latin did not use rhyme, nor did Anglo-Saxon, nor did the Nordic poets. Meter in its various forms, with the internal devices of alliteration, assonance, caesura, and the like, were the basic tools. The standard metrical line of this verse conformed to what Fred Turner and Ernst Pöppel have shown, in a towering, definitive study, to be much the same length for all forms of verse, in all languages (including the unwritten ones). This universal line has an average neural processing period of between three and four seconds. (The "specious present" of William James?)

The average number of syllables per line from a short of seven to a long of seventeen, is about ten. (Tone languages halve these numbers because the syllables take twice as long to articulate.) This "line" is an acoustical unit, not a written one (and has nothing to do with breathing). It "is tuned to the three-second present moment of the auditory information-processing system." But it corresponds remarkably with the actual line of epic verse, as it came to be written, like the iambic pentameter (ten syllables) or the Alexandrine (twelve). The Latin hexameter was at the outer limit with fifteen, but like other long-lined forms was broken with a caesura. Similarly, classical Sanskrit used a line up to twenty-three syllables long, but this was a purely artificial literary device. The Japanese Haiku has seventeen syllables but is broken into three lines: five–seven–five:

> A quick breeze crackles
> dry snake skins in the broken
> geranium pot.

This three-second-plus line was a kind of outer limit that prescribed the metric unit. Within that limit the line could be broken up and varied in many ways by the "meters" or rhythmic patterns of the verse lines. Ballad verse typically uses short lines of a few feet with rhyming endings.

Stressed and unstressed syllables, in the languages where they occurred, like English, formed the basis of "feet," which were the subunits of the line. Anglo-Saxon verse demanded three alliterative consonants per line. Homeric verse used internal devices like fixed adjectives that were simply moved about according to the meter—"rosy-fingered dawn," "horse-tamer Hector," "Ajax destroyer of cities," and so on. These imposed their own kind of discipline, because, like rhyme, they were a fixed stock of devices to which the poet must adapt. Semitic verse, whether Hebrew Psalms or Bedouin praise poems, used the major device of antiphony:

> I will lift up mine unto the hills: From whence cometh my help.
> My help cometh even from the lord: Who hath made heaven and earth.

A tradition of English verse arose following William Blake that used a deliberate imitation of the sonorous rolling cadences of the psalms, most notably in Walt Whitman and in, for example, T. S. Eliot's "Choruses from the Rock" or Kahlil Gibran's "The Prophet" or even Allen Ginsberg's "Howl." I must admit to using it myself in the appropriately named "Psalm 151" (in *The Passionate Mind*). We might call this the declamatory or prophetic style, and it is perhaps best seen as a kind of poetic prose, for it does not obey the Law of the Neural Line. It is more like music, in that it depends on how much you can say in one breath. But it is worth noting that a lot of the effectiveness of poetic prose lies in its use of cadences somewhere near to the meter of the neural line: in English the iambic pentameter. Think of the Gettysburg Address. This echoing of the verse line in prose gave the modernist fathers, Eliot and Pound, a lot of wriggle room in suggesting a more "flexible" line of verse, to the point of losing the distinction—a loss that still afflicts us.

Rhyme in History

Turner and Pöppel have shown decisively the neural basis for the universality of a standard metric line, and I cannot match this with anything similar about rhyme. So we must start with the universality of meter and ask what rhyme adds where it happens. Apart from scientific evidence from studies of the auditory cortex, it seems to me sheer common sense that the repetition of like sounds has a deep appeal. Repetitive action of any kind tends to increase brain levels of serotonin and dopamine (the brain's natural opiates) and hence feelings of well-being. Witness the repetitiveness of most rituals, meditations, and such, from the chanting of mantras to the telling of rosaries, and the nodding and swaying during prayers and recitals of scripture.

Rhyme involves, at its broadest definition, the systematic repetition of like sounds at fixed points within, but mostly at the end of, metric lines. This might seem to cover alliteration, but that involves only letters. "The murmuring of innumerable bees" (Tennyson) is smoothly alliterative, but not rhyming. Like sounds must occur in all languages, but they do not result in rhyming verse. So while rhyming verse does not appear to be universal, it does, interestingly, occur in those civilizations that advanced the farthest in material and intellectual progress and social complexity: China, India, Persia, the medieval Arab societies, and finally the Europeans. This may be a massive coincidence, or there may be a connection to do with cognitive processing—particularly the packaging of information at a level deeper than we understand at the moment.

The rhyming schemes were often complex and did not always involve "hard" rhymes, as we understand them. Often "vowel harmony" or assonance, or even the clustering of any vowels round a common consonant, or, as in Chinese, a repetition of a like tone, or common case endings, was used. It is hard, if not impossible, to convey these devices in any English transliteration: In his *Sanskrit Poetry,* Daniel Ingalls gives an example of a vowel harmony AAAB scheme with endings in:

hayiah : teksaniyiah : kesariah : mahodadhāu

as near as I can make it.

To illustrate Arabic rhyme, or *qâfiyah,* the Lebanese poet Mansour Ajami (no relation to Fouad) gave me an elaborate transliteration of a classical Arabic tenth-century text of Ibn al-Anbārī's *Elegy on the Vizier Ibn Baqiyya.* Here again I can try to render the endings of the first quatrain as:

'l-mamāti : 'l-mu'jizāti : qāmū : 'ṣ-ṣilāti.

This goes on amazingly through sixteen stanzas *(li-ṣ-ṣalati/hibati/'s-sāfi-yāti . . .).* It is an example of similarity of case endings as rhyme; here the genitive case in *"-ti"* is used with astonishing versatility. Ajami says, however, that the introduction of rhyme led to "enough padded doggerel to fill a few football stadiums." This is, of course, always the downside to the use of rhyme, unless we think of doggerel as a kind of low-level practice.

The common Arabic form was the AABA quatrain, also used by the Persian poet Omar Khayyám (1048–1122) in his *Rubaiyat* (the Arabic plural for quatrain) and famously imitated by Edward Fitzgerald in his translation, as in this eighteenth stanza:

> They say the Lion and the Lizard keep
> Their Courts where Jamshyd gloried and drank deep:
> And Bahram, that great hunter—the Wild Ass
> Stamps o'er his Head but cannot break his Sleep.

Arabic rhyme could be "hard" as we understand it, or "slant" as when it rested on the repetition of a single consistent consonant while varying the vowels.

Rhyme came into European poetry from Arabic, along with the Arabic system of numerals, which was the foundation of modern science, mathematics, and finance, via the genius of Fibonacci. Rhyme came probably from the genuinely multicultural Norman kingdom of Sicily in the eleventh and twelfth centuries, and spread northward via the troubadours. Medieval writers introduced rhyme into Latin, as in the *Carmina Burana*:

> O fortuna, velut luna,
> statu variabilis.
> Semper crescis, aut decrescis,
> vita detestabilis.
>
> O fortune, like the ever-changing moon,
> Waxing, waning: execrable life.

Very similar to al-Anbārī's use of identical case endings (desinence) as rhymes is the technique of St. Thomas Aquinas in his *Pane Lingua*:

> *Tantum ergo sacramentum*   To laud so great a sacrament
> *Veneremur cernui:*   We can do nothing casual:
> *Et antiquum documentum*   So let the ancient document
> *Novo cedat ritui:*   Give way to a new ritual
> *Praestet fides supplementum* Allowing faith to supplement
> *Sensuum defectui.*   The defect of things sensual.

Aquinas is here using the Latin accusative and dative cases to form rhymes. This is hard to render into English to get both the meaning and a sense of the rhyme scheme: I have tried. My line 2 is pure invention. Literally the Latin means something like "let us venerate by falling headlong." (You will find that the Latin words fit exactly with the tune of Patsy Cline's "Walkin' After Midnight.")

The other source was Celtic poetry, where, unlike its continental cousins, various forms of rhyme were in use, but as in Sanskrit and Arabic not always hard rhymes but the more subtle assonance and pararhymes. Since we have had an Arabic threnody, let us use the example of the famous "Lament for Art O'Leary." This great anonymous poem was composed late—in about 1773 (but not written down until a hundred years later) when the bardic prosody of the classical schools, alliterative and syllabic, had given way to the more popular stressed verse of the people. I learned a variant of it from old singers on Tory Island in Donegal. Its simple directness helps make the point. Eibhlín Dubh O'Leary (Dark Evelyn) mourns for her murdered husband, Art:

Stadaih anois d'bhúr ngol,	Cease now your wailing
A mná na súl bhliuch mbog,	Women of the soft wet eyes,
Go bhfaghaidh Art Ua	Till Art O'Leary drain his cup
Laoghaire deoch,	
Roimh é dhul isteach 'sa sgoil,	Before entering the school,
Ní h-ag foghlaim	Not for music or learning
léighinn ná port	
Ach ag iomchar cré agus cloch.	But to bear up clay and stone.

This is from Daniel Corkery's *The Hidden Ireland*. The translation is his; I cannot better it. The "school" the murdered Art is to enter is of course the bardic school, which becomes metaphorically the school of death: the grave. Even if you do not read Gaelic, it is easy to see that this is an AABAAB scheme, with assonance in the A lines (*ngol, mbog,* and *sgoil, port*) and a true hard rhyme in the B lines: *deoch* and *cloch*. Yeats did not speak Gaelic, but he heard it and appreciated its subtleties, and they are reflected in his own special versification.

In languages that lend themselves to it (Sanskrit, Chinese, Persian, Arabic, Indo-European—all of which produced literate high cultures), the addition of rhyme to meter doubles the effectiveness of repetition. If meter is as powerful as it seems to be, for the physiological reasons that have been demonstrated, then consider the doubling of this effectiveness and its arousal potential. Rhyme assists nobly in the essential process of "chunking" described by neurophysiologists as "tying together units of information into groups and remembering the group as a whole." This is from Daniel Levitin's *This Is Your Brain on Music*—an inviting introduction to brain and memory that does not underestimate the role of emotion in remembering, which we shall see is crucial.

A poem is exactly an exercise in chunking, with the rhythm, and the rhyme where it occurs, serving the tying-together function. In an oral culture this was an almost essential service if large amounts of material had to be preserved and transmitted over the generations. Oral epics like the *Iliad* or the *Táin*, which are preserved in the early written versions, are what Eric Havelock *(Preface to Plato)* called "tribal encyclopedias," with their information chunked into metrical verses, stanzas, metaphors, and similes. We don't know how early in time rhyme came into Chinese, Arabic, and Sanskrit, for example, because of course we only have the written record. It always seems to have been there in one form or another in the Celtic languages, but again we are limited to the record. The relationship between rhyming verse and literacy itself has really yet to be explored. I am forced again to note that rhyming and literacy go together with the development of the high intellectual cultures (the Arabs transmitting it to Europe) but cannot take it further than that.

Dreams, Metaphor, and Memory

Flashback to the hominid brain and its evolution of *lateralization:* the division of functions between the hemispheres, the most amazing development since the origin of the brain itself. *Words* that rhyme are processed in the left hemisphere of the brain, the home of language, linearity, and analysis. The *pattern* of a rhyme scheme, its chunkiness, is detected by the right hemisphere, the home of wholeness, of gestalt. The confluence of the two unites the hemispheres (via the corpus callosum) and drives the whole brain, including the emotional functions of the limbic system and the arousal of the pleasure centers and their opioids. When linked to metrical rhythm, it involves the movement-control activities of the cerebellum and the *motor cortex*. Literacy and rhyme together change the brain; they set up new neuronal patterns, but patterns that tap into the most basic of that organ's basic processes.

Memory was the mother of the muses, and so a major function of the meter–rhyme combination is mnemonic. I have described elsewhere (in *The Red Lamp of Incest* and *The Search for Society*), following the neglected but pathbreaking work of Jonathan Winson, the chemical process by which language (along with all other experience) is first stored in the *cyngulate gyrus,* in preparation for processing into memory. During rapid eye movement (REM) sleep, or "dreaming" as we know it, this chemical material, along with other "day residue" (Freud's term), is passed through the hippocampus, where "neuronal gates" progressively release it to circulate through the limbic system, the old mammalian emotional center of the brain.

We cannot remember everything. Memory has to be selective, but on what principle? For any material, including concepts couched in language, to get into long-term memory, the dreaming brain must first translate it into images so that it can be emotionally "vetted." This is done by input from the emotional brain, especially the amygdala but also the *septum* and the cerebellum, and then it is transmitted back to the frontal lobes for storage, via the hypothalamus and the thalamus. This happens about four times a night, and deeper levels of retrieving and processing are reached and then recede as the REM dream-sleep continues. There are dreamlike states outside REM sleep, but they do not seem so connected to memory, long- or short-term. It is REM sleep deprivation that affects memory.

Memory is older than language; it worked entirely on images before language came along, very late in primate/hominid evolution. In consequence words must be accompanied by, or be converted into, images, in order to enter memory. Primate dreaming had accommodated sound, but words are more than sound: they are concepts and categories; they have meaning. Dreams are always visual; there is no such thing as a purely linguistic dream—sound without symbol. Metaphor and simile are two basic ways to provide the memory with ready-made images and symbols, and they must have been there in the Ur-language of mankind, which was probably closer to poetry than prose, as Giambattista Vico proposed in the eighteenth century.

But, as Winson insists, "abstract concepts arising with language . . . can only be integrated into our unconscious brain mechanism by translation into visual scenes and action." Thus concepts must become images before they can be lodged in long-term memory. Some of the strangeness of dreams is a result of this conversion process, this "need for representability," as Freud called it. It also explains why our concepts and categories, like our concept of time, for example, are not simply abstract and logical but are loaded with emotion. Time is an old father, with tide it waits for no man, it marches on, there is a nick of time, we beat time, we mark time, we keep time, we spend time, we waste time, and if we commit a crime, we *do* time, perhaps until our time is up.

The "stamping in" to long-term memory takes about three years, studies of memory loss have shown. During this stamping-in process the human brain compares incoming material with already-stored experience and not just with basic instincts, as in the "theta rhythm" of other mammals. This may be one huge and crucial exception to the rule that we do not lose anything in evolution. The human loss of theta rhythms may have been one of the most liberating developments in our evolutionary history. It released memory from instinct so that memory could build directly on memory itself. The brain then stores only that which meets the test of emotional appropriateness. That is, it stores material seen as relevant to stored experience—a lot of this being experience from early childhood, and therefore retained. Charles Dickens understood this uncannily well. Pip asks Estella in the 1946 film version of *Great Expectations* if she remembers making him cry as boy. She tells him no, and adds that he meant nothing to her so why should she remember? She says: "You know Pip I have no heart. Perhaps that is why I have no memory."

I used the example of totemic categories and their instillation during the initiation ceremonies of young men, to make the point, and this refers us back to the discussion of Lévi-Strauss in Chapter 1. The rules of the totem clan or moiety (rules of marriage and exogamy, for example), perhaps the most archaic of social rules, are concepts that are most effectively learned as dramatic images—snake, bear, wolf, eagle, raven, crow, coyote, emu, and the legends associated with them. These are instilled into the boys during often-painful and dramatic rituals over a long period, and dreamed into memory. In fact we learn better from trauma than from normality, and male rats seem to learn more from "inescapable stress" than female rats do (Shors 2001, 2002). The actual process is complicated, and the reader must look to the details in *The Red Lamp of Incest* and *The Search for Society*, and to the theory proposed by Francis Crick and Graeme Mitchison (at much the same time as Winson) that dreaming is an aid to selective forgetting. But despite the complexities, the general point about meter, rhyme, and memory is obvious.

The rhyme schemes we have been investigating are *compressed and powerful images* like *death/breath—womb/tomb/doom—lust/thrust/dust*. Every rhyme scheme is a little metaphor; every poem is a little ritual. Ted Hughes, in his book on Shakespeare's "ritual drama," sees metaphor as a result of the brief perfect combination of left- and right-hemisphere interaction (which we shall reencounter in Chapter 13) that produces a momentary "convulsive expansion of awareness." So rhymes, added to the power of meter and embodied in the "heightened reality" of metaphors, are a ready-made system of images for the dreaming brain to work on in its task of vetting the emotional appropriateness of potential memories. Repetition of course does the trick if we are to set up neuronal pathways, and we must repeat to remember. It is not, then, just that rhyme helps memory; rhyme is part of the metaphorical process of memorizing itself.

The Music of Verse

When I was praising the power of Swinburne's verse to the lady critic, she dismissed it as "mere rhythm." "You might as well bang a drum," she added. Well yes, if that is all you hear.

Di di dum di dum di di dum di dum di

It might as well be a drum: and with several drums playing cross rhythms, as in Africa, it can be exciting as rhythm per se. But when we add, as in the first of the magisterial choruses in *Atalanta*:

When the hounds of spring are on winter's traces,
The mother of months in meadow and plain
Fills the shadows and windy places
With lisp of leaves and ripple of rain;

We are almost lifted off our feet with a blast of cleverly varied meter, pulsating rhythm, hard rhyme, part rhyme, classical allusion, striking metaphor, alliteration, assonance, and onomatopoeia. You might say all of English poetry is here. His "lisp of leaves and ripple of rain" was condemned at the time as "sensuous." And so it is. There was no Thomistic nonsense here about letting faith make up for the deficiencies of the senses. Swinburne went straight for the sensual jugular. The appeal is almost directly to those limbic emotions and the deep structures of rhythmic movement in the cerebellum. You don't just hear these lines—perhaps his most famous (think of the Thurber cartoon that uses them)—you feel them physically. For those who don't know them it would be unfair not to complete the stanza:

And the brown bright nightingale amorous
Is half assuaged for Itylus,
For the Thracian ships and the foreign faces.
The tongueless vigil, and all the pain.

Swinburne collapses several Greek myths, including that of Aedon, who killed her son Itylus by mistake, and Philomela, whose tongue was cut out to prevent her disclosing a rape. Both were turned into nightingales to sing forever of their sorrow. I would have probably written "silent vigil," which is why I am a so-so poet and Swinburne is a very great one. The lady critic (she's a composite, but you've met her) condemned the "metrical monotony" of this poem. But note that in fact no two lines are the same metrically, except for the four beats. This kind of infinite variation was the sublime skill of Swinburne.

"The Hounds of Spring" was in its day perhaps the best-known poem in English. It was killed by overfamiliarity, and then forgotten, since the days when Oxford undergraduates of the aesthetic persuasion used to link arms and march through the streets chanting it along with "Faustine" and "Dolores" to annoy the hearties (jocks). It was their version of a Grateful Dead concert, and we can see the odd affinity. Add music to meter and rhyme, and you have the scary mix that made Plato shudder and fear for the Forms.

But in great musical poets like Swinburne, the music is there in the verse itself. Consider his perhaps most intrinsically musical poem, "A Forsaken Garden"—you must read it aloud for the effect:

> In a coign of the cliff between lowland and highland,
>   At the sea-down's edge between windward and lee,
> Walled round with rocks as an inland island,
>   The ghost of a garden fronts the sea.
> A girdle of brushwood and thorn encloses
>   The steep square slope of the blossomless bed
> Where the weeds that grew green from the graves of its roses
>   Now lie dead.

This is sustained over ten perfect stanzas until:

> As a god self-slain on his own strange altar,
> Death lies dead.

We have forgotten about beauty in verse. The Chinese, Sanskrit, Arabic, and Gaelic poets would have welcomed Swinburne to their circles. They would have known.

Rhyme and Translation

While English and its Germanic relatives have a more sparse stock of rhyme than their creolized-Latin cousins, English poets have always gloried in it. Because it is more difficult to find rhymes in English than in Italian or Spanish, it is more challenging and more satisfying to master the challenge, and the early English poets were already in its thrall. The introduction of blank verse to English (by Henry Howard in his *Aeneid* translation of 1561) was in direct imitation of the classical model: as though somehow rhyming was inherently less dignified. But the rhyming heroic couplet has since Chaucer also been a vehicle of choice. Thus we have in English a basic stock, as it were, of rhymes.

Rhyme is a totally arbitrary linguistic system. The words all have their own meanings and often elaborate connotations, but they could have been different: it is pure linguistic accident that "death" and "breath" *sound* the same. In French they don't rhyme: *mort* and *souffle* have no relationship as sounds. *Mort,* however, as "death," does rhyme with *port* (harbor), for example, and *morte* as "dead" rhymes with *porte* (door/carry). French (and Italian) poets take advantage of this, because there is not only a re-lationship of sound, but also a relationship of sense, between the two words. Death is a portal, and death "carries" us through that portal, and *forte* is waiting in the wings: the strength of both death and the courage we need to face the gateway to death. Even the children's rhyme takes advantage:

> Ma chandelle est morte,
> Je n'ai plus du feu;
> Ouvre-moi ta porte
> Pour l'amour de Dieu.

Dante hits it right up front in the second stanza of the *Inferno* (he had used it already in the first):

> Ahi quanto a dir qual era è cosadura
> Esta selva selvaggia e aspra e forte
> Che nel pensier rinova la paura!
>
> Tant'è amara che poco è più morte.

And in Canto III, after being told to abandon all hope at the Gate of Hell, he hits us with the rhyme:

> Vid' io scritte al sommo d'una porta . . .
>
> Ogne viltà convien che qui sia morta.

Longfellow translates *morta* as "extinct." "Dead" is better. Italian, it is said, with its vowel endings makes rhyming too easy: everything rhymes with everything else. Perhaps. But it really is about knowing how to use it, and we can never fault Dante. He of all poets understands the subtle relationship between the meaning of the statement and the implicit meaning of the rhymes, and sustains it throughout his marvelous verses.

This implicit system of meaning contained in rhyme is a constant problem for translators, of course. The very existence of this chapter will reduce the book's chances of being translated. All the points would be automatically lost in translation. There have been marvelous attempts, for example, to translate Dante's *Inferno,* including Longfellow and my favorite contemporaries, John Ciardi and Robert Pinsky, and they all have either had to abandon rhyme or contrive some method of conveying the effect of his rhymes, which are essential to the original intent. But because the rhymes cannot be reproduced in English—if you translate you lose them—then every translation, as the translators recognize, can give us only a ghost of the original. English cannot convey the implicit connection between *porta, morta,* and the Gate of Hell. Pinsky gets the correct words in there:

> Abandon all hope, you who enter here.
>   These words I saw inscribed in a dark color
>   Over a *portal* . . .
>
>   "All fear
>   must be left here and cowardice *die*."

(My italics.) He beautifully preserves the intent of Dante's words, but the play on death and the gate is gone.

Sound, Sense, and Rhyme

Such inbuilt relationships of sound and sense are there in the English words also. *Death* and *breath* do make a meaningful pair, because breath is the essence of life and death its termination. Thus whenever they occur together, whatever the meaning of the lines in which they are contained, there is always also this underlying meaning that is inherent in the words themselves. A poet using the rhyme is always playing with this duality of meaning, and rhyme-sense always therefore exerts a discipline on the line-sense, if we may use these neologisms. Bad lyric writers are trapped in the rhymes; great poets use the tension creatively. In the second luminous chorus in *Atalanta,* Swinburne continues his anger at the fate of man's transient existence, an existence cursed with the consciousness of death:

> Pleasure with pain for leaven,
>   Summer with flowers that fell;

Remembrance fallen from heaven,
   And madness risen from hell;
Strength without hands to smite;
   Love that endures for a breath:
Night, the shadow of light,
   And life, the shadow of death.

He knows he is going to end this sequence with "death"; that is where it is leading; that is where everything leads. English gives him the compulsory rhyme and he inserts it. Love is transient like everything for man, so it "endures for a breath," a breath that is itself the essence of transience. Yes. He must use the rhyme, and that discipline carves his meaning into shape, not by a slavish following of a convention but by the demand that he make the line-sense and the rhyme-sense come into conjunction. A few lines later, he repeats the idea, speaking of man:

His speech is a burning fire;
   With his lips he travaileth;
In his heart is a blind desire,
   In his eyes foreknowledge of death.

Here he can use the archaic verb form, which gives him a little freedom, but he is also constrained by its meaning. So he must use it to his end. Man labors with his speech to make sense of—what? Of life and death of course. But "travail" conveys so much more; this is not mere effort but anguished effort, like the "travail" of childbirth. It is the hard road of life toward inevitable death. The meaning of the lines is clear (note the balance of "blind" as with "desire," against "eyes" and the contrasting "knowledge"), but the rhymes carry their own weight as a counterpoint and anchor to the overt meaning.

So far from being stuck with rhymes and limited by them, the poet who accepts to play by the rules of rhyme faces them as a challenge: they are fixed points around which he must navigate skillfully to bring his ship of verse home to harbor: the understanding of the audience (for all poetry was initially oral). When skillfully used, the inherent connotations of the rhymed words add the second layer of meaning we have been discussing. If we may use another analogy, the rhymes and their inherent meanings are topological points: they are like fixed dots on a rubber sheet. However you stretch the sheet, the relationship between the points stays the same. Your geometry must always be developed with this in mind. You can change the appearance of the shapes, but never the basic relationship between the points.

In reading through Swinburne we can see on every page examples of the repetition of certain key rhymes. And note that Swinburne, unlike Browning, was not one for making up clever original rhymes. He took what was there. But this was not for lack of skill in ingenious rhyming. In fact he pokes elegant fun at Browning's rhyming ingenuity, and his quirky style in general, in "On the Sands":

> Those who've read S. T. Coleridge remember how Sammy sighs
> To his pensive (I think he says) Sara—"most soothing sweet"—
> Crab's bulk's less (look!) than man's—yet (quoth Cancer) I am my size,
> And my girth contents me! Man's maw (see?) craves two things—wheat
> And flesh likewise—man's gluttonous—damn his eyes!

and wickedly on and on.

Let us just take his monosyllabic rhymes (with the odd exception: he was fond of feminine rhymes and used them with skill, but that is another essay). Like "death" and "breath," these rhymes are arbitrary likenesses of sound that carry fundamental affinities of sense. The great poet must work with this dual system; he must form his geometry of meaning around these fixed points.

Take one of Swinburne's favorites: "God" and "rod." A diligent student could go through and do what I have done for my chosen rhymes, and find all the examples and note how the resonance of the two words is utilized. We can stay with *Atalanta*:

> A landmark seen across the way
> Where one race treads as the other trod;
> An evil sceptre, an evil stay,
> Wrought for a staff, wrought for a rod,
> The bitter jealousy of God.

He is speaking of Fate, and the succession of peoples who cannot escape it/ her: hence "tread" and "trod" suggesting weary inevitability. He then hammers away with the related "sceptre," "stay," "staff," and "rod"—the rhyme picking up the trapped and doomed races, and giving a harsh ending to the list, and leading the ear of course to the grimly inevitable "God." The affinity of sound and sense with these two words echoes the harsh and punitive nature of the Judeo-Christian deity (as Swinburne sees him), just as in

Christian hymns "love," "above," and "dove" link their version of God's heavenly compassion descending to earth. But for Swinburne the rod is a scourge, although God does not need a physical rod to torment his creatures:

> Who makes desire and slays desire with shame;
>> Who shakes the heaven as ashes in his hand;
> Who, seeing the light and shadow for the same,
>> Bids day waste night as fire devours a brand,
> Smites without sword, and scourges without rod,
>> The supreme evil, God.

(T. Earle Welby said in his *Study of Swinburne:* "The very last lines he had written had been an appeal to eternal justice to determine which was worthier of chastisement, God as the maker of man, or man as the maker of God.") I won't belabor the point. The affinity of sense that goes with the arbitrary affinity of sound is a series of challenges to a good poet to marry the two levels of meaning to give the listener a double richness of connotation. Here is a list of some of Swinburne's favorites, other than those we have considered, with some of the common alternatives. The reader can write his own commentary.

Tomb : womb (gloom, loom)
Earth : birth (mirth, girth)
Dead : bled (head, red)
Hand : land (stand, grand)
Name : shame (blame, fame)
Gold : old (told, sold)
Years : tears (fears, appears)
Night : light (flight, sight)
Sigh : die (cry, fly)
Rain : pain (again, plain)
Sleep : deep (weep, creep)
Lust : dust (trust, thrust)
Wife : life (strife, knife)
Blood : good (flood, stood)
Bride : pride (side, guide)
Desire : fire (lyre, pyre)
Worm : germ (term, firm)

We could go on, but the point is made. The resonances of *tomb* and *womb*, and *earth* and *birth*, and their rhyming cousins are a fund of connotations,

and are richly plundered by the poets. The rhymes on the list are particular favorites of Swinburne's, for obvious reasons. Jonathan Bate
quotes Edward Thomas on Swinburne: "He kept, as it were, a harem of
words to which he was constant and absolutely faithful." On the list
were: *sea, wave, sleep, dream, kiss, mouth, fire, light, bright, shine,
ache, desire, delight, high, sky.* Bate finds, correctly, that these become
in his later work (in his sober reclusive years) repetitive and dulled by
use. Swinburne lived too long, maybe, and wrote too much. But in his
youth he revolutionized poetry, and in his older years he wrote some
of our most perceptive criticism. (For some digressions on rhyme in
Basque poetry and its surprising occurrence in Mayan poetics, see the
notes.)

Rules, Rhyme, and Comic Verse

Rhyme may have originated in poetry for sheer fun in the play of sound;
or more likely the "memorability" of rhyme added to its value in an oral
culture. Married to the older discipline of meter, it more than doubled the
chances of remembering, as we have seen. How much more easily we remember rhymed verses than paragraphs of prose. But the arbitrariness of
rhyme, the sheer coincidence of etymologically unrelated words sounding
the same, has always given the poets who could master it a double layer of
meaning to work with.

Poets who are the slaves of rhyme, like the bad lyricists we so often invoke, simply do not understand what they are dealing with. Poets who are
the masters of rhyme, like Swinburne, use it like the masters of color in
making a picture. A bad artist is the slave of color: a great artist its master.
A great artist does not see a restriction in the fact he must use the colors in
the range of the palette; neither does a great poet feel rhyme (or meter) to
be a restriction. In each case the arbitrary given exerts a discipline, but that
is what the true artist welcomes.

The rules of any game exert a discipline, but without the rules and the
discipline there would be no game: the rules are what the game is about.
The analogy with real games is obvious: if we threw an inflated pig's blad-
der between two groups of boys in a village and said, "Do what you like
but get it to the opposite end of town," we would get mayhem. This is in
fact how soccer, rugby, and football began: a goal but no rules. They
evolved into games with exquisitely exact rules, and these rules are arbitrary but they are the game. To play within the rules yet still achieve the
goal is what makes the game exciting and aesthetically, and even morally,
pleasing to us and to the players.

Light or comic poets are governed by the same rules. That rhymed verse can devolve into jingle and doggerel only reveals the banal truth that not all men are great artists. A great deal of comic verse—think of W. S. Gilbert, Ogden Nash, or Lewis Carrol, Edward Lear, Cole Porter, or Noel Coward—depends on the witty use of unusual rhymes that surprise our ears:

> Because the simple creatures hope he
> Will impale his solar topee
> on a tree.

The more outrageous the better:

> Because the sun is much too sultry
> And one must avoid its ultra-
> violet ray.

> But Englishmen detest a
> siesta.

But Noel never puts his rhyming foot wrong, and unlike doggerel, as in say *The Cat in the Hat*, the meaning here drives the rhyme, however weird the latter may become. To be fair, *The Cat in the Hat* is meant for children, and such doggerel, like nursery rhymes, is part of their education in rhyme, and also plays to the sheer fun of the repetition of like sounds that is the basic appeal of rhyming.

Iona and Peter Opie showed for us, in their *Lore and Language of Schoolchildren,* what a huge inventory of rhyming verses existed within the culture of British children: verses that often enough bypassed the adult culture completely and were transmitted down the generations from child to child. Children are particularly good at spontaneous insult rhymes: "Dickie Sweeny is a meanie" I remember among many from my own childhood, and that is one of the printable ones. "Robin Fox, Robin Fox /Put your bollocks in a box" was one they couldn't resist, the little darlings.

It is not that much a remove from the spontaneous rhyming of children to the great epic poet ringing endless changes on the same rhymes, but moving his meaning around them and their intrinsic content. The great comic poets delighting us with anticipation of witty new rhymes are playing the same game, for example, Tom Lehrer (worthy of Browning!):

> When they see us coming the pigeons all try an' hide
> But they all go for peanuts when coated with cyanide.

They do not seek to escape the rules; they beat the rules at their own game. They are the field-goal kickers who become so accurate that the goalposts have to be narrowed to make it harder, or the kickoff pushed back to the thirty yard line to give the returning team a chance.

One day there will be kickers who so regularly punch it through from seventy-five yards that we will have to rethink the whole business of field goals. This will not be because they broke or abandoned the rules, but because they played them so well they went beyond what the rules were designed to control and hence forced a change. When the immortal William Webb Ellis at Rugby School in 1823 picked up the soccer ball and ran it into the goal, he was not breaking the rules. There was no rule against carrying the ball into the goal, but no one had thought to do it until then. That the story is probably a myth helps to make my point: someone ran with the ball; Ellis became the icon. Think of John Heisman (or was it Walter Camp?) and the forward pass in football. And from that one creative play, a whole series of wonderful team games arose:

> And so their Ur-Rules
> spawned more rules.

(Sorry, Noel!)

We love games because we love their telescoped, dramatic analogy with life. We make everything we can into a game with rules. Poems are themselves little games with rules that appeal to our sense of the dramatic. Poets can create rule changes in a similar way. Most poets, and Swinburne in particular, use "hard rhymes" of the *death/breath* variety. These are the most obvious and the most memorable for they strike an automatic chord of absolute sameness. But W. B. Yeats taught us (learning as we have seen from the Gaelic) that consonantal rhymes, or assonance, for example, can be effective in their suggestiveness (*swans/stones, south/both*). Leonard Cohen is a master of the suggestive half rhyme— the production of a haunting echo along with a hard repetition, as in "I'm Your Man:"

> If you wANt a pArtNer
> Take my hANd
> Or if you wANt to
>   strike me down in ANger
> Here I stANd
> I'm your mAN

Swinburne had done the same thing with his rhyming masterpiece "Faustine" and its use of *-in* pararhymes to match the *-ine* of Faustine itself. He did the same thing, as we have seen, in softening the hard-rhyme impact in "The Hounds of Spring" by rhyming "amorous" with "Itylus." Wilfred Owen made a tragic brilliance out of consonantal rhyme *(escaped/scooped, groined/groaned)* in his war poems. C. Day Lewis followed with *coinage/carnage* and *ashes/unleashes* in *The Nabara.* But it took Pinsky in his *Inferno* translation to make this into a systematic way of conveying the insistence of rhyme in Dante without, as he says, making it sound like a limerick or W. S. Gilbert.

The sustained virtuosity of Pinsky's effort provides a new standard and will be much imitated. But it wavers on the outer edge of sophistication, suitable in a Yeatsian lyric, but foreign to Dante. The hard rhymes appeal to something hardwired, and even Pinsky uses them frequently enough to provide that anchor that the auditory system craves. If he does not, then the verse tends to float away from us in a way Dante's never does. But that is just my subjective feeling. After all, the *Chanson de Roland* throughout uses assonance or vowel rhyme and is very effective as a tough epic (see Chapter 8). The important thing is that Pinsky does not break any rules; he creates subtle variations on them.

In the midst of writing this I had a particularly strange dream (that is, REM sleep episode) with a juxtaposition of Sartre and Dali that vouchsafed me, among other things, an example of assonantal rhyme in French that went along with being lost among giant mollusks:

> Vraiment si l'enfer c'est les autres,
> Ne t'engage qu'avec les huitres.

"Truly if hell is other people, only get involved with oysters." The hippocampus was checking my day residue of concern with assonance and French verse against related memories of what was emotionally important to me in the past and was itself already in storage. Aficionados of existentialism, a passion of my student years along with shellfish and surrealism, will recognize *engagement,* and the wittiness of dreams is confirmed. The unconscious, as Freud said, is diabolical.

The Rules of the Game

A generation arose after the rebellious sixties that decided the only way to deal with rules you don't like is to abandon them. Thus you are rule-free and hence happy. You are never rule-free. If you abandon one set of rules, then you must invent another with the same ratio of arbitrary content to noise, because the essence of rules is redundancy: they enable you to predict the world and live forward in time, which is what the neocortex is for in the first place. We do not respond like lower animals to immediate emotional demands; we mediate them with rules; our neocortex controls our limbic brain. And like rhyming, it is all about anticipation and predictability.

What in the jargon we call "equilibration" involves the evolution of the ability to see the consequences of actions and hence to inhibit and time them. Those of our ancestors who could do this survived in the struggle for reproductive success. They did not die in out-and-out competition, they were able to live in rule-governed communities, however rudimentary those rules might have been at first: rules about mating and hierarchy mostly. (See my *Red Lamp of Incest*.)

With the advent of language these rules could be articulated and codified in memory. They could be recited and chanted and taught to young men at initiation and young women at childbirth. We became rule-making organisms: we acquired the ability and necessity to make rules and hence to be able to anticipate the future and orient to it became part of our being. It occurs spontaneously in children, as Jean Piaget meticulously demonstrated with his observations of boys playing marbles, in those crucial learning years of "middle childhood"—Freud's "latency period." The embodiment of the rules in the chanting and the storytelling, in the songs and myths, the praise poems and sagas, was essential to their preservation. We go beyond adaptation and survival in our obsession with rules.

Rule creation is an "appetitive" activity for us. One might even say (metaphorically) that we have an instinct to make rules, as we have an instinct to classify and exchange (so Lévi-Strauss taught us). In some sense it does not matter what the rules are as long as we have some; which exact rules we have will be determined by adaptation and history and no little accident. We are not always conscious of the rules, by any means: the rules are sometimes imposed, but mostly they develop organically. This is why we have grammarians and anthropologists: they make explicit the implicit rules of language and society. For a recent example of the latter, see Kate Fox's ingenious decoding of the rules in *The Racing Tribe* and *Watching the English*.

Think of the great defining drama, the *Oresteia,* the *Hamlet,* of the post-sixties generation: it was *Seinfeld. Seinfeld* was to the post-sixties people what *Siegfried* was to the Third Reich. And it was about rules. Every episode dealt with the search for rules in a generation that had dispensed with them. What are the rules for dumping a girlfriend; for the copyright on children's names; for breaking a date; for double-dipping; for putting people on your speed-dial list; for calling after a one-night stand; for make-up sex; for what counts as garbage; for being seated in a Chinese restaurant; for "regifting" unwanted Christmas presents; for calling after ten at night; for keeping greeting cards; for referring to homosexuals? "Not that there's anything wrong with that." George tells Kramer, "You can't abandon people in the middle of an airport pickup. It's an unbreakable social contract." When George is accused by his boss of having sex with the office cleaning lady on his desk, his immediate response is: "Was that wrong? Should I not have done that?" This theme of the search for rules was part of the genius of *Seinfeld* originator Larry David. In his own TV series, *Curb Your Enthusiasm,* he frighteningly pursues the bafflement of the rule-free generation in its search for those absolutely necessary points of order in an otherwise unpredictable universe. Who owns the bouquets of flowers that people leave at the scenes of tragic accidents? May you take one for your wife's birthday?

Turner and Pöppel add the idea that "free verse" that abandons the rules is favored by bureaucratic systems because such systems prefer people not to put their whole brains to work, but to remain specialized and personal: "lyric descriptions of private and personal impressions." This makes them easier to control. This is ingenious but perhaps a little too sinister. I doubt that even totalitarian systems are that smart. It is perhaps more likely to be an effect of the democratization and vulgarization of culture favored by egalitarian democracies. Great skill in verse demands unusual imagination, outstanding education, long practice, and perhaps even leisure; it is not something anyone can do. It is therefore anathema to the egalitarian mentality.

It never helps my case, I find, that Swinburne was an aristocrat with a classical education and a lot of spare time. To the egalitarian, verse should be something everyone can do with very little effort: what my daughter's creative writing class in college always referred to as "lazy poetry." They were happy when that was the assignment. It called for very little thought, and because there were really no standards, every piece was as good as any other as long as it was "sincere." Self-esteem was assured. Gandhi said that it was unfortunate that the inevitable result of democracy seemed to be corruption and hypocrisy, but there it was. The inevitable result of the democratization of knowledge seems to be intellectual laziness; it pervades the whole culture. It is a pity, but there it is. Tocqueville understood this very well. It is also a great irony that the lead practitioners of this egalitarian verse form should be an elite group of tenured English professors who write only for each other and operate in self-congratulatory cliques, largely unread except by themselves. "The people" on whose behalf they are so vocal prefer rap, hip-hop, country and western, or anything with meter and rhyme.

Rules are always negotiable. Look at the enormous variation on a strict form in the *ottava rima* of Spenser, Milton, Byron, Keats, and Yeats. They scarcely sound the same, despite the unvarying rule. Look at the heroic couplet from Chaucer to its perfection in Pope, to the eccentricity of Browning's *Sordello,* and even to Swinburne's own *Tristram of Lyonesse* or more recently Frederick Feirstein's detective story in verse, *Manhattan Carnival.* Again, a simple direct rhyming rule can produce effects that sound like a different language. But like Seinfeld's ingenious characters, the real poets play by the rules and try to push the envelope.

The abandonment of rules is an abdication from the game. It *is* playing tennis without a net (Robert Frost). *The New Yorker* and its like no longer publish poetry. They are trapped in print and the foolishness that print allows. We can't abandon print, of course—and it gives us another dimension to play with that can be fun: we can see the *shape* of poems. But neither can we abandon the Drumbeat of the constraints on our cognition of which poetry is both the producer and the product. Or rather we can abandon them, but it is our great loss if we do so.

Epilogue

The music still comes through to modern ears. Put the following gracious sonnet by Frederick Turner alongside Swinburne's death sonnet. They couldn't be more different, and yet they couldn't be more the same. Swinburne's poem makes me afraid of Death, and this fear is reflected in my own sonnet. John Donne, in the "Death Be Not Proud" sonnet we touched on earlier, pities Death because, for a Christian, Death hath no dominion. Fred Turner softly questions Donne: Death is not the loser, we are. He has no need for pride. Turner gentles Death, and makes me almost indulgent of him. This Death, like the Cyrano he brings to mind, is a gentleman, but of course not any less deadly for all that. Was Swinburne's gladiator, with his plea for more time, a "loser" by Turner's standard? Perhaps. But the point is: we all are. The rhyme of the couplet is inspired. Savor its connotations and my case is made.

Donne in His Coffin

Death is not proud, but patient. He can wait,
For time, and tact, are always on his side.
Death's humbleness is famous in debate,
The fated winner has no need for pride.
Let losers ponder what they have in hand,
What still remains of time and energy:
No need of a reminder where they stand! –
They will soon bow to the necessity.
Indeed, why take offense at their distress?
Death pats them on the back as they come round.
It could be worse—worse would be witlessness –
At least they knew they could not hold the ground.
Death lets us keep our swords and minds his manners,
Doffing his black hat as we strike our banners.

Frederick Turner

CHAPTER TEN

Seafood and Civilization

From Tribal to Complex Society

MONG THE MIRACLES in the ascent of humanity was the decisive shift from hunting and gathering to the domestication of animals and plants: the Neolithic revolution. We encountered it in the "Neolithic Paradox" in Chapter 1. It was the beginning of what we choose to call civilization, which literally means living in cities. We saw how the Israelites struggled with this in their later stage of the transition, once bronze and iron had been introduced. They moved from being primarily pastoral nomads to being cultivators and town dwellers, and their labor pains in this rebirth, and the role of religion and conquest in it, provide insight and drama second to none. But for many of the peoples that made the initial transition there is no such record, and we must learn what we can from their material remains, from what archaeology can tell us about them. We are the heirs of the civilizations they created, and we carry within our cultural DNA many of the conflicts that they both inherited and created.

Civilization and Complexity

So we must ask ourselves a basic question: What are the necessary conditions for the rise of civilization? Ten thousand years ago our ancestors were all hunter-gatherers, living a nomadic existence in small bands. Two thousand years later there existed, in the Middle East, farms and small settlements. Five thousand years ago there were city-states in Sumeria, in what is now Iraq. The rest is, indeed, history. The move was momentous. For more than 2 million years hominids had lived successfully as nomadic hunter-gatherers. It is, in a basic sense, what we are, what we evolved to be.

We were at the top of the food chain; we expanded to fill the habitable globe; resources were plentiful. The great mystery is why we ever decided to change to the turbulent and uncertain state of agricultural and urban society: to history and civilization. In hindsight it appears an inevitable shift; we label it "progress" and see it as a series of "upward" steps to our present exalted state. But in evolutionary terms it is an afterthought, a brief episode whose outcome is in serious doubt. Our very success looks like backfiring on us.

The move from "simple" hunting societies to "complex" urban-industrial ones seems less like inevitable progress and more like a true loss of Eden. If our hunting ancestors could have seen the end result, would they have been so eager to save those wild barley seeds and sow them in the spring? Perhaps. They were using their ample brains to help themselves and their relatives survive and reproduce. They were doing what they had always done. The ultimate consequences were not their concern, but they must be ours. Was it inevitable? What had to happen to get it started? If we know more about our improbable beginnings, perhaps we can be wiser about our probable end.

In 1994 (in *The Challenge of Anthropology*) I attempted to pin down the necessary conditions for the rise of complex societies. I contrasted the rise of Anasazi civilization in the American Southwest with the achievements of the Calusa Indians of southwest Florida. My point was to show that a society whose main resource was seafood (fish, shellfish, and sea mammals) and that lacked agriculture entirely could achieve a high level of social complexity. This was contrary to the orthodox opinion, which held that intensive agriculture was a necessary precursor to civilization. At the time, while mentioning the Northwest Coast Indians, I argued that the Calusa remained an exception to the "intensive agriculture" rule, but discoveries on the Norte Chico of Peru show clearly that such a transition was possible in other coastal communities lacking intensive agriculture and a storable staple crop.

Here I shall try to show how these three coastal fishing societies in the Americas advanced toward complexity while still being technically "hunter-gatherers." I shall also test my own hypothesis: that the four correlates of the emergence of true civilization from incipient social complexity are (1) a critical density of population, (2) the division of labor and specialization of tasks, (3) expansive warfare and conquest, and (4) elite literacy and record keeping.

Fishing for Answers

John Haywood in the *Historical Atlas of Ancient Civilizations* (2005) puts it bluntly: "Where intensive agriculture is not possible, civilizations cannot arise." He recognizes that there are either lax or very tough criteria we can invoke to define civilization. Gordon Childe (as quoted in Haywood) proposed ten, in order of appearance, of which the first five are crucial: cities, specialization, surplus, classes, states, monuments, trade, artwork, writing, and numeracy (I summarize). But to try to decide fringe cases gets us into a quagmire of definitions. That is why I prefer to use the criterion "social complexity." In this, as in much else, I am following Julian Steward (in *Theory of Culture Change*), who preferred to speak of "complex society." I added the proviso that what was at issue was "vertical complexity"—or stratified society.

Primitive hunters can have, for example, very complex kinship systems, but they do not have ranks and classes and the specialization of labor. They have what Émile Durkheim in *The Division of Labour in Society* called "mechanical solidarity"—the multiplication of like parts, each part being self-sustaining. This he opposed to "organic solidarity"—the necessary dependence of unlike parts, as in the division and specialization of tasks. A society could advance in complexity and, as Adam Smith saw, in wealth, to the degree that it expanded the division of labor.

This latter in turn depended on an increase in population, which depended on settlement, the domestication of animals and crops, and above all the development of an agricultural surplus. The economy had to move above subsistence to the production of a surplus that could be stored. All those kings, courtiers, nobles, priests, scribes, judges, warriors, smiths, armorers, builders, artists, jewelers, weavers, potters, and traders, and even slaves, had to be fed if they didn't raise food for themselves. All this had to be administered. Once competition over land and water led to war and conquest (and inevitably slavery), some kind of literacy (or at least numeracy) was needed, with an administrative, usually priestly, class to run it all. They had to collect taxes from the great mass of peasants who raised the food, and tribute from the beaten enemies, and they had to keep records of it. This is why writing was invented in the first place.

Jared Diamond, in his large-minded *Guns, Germs and Steel*, illustrates the progress of this very well in his diagram of the "factors underlying the broadest patterns of history" (in his chapter 4). On his model, there must be natural resources in the form of easily domesticable species of animals and plants, the domestication must occur, and from it a storable agricultural surplus must be produced. From this will follow "large, dense, sedentary, stratified societies." Diamond's scheme does not necessarily rule out fish as a source—fish are technically "animal"—but to fit his model they would have to be domesticated and stored. Let us keep this in mind. There is a long history of prejudice against fish. The "finny prey" is at best seen as an ancillary source, and at worst as a barrier to progress because it is wild and must be hunted, and so holds civilization back to the hunting stage. Even if it can be domesticated and stored, it can never compete with grains and roots, particularly the former.

The social evolutionist L. H. Morgan, in his *Ancient Society* of 1877, who will be the subject of Chapter 11, thought that any society dependent on fishing was of necessity at the bottom of the ladder of progress; it could not rise above the level of subsistence. Thus for him the Indians of the American Northwest were still hunter-gatherers and did not even rise to the level of primitive horticulture, the necessary precondition for agriculture. He thought the human consumption of fish meant that fire must have been invented because the fish had to be cooked. He obviously didn't know about sushi, and of course shellfish can be eaten raw and are often preferred that way. He did see that fishing could lead to the spread of populations along rivers and shorelines, but it could not take society beyond a very primitive subsistence stage. The prejudice persists, and it has some basis: it is hard to see how the unreliable and precarious pursuit of fish can be the source of the storable surplus necessary to build a complex society.

Diamond's paradigm fits very well the rise of early city-states in Mesopotamia: the cradle of civilization. In the Fertile Crescent, from Palestine through southern Turkey to the plain between the Tigris and Euphrates rivers, Neolithic agriculture (wheat, barley, cattle, sheep, goats) was underway by 8000 BC. The first small towns (or large villages) had appeared by 6000 BC. Intensive agriculture (taking crops repeatedly from the same area of land), the plough, the domestication of animals, and irrigation were in place by 4000 BC. By 3500 BC city-states had arisen in Sumeria, with all the appurtenances of stratified complex societies: kings, warriors, priests, nobles, specialists, traders, workers, peasants, and slaves.

The story unfolded in remarkably similar sequences, as described by Julian Steward, although at different times on different continents, from hunting and incipient agriculture, through formative and regional states, a dark ages, cyclical imperial conquests, to the Iron Age cultures, where the Israelites pick up the story. We are here concerned with that initial push during the Neolithic revolution, from 10,000 to 2,000 years ago.

The initial sequence was repeated in Egypt, India, and China, in the great river valleys: Nile, Ganges, Indus, Yellow, and Yangtze. In each case the sequence was, as Diamond presents it, with "intensive agriculture," the domestication of animals, and the agricultural surplus being the basis for the development of complexity. Because arable land was scarce (both naturally and as a result of population growth) and water had to be controlled for irrigation, there was inevitably conflict over both. This led to the development of central authorities, warfare and conquest, and the development of a peasant and slave class. Karl Wittfogel considered the control of irrigation to be absolutely central to this development: what came to be known as the "hydraulic hypothesis." Literacy of a kind had appeared in Sumeria by 3400 BC, and was originally largely a matter of lists and brief injunctions on clay tablets for the use of the growing class of bureaucrats needed to administer the conquered territories and keep records of tribute and taxation. With the perfecting of metal weapons this process was further intensified, specialized classes of metalworkers came into being, and the age of empires began in earnest.

In the Americas the same pattern was followed (from about 1200 BC), with the development of some staple crop—usually maize but in the Andes potatoes—forming the basis of population growth with all its consequences. Maize was domesticated in Middle America, and the Olmec, Aztec, and Maya civilizations, with all the characteristics listed above, including advanced literacy and astronomy, grew out of the surpluses made possible by intensive agriculture in maize. Diamond notes that there were no domesticable large animals available to use for either food or as draught animals, which probably slowed development. Maize diffused to North America, and in the Southeast kingdoms like the mound-building Cahokia arose, but did not last.

The most astonishing development of a society based on maize cultivation was that of the Anasazi in the arid Southwest. The great stone buildings of Chaco Canyon, for example, may well have been built partly as ceremonial centers and partly as grain storage houses. The Anasazi management of scarce water resources was extraordinary. But I have argued that there is no evidence of a large population, complex hierarchy, or much specialization, warfare, conquest, or literacy among the Anasazi. Their level of political and social development was probably about the same as that of the known Pueblo Indians. Their end is mysterious, but probably came as a result of prolonged drought in the 1200s when the towns, and later the spectacular cliff dwellings, of Mesa Verde and the San Juan valley were abandoned.

The three areas of the Americas we have mentioned, though, did not follow this pattern. Steward sees the story of complex societies in the Americas beginning only with the domestication of maize in Middle America and the potato in the northern highlands of Peru; the previous period is simply "pre-agriculture." But this was before the astonishing findings by Michael Moseley and others on the Norte Chico (the North-west Coast) of Peru. Haywood does recognize that Peru may have been an exception to his rule. We shall look first at the Northwest Coast Indi-ans, then at the Calusa, and finally at the Peruvians of the Norte Chico, to see how far societies could go toward social complexity without the necessary conditions of the orthodox theory, but with an abundance of seafood.

The Northwest Coast of America

The tribes of the Northwest Coast (Map 10.1) reached a height of social and cultural development in the eighteenth and nineteenth centuries. At first they flourished with the opportunities of trade with the Russians in what is now Alaska, the British in Canada, and the Americans pressing from the south. By the end of the nineteenth century they had succumbed to the pressures of acculturation, disease, and population loss, and their traditional way of life was all but gone. But by then they had become part of the legend and literature of America. The work of Franz Boas in ethnography, the popularization of the Kwakiutl by Ruth Benedict in her best-selling *Patterns of Culture* (1934), and their incorporation into so-cioeconomic theory with Thorstein Veblen's *Theory of the Leisure Class* (1902) made them one of the most famous of all tribal societies. Even in European anthropology they were well known through the work of Mar-cel Mauss on primitive exchange systems in *The Gift* (1925), where the institution of the potlatch was central. But it was Veblen, who used the potlatch as an example of "conspicuous consumption," that ensured their fame.

The "tribes" are in fact linguistic and cultural divisions; there was no formal tribal organization. The narrow coastal area was densely wooded with fir and cedar, and there was no room for agriculture, but some hunt-ing of land mammals. At best small gardens could be cultivated, but mostly plants were gathered. The main source of food was the sea, with its plenti-ful supplies of salmon (five species) as well as smelt, herring, and candlefish rich in oil, and cod and halibut. The salmon spawned annually by swim-ming up the rivers and were caught in both nets and traps. All these fish, especially the oily ones, can be smoked, dried, or cured and thus provide

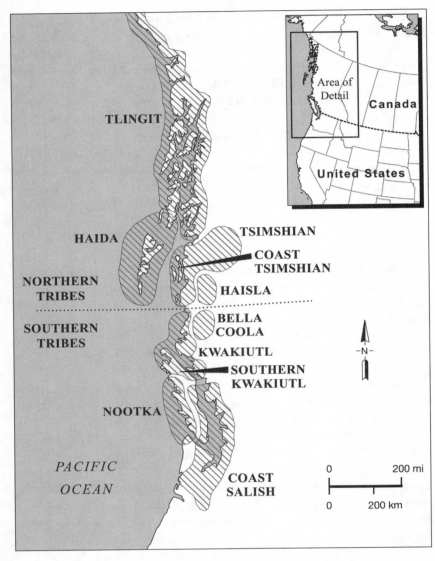

Map 10.1 Tribes of the Northwest Coast (after Drucker, *Indians of the Northwest Coast;* map by Rutgers Cartography)

food over the winters. Large seagoing canoes were carved from the forest woods, and whale and other sea mammals were hunted for their flesh and their fur. Recent archaeology has found extensive "clam-gardens" where clams were systematically farmed (Rick and Erlandson 2009). Trade was established over a wide area, and with the coming of the Europeans great wealth was amassed from furs and fish.

This was a culture of wood, which does not survive, so its monuments are forgotten and its achievements underestimated. Their large, superbly decorated 150-foot-long communal plank houses decayed and disappeared (although the tradition has been revived). But these tribal peoples reached great heights as wood-carvers, and their totem poles, masks, canoes, storage chests, and house carvings achieved worldwide fame and had a deep influence on modern art. They had no pottery but skillfully wove baskets as containers. Fibers of the versatile red cedar were ingeniously woven into nets, mats, and baskets, and when added to goat hair, into colorful blankets and often elaborate clothing. They had no metal until the Europeans brought it. There was no writing, but crests, boards, and poles carried pictorial lineage histories. But despite all these achievements, technically these people were hunter-gatherers, although of a settled, not nomadic, variety.

Their society, however, was complex and hierarchical, but politically it rose only to the level of chiefdoms. The "chiefs" were strictly local, and at best they achieved loose confederations of local units for warfare—which was largely raiding. The basic unit of the society was a local group or village of, on average, 200 to 400 people, which owned land and fishing rights. It would have a chief, who was in fact a headman or village manager. It was a kinship group always, although variously constituted, and there was a lot of local variation. To the north, the Tlingit, Haida, and Tsimshian were poster boys for the perfect structure of "primitive society" as the evolutionists and functionalists saw it. They perhaps preserved the pristine structure that was carried into the New World. Among the Tlingit, for example, the linguistic group was divided into exogamous moieties: people belonged to one of two divisions of the tribe, called Ravens and Wolves, and descent was matrilineal: you got your moiety membership from your mother, and you must marry into the other moiety. The moieties were not localized, but spread throughout the tribe.

The moieties were further subdivided into named totemic clans, which were again matrilineal and exogamous. The Haida had two moieties, Raven and Eagle, but no clans. The Tsimshian had four matrilineal phratries—Eagle, Raven, Wolf, and Black Whale (think of them as large clans)—but no moieties. In all these northern tribes, the local group was a lineage or segment of people related by matrilineal descent with the wives, sister's sons, retainers, and slaves—the latter being obtained in raids. Cross-cousin marriage, especially with the mother's brother's daughter was favored, and so was avunculocal residence—at puberty a boy would go to live with his mother's brother, his nearest matrilineal relative from whom he could hope to inherit property and titles.

This picture-perfect primitive society was not so well represented in the southern tribes, the Kwakiutl, Bella Coola, Nootka, and Coast Salish. Descent here was bilateral rather than matrilineal, with even a slight preference for the father's line. But the local unit was still the autonomous kinship group—an extended family. Ranks and titles were here even more important, especially as bestowed on sons-in-law. The northwestern tribes generally put a huge emphasis on rank and title. In Benedict's description it is an almost maniacal obsession. In the north, the more structured and traditional, ranks were determined mostly by matrilineal heredity; in the south there was more of a free-for-all and competition was encouraged. In all of them there was a broad grading of society from chiefs through nobles to commoners and then slaves. The slaves were stuck, their lives were miserable, and they were sometimes killed for show, but the top three ranks could be negotiated. Each was graded into fine divisions of status, and individuals could move up or down in rank, but to do so depended on the accumulation of goods, and through the disposition of these the obtaining of crests (heraldic devices) and titles.

This is where the famous potlatch comes in. The chiefs in particular had always been redistribution agents, and a great deal of their lives was spent moving wealth around, usually by means of lavish feats and giveaways, including the distribution of titles. By these they both established their own prestige and benefited the community. In the north, potlatches were mostly used to establish hereditary rank, and were held particularly at funerals with the passing on of the chiefly titles. But in the south a lower-ranking individual could use the wealth he had accumulated to challenge his superiors in rank to contests of feast- and gift-giving in an attempt to better them and increase his rank. At its height this potlatch could include those displays of the destruction of wealth that so impressed and shocked white observers. To illustrate his superiority a man could destroy objects of value such as "coppers"—the nearest thing to currency—burn canoes and valuable woven blankets, and even kill slaves.

The lavishness and destructiveness of these feasts seemed to observers like Veblen to be a kind of nightmarish metaphor for status-seeking consumption in Western societies, which were also obsessed with status and rank. It is more than possible that the potlatch reached these extremes only as a result of the relatively rapid accumulation of wealth derived from the fish and fur trade in the nineteenth century. This went along with the dissolution of traditional social bonds and the agglomeration of the declining population into larger settlements. But the image of the secret societies holding their masked rituals by firelight, with the cannibal dancers taking bites of human flesh, together with the deliberate orgies of destruction in search of superior rank, remain lodged in the collective subconscious of the West.

This was a social order whose major source of protein was the sea, especially salmon. It completely lacked agriculture and the cultivation of a staple crop. It was not literate, but its level of artistic development was second to none in the preindustrial world, given that it worked in wood, which, as we have seen, perishes. It had a division of labor (fishermen both local and deep-sea, hunters, trappers, artisans in wood and bone, warriors, shamans, managers) and supported a nonworking noble caste. It had one of the most elaborate systems of rank and status in the nonagricultural world. Helen Codere called it "rank without class." It had almost constant warfare, which was perhaps like that of ancient Greek society, with local chiefdoms raiding each other and carrying off goods, women, and slaves. This warfare did not include conquest and expansion, however; there was no mechanism for that.

Its level of political development did not rise above the local chiefdom and the loose tribal confederation, but despite this lack it dominated the Pacific Northwest until the inevitable corrupting forces of the Western nations brought it down. If it was not a civilization in the strict definition, it was a hierarchical, complex, wealthy, and artistically spectacular society. For our immediate purposes it illustrates how far in the direction of complexity a people can go without any agriculture or agricultural surplus, but with a secure base of protein in the fruits of the sea.

The Calusa of Southwest Florida

The climate of southwest Florida is semitropical and therefore conducive to horticulture, but its coastline is a tangle of dense mangrove forests where any kind of cultivation is impossible. The inland southern part of the peninsula was the vast and uncultivable swamp of the Everglades. Nevertheless, the Calusa Indians, who were in place by AD 200, developed a complex kingdom there that held off the Spanish and finally the British and Creek Indian invaders until the early eighteenth century (Map 10.2). These were the Indians who famously killed Ponce de León in 1521 during his search for the Fountain of Youth.

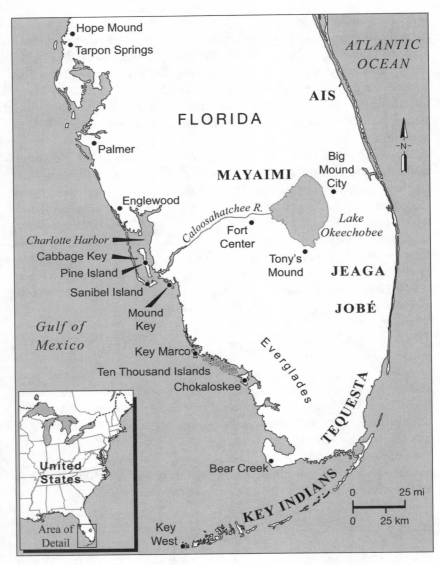

Map 10.2 Calusa sites of Southwest Florida; tributary tribes are shown in capitals (map by Rutgers Cartography)

Their society, which was flourishing by AD 500, was built literally on shellfish. Temple and dwelling mounds as high as forty or more feet were built from used seashells and, in the historic period at least, faced with shell. The remains of these shell mounds (and burial mounds, after about AD 1000) are the only high places in this otherwise totally flat country. Whole islands rising thirty feet out of the water, like Cabbage Key in Pine Island Sound, are in fact Calusa shell mounds. Shells provided most of the tools, weapons, and fishing gear, there being little stone that could be used. The warm waters of the Gulf of Mexico provided forty varieties of shellfish and more than fifty varieties of fish, from the tiny pinfish, pigfish, and catfish—the staples—to the abundant mullet, grouper, snapper, and sheepshead, up to the formidable tarpon. The easily caught and plentiful mullet was the staple for winter fishing, making it unnecessary to dry and preserve the fish as in the Northwest. Then there were sharks (and occasional monk seal), more difficult to catch and probably prestige foods.

Sharks' teeth were used as knives and carving tools; plant fiber provided nets and lines; conch and whelk shells became sinkers; easily cultivated gourds were floats. Supplemented by some hunting of deer, turtles, and alligators, and the gathering of plants and the cultivation of small gardens, the teeming sea provided for a population of probably 10,000 to 15,000 at its height. Fishing, trade, war, and rapid communication were made possible by the use of large dugout canoes that could hold up to forty or sixty men. Two canoes lashed together with planks made a catamaran for especially bulky loads. Most of their artwork, being in wood, has perished, but what has been found rivals the best in native North America.

One of the mysteries of the Calusa is their relationship to the great earthworks or ceremonial mounds found around Lake Okeechobee to the northeast (see Map 10.2). These are massive structures. Tony's Mound is 1,665 yards long and 580 yards wide. Big Mound City covers half a mile across in two directions. The mounds, often semicircular with "fingers" leading off them, must have required a tremendous amount of labor to construct; yet there is little evidence of habitation around them. They were perhaps purely ceremonial centers, like Stonehenge, where all the south Florida tribes gathered.

Another theory has them as dwelling mounds built to escape the rise in swamp levels (and sea levels) during the warm period of AD 100–400. They may even predate the Calusa. They are associated with a pottery style (Belle Glade) from about AD 200 that is found among the Calusa after about AD 500. This could mean that the Calusa came from that area and moved to the coast, or simply that they borrowed the pottery style. But someone built those huge mounds at massive cost, and there are so far no other candidates than the pyramid-building Calusa or their immediate ancestors.

At one period during the fifteenth and sixteenth centuries the Calusa empire and its vassal tribes covered the whole of south Florida. It was linked by a system of well-constructed canals up to twenty feet wide and lined with shell. It stretched from the present-day Fort Myers area in Charlotte Harbor to Miami via the Caloosahatchee River and Lake Okeechobee, and south via the barrier islands to the Florida Keys (Map 10.2). The barrier islands were storm derived, and at their edges oyster beds provided an anchorage for mangrove trees in whose long finger-like roots soil gathered. These mangrove forests then expanded to cover whole islands.

The main towns were large and prosperous. On Pine Island the site of one town covers three miles of shore by three-quarters of a mile inland. Like the Calusa capital on Mound Key in Estero Bay, it included as well as the pyramid mounds, large plazas, and water courts with pile dwellings around the sides and burial mounds in the centers, internal canals, fish tanks, and gardens. Spanish descriptions of Mound Key ("Calos") describe the main mound as supporting a royal palace that could hold 2,000 people.

Here elaborate rituals took place, including human sacrifice (with heads on poles)—the fate of most Spanish captives. Children and captives were sacrificed on the death of a queen or a nobleman. Spanish records describe ceremonies with masks, processions, songs, dances, and retreats. There was a belief system that included a doctrine of three human souls, and a trinity of "great" gods controlling the sea, the weather, and war, together with totem animals and finely carved idols. During their long contact with the Calusa, while not conquering them, the Spanish did record many details of their life and society, as did Spanish captives who survived.

The ruler of this ambitious empire was called "Carlos" by the Spaniards (obviously a version of "Calus"). He was a "sacred king" who took as one of his wives his own sister, Inca style: the only case in North America of incestuous royal marriage. The king was surrounded by a caste of nobles and a body of priests and full-time warriors, all of whom were exempt from work. The throne seemed to pass from father to son (with much of the usual royal intrigue), but we do not know what was the rule of descent for the commoners. The Indian tribes of the Southeast were uniformly matrilineal, and it may be that the commoners still traced descent through the female line while the nobles and king, consonant with their practice of polygyny, had moved to a patrilineal system.

Carlos, the king, is reported to have had a war chief—called "captain-general" by the Spanish—and a chief priest, both of whom were relatives. This sounds like the basic Amerindian "war chief and peace chief" system, but both of these officials are here subordinated to a ruler. This represents a step up the social evolutionary scale from chiefdom to kingdom, and a definite step toward serious vertical complexity. It was the step the Northwest Coast tribes never took. However, the Calusa did not attempt to conquer and administer the other tribes in south Florida; it was enough to hold them in vassalage and take tribute from them, including European trade goods and captives. It was not enough to spur the development of a class of literate administrators.

The whole story of how the Calusa held off the Spaniards—missionaries and colonists—by a mixture of diplomacy and force (the Franciscans were stripped naked and dispatched) is fascinating, but too long to tell here. In the end they succumbed to disease, and slave raiding by the renegade Creeks armed with British guns we now call Seminoles. Guns, germs, and steel did them in. It may be that their last stand was in Key West, which is "Cayo Hueso" in Spanish: the island of bones, named for the many skeletons found there, which could be those of the last Calusa.

But this empire did not fall from internal collapse. It was a staggeringly successful kingdom and empire that was sustained almost entirely from the sea. There was only minor horticulture and absolutely no intensive agriculture, but there was intensive fishing from a boundless and reliable source. There is good evidence of a division of labor, of a specialization of tasks, especially in the production of shell artifacts for trade after AD 800. The bulk of the population was involved in fishing and did all the things associated with a fishing economy. There may have been some fish farming, but mostly fish were still "hunted" day by day. Yet this oceanic predation supplied the staple and surplus needed to sustain a complex urban kingdom of ranks and castes that flourished in south Florida for a thousand years.

The Norte Chico of Peru

Andean civilization peaked with the Incas in the sixteenth century, before its destruction by the Spaniards. The Incas have every one of the qualifications for complexity except literacy. They did have the *quipu*, a form of abacus made from rows of knotted strings, which allowed them to keep records of quantities and perhaps even code simple messages. The Inca civilization certainly developed its high point through intensive agriculture, largely potatoes, beans, and squash, in the incredible terraced mountainsides of the Andean highlands that are one of the wonders of the ancient world. But it did not start there. Maize diffused late to the Andes and could not have been at the source of this particular fountain of civilization. There was one kind of domesticable animals, in the form of the llama and its relatives, but they were of limited use as food or as draught animals, being used mostly as beasts of burden and for their wool. The earliest signs of cities and complex society came from the Andean coast, and thereby hangs a tale.

The coast of northern Peru, where we find these stirrings—as early as 3500 BC—was one of the most arid areas on earth, and intensive agriculture, even if there had been a suitable staple crop, was impossible. There is less than one inch of rain a year on this narrow barren coast; in some parts there is none at all. The whole area sits in the shadow of the

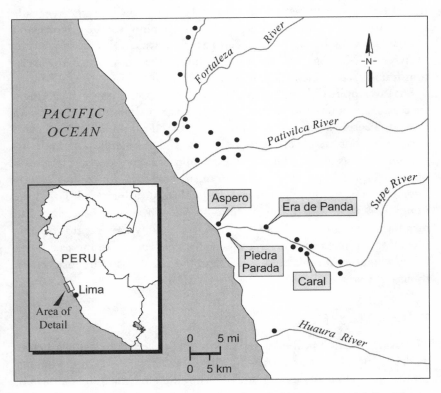

Map 10.3 The Norte Chico of Peru; only selected cities are named (after Mann, *1491;* map by Rutgers Cartography)

Andes, and rain falls only to the east of the mountains. The whole coast is, however, like the Pacific Northwest Coast, crossed by numerous rivers, which flow down steeply from these very rain-fed mountains, creating small areas where, with careful irrigation, some production of crops is possible: perhaps 10 percent of the land. The Pacific Ocean here, particularly the Humbolt current, is both extremely cold and extremely abundant. These icy waters teem with an endless supply of fish, mostly anchovies, sardines, and shellfish, and Peru still has the third largest fishing industry in the world. Even so, it is hard to imagine that what ultimately became the high civilization of the Incas can have originated in this bleak place, and before the Egyptians built their great pyramids. But it did.

The four river valleys (some seventy to ninety miles north of Lima) that were the axes of development were, north to south: the Fortaleza, the Pativilca, the Supe, and the Huaura (Map 10.3). The original settlers of the area, moving down the shoreline from North America, drew more than 90 percent of their protein from the sea and lived in small communities along the coast. But somewhere around 4000–3500 BC, at the mouth of the Supe River, larger settlements began to appear. By 3255 BC, at Aspero, there were ceremonial platforms and temples, and evidence of genuinely urban life. These dates are incredible because they put the origins of urban life in the Americas at least a thousand years before it was thought to have occurred. It is all the more remarkable because these coastal peoples had no metal tools and had not even developed pottery: they were, in the jargon, "pre-ceramic," like the Northwest Coast Indians and unlike the Calusa, who had pots. For Morgan, pottery was the sign of the emergence from savagery. But these "savages" were in fact the first town dwellers in the Americas.

As you go up the valley of the Supe you find even larger and more complex cities. Their platforms, temples, and pyramids, like those of Aspero, were built in "step-pyramid" fashion with blocks made from mesh bags filled with stones, which were then faced with stone or plastered. The organic material used in the meshes gives the excellent carbon dates. Piedra Parada lies on the south side of the river. Era de Panda is the largest, with mounds and courts filling 79 hectares. The best known, and probably the "capital"—or at least center-city, Caral (69 hectares)—is about 23 kilometers inland.

Caral which has been firmly carbon-dated to between 2627 BC and 1977 BC, was a truly complex city with many different pyramid temples, and elite living areas with plastered and painted walls, matched by barrios for workers with houses of cane, and workshops for artisans and jewelers. The main pyramid is 153 by 109 meters, and rises to 28 meters. In front of it was a large sunken circular court topped by fire-altars. This Caral pattern was to be repeated throughout the Andes as urban civilization spread. There are some thirteen other similar mounds in Caral. By any standards this was a large and complex ceremonial city, made by people who had no pottery or metal tools, few textiles, and seemingly no art. A large number of conch trumpets and bone flutes were found, however; they had organized music.

In the Supe valley there are seventeen such city complexes, and in the other river valleys as many more, only apparently of later dates. The valley could have supported a population of 10,000 to 20,000; the whole region's population could have been as much as 50,000. Although the cities were built in stages, the population of the Supe valley could scarcely have built them alone. Supe, it seems, was the center of what begins to look like a genuine state, and if so, the first state in the Americas. But how did they live, if so little of the land was cultivable? Where was the "intensive agriculture" that is integral to the orthodox view? Caral actually did have serious irrigation works, and there was cultivation. But let us return to the coast for a moment to the older settlement of Aspero.

The people of Aspero lived largely on fish, as we have seen. There were bottomlands of the river that flooded and could have been farmed, and some items were planted. Among these, three items rank high: fruit trees, gourds, and cotton. All these can be planted and largely left alone; they do not need intensive care. The trees provided fruit, of course, but also wood, which was needed for boats, although boats could have been made from bundles of reeds, as is still done today. The gourds provided a little food but were essentially used for net floats and containers. The cotton was used for textiles, but largely for fishing nets. There was no large crop of cotton.

Other plant fibers were also used for nets and for the mesh bags used in building. Thus there was no crop of staples that could be stored at what was still a horticultural level of production. The basic food items were the anchovies and sardines and the other fruits of the sea that could be fished by net and line. Unlike on the Northwest Coast, there was no development of the harpoon and the large seagoing canoe that could reap a harvest of sea mammals. These conditions seemed to set a limit to further development.

Yet if we return upriver to Caral, we find that all the irrigation and farming did not involve any staple food crop. Fruits (guayaba, pacae) were planted as on the seashore, but the most abundant crop was cotton. You can't eat cotton. What you can do, as well as make textiles with it, is make more and better fishing nets and lines. Add to this that remains at Caral show large amounts of anchovies and sardines, and that these were the only source of animal protein (there was little hunting and no domestication of animals or birds), and the answer is clear.

The coast is only 23 kilometers away; communication up the valley is easy; you could go up and down in a day. There was a symbiosis between the great inland cities and the smaller cities and fishing villages of the coast: either cotton was traded for anchovies, or the seafood was tribute exacted by the inland priests who provided the cotton to the shore folks, or whatever other combination. But the seafood came inland and the cotton went to the shore, and the result was the first complex urban society in the Americas and one of the oldest in the world.

The relative part played by horticulture and fishing, and which came first, is still debated by archaeologists. Did the cities start inland and expand to the sea in search of anchovies, or did they start by the sea and then send colonies inland in search of cotton? The coastal cities seem to be the oldest and to have come first, but it may be more complicated than that. For our purposes it does not matter. It is what sustained this early complex society that matters, and that was fish.

The cycles of El Niño, the bitter winds that periodically disturb the West Coast of the Americas and cause devastating losses of cold-water fish, could have played their part. As population grew on the coast, it could have been forced to develop horticulture in the river valleys as a hedge against these losses. But for whatever reason, the expansion happened, the population boomed, trade goods from the north (now Ecuador and Columbia) and the Amazon (including hallucinogenic snuff) appeared, and a hierarchical, ceremonial, urban, differentiated society (priests, artisans, farmers, fishermen) arose as a basis for the high Andean civilization that followed.

But there was no evidence of warfare, certainly not of expansive warfare and conquest. So along with literacy (unless we count the *quipu*) this pillar of my quadripartite theory must go, even if dense population and the division of labor survive. At some point Caral was abandoned like the cities of Chaco. There was no destruction, no burning, no shattered buildings, no bodies. They just moved up into the Andes and produced other wonders like the Chavin civilization to the north.

Somehow this complex union of city-states developed without evidence of armies, barracks, palaces, fortifications, armaments, and all the appurtenances of statehood and expansion that characterized the rest of the civilizing world. There is evidence of large feasts—the remains of them were actually built into the monuments; the major buildings were religious; and there were all those flutes and trumpets. In a people lacking art (except for geometrically decorated textiles), a figure like the Inca god Wiraqocha was found incised on a gourd at Caral. Did this primitive state hold together by the power of the religious hierarchy, by ceremony and ritual, and by voluntary labor given as religious service? Why not?

We shall probably never know why they moved. They had a booming population that had to be fed. Did they discover the value of the potato as a staple, capable of "intensive agriculture" and storage? They needed to produce a surplus, so perhaps they just had to go somewhere where more extensive irrigation and terraced farming could be practiced, and where llamas and alpacas could be used as beasts of burden and providers of wool. But why abandon the abundant harvest of the sea? Maybe a more than usually devastating El Niño hit them and robbed them of the seaborne staple that was their lifeblood—or earthquakes, or flooding, or sand dune incursion (see Sandweiss et al. 2009). For whatever reason, by about 1600 BC, like the Anasazi, they just moved away. They may have abandoned the arid coastal desert and narrow valleys of the Norte Chico, but their civilization was born there, and its secret was seafood.

The Hill with a Navel

The rise to civilization may be older and much more complicated than we have thought to date. In southeastern Turkey lie the remains of an early Neolithic monumental building complex some 11,000 years old—8,000 years older than Aspero. This corresponds in time to the odd phenomenon of the abandonment of cave art in Europe. It is as if populations came up out of the caves and started building megaliths. Göbekli Tepe ("Navel Hill") would be remarkable enough with its artificial hill and hand-quarried and carved T-shaped limestone pillars, in circular stone or oval enclosures. There may be as many as twenty of these enclosures, with the pillars, carved with animal figures (lions, bulls, boars, foxes, gazelles, snakes, reptiles, and birds, including vultures) rising to twenty-two feet in the center, weighing up to twenty tons: the largest known stone circles before Stonehenge. The floors are of burnt lime, and a bench runs round the interior wall, as in Anasazi kivas. The pillars may have supported log roofs. This collection of large stone structures is the oldest man-made place of worship in the world, and *it was built by hunters and gatherers.*

The plains and rolling hills, which are now barren, were then lush and teeming with game: deer, gazelle, pigs, geese, goats, waterfowl, and wild donkeys. This attracted bands of hunters who, starting even in the Meso-

lithic, began to build ritual centers. Before there was settlement and domestication, then, there was monumental ritual building activity requiring
the labor of thousands, with only stone tools, yet without any evidence of
a state or of central control. But the level of ritual activity, along with evidence of feasting, suggests, as at Caral, the presence of a priestly elite, as do
the carvings of arms and hands and "stoles" on the T-shaped pillars. The
frequency of vultures in the carvings, including one showing a decapitated
corpse surrounded by vultures, suggests that the practice of exposing bodies to be stripped by the birds (Zoroastrian "sky burial") may have started
here. It is a mystery on the scale of Stonehenge, only it is 7,000 years older
and the builders of Stonehenge already had domestication and settlement.
Clearly there was no intensive agriculture here, no Neolithic revolution.
Then the plot thickens.

On nearby Mount Karacabag geneticists have found what they consider to be some of the earliest ancestors of the cultivated grains that
sparked the Neolithic revolution, particularly Einkorn wheat. The beginnings of grain cultivation, then, could have taken place here, and even
perhaps were spurred by the need to feed the large labor force building
the megalithic temples. Could the agricultural revolution then have be-
gun, not with thousands of small cultivation events, but with a "big bang"
of grain production needed for essentially religious purposes? We don't
know for sure. We do know for sure that a degree of social complexity—
hunters, farmers, priests, stone carvers, and laborers—was achieved here
well before "intensive agriculture" was common. We know that it could
be sustained by a lush hunting-and-gathering economy, and that it may
well have given rise to that very intensive agriculture that was supposed to
be its cause.

Somewhere about 8000 BC the whole thing imploded, destroyed by its
own success: a pattern to be endlessly repeated in the millennia to come.
Perhaps overuse of the valley caused a drastic decline in the number of
prey animals, and even primitive agriculture and the domestication of the
local goats might have caused a depletion of the soil. Perhaps there was a
great drought. But as with the Anasazi and other of the collapsed "civilizations," they did not just leave: they made a measured exit and modified
their habitation. They began to backfill the complex and over time to bury
it under 500 cubic meters of soil, flints, and refuse, until it looked like a
natural hill and was thought to be so until very recently. But as the buried
complex is gradually retrieved, its story adds to that of the examples here
as a complication in our record of the origins of civilization, and another
challenge to the orthodox hypothesis. The bounty of the hunt, like the
bounty of the sea, could initially sustain complexity.

Terra Ardua: Oceanus Benignus

On the rainy Northwest Coast, on the basis of seasonal salmon fishing and the general bounty of the sea, there grew up a complex, extremely wealthy, densely populated society of local chiefdoms and tribal alliances. It had specialization of labor and a finely graded system of ranks, including slaves and nobles. It lacked writing, but was rich in artistic and ceremonial traditions, and if politically it did not rise to the level of a state, socially it showed a true vertical complexity. In the warm semitropical Gulf of Mexico the Calusa, with their winter supply of mullet and equally abundant resources of fish and shellfish, developed a true state with a monarch, towns with pyramids, ranks and classes, and effective control over the whole of south Florida. On the arid coast of northwestern Peru, the stone cities of the Supe valley, fed by anchovies and other fish from the Pacific, formed the nucleus of an urban state system that in turn was hierarchical and ceremonial, and had a specialization of tasks. None of these societies had elite literacy, unless one counts the *quipu,* but that is more like incipient literacy. The Northwest Coast had raiding but not conquest, the Calusa had war and intimidation but not acquisition, while on the Norte Chico there was no sign of such conflict but nevertheless there was a complex state system sustained by religion.

Archaeologists have been reconsidering the role of seafood in an earlier surge forward: that from the Mesolithic to the Neolithic in Europe some 15,000 to 10,000 years ago. The Old Stone Age hunters had always fished, as Morgan recognized, but fish was thought of as an ancillary source of food. Recently, however, discoveries in Britain and the European coasts have led to the view that there might have been an almost total dependence on the sea. Chris Stringer proclaims in *Homo Britannicus* (2006): "Early in our present interglacial, such dependency was widespread across western Europe, from Scotland and Denmark in the north, to Portugal in the south. In some sites, massive accumulations of shellfish middens and isotope data suggest that marine foods could have made up almost all of the diet." He continues: "Some experts see this Mesolithic reliance on a single source base (the sea) as a prelude to the similar narrowing that followed in the subsequent Neolithic period, with the switch to agricultural and pastoral foods." I quote him verbatim lest I be thought, in my enthusiasm for seafood, to be exaggerating its role. But there it is: an almost total dependence on the sea that pushed mankind forward into the Neolithic and into history.

Rick and Erlandson in the article already cited show how so-called hunter-gatherer populations "substantially altered and enhanced marine eco-systems" in the Americas from as much as 23,000 years ago. Springer sees the Neolithic move to agriculture and pastoralism as the next necessary step after the stage of "mariculture" in Europe. Göbekli Tepe, with its initial dependence on game animals, may have been the crucial intervening step in the Eurasian development. But the three examples from the Americas looked at here show that seafood alone could in fact sustain the move. They show three stages in the growth of social complexity. They show how far it is possible for society to evolve toward vertical complexity without intensive agriculture: a staple food crop and a storable surplus of that crop. They can do this by using the continuous surplus provided by the limitless bounty of the sea.

The leisure class in each case must expropriate that surplus and exploit it to its own advantage. How exactly it does this is still a mystery to be solved; fishermen in their boats are somehow more difficult to control than peasants who are attached to a fixed piece of land. But in a system based on fishing, as opposed to a system of heavily taxed and exploited agricultural peasantry, no one (except perhaps the few slaves) really loses. While the upper classes certainly have *more* than they need, the fishermen have *all* that they need. The sea provides.

CHAPTER ELEVEN

The Route to Civilization

From Tribal to Political Society

I F WE are to understand the meaning of the tribes and the tribal, the nature of the Drumbeat and its contribution to, or undermining of, the world of the Miracle, then we should have a science that studies that meaning. Anthropology began life in the nineteenth century with a firm mandate to look at the primitive peoples of the world, the "simpler societies" as they were often called, in order to understand better how mankind had managed to "rise" to the level of civilization. To this end the extant tribes had to be seen as in some way representing the various stages of this ascent. Archaeology would then tell the story of the progress through the stages of civilization itself, until history took over once there was a written record.

After Darwin, anthropology added the task of investigating the beginnings of the human story, of how mankind had come about in the first place: the transition from ape to man. This would complete the story, and so paleontology was added to the agenda, along with linguistics, given the fundamental and defining importance of language in human society. Thus was the necessary science born, and though it was not strangled at birth, its subsequent history was subject to the unforeseeable twists and turns of human ideology that are both its subject matter and its fate. In this chapter we shall look at one of its founding fathers, Lewis Henry Morgan, who dominated its early days and then was discarded along with the mandate. If we can recapture some sense of the mandate as he saw it—and helped to create it—then perhaps we can recover some idea of what such a science should be like if it is to uncover the meaning of the tribes and the persistence of the tribal imagination.

Morgan the Man

Lewis Henry Morgan (1818–1881) was one of those remarkable Victorians at once very much of his time and yet very much beyond it. He is most readily, and justly, compared with those other giant intellects of his age, Charles Darwin and Herbert Spencer. All three were in their lives conventional men, not radical and certainly not revolutionary; but they all developed theories with radical and revolutionary implications in the world of ideas. Collectively they helped to shape the intellectual landscape of the succeeding generations.

All were amateurs, not academics, and their work was directed to educated people in general, not to a disciplinary clique. All were concerned with evolution in one form or another, and hence in conflict with religious and intellectual orthodoxy. Spencer was an overt agnostic: religion was the realm of "The Unknowable." Darwin in his youth accepted that he might become a clergyman, but spent his later life feeling uncomfortable about his inability to share his wife's piety. Morgan remained a nominal Christian, a Deist in effect, but suspicious of religious ritual and, like Darwin, uncomfortable with his wife's devoutness. Morgan, like Darwin (and unlike Spencer), married his first cousin, and both men were devastated by the death of a young daughter. Spencer never married, although in his youth he was romantically linked to the novelist George Eliot (Mary Ann Evans), whom we met in Chapter 7 as the author of *The Mill on the Floss*.

Of the three, Morgan was the worldliest, most unlike the reclusive Darwin and the socially reserved Spencer. He had a classical education in the best New England tradition; as a boy he formed a club for the study of the classics. In this he was unlike Darwin, who was forced to study the classics but disliked them, and Spencer, who had a positive hatred for them and campaigned against classical education all his life. The results of this devotion to Latin and Greek studies are obvious in what follows. Morgan then became a lawyer and astute railroad investor in his native New York State. (Spencer, in comparison, became a railroad engineer but failed at it and fell back on his family and its income.) The fortune Morgan amassed enabled him to devote himself both to ethnological studies based on his local Iroquois—largely Seneca—tribes, and to a successful career as a legislator in the New York State Assembly.

In founding his eventual theoretical ideas on the solid factual basis of detailed ethnographic studies, he was more like Darwin than the library-bound Spencer. *The League of the Ho-de-no-sau-nee or Iroquois* was his *Voyage of the Beagle*. He was more like Spencer in his personal involvement with public affairs. But while Spencer sought to influence ideas, Morgan tried, successfully, to influence law and legislation on behalf of the Indians in his state. He was Commissioner of Indian Affairs for New York for some years, and helped the Iroquois resist attempted land grabs by powerful commercial interests. He was also a conscientious representative of his Rochester constituency. He was elected president of the American Association for the Advancement of Science and founded its anthropology section.

After having for many years resisted the idea of physical evolution—and the whole theory of the survival of the fittest—he eventually visited Europe; met Darwin, Spencer, and other evolutionists; and became a convert to the general idea. His journal of his European visit is a fascinating window both on the intellectual life of the time and on his own firmly held and very American views of democracy and equality, and his distaste for the lack of these in the countries he visited. It is perhaps prophetic, considering his later adoption by the Marxists, that he considered it inevitable that the dispossessed of Europe must eventually rise up against their oppressors.

One of the greatest ironies of early anthropology is that Morgan, a Christian and special creationist, should have made one of the most convincing arguments for the continuity in intelligence and ability between man and animal. This conclusion was reinforced by his intimate knowledge of, and deep study of, the American beaver. That it had no influence on later anthropology is perhaps due to its zoological subject matter. But his unjustly neglected and yet very great work of natural history, *The American Beaver and His Works* (1868), shows again the devotion to the factual, detailed study of cases in order to form theoretical conclusions, that was to characterize Morgan's work.

He had, in 1843, made a powerful argument to the general educated public in the *Knickerbocker* magazine—a New York periodical—where he insisted that animals showed intelligence, memory, abstraction, and imagination, and that "instinct" in animals should be understood to be a manifestation of these abilities. His insistence on the detailed observation of behavior in order to arrive at conclusions about its nature anticipated the later ethological approach to animal and human comportment. This was an approach that his successors—rather usurpers—in anthropology so stubbornly resisted in their devotion to the ideal of culture as "superorganic"—a term borrowed, ironically, from Spencer.

Perhaps the most moving tribute to him as a human being was his lifelong friendship and collaboration with a young educated Seneca he met browsing in an Albany bookstore. Hasanoanda, known in English as Ely

Parker, was a remarkable Native American, who was to become a civil engineer, aide-de-camp to General Ulysses Grant, and Commissioner of Indian Affairs. Morgan dedicated *The League of the Ho-de-no-sau-nee or Iroquois* to him, and he remained living proof to Morgan, and the world, that "savages" were equal in ability to ourselves, and that they too could achieve "civilization" as readily as Europeans. Why some peoples had achieved this status, while others had not, therefore, became something he urgently needed to understand. This was the route to *Ancient Society* (1877).

He paved the way with his stupendous *Systems of Consanguinity and Affinity of the Human Family* (1871), surely the most ambitious and impressive work of social science in the nineteenth century, or for that matter, the last 200 years. This too grew out of his detailed knowledge of Iroquois kinship—via Ely Parker and his family and people. It led to his epiphanic insight that this type of kinship system was not peculiar to the Iroquois but was found throughout native North America and in large areas of the globe elsewhere. To the examination of this then-startling finding, he gave his life, and gave us anthropology as a science.

The Development Hypothesis

Morgan was without question one of the great figures of nineteenth-century social science. With Herbert Spencer, Henry Sumner Maine, and Edward B. Tylor he laid the groundwork for what would become the modern sciences of social development. The idea of development did not originate with them; it was part of the eighteenth-century Enlightenment project of the "Universal History of Mankind" and, among others, the scholars of the Scottish Enlightenment had helped lay the foundations.

At this point, the differentiation into sociology and anthropology had not crystallized. The germs of it were there in the work of Émile Durkheim, for example, and his attempt to carve out a realm of "social facts" that would be the exclusive domain of sociology—an approach that had its roots in Auguste Comte and the French Enlightenment. But even this "sociology" was not defined as something exclusively concerned with modern industrial society, far from it. Such a concern would be articulated later and largely in the United States. The nineteenth-century social scientists, whatever their particular concerns, were all social developmentalists of one sort or another. Both Morgan and Durkheim felt it necessary, when dealing with either kinship or religion, to start with the Australian Aborigines. Karl Marx and Friedrich Engels, in their turn, although with a different twist, were just as firmly part of the pattern and, as we know, assimilated Morgan (Engels working from Marx's ethnological notebooks after his death) into their orthodoxy with enthusiasm.

We cannot understand or appreciate Morgan's contribution without first understanding the general background of social developmental thought. It is often referred to as "social evolutionism," but this is perhaps confusing, because it suggests a direct link with the Darwinian theory of evolution by natural selection. But one of the major cleavages among the developmentalists was between those, like Morgan, for example, who owed little or nothing to Darwin's theory, and those like Edward Westermarck who owed everything. So the best general term is "developmentalists."

The idea of social development of course preceded Darwin. There is a venerable history, stretching at least as far back as Lucretius in his *De Rerum Natura,* of thinkers who saw mankind developing from a primitive to a more civilized state through a series of stages and for a variety of suggested causes. The major cleavage had been, before Darwin, primarily between those, like Auguste Comte or G. W. F. Hegel, who saw the "progress" of mankind largely in terms of ideas, and those, like the Baron de Montesquieu and the Scottish school, who looked rather for environmental or material causes. Marx, in "standing Hegel on his head," was in effect a convert from the former to the latter (while keeping the basic Hegelian dialectical method as his explanatory tool). But without doubt Herbert Spencer set the terms of the debate in the nineteenth century. He even coined the term "the development hypothesis."

Like virtually everyone else but Darwin, Spencer assumed that evolutionary development must be progressive—in his case he saw the universe, and then life, moving from homogeneity to heterogeneity; from simple to complex. Societies moved likewise, and he established a typology of stages of such development, elaborately illustrated by examples from the "lowest" to the "highest" levels of social complexity. For Spencer this was in the nature of an inexorable natural process; there was no need to look for contingent causes. Most other developmentalists looked, however, for the causes of the social development they observed. However, all the developmentalists had in common this concern with the whole sweep of human society from its most primitive beginnings to at least the advent of civilization and often beyond. This is why there was as yet no clear distinction between anthropology and sociology: even self-identified sociologists, such as L. T. Hobhouse and Edward Westermarck, for example, were of necessity concerned with "primitive man" and "early society" and even with their prehuman foundations.

One thing also they took for granted: the validity of the "comparative method." This meant different things to different scholars, but in general it was the assumption that surviving "primitive" peoples were, in a sense, social fossils: glimpses into "the infancy of the human race" and the "stages of moral development" of mankind. Again the theorists differed among themselves, often acerbically, about what these stages were and what the causes were of the upward movement from one stage to another. But they were united methodologically in their acceptance of the principle that modern primitives ("savages," in their terminology) were essential clues to the universal history of the human past. As long as both sociologists and anthropologists were committed to the development hypothesis and the comparative method, then their work was bound to be largely indistinguishable.

Both, however, should be clearly distinguished from the "Social Darwinists" (William Graham Sumner, Lester Ward, Benjamin Kidd, Walter Bagehot), who were really very un-Darwinian and mostly an American political offshoot of Spencer's individualism and "survival of the fittest" doctrine (his phrase, not Darwin's). They might have superficially seemed like developmentalists in that they accepted the doctrine of stages and considered the progressive societies to be the "fittest." But this was both a misapplication of the Darwinian notion of fitness, which referred solely to individual reproductive success, and did not represent the views of developmentalists, like Morgan, who did not necessarily share the idea of favoring those individuals, societies, or races most ruthless in contemporary social competition. The confusions engendered by lumping all these late nineteenth-century thinkers about social evolution together remains with us today, and hinders attempts to get the social sciences to take seriously the findings of, for example, evolutionary biology.

For anthropology, the unity of purpose and method imposed by the developmental or social evolutionary thesis had even more profound implications. When Tylor and Morgan first began to define the subject as such, they saw the distinction between it and sociology more or less as a division of labor. Tylor's definitive work was called *Researches into the Early History of Mankind and the Development of Civilization*. This was defined as anthropology's task: it was assigned the early history of the species, the clues to which lay in the customs of the contemporary primitives. And this led, of course, to an immediate connection with pre-history (archaeology) and paleontology. The comparative method allowed us to read off the past from the present and hence to interpret the archaeological record. Present day "stone-age" peoples were the clue to the life of our stone-age ancestors as revealed to us by archaeology. As John Lubbock's book title concisely put it, *Pre-historic Times: As Illustrated by Ancient Remains, and the Manners and Customs of Modern Savages*.

This again merged smoothly into the post-Darwinian concern with human origins and the prehuman past: they were simply the natural continuation into the furthest past of the history of the human species. Darwin's neighbor and friend Sir John Lubbock (later Lord Avebury) was one of the first to make this connection as early as 1865. Morgan, in his mammoth researches into the development of the kinship terminologies of all the human language families, added comparative philology (modern linguistics) to the mix. Thus, in a simple, grand manner, all the classical anthropological concerns came to hang together. While there could be many different theories and emphases about the nature of human social and cultural development, there was a unity of purpose, material, and method, which the present fragmented discipline (and the chaotic social sciences in general) can only look back on with awe and envy.

Progress and Moral Development

We of the age of sensitivity, relativity, and political correctness have to make a serious leap of the imagination to find sympathy with—and in consequence to learn from—the developmentalist position. It is impossible today to claim with the confidence of our nineteenth-century forefathers that there is a clear ladder of progress and that we are at the top of it. There is no difficulty in the economic and scientific/technological realms, and no one but the most lunatic cognitive relativists (who unfortunately do exist) would ever challenge that Western industrial civilizations are the wealthiest and most scientifically and technically advanced societies the world has known. The problem lies in the confidence with which our forefathers claimed a corresponding *moral* advancement.

Non-anthropologists might have cited, perhaps, Christianity with confidence as clearly superior to heathen religions. Even the stoutest antirelativists among us would not have that conviction today, with large numbers of people turning to Eastern religions and even reviving paganism. Some countries once solidly Christian now have churchgoers as a tiny minority (England, for example). Two devastating world wars in which each alliance called down the Christian god to its altars have helped to increase skepticism. Christian belief and Christian morality no longer seem so self-evidently superior, except to unregenerate fundamentalists.

But in the nineteenth century even the non-Christian anthropologists could still, given the development hypothesis, claim the Western industrial civilizations as the end product—and ipso facto the superior product—of social and cultural evolution. To them this inevitability meant a corresponding moral superiority. Clearly moral reasoning or "the moral idea"

(Edward Westermarck, L. T. Hobhouse) had improved, expanded, and developed. The savage knew no morality outside his tribe; the barbarian was clearly not a superior moral reasoner. Some thinkers, like Émile Durkheim and Ferdinand Tönnies, saw that increasing social complexity could lead to *anomie* or loss of "community" and the like. In fact this became a central theme in sociology. But even they did not challenge the basic developmental thesis.

Obsolescence and Moral Obligation

So the issue is: if we follow ruthlessly the logic of the thesis, then all those societies that are not Western industrial civilizations are in some real sense obsolete. They did not develop. They exist, but in the same sense as the coelacanth or the echidna exist: as living representatives of past stages of evolution. They have therefore the same theoretical interest to us as a newly discovered still-living dinosaur or ape-man would have: they present previous stages of our own evolution that continue to survive. They are side branches of the main trunk of the evolutionary tree, and as such enable us to reconstruct that tree, to define its successive stages. Above all, then, they will help us answer the key question of why development takes place: Why did some societies progress and others did not? By examining those that did not, and by assigning them their proper place on the ladder of development, we can understand how progress takes place, and even further it. Thus societies other than Western industrial civilizations have their place in understanding how the latter occurred in the first place.

As to our own moral obligations to these societies, we of the most advanced version obviously should do all in our power to assist them in attaining the same high status. Here anthropology divided on the issue of the relationship of progress to race. To one wing the choice was obvious: the clue to development actually lay in race, with some races displaying superior abilities as a result of natural selection. Thus the inferior races could not be promoted to higher status. Exactly what could be done with them was disputed. Answers ranged from benign and responsible trusteeship—"Take up the white man's burden" (Rudyard Kipling)—to incarceration and neglect, and even outright elimination, as in the murder by King Leopold II of Belgium of 11 million Congolese in furtherance of his personal gain. Closer to home was the illegal and inhuman removal of the Five Civilized Tribes from the Southeast to Oklahoma by the evil Andrew Jackson and his cronies, in defiance of a Supreme Court ruling.

To the other wing, to which Morgan belonged, all human races were equally able. They all shared in Adolf Bastian's "psychic unity of mankind." This was an idea stemming from eighteenth-century rationalism, particularly Immanuel Kant, almost lost in the hereditarianism-racist early nineteenth century, and then revived by Spencer and the developmentalists. For Tylor and Lubbock it was fundamental, and external circumstances of one sort or another, not inherited racial traits, were responsible for differential progress.

This division plagued anthropology throughout its own development, and unfortunately to many anthropologists the equation of social evolutionism with "racism" has become absolute. It is, then, important to note that it was only one wing and not the predominant one. Because of the subsequent misuse of evolutionary argument by unsavory political regimes, it is hard for us to look at this dispassionately. But to the progressive-liberal wing of developmental anthropology, "assimilation," far from being a destruction of valid alternative cultures, was a supreme act of social responsibility. These cultures had not made it on their own, but because they shared in the psychic unity of mankind, they could learn civilization without the agony of the intervening, often traumatic, developmental stages. They could piggyback to Western industrial civilization status.

Horrified as we may now be at what was done, for example, to young Native Americans in Indian schools ("tradition is the enemy of progress") with their total suppression of native culture and language, this was all part of a totally well-meaning effort to jump-start them into the civilized state. There could be no argument for their continued existence at "lower" levels. Our progressive reforming forebears (Tylor—"anthropology is a reformer's science" in *Primitive Culture*) would not have understood the relativist argument that these were valid and alternative lifestyles; they certainly would not have used that barbarous coinage.

The cultures that had not achieved Western industrial civilized status were certainly extremely valuable intellectually in preserving for us examples of the early history of mankind (Tylor), or of the "ages" of human growth (stone, bronze, iron—Lubbock 1865), or of ancient society (Morgan). But to then argue that primitive cultures should be deliberately preserved in these primitive states would have seemed, to our intellectual ancestors, morally perverse. It would have elevated their antiquarian status over their human status. To leave them deliberately, on such grounds as "diversity" or "multiculturalism," in a state of undeveloped savagery or barbarism would have been unchristian, unkind, and flatly immoral. Reasonable multiculturalists would rightly object that they only mean that tribal peoples should have an effective say in what happens to them, and no one can object to that.

Social scientists do not have to make too much of an imaginative leap, if they think about it. Over the postwar decades they too were obsessed with "development" in the sense of helping the backward (renamed "developing") countries of the colonial past to achieve industrial, and hence democratic political, status (it was hoped). The argument was largely between the socialists/Marxists, who wanted planned centralized economies and one-party politics, and the democratic-liberal wing, which wanted to achieve "takeoff" conditions into a laissez-faire economy and multiparty polity.

This whole movement in sociology and economics—the "modernization" movement—would have had equal difficulty in understanding an argument that seriously proposed leaving "underdeveloped" peoples in their unmodernized state. The "natives" in these very countries who demand developmental aid from their ex-colonial overlords would not understand it. Indeed, no one but theory-befuddled academics would propose it.

The Comparative Method

It would be interesting to hear how Morgan or Tylor might have answered the modern relativist position. But we must confess that such an argument could, in modern times, be only hypothetical. Modern anthropology from functionalism through post-structuralism to postmodernism is so completely rejecting of the development hypothesis and the comparative method that there would be no grounds for debate. It would be like geographers debating flat-earthers or evolutionary geneticists debating Lamarckians. It is not that the moderns do not accept that development has taken place; they could scarcely do that. But what they do not accept, and have not accepted since Franz Boas led the way in 1896, followed by A. L. Kroeber, A. A. Goldenweiser, Robert Lowie, Bronislaw Malinowski, A. R. Radcliffe-Brown, et al., is the validity of the comparative method. The developmentalists had been sure that previous stages of human development could be "read off" from the living—or surviving—examples of those stages. They differed only as to what the stages were and how the examples should be read off.

To be fair we should note that the developmentalists had their contemporary critics. But these were "diffusionists" (W. J. Perry, Grafton Elliott Smith) who challenged the psychic unity thesis—with its corollary of independent invention—and insisted that culture was in fact "diffused" from a few creative centers. Egypt was a favorite. But the modern schools are equally rejecting of diffusionism. (We should note in reading Morgan that he is not averse to invoking diffusionist—or contact or acculturation—arguments, when faced with anomalies that defied a unilineal interpretation. Thus societies that had progressed could affect other societies at a lower stage by conquest, trade, or other contacts, and help them skip a stage, or more likely substage. We can see this either as a contradiction in Morgan or, as Eleanor Leacock prefers, as an example of his undogmatic pragmatism.)

The idea of "reading off" the past from the primitive present—the essential tool of the comparative method—has been thus rejected for most of this century since the end of World War I. Morgan's three grand stages of savagery, barbarism, and civilization were usually cited with the loudest disapprobation. Actually they were implicitly retained but renamed "hunting and gathering" (savagery), "domestication" or "horticulture" or "slash-and-burn cultivation" (barbarism), and "urban society" or "the great tradition" or "the urban-peasant continuum" (civilization).

But in the enlightened view, all contemporary cultures have been evolving for exactly the same length of time, and consequently none is, in that sense, more primitive than any other; they simply represent different modes of adaptation. If they were primitive (and the word was stubborn in its persistence), then this was not because they were "stuck" in the stone (or iron or bronze) age, but because their degree of social complexity or their technology was "simpler." But this simplicity did not represent a prehistoric state; it was a purely contemporary state, the end product of its own particular evolution.

Unilineal Uniformity

The most endearing examples of the living Paleolithic, the Australian Aborigines, had been so fascinating to Morgan, and Durkheim, as well as James Frazer *(Totemism and Exogamy)* and Sigmund Freud *(Totem and Taboo),* because they did seem to be living representatives of the Old Stone Age. Their stone tool industries were indeed, technically, Paleolithic. If this were so, and if they were in a pristine condition, then their beliefs and social institutions must be similarly living fossils of the "infancy of mankind." We could read off what our earliest ancestors had believed about the supernatural, what they had practiced regarding sex and marriage, what their ritual and art represented, what forms of government they favored, and so on. And these would be the most elementary cultural and social forms: the Ur-culture of mankind. That acknowledged father of sociology, Émile Durkheim, meant it literally when he called his book centered on the Australian Aborigines, *The Elementary Forms of the Religious Life.*

It was heady, exciting, and even mind-blowing as we might say today. Our tight-collared ancestors didn't say that, but they felt the excitement at being given these moving pictures from the middle Pleistocene—a kind of human Jurassic Park. I remember the very old Lord Raglan, a former president of the Royal Anthropological Institute, showing interest in my studies of the isolated Gaelic-speaking crofters of Tory Island because they represented an example of "the Indo-Aryan village community practicing common ownership as it existed before the coming of capitalism" And in a sense he was right, of course. But only in one sense, because, as all antidevelopmentalist pro-functionalist relativists would chorus, "they too had evolved!" And herein lies the problem. In some sense preindustrial tribes do represent the state of affairs in "preindustrial" society, and even different "stages" of development toward such a society. But at the same time they too have changed/evolved/developed, and we cannot be certain that in all things, or even in most things, they are true representatives of the past.

This was not the only weakness of developmentalism. The relative isolation of the Australian Aboriginals (for 40,000–60,000 years) made them tempting as a "pure" example of the fossilized Paleolithic. Also, the Americas, with between 20,000 years or more of isolation, and showing all "levels" of development from hunting and gathering to urban, literate (but nonindustrial) civilization, were pristine enough to be tempting. The same was true of other areas of relative isolation, like New Guinea, with, as it is now known, more than 8,000 years of independently developed horticulture. But elsewhere, the ebb and flow of historical contact has left very few pristine examples, and contact and diffusion were more easily invoked, as we have seen, to explain differing levels of development. Even in the Americas the higher civilizations rose and fell and influenced the tribes around them. Many of the current South- and Middle-American "tribes," for example, as well as many tribal peoples in southeast Asia, are descendants of the fallen civilizations, not pristine remnants of "savagery."

The assumption of "uniformitarianism" also weakened the developmental case. This assumed that all societies, everywhere, passed through the identical stages of development, though not necessarily at the same speed. But this "unilineal evolution" meant that there was only one route and that they all took it. The most that contact and diffusion could do was help the struggling societies to skip a stage (more likely a substage) by introducing the higher technology, idea, art form, morality, or whatever. The white man's burden, in fact, was to do precisely this.

To generations reared on the knee-jerk abuse of colonialism and imperialism as a moral absolute (and unfortunately a substitute for thinking in the social sciences) it will seem incredible that these movements could be imbued with as much genuine high-minded moralism as are their contemporary abusers. But the imperial-colonial powers, while most certainly out for power and profit, were also—the best among them—on a massive mission to bring the benefits of civilization to their less fortunate brethren. Given the logic of the developmental argument, the powers had indeed a moral obligation to raise their wards. In many cases they horribly failed—the Congo was the worst but not the only such example, but in many cases they tried decently to do their best within the limits of their developmentalist thinking.

We shall need a period of calmer reflection—a period in which we climb down from the moralistic high horses now being ridden, before we can assess this realistically. My point is that it was a natural outcome of uniformitarianism, which informed the whole culture, not just the anthropologists. Yet we should note what I observed earlier: that this was a decidedly nonracist position. The psychic unity hypothesis on which it depended insisted that all races could ascend the ladder. Those that had gone up more quickly could help the laggards. This might be paternalistic, but it is not, in the modern sense, racist. (The qualification is because the language of "race" was often used in a very loose sense that meant nationality, or linguistic group, or culture, or strain, or population.)

But I have already said that this was a weakness, and it was a weakness of the theory. For as many critics (Goldenweiser and Lowie perhaps the most eloquent) pointed out, there was simply no actual historical or archaeological evidence that all people in all places had passed through the stages proposed in the sequences proposed. Sometimes these stages were vague and ideological, like Frazer's magic-religion-science, and could perhaps be roughly accepted. Sometimes, however, as in Morgan's case, they were so highly specific that it was easy for critics to show that there was no evidentiary basis for them and that they derived from theoretical assumptions only.

Thus the twin problems loomed for developmentalism: highly specific stages—as we shall see with Morgan—were proposed, and all societies must have gone through them in order. The conditions of uniformity and psychic unity demanded this. Some, like Western industrial societies, had made it up through all the rungs of the ladder; others, like the Eastern civilizations and "our primitive contemporaries" (G. P. Murdock) were stuck along the way. And, of course, we read our own past off from these social fossils. Among other things this would help alert us to what Tylor chose to call "survivals": institutions, practices, and beliefs that were simply hangovers from a more primitive past and that therefore hindered further progress. Religion and magic ("superstition") were prime targets (for Spencer it was "militarism"), and this was what made anthropology for Tylor and his followers "a reformer's science," as we saw in Chapter 1.

For this to work, the assumption of uniformity had to be true—there can only be one route of developmental progress, and above all one had to get the stages right! The problem for the hypothesis was that when one descended from the very general (and usually three) stages of the broad scheme to the highly specific stages of the subscheme, the stages became more improbable as rungs in a universal ladder, and in themselves became less credible as successive stages. Thus, when Morgan stuck to his stages of savagery–barbarism–civilization, with hunting characterizing savagery, pottery barbarism, and writing civilization, he couldn't help but be more or less right. But when he broke these down into seven substages and assigned, for example, a different form of the family and kinship system to each substage, taking examples from the world's different language families to illustrate the system appropriate to each stage, he created an impossible monster.

It was a ladder that no contemporary civilization could have climbed. The struts of the ladder, to pursue the metaphor, made sense, but the rungs were totally misconceived. That we moved from hunting through agriculture to urban civilization is of course true. But that we moved—all of us who made it to the top—through Promiscuous Intercourse to the Marriage of Brothers and Sisters with the Consanguine Family and the Malayan system of kinship, to Group Marriage and the Punaluan family, to organization into Gentes and the Turanian and Ganowanian systems with the Syndiasmian family, to the Patriarchal family and finally the Monogamian family and the Aryan, Semitic and Uralian systems (see part 3, chapter 6 of Morgan's *Ancient Society*)—then, even as he recognizes himself, we are in the realms of pure hypothesis, not empirical history.

The whole scheme had a nice logicality, given its premises, and is not without some particular insights—when dealing with real historical sequences—as we shall see. But any scheme that claimed to be historical and yet lumped together the kinship systems of the Iroquois of New York State, the Australian Aboriginals, and the Tamils of South India, thus proving they all had a common origin, and that assigned the sophisticated civilizations of Polynesia to the lowest level because of their supposedly "primitive" system of kinship terminology, was clearly putting the logical requirements of the theory before the chronological realities of history. While recognizing this now-obvious weakness of Morgan's particular developmental scheme, I am still going to argue that in throwing it out, we threw out both a vision that unifies anthropology and a lot of interesting theoretical babies along with the developmental bath water.

Biology, Terminology, and Gentile Society

Perhaps by way of illustration we should get a bit (but only a little bit) technical here, because out of the complexities of Morgan's scheme— improbable as it was—technical kinship studies crystallized and serendipitously emerged. And because kinship has been subsequently central to the science of anthropology, it does no harm to examine its origins as a discipline, even if it has repudiated those very origins.

We must first note that the moral dimension in the developmental scheme helped inform its theory. If our current version of civilization represented the apogee, then by definition the earliest conditions must have represented its opposite. If we had developed to the level of the "monogamian family" then the "lowest levels of savagery" must perforce have been in a state of "primitive promiscuity." The "moral idea," as Westermarck had it, must have had an "origin and development." That bottom-feeding savages could have been just as moral as ourselves, and therefore just as likely to have monogamy and marital fidelity, was simply, self-evidently, impossible.

Darwin (and later Westermarck) emphasized the tendencies to possessiveness and sexual jealousy in male apes, and hence primal humans. This suggested a different starting point in an organized family. Maine posited the "patriarchal joint family"—as found in the proto-Indo-Aryans, as the Ur-family of mankind. But the majority of the developmentalists followed J. J. Bachofen's *Das Mutterrecht* (1861)—and Morgan fell in line—in positing primitive promiscuity as the original state and hence, because paternity would be unknown, "motherright" or descent through females as the first form of kinship.

Travelers' tales were ransacked and the opinions of missionaries polled to prove the point. The reports on "the morality of the lower races" were notoriously unreliable. To one of Frazer's questionnaires regarding the "manners and customs" of the natives, a district officer replied tersely: "Manners none, customs beastly." Morgan never fell into the trap of picking hundreds of random examples and lumping them together as a picture of the moral state of savagery. To his credit, he surveyed in detail what was known, for example, about the kinship systems of the North

American Indians, and was impressed at the overwhelming preponderance of matrilineal systems. But he did not hesitate to attribute, on logical grounds, a previous state of "promiscuity" to all such peoples.

Morgan actually makes little of this supposed earliest stage. It is in effect a typical Enlightenment-style "state of nature"—more dependent on the logical needs of the theory than any facts about nature or history. But Morgan was anxious to show that a crucial stage intervened between the proverbial promiscuity and the well-documented "motherright." This is the stage he discusses in part 2, chapter 1 of *Ancient Society*—"Organization on the Basis of Sex."

Thus, for Morgan, out of promiscuity (or what today we might more cautiously call random mating) there grew the "consanguine family" and consequently "group marriage." Because paternity was unknown, individual fatherhood was impossible, so what ensued was first the incestuous marriage of brothers and sisters—the consanguine family. The next stage was the marriage of groups of "brothers" with groups of "sisters"—the "Punaluan" family, in which one's own brothers and sisters were excluded as marriage partners but collateral or classificatory brothers and sisters were allowed (rather required) in marriage.

This exclusion of consanguines as marriage partners, but marriage in effect of groups of cousins by other groups of cousins, was for Morgan the first great breakthrough on the upward march of development. And he did not simply make this up; he deduced it from the logic of kinship terminologies. To follow through his reasoning, at however superficial a level, is to see a great and logical mind at work. No one since, except perhaps his disciple G. P. Murdock and the great French anthropologist Claude Lévi-Strauss, has known more about comparative kinship. We all look to Morgan's *Systems of Consanguinity and Affinity of the Human Family* (1871) as the bible of kinship studies. But like the Bible, although it contained much wisdom, it had serious gaps and came to some wrong conclusions.

Morgan deduced the "consanguine family" and "group marriage" from kinship terminologies that equated the terms for father, mother, brother, sister, and child with a number of other relatives. Without bothering with the technical terms, and using the equivalent English words for kin, let us take two examples that Morgan used to make his argument. Thus (let us call it Type A) the father and his brother might both be called "father" and distinguished from the mother's brother ("uncle"). Then the mother and her sister would both be called "mother" and distinguished from the father's sister ("aunt"). The children of those called "father" and "mother" would, logically, all be called "brother" and "sister." The others could be classed in various ways (including as grandparents, as we saw in Chapter 1) but we shall put them for convenience under "cousin." A cousin in these systems was usually a prescribed marriage partner, so this term could also mean "spouse."

Type A

FZ	FB	F	=	M	MZ	MB
aunt	father	father		mother	mother	uncle
cousin	brother/sister		**Self**	brother/sister		cousin

Alternatively (let us call it Type B), *all* the male members of the parental generation could be "father" and *all* the females "mother"—one's own generation would *all* be "brother" and "sister"—and so on.

Type B

FZ	FB	F	=	M	MZ	MB
mother	father	father		mother	mother	father
brother/	brother/		**Self**		brother/	brother/
sister	sister				sister	sister

This kind of classification of relatives—the lumping together of different types under one term—he called a *classificatory* terminology, as opposed to a *descriptive,* which named each relative individually. He saw the second example, our Type B—the lumping of all members of a generation of the same sex together under one term, as a "survival" (Tylor) of a stage above the simply promiscuous: the stage of the "consanguine family," as we have seen. At the consanguine stage brothers and sisters systematically interbred—which would logically produce such systems: everyone in the parental generation is a "father" or a "mother." The first type, our Type A, he saw as coming a stage further on: his Punaluan stage. At this point, groups of brothers ("fathers") married groups of sisters ("mothers"), all their children being "brothers and sisters."

There is no doubt that the discovery of the classificatory principle, which we saw early on in Chapter 1 with the example of the lumping together of different generations of a clan or lineage under one term (GM, or GF, or FZ, for example) was one of the major discoveries in anthropology in the nineteenth century. The discovery of this classificatory principle was as significant for the social sciences as the discovery of natural selection was for the natural sciences. The problem with Morgan's immediate use of it to reconstruct the history of kinship systems was that his deductions rested on a shaky first principle: that *the kinship terms literally stated actual biological relationships.* Because language is more conservative than institutions, he argued, present-day kinship terminologies are the clue to the earlier stages of the family and kinship.

Critics like John Lubbock and John McLennan noticed at the time that these terms did not necessarily denote relationships of paternity and maternity in a biological sense, and others, like Robert Lowie, were to elaborate this criticism later. The mistake rested on a simple ethnocentric confusion: Morgan assumed that the kinship terms such as "father" and "mother" were, as in our case, indicative of a specific biological relationship as "male and female begetters." Thus "brothers and sisters" would be, biologically, "children of begetters." Only an assumption of consanguine marriage (and later group marriage) would account for these biological facts. (See his argument in part 3, chapter 2, of *Ancient Society*.)

But if the term he translates as "father" and equates with "male begetter" (or "genitor," to use the correct Latin legalism) should really be translated as "related male of my parental generation"—as in his favorite Malayo-Polynesian example—then there is no necessary implication of immediate biological "fatherhood" in this term. McLennan saw this: the terms were "a system of mutual salutations," he said, not biological designations. (See Morgan's long "Note" on McLennan, in *Ancient Society*, pp. 516–531.) They were surely, as such, of great significance, because they told us how people saw their universe of kin: whom they equated with whom. But they did not necessarily indicate actual reproductive biogenetic relatedness. "Father" was not necessarily to be translated as "biological parent."

"Morgan's mistake" led him to one of his most serious errors regarding the aforementioned Polynesian societies. These were elaborate, sophisticated, hierarchical, monarchical, socioreligious complexes of an obviously very advanced stage of development. But because their kinship terms, arranged in generational layers as we have seen (Type B), betrayed them as immediate heirs to the "consanguine family," they had to be assigned to one of the lowest levels in the developmental ladder. Had Morgan known as much about the Polynesians as he did about his own Native Americans, he might not have made such a mistake. This was a case where factual ignorance really was theoretical bliss. Morgan repeatedly had to juggle whole civilizations in this way in order to fit the equation "kinship terms denote biological relatedness." But the critics were right: classificatory terms did not equal biological relatedness. Yet this equation was the linchpin of Morgan's theoretical scheme.

We might well ask, "If the linchpin is broken, how can the building stand?" Here the promised excursion into the Australian case will perhaps help illustrate both where Morgan was wrong about specifics and why his general idea of a progressive and logical movement from one type of kinship system to another remains useful, and why its neglect has been fatal. He was anxious to look for the origins of the crucial "stage" that he found exemplified in his beloved Iroquois and the North American Indians generally, that of the *gentes*. The word was borrowed from the Latin *gens* (plural *gentes*—properly pronounced with a hard *g*, commonly with a soft one). This referred to the named Roman patrilineal lineages—the Claudian *gens* (Claudii—as in Claudius Nero), the Julian *gens* (Julii—as in Julius Caesar), the Fabian *gens* (Fabii—as in Fabius Maximus), or in the case of an author we met earlier, the Ovidian *gens* (Ovidius Naso). The term now used is usually "clan," later borrowed from the Gaelic *clann*.

Morgan called this gens or clan stage, perhaps confusingly, the stage of *gentile society*. His discovery that this form of what we would now call "unilineal descent" characterized not only the whole of North and South America, but also the original societies of Greece and Rome, was a stupendous revelation about the universal history of mankind. He knew little of Africa and Asia, but they would have supported his observation, the gentile organization—the clans—lasting in China, for example, until modern times. If we knew how mankind came to acquire the gens (I will drop the italicization) then lose it and develop something else ("political society"), we had the great clue to our history. A major defining task of anthropology—something that would give it its pivotal distinction from the other social sciences—would become the *identification and analysis of the forms of gentile society*.

And the royal route was to be via kinship terminology: this was the "survival" clue to the past states, since terms changed more slowly than actual family or kinship organization (thus being a kind of "survival," à la Tylor). We must try to make an imaginative leap back in time in order to empathize with the excitement Morgan and his contemporaries must have felt as these great clues to human history seemed to fall into place. Huge areas of the globe that had simply been a puzzle to generations raised on the biblical chronology of history suddenly made sense in the great developmental scheme of things. As we saw in Chapter 1, a crucial change in classificatory kinship both reflected and helped to accelerate the changing human notions of time. Anthropology, in consequence, became the queen of the sciences, for she alone had the tools to analyze the mechanics of the most vital change in human history.

The Amazing Australians

Thus the Australian Aborigines, still living in what was technically a Paleolithic stage of technology and *in situ* for 40 to 60,000 years, became crucial. For Morgan they were one of the only living examples of the stage before the true flowering of gentile society itself: the movement from "group marriage classes" to the gens proper.

He was dealing with personal communications from the earliest Western explorers of Aboriginal society, particularly the Rev. Lorimer Fison (and his collaborator A. W. Howitt) on the Kamilaroi of the Darling River in Northern New South Wales. Mr. Fison and his collaborator, like all early students of Australian kinship, were dazzled by the system of "marriage classes," which is not surprising—this is the way the Australians describe and explain their own system. And at one level it does explain it, and interestingly at much the same level as an anthropologist's theoretical models of a kinship system.

But this way of interpreting the system gave rise to a fateful misconception: Morgan saw the "classes" as logically and hence chronologically preceding the "gentes"—which existed in Australia but, he thought, at a more rudimentary level than, say, among the Iroquois. The gentes, in his view, in the rest of the world had ousted the marriage-class system, thus illustrating how the gens eventually superseded group marriage. The problem with this is that there never was group marriage among the Australians—or anywhere else that has been documented. The division into "classes," as we have seen, is a way the natives have of explaining how the system works at an abstract level, not a previous stage of the system. Later scholars renamed the marriage classes with the more neutral term "sections."

Here let us simplify things by taking the simplest possible Australian-type system and showing how two intermarrying descent lines automatically produce the fabulous marriage classes. The Kamilaroi represent, in fact, a complicated expansion of such a system, and the reader may easily be put off trying to follow Morgan's description of it. The description here may look complicated, but it is no more difficult to follow than the average crossword puzzle. However, readers who are understandably impatient with the following of diagrams may skip to the next section.

Let us just take a system where the tribe is divided into two exogamous unilineal moieties; that is, everyone belongs to either moiety **A** or moiety **B**, and the moieties systematically exchange spouses with each other on a generation-by-generation basis. Men of **A** marry women of **B** and vice versa, just as we saw in Chapters 2 and 6, with the resulting "cross-cousin marriage."

Let us also assume these are patrilineal moieties; that is, membership is gained through the father. (They could be matrilineal, as with the Kamilaroi—from a structural point of view it makes no difference.) This form of moiety organization did in fact characterize most of Australia and many tribes of Melanesia and the Americas, and its terminology exists among the Dravidian speakers of South India, although it seems absent from Europe and Africa.

We can diagram this as in Figure 11.1, where the triangles for the moment represent all the men of a generation and the circles all the women, in each moiety. We shall call the moieties just **A** and **B** since this is an abstract example, but with actual tribes they would have had much more colorful "totemic" names like "Emu" and "Crocodile" or "Bear" and "Raven" or, as with the Pueblo Indian tribe I studied, "Pumpkin" and "Turquoise." The items in black are for future reference.

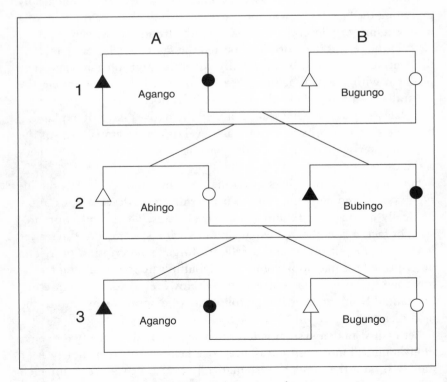

Figure 11.1 Moieties, generations, and marriage classes

This is in fact the very simplest form of systematic kinship system known, but it is not as simple as Morgan would have liked it to be. You have already seen the bones of it in Chapter 7, and how it results from continuing "sister exchange" over the generations. You can also see how it corresponds exactly to our Type A system of terminology and why it makes the equations it does, including the vital "cross-cousin = spouse" rule.

But let us follow the logic of the classes. Because this is a type example, not an ethnographic case, I have invented some names for the "classes." If the natives are asked to describe their marriage rule, say by a Western missionary like Mr. Fison, they would reply as follows:

Agango men (A1) marry Bugungo women (B1) and their children are Abingo (A2)

Bugungo men (B1) marry Agango women (A1) and their children are Bubingo (B2)

and so on, the third generation repeating the first, giving a pattern of the "identification of alternating generations" that we found to be so basic in Chapter 1.

Abingo men (A2) marry Bubingo women (B2) and their children are Agango (A3)

Bubingo men (B2) marry Abingo women (A2) and their children are Bugungo (B3)

Thus the "marriage classes" alternate over the generations:

Agango = Bugungo
Abingo = Bubingo
Agango = Bugungo
Abingo = Bubingo
Etc.

with the children joining the father's moiety.

The missionary would see the intermingling chaos of an Aboriginal camp, where often an older man did not know which among the young girls were his daughters and which his wives (he had to be told by the women). The missionary would also see "wife lending" and other forms of sexual hospitality, and could well conclude that "group marriage" was taking place, and that the existence of the marriage classes demonstrated this.

Thus it was supposed by these early observers that *all* the Agango males collectively married *all* the Bugungo females and so on. This turned out not to be the case, but it was a natural mistake to make. The fascination with the idea that marriage classes were either a clear example of, or again a survival of, a prior state of group marriage, was, when wedded to the archaic status of the Australians, quite understandable. And the kinship terms were compatible with such an arrangement: our Type A above. All the men of the ascending generation in one's own moiety would be "father"; all the women of the same generation in the mother's moiety would be "mother"—and so on.

Fison and Morgan, however, did recognize that "gentes" were present but, as we have seen, thought them to be at this point matrilineal only and very undeveloped. Unfortunately for his elaboration of the idea, the Kamilaroi had matrilineal moieties and matrilineal gentes divided between them, like the Iroquois. This is a minority pattern in Australia, occurring largely in the southeast where these early studies were done. But it was to color Morgan's view of the stages of development. Ironically, gentes (clans) are relatively well developed among these particular Australians, but their attachment to moieties and their supposed attachment to marriage classes and group marriage put them, for Morgan, at an archaic stage in the developmental system.

As far as the change from marriage classes to gentile society was concerned, it was Morgan's opinion that group marriage "would not endure" and that "pairing" would start to take place, thus changing the system toward a gentile one. Given his theory, this must be a matrilineal system (motherright), not patrilineal as we have illustrated it. The truth is the Australians have it both ways. Consider the triangles and circles we have shaded in Figure 11.1; take them out and show them independent of the patrilineal moieties, and they will constitute a matrilineal group (descent through females) as in Figure 11.2.

Equally, B1–A2–B3 (Bugungo–Abingo–Bugungo) would be a matriline. Again, the Australians recognize this and name "submoieties" that are

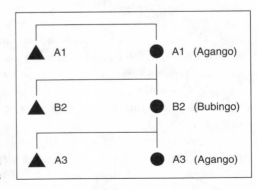

Figure 11.2 Matriline and marriage class

matrilineal in descent. Thus we could "explain" the system as one of inter-secting patrimoieties and matrimoieties, which would also produce four marriage classes as follows (Figure 11.3).

What is important to note is that *all* these elements—patriclans, matri-lineages, patrimoieties, matrimoieties, and marriage classes or sections—are *all ways of describing the same system.* The so-called marriage classes can be seen as mnemonic devices for remembering what moiety, gens, matriline, and, above all, generation one belongs to. They are a short-hand way of keeping the system straight. One must then marry a spouse of the appropriate moiety-generation "class." The classes turn out to be more important as ritual units than marital groups, and their members, as a unit, have nothing to do with the actual marriage choices and ar-rangements, which are handled by the members of ego's gens in his own moiety in conjunction with his personal matriline. (For more details, see my *Kinship and Marriage,* chapter 7, and *The Challenge of Anthropology,* chapter 12.)

It is very important to note that, as we have stressed before, structur-ally it does not matter in such a system whether the moieties are patrilin-eal or matrilineal. If we start with matrilineal moieties, then the submoi-eties would be patrilineal, and we could abstract out patrilineal gentes from alternate generations of the matrimoieties. The system of classes/

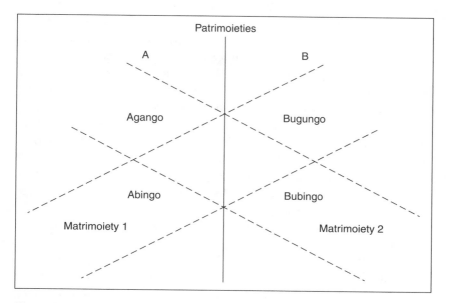

Figure 11.3   Patrimoieties, matrimoieties, and marriage classes

sections would be the same. The Iroquois (like the Tlingit we met in Chapter 10) have matrilineal moieties with the matrilineal clans divided between them, like the Kamilaroi. They do not, however, name the classes/sections that are implicit in this form of kinship system, nor do they recognize patrimoieties. This is really the difference between them and the Kamilaroi, not a basic change in the moiety-clan relationship to a higher stage of kinship, as Morgan thought.

Classes, Clans, and Kinship

This is the crux of the mistake that plagued not only Morgan but several generations of developmentalists: by calling these ritual units "marriage classes" they begged (in the correct sense) a massive question. Marriage, it turns out, after many years of careful genealogical research, is not "group" at all, nor does it have to do primarily with the "classes." Aboriginal marriage is organized by the gentes ("clans" as they have come to be called) and by the individual's personal matriline—the relatives related through the mother and sisters as in Figure 11.2. It involves individual unions (polygynous) with a man's quite specific cousins, from the commonest case of mother's brother's daughter / father's sister's daughter (taking the triangles and circles in Figure 11.1 as individuals, one can easily trace out this relationship), to the mother's mother's brother's daughter's daughter (as among the Kamilaroi), and other complications.

And this is the point: Morgan was correct to see at least certain forms of gentile organization as evolving from "marriage class" systems. But he really could not find the mechanism for this transformation—he proposed the origination of "pairing"—because he did not understand that *marriage was not between groups to begin with,* so "pairing" was already present. What is more, marriage was always with a specified first or second cousin. When this "individual marriage" rule was followed—even with a classificatory as opposed to real relative—then the "marriage class" rule would be automatically observed. A man marrying the woman he called by the term for "mother's mother's brother's daughter's daughter" would automatically marry into the correct class. This is why the natives could use the "marriage of classes" to describe their system; but they could not just marry anyone in that class, and certainly groups of men did not marry, collectively, groups of women.

Another basic mistake of the developmentalists, as we have seen, was to assume that the systems of kinship were *exclusive* of each other: that matrilineal kinship meant "kinship through females only" and thus excluded patrilineal relationships or cognatic relationships as in "the family."

Indeed, "families" on this logic must have been later developments, after the "discovery of paternity." Thus for the developmentalists, "matriarchy" or "motherright" (from German *Mutterrecht*)—kinship through females only—meant just that, and must have preceded "patriarchy" or "father-right." We now know that these are not exclusive, and that different forms of descent can exist for different purposes in the same system, and that some form of "family" exists everywhere with corresponding cognatic (or bilateral) relationships. "Kinship" is in this sense always bilateral, involving the kin of both the father and the mother.

Unilineal descent groups, like the gens, can then exist for specific purposes, such as inheritance or group membership or, most commonly, exogamy: defining the rule of marriage. Thus in "double-descent" societies there can be matrilineal clans that determine marriage, and patrilineal lineages that are cattle-inheritance groups (as in Central Africa). Or as in the Keresan Pueblos, there can be patrilineal moieties for ritual purposes and matrilineal clans as exogamous units. And in all cases there will be a "web of kinship" (Meyer Fortes) for any individual, which includes paternal and maternal kin.

Once this is understood, then we see that there is no warrant for treating systems of descent as exclusive of each other or of the family and kinship, and hence positing that they must succeed each other in time. Kinship is never "through females only," but kinship through females (uterine kinship) can be used for some purposes. This may seem obvious to us now, but it took some time for this to displace the evolutionary notion. A. L. Kroeber wrote one of the greatest ethnographic descriptions of a tribe, his *Zuni Kin and Clan,* in 1917, to show precisely that the two items of his title could indeed exist together. He was deliberately countering the view that Zuni had moved from a "stage" where it had matrilineal clans as exclusive kinship units ("kinship through females only") without bilateral families.

Hindsight is a wonderful thing, and we now know "how the system works." But in the meantime, since anthropologists have declared developmentalism to be anathema, we have no language in which to couch the problem of change in kinship systems. I have, in my studies of Pueblo society, tried to approach it by ditching Morgan's universalistic language and treating the emergence of certain types of gentile organization—the famous Crow-Omaha systems—as one logical, and hence chronological, outcome of the basic moiety type of organization of the Australians.

Morgan's Iroquois have, as we have seen, matrimoieties and matriclans, but they do not organize them in classes/sections like the Australians. Their kinship terminology—and this impressed Morgan—was not unlike that of the Australians (our Type A) or indeed even the Dravidians of south India, who do not have gentes or moieties but who marry the same first "double cross-cousin" as we find in Figure 11.1. Clearly there is some logical or developmental connection.

Across North America we find hundreds of examples of systems with matrilineal clans/gentes (and some with patrilineal), and often moieties. They have terminologies that "hover" between those that logically belong with an Australian or Iroquoian system and those characteristic of matrilineal clan systems without any trace of moieties or classes. These are the transitional types that are discussed in the Appendix, when interrogating Lévi-Strauss on Pueblo genealogy and time. They may indeed be the secret to the unexplained diversity of the Crow-Omaha type. For details the bold reader can look at my essay on "The Evolution of Kinship Systems" in *The Challenge of Anthropology*, and the even bolder reader can follow up on Nick Allen's remarkable "tetradic" theory of the evolution of kinship terminologies (see the Digression on tetradic theory in the notes for this chapter).

So the developmental logic is there, but it is not, as Morgan thought, a universal logic of universal stages through which all of mankind must of necessity pass. In throwing out this universalistic idea, however, the functionalists and their successors dumped the baby with bath water. What Morgan reminds us is that we should not just ignore the question, but go back and get it right this time; that is, with specific developmental lines rather than universal stages. His better successors, like Murdock, tried this, but unfortunately introduced as many new errors as the old ones they discarded. This is a fascinating piece of anthropological history, but it is a story outside our brief.

Iroquois, Aztec, Greek and Roman

Morgan concluded, on theoretical grounds similar to those of Bachofen and McLennan, that gentile organization based on descent through females (motherright) had of necessity preceded in time both descent through males and the Monogamian (monogamous) family. This logical— not empirical—conclusion was then to color all his discussions and classifications of kinship systems. Even if they might show uncompromising descent in the male line, and a consequent patrilineal gentile organization, and with no known history of anything else, they must, in the Morganian system, have gone through the obligatory matrilineal stage, preceded by the promiscuous and consanguine stages. He was able to show that the overwhelming majority of tribes in North America had matrilineal kinship systems. The tribes that were unquestionably patrilineal, and the great civilizations of Central America, were therefore, for him, later developments.

For Morgan, the Iroquois and the Aztec remained the type cases of gentile society. Ironically, as it turns out, Iroquoian kinship terminology is less compatible with a developed matrilineal clan organization than the "Crow" terminologies of Southwestern, Southeastern, and Plains Indians. Morgan missed this crucial point. But his type-case Iroquois showed in detail how far the matrilineal stage could progress. And it was quite far. The Iroquois developed a sophisticated form of political confederation among their tribes, which Morgan described definitively in his *League of the Ho-de-no-sau-nee or Iroquois* . Yet they never advanced to the stage of a nation, city-state, or empire. For Morgan the stage of gentile society could not do this. Superordinate political authority belonged to a stage beyond the gentile; it was the next stage of "political society." This worked for the League of the Iroquois, which had the correct combination of kinship and politics, but it caused Morgan to indulge in some shaky special pleading when he came to more complex forms of political organization that were nevertheless still at the gentile stage.

The Aztecs (along with the Inca) showed perhaps the most advanced form. To most observers they were clearly a monarchy with a priestly and warrior caste. But for Morgan, because they were organized into patrilineal gentes, they could not have had an absolute monarchy, or any kind of monarchy in a political sense. Thus the Aztec kingship had to be downgraded. The basic form of government must have been, as in all gentile societies, a "democracy of equal gentes." Consequently, Montezuma and his predecessors must have been a kind of "war chief" on the North American model: in command in time of war, but with no real civil powers and subject to deposition, like the sachems of the Iroquois.

Following this logic, and looking at the early history of Greco-Roman society, Morgan came to the same conclusion regarding the *rex* in Rome and the *basileus* in Greece. Because both societies were at this point still in the gentile stage, these officers could only have had "war chief" status, and could not have been "kings" as is commonly assumed. Morgan actually argues his point well—it deeply impressed Marx—and it is for the informed reader to judge how convincing he is. But right or wrong it is a clear case of the demands of the theory determining the interpretation of the facts. Morgan did not try to deal with the great civilization of China, but he might have had trouble there because gentile organization, combined with an imperial and bureaucratic system of government, persisted in China for many centuries, well into their stage of "political society"; in the end the gentile system did give way, but only really with changes forced on the society by the modernizing West, and eventually state Communism.

We see the same problem in his insistence that although Aztec, Greek, and Roman kinship was uncompromisingly patrilineal even in these early stages, it must have gone through a previous matrilineal (Iroquoian) stage (*Ancient Society*, part 2, chapter 4) The evidence adduced for this is very dubious, and all modern analysis suggests that these Indo-European kinship systems, even in their earliest proto stages, were clearly of the Omaha type, and were hence never anything but patrilineal since before 3000 BC (thus vindicating Maine). The insistence on previous matrilineality by Morgan and the other matriarchalists strangely persisted in, among other areas, classical studies, and has even had a passionate revival under feminism. That some of the pre-Greek Mediterranean peoples worshipped a mother goddess, and that some have hints of matrilineal-like customs, does not affect the status of the Latin and Greek families as purely patrilineal.

Despite these particular flaws, Morgan was again, in this instance, raising in general a very good question. Though the transition from gentile society to political society was not a universal progression that all advanced societies had gone through, the transition from societies based largely on kinship—of whatever specific form—to those based on citizenship and state organization, was a universal reality for all "civilized" societies. In making this transition a primary focus and something requiring an explanation, Morgan posed one of the basic questions of modern social science. If we forget his insistence on gentile society per se (remembering that at the time this was an exciting discovery and did seem to hold a vital clue) and ask the general question, we see that Morgan was one with the other theorists of the great transformation we met in Chapters 1 and 2. He was with Spencer (military to industrial), Tönnies (*Gemeinschaft* to *Gessellschaft*), Maine (status to contract), Durkheim (mechanical to organic), Max Weber (traditional to rational-legal), Robert Redfield (folk to urban), and all the others who saw this breakthrough as crucial to understanding the route to civilization and modernity.

And to Morgan's credit we should recognize that it was, in many cases, truly a transition from gentile (unilineal/clan) kinship to a state system. Rome and Athens were correct examples. The process of change from kinship to citizenship was difficult. Even in the late Roman Republic, candidates for office were still voted on by the *comitia tributa,* the "assembly of tribes." These tribes, which voted as blocs, were originally geographical constituencies, but membership in them was through the father.

But today we are faced with the knowledge that the cultures that developed the most advanced technologies and democratic societies first—namely those of northwestern Europe—arose not from gentile society as such, but from systems of non-unilineal or cognatic kinship like our own. Their relatively rapid development of democratic, industrial, individualistic, entrepreneurial states (especially Britain and Holland, but also France and Germany—and for that matter Japan) could even have its roots in the very "nongentile" nature of their kinship systems.

It is precisely this lack of need to "shed" the clan system that made the transition to individualism and contract relatively easy. We noted this in Chapter 3, where we also saw how the Arab and other Muslim societies are struggling with a similar transition from a system dominated by patrilineal descent groups to one based on individual citizenship. The northern European countries had indeed gone through a gentile phase. They were, as we have seen, like all Indo-European communities originally of a patrilineal Omaha type. But they had shed their unilineal character earlier and moved to a bilateral system, with England moving furthest toward the dominance of the nuclear family and the individual citizen.

But in Morgan's day no one was thinking this way. He was overwhelmed by the ubiquity of the gentile system among savages and barbarians, and he lays out the evidence for it at length in *Ancient Society*. In the Greek (Athenian) case he saw clear documented evidence of the transition from the kin-based *genos* and *phratria* to the city-state based on the territorial unit of the *deme* and universal citizenship. This is what the reforms of Cleisthenes (sixth century BC) were all about (see my *Reproduction and Succession,* chapter 3). Historians and classicists had of course known this, but they had not made the connection with the widespread phenomenon of gentile society. They had not seen the Athenians and Romans, in their early stages, as part of a worldwide phenomenon represented by "savages and barbarians." They would indeed have found such a view distasteful.

But Morgan forced this realization upon them, and revolutionized the way we look at these "classical" societies that we regard as the foundation of Western civilization. They arose out of barbarism, and we could look around at living examples of the savage and barbaric stages in order to understand the principles on which they worked. But because Morgan's insight was so tightly bound to his theory of universal stages, when that went down the insight went with it, and we do not today find many historians or political scientists feeling the necessity to acquaint themselves with comparative ethnography to do their jobs.

Morgan was consigned, with other "philosophies of history," to the wastebasket of "evolutionism."

Morgan and Marx

This neglect, in both history and social science, has been reinforced by the overtly puzzling adoption of Morgan by Marx and Engels and his consequent enshrinement in the Marxist-Leninist pantheon as a pillar of Soviet orthodoxy. In the Soviet Union, my own book *Kinship and Marriage* was banned from translation because it criticized Engels on kinship. An attempt to translate it into Georgian was suppressed by Moscow. This is no place to go into the details of this development, but it is worth noting that the excitement Morgan felt over the discovery of the necessary stages of social evolution, and especially of the absolutely crucial role of gentile society, was readily communicated to thinkers like Engels, themselves in search of "necessary stages" leading inevitably to capitalism. They were entranced by the idea of "primitive communism" in property (in the stage of savagery), because this showed that private property was not a law of nature, as the eighteenth century had thought, but a late stage of social evolution. They could then envisage the perfect communist society of the future as a return to what was in essence a "state of nature."

This, for Engels, applied equally to the monogamous family, and the State itself, as demonstrated by Morgan. If the State was eventually to "wither away," then it could not be a necessary institution but a passing phase, and Morgan had shown this to be so, and again shown the stateless communist society to be the natural condition from which we sprang, and hence to which we might return. Morgan himself had no such notion of an eternal return to the simple life. He had not read Hegel. For him there was no predicting what future stages might be, except that there would be some. Evolution was continuous for him, and forms of marriage and the family and such would change as means of subsistence changed. He would have had no truck with current movements to restore "family values" belonging to an earlier mode of subsistence. Change was inexorable.

But even so, he was attractive to Marxists because of his uncompromising materialism. The causes of change lay in increasingly effective control over "the means of subsistence." He never worked this out very systematically, but it was for him the only explanation of progress. It was easy for Engels to marry "means of subsistence" to "mode of production" and graft this onto Marxist orthodoxy. But if we are truly to appreciate Morgan today, we must make a conscious effort to ignore his adoption by the Marxists. For while this is yet another a fascinating episode in intellectual history, it can only distract us from a useful understanding.

Morgan's Legacy

What then is this useful understanding? Does Morgan have anything to say to us today, or is his version of anthropology itself a fossil: a stage on the way to more enlightened postmodern and certainly postevolutionary understanding? We have noted the more obvious mistakes. There were no universal stages in the development of the family and kinship. These conjectures were themselves based on a wrong assumption about the relation of kinship terms to real genetic relationships. Morgan insisted that matriliny must everywhere have preceded patriliny, and where it did not appear evident, he inserted such a "theoretical" stage. The gens did not precede the family as a form of organization; they always appear together.

But look at the positive side. If we drop the requirement of universal evolution/development and, like some modern evolutionists (G. P. Murdock, Julian Steward), try to find multilinear pathways (Chapter 10), we do find a number of developmental sequences that echo Morgan's schemes. Thus when unilineal kinship systems change from one form to another—and they do in regular ways—the direction of change is always from matrilineal to patrilineal, never the reverse. The whole of mankind may not have gone through this process, but in all documented cases this is the direction. Morgan had indeed deduced a correct law of development; he just misunderstood the range of its application. Again, we have seen how the change from "marriage class" to "gentile" kinship, though not being universal, does occur in many cases, and indeed the previous existence of moiety organization may be the clue to most North American systems.

As a last example of Morgan's accuracy (once we drop the universality requirement): the transition from gentile society to political society accurately describes the transition that took place in Greece (in Athens) and Rome, and Morgan's description of this, in broad outline, is masterly, scholarly, and accurate. It is almost sad that this is not a universal stage embodying a true law of development, for this would have been a discovery of monumental importance, as it seemed to Morgan's contemporaries. And as I have argued, even if this is not a universal process, it is so widespread that historians would still do well to pay attention to it, and hence to understand why they should try to grasp the structure of Iroquoian kinship!

Finally, on this positive note, let us remember that Morgan was not guilty of the offense for which Goldenweiser pillories the evolutionists in general. He did not set up stages and then cull random examples from around the globe to fill them in. He undertook detailed scholarly and historical studies of his main examples—Iroquois, Aztec, Athenian, and Roman societies. He married these to widespread but intensive comparative ethnographic materials. He always tried to deal with whole culture complexes and their changes in time, not isolated examples unnaturally thrown together because they fit the relevant stage. He dealt sweepingly with whole language families—Semitic, Aryan, Polynesian, and so on—because these were the repositories of the kinship terms so crucial to his theoretical constructions. With hindsight we can spot the errors in his assumptions, deductions, and materials. But those of us doing the spotting have not even come close to the grand, ambitious, and intellectually exciting adventure that Morgan undertook when he thought he had the glorious key to the secret of human progress.

The grand scheme collapsed, but Morgan had nevertheless set the agenda for anthropology. His fascination with gentile society—renamed "the structural-functional analysis of unilineal descent systems"—was at its defining core for half a century, however hostile to "evolutionism" this later school may have been. It is not too much to say that the whole school was Morgan without social evolution. He defined the terms of subsequent debate, and while kinship terminology was no longer seen as the clue to historical development, its relationship to social organization, and its role as a determinant or index of social structure, became an obsession with structural-functional anthropologists.

Furthered in Britain by W. H. R. Rivers, who retained the evolutionary approach in his history of Melanesian society, it reached its apogee with the work of the British Commonwealth school. It was behind the structuralism of Lévi-Strauss and his followers in post–World War II Europe, and the Chicago and Yale schools—and even the surviving Morganians at the Smithsonian—in America. The strict adherence to unilineal social evolution even had continuing support in the work of archaeologists like V. Gordon Childe and the anthropologists Leslie White and Elman R. Service, and strongly influenced the cultural ecologists and materialists, like Marvin Harris and Richard Lee.

We might look, as an example of the persistence of the Morgan agenda, at the burst of postwar activity that resulted in the publication in 1949 of four of the most important anthropological books of that period. These were: Leslie White's *The Science of Culture*, Claude Lévi-Strauss's *Les structures élémentaires de la parenté*, G. P. Murdock's *Social Structure*, and Fred Eggan's *The Social Organization of the Western Pueblos*. White's book was wholly in the Morgan tradition, taking as its point of departure the evolution of control over energy conversion rather than Morgan's control over the means of subsistence. Lévi-Strauss's great work became the bible of structuralism, but its concerns with "elementary" kinship systems, their terminologies, and their *passage* into complex systems, were in the true spirit of Morgan, and we should note the book was dedicated to Morgan.

Murdock's book (also dedicated to Morgan and several others) was avowedly about the evolutionary changes in kinship systems—although not unilinear changes—and again in particular their terminologies. It established among other things the principle we have mentioned that when unilineal (gentile) systems did change, the direction of change was exclusively from matrilineal to patrilineal. Following a lead established by E. B. Tylor in the study of social evolution, Murdock revived the use of the cross-cultural statistical method. He used it to test hypotheses about the evolution of systems of terminology and social structure.

Eggan's book might seem more parochial, but it is important as the culmination of Radcliffe-Brown's influence on the Chicago school and in setting the style for the subsequent study of native North American kinship. While being avowedly functionalist, it too bore the inevitable stamp of the Morgan agenda on change in kinship systems as reflected in terminology. All these impressive books—books that helped set the agenda for postwar anthropology and had their profound influence across the social sciences generally and even into philosophy and literature—can be seen, then, as essentially in the tradition of Morgan's evolutionary materialism. They especially echo his insistence that kinship and the categories of kinship were the royal road to any kind of understanding of the nature of society, evolutionary or not.

The Blind Men and the Elephant

Things have now changed. The study of kinship has been in a long decline (but showing some recent signs of revival—see the notes for this chapter). The analysis of kinship was the main tool for the reconstruction of social evolution. As long as it remained central there was still a hope of a return to the analysis of social development. That hope has almost faded. One might say that anthropology has been taken over by those post-1968 students who found kinship analysis too difficult. Also, for their idealistic sensitivities, it was not "relevant" enough. I said, in *Kinship and Marriage*, "Kinship is to anthropology as logic is to philosophy and the nude is to art." These words are often quoted, but I think mostly out of amusement at the archaic sentiment. Logic is no longer required in philosophy; anatomy and figure drawing have disappeared as requirements in the art school curriculum; poetry has been hijacked by those who can't handle prosody; Anglo-Saxon is no longer needed for degrees in English; statistics is not a requirement in sociology, and even classics is largely taught in translation. We live in an intellectually lazy age. We have become relevant at the expense of being interesting.

Kind critics, like Adam Kuper, might say that the current trend in anthropology is simply a swing back to the tradition of Tylor, Frazer, Boas, and Kroeber: the anthropology of "culture" rather than that of "social structure." Perhaps. But this further decline from exacting Morganian standards in the post-structuralist world is moving anthropology even farther from its raison d'être as a science. Under the equally baleful influence of Clifford Geertz's "interpretive" and "humanistic" approaches, "cultural anthropology" becomes a writing exercise that ends up as the reorganization of field notes under fashionable buzzword headings, or as routinized indignation about social injustice of one form or another. Thus anthropology becomes just another "humanism," subject to shifting fads and fashions of interpretation. (See my "Scientific Humanism and Humanistic Science" in *Conjectures and Confrontations*.) Other subdisciplines of anthropology, such as medical, cognitive, and ecological, at least retain their commitment to causal analysis and thus the possibility of cumulative science, even though they also long ago abandoned the developmentalist problems.

This returns us to the point I was making initially. The problems the developmentalists posed were never solved; they were simply abandoned. The developmental scheme, and in particular its Morganian version, created a consistent approach that helped define a specific area of inquiry— anthropology, which was therefore a unique, distinct, and different science in its own right. It was not history, philosophy, biology, or philology— although at that point it was not differentiated from sociology, because both shared the development hypothesis. It could incorporate some of these disciplines, for it was a synthesizing effort and needed, as Morgan admirably shows, the material of history and philology (linguistics) and particularly archaeology, and latter would need, logically, that of evolutionary biology. But its concern with the "origins and development" of man—of the universal history of mankind in its deepest (i.e., phylogenetic) sense—made its use of these materials wholly consistent and logical.

Above all, its particular concern with nonindustrial societies, and its even greater concern with the simplest of these, made logical sense within the context of the total science. The interest was not in these societies for their own sakes, or as alternative "lifestyles," or simply as part of comparative sociology, or as tools to attack colonialism or capitalism. It was not a pursuit of "fieldwork" as some kind of literary art form ("thick description") one notch above the travelogue. No. Anthropology needed the intense ethnographic study of primitive and preindustrial peoples— and needed it urgently before they disappeared—as crucial evidence for the stages of development that were part of the "early history of mankind." We needed the information as the best approximation that we could make to the social, cultural, and economic conditions of our own past. ("Salvage anthropology" understood this very well.) True, many of the primitive societies had changed themselves, particularly through contact with us. This would be a problem we would have to face in winnowing through the material.

But having thrown out the *specific* stages (rightly) of Morgan et al., without accepting the basic validity of the comparative method even minus the stages, we destroyed the elegant unity of anthropology this provided. The stages were like a ladder leading up vertically from the past. We simply took the ladder and moved it to the horizontal. It no longer led from anywhere to anywhere. We were left staring at all these rungs. What to do with them? We had acquired them because they *were* a ladder, and this ladder had given them an order and a meaning. But now they were simply there.

Anthropology has been admirably ingenious in adapting itself to the problem of what to do with the rungs once the ladder is no longer vertical. After all, it had to keep a constantly expanding number of practitioners in employment. We could pick a couple of the rungs and study them intensively and then compare them with a couple of others, which is what functionalism did. We could use them as examples in exploring universal aspects of mental functions, which is what structuralism did. We could perhaps devise a way to compare a lot of items across the different rungs to see what went with which, as with the cross-cultural method. There were endless fascinating questions we could ask about them, particularly about how they are changing: itself an endless process. This then leads to a theoretically endless string of sensitive interpretive studies, many of them intrinsically interesting: but to what end?

The rungs were no longer related chronologically and causally to each other; each was just a different example of "cultural construction" in an unwinding and inexplicable diversity of cultural schemes. And none of them was connected to the biological processes of evolution in which the vertical ladder had logically placed them, its bottom rungs plunging into the evolutionary past. Nor were they connected to the societies of the past revealed in more and more detail by an improving scientific archaeology.

We are now like the bewildered blind men trying to identify the elephant. We are all doing these disparate things, but we have in fact no elephant to hold them together. So we all identify the elephant with the particular thing we happen to be doing. And there is basically, therefore, no good reason, except long habit, why we should even be doing them in the same department and under any collective heading. For those of us who still believe that anthropology is a discipline anchored in evolution and needing all the forces of paleontology, genetics, archaeology, linguistics, history, and ethnography to tell the whole human story that is its brief, a hard second look at the perfect integration that Morgan's comparative method offered us will do no harm. (Some archaeologists are recognizing this: see "Left Anthropology and Right Archaeology" in my *Conjectures and Confrontations*.) An understanding of the persistence of the tribal imagination will restore the importance of the study of the tribes. We can clean up the obvious errors, but we should not let these blind us to the great vision that is Morgan's High Mandate for anthropology: to explore the Universal History of Mankind. Without a vision, as we know, the people perish; or at least they become so little as not to matter very much.

CHAPTER TWELVE

Open Societies and Closed Minds

Tribalism versus Civilization

A T THE London School of Economics (LSE) in the early 1950s, in the building that housed the student bar (The Three Tuns) and the student newspaper *(Beaver)*, there was tucked away a small but delightful tearoom run by Mrs. Popper. She was no relation to the great philosopher, but the coincidence was too good to overlook. Karl Popper's devotees (of whom I was one) gathered there for tea and crumpets and strawberry jam, and discussions of *The Open Society and Its Enemies* and *The Logic of Scientific Discovery* (at that point not translated into English). The School's Marxist students from time to time demanded a cooperative tearoom run by the Student Union. Their demands were always resisted. The general run of students may have been predominantly Left, but they weren't stupid. The notice on the tearoom door read:

MRS. POPPER'S
SOCIETY
ALWAYS OPEN

Karl Popper taught us perhaps the most important lesson in the philosophy of science: the absolute importance of being wrong. If you could not be proved wrong, you were not doing science; you could even be doing the antiscience of metaphysics. Any crackpot proposal of a metaphysician—say, that everything is an event in the mind of God—can in principle be proved *right*. The philosopher could, in principle at least, produce the mind of God and the events within it. The problem is it can't ever be proved *wrong*. There is no experiment or piece of evidence that could show there were not such events. The proposition is perfectly invulnerable. A scientific proposition, on the other hand, was not only open to verification, it was open to falsification: it was always in doubt. Popper had a student who came to him in despair. "I have done all these experiments," wailed the student, "and all my hypotheses have been disconfirmed." "That's wonderful," said Popper, "it means, young man, that you are doing *science!*"

This kind of systematic doubt, this constant challenge to the orthodox, this posing of conjectures that invited refutations, may have been the essence of science, but it required a particular kind of social system to exist and flourish. We have seen how in northwestern Europe in the sixteenth and seventeenth centuries this kind of society began to emerge, especially in England. As Lewis Feuer in another neglected book *(The Scientific Intellectual)* showed us, a strange and unlikely alliance of Calvinism and Hedonism moved science and education forward. It was inspired by the search for heavenly salvation, on the one hand, and the earthly memory of the Roman Republic and Athenian democracy, on the other. We have seen how, under the umbrella of a constitutional monarchy, a democratic electoral system emerged, and how science and industry finally exploded and the Miracle was made.

Free inquiry, skepticism, experiment, all became possible. Above all, personal responsibility replaced the observation of custom as the basis for moral action. Popper understood how precious was what he called the "Open Society" that emerged with fits and starts in this process. (Here capitalized when used in Popper's special sense.) He also understood better than most social commentators what we have been stressing throughout this book: how recent it is and how very fragile it is and how easily it can slip back into its opposite, the "Closed Society." This latter for Popper was unquestionably the tribal society, which brings us back round to where we started this journey.

These ruminations were prompted by reading Roger Sandall's comments on Popper in *The Culture Cult,* a brave book that examines Popper's insight in the context of the neoprimitivism that we noticed in Chapter 1. Sandall reminds us that Popper shared Freud's concern with the fragility of "civilization." In a footnote Popper says: "I suppose what I call the 'strain of civilization' is similar to the phenomenon which Freud had in mind when writing *Civilization and Its Discontents.*" Why did Open Societies seem so ready to reject the very openness that was the secret of their success?

When pondering the intellectual attraction of Nazism and Communism, says Sandall, Popper asked:

Why do these social philosophies support the revolt against civilization? And what is the secret of their popularity? Why do they attract and seduce so many intellectuals? I am inclined to think that the reason is that they give expression to a deep-felt dissatisfaction with a world, which does not, and cannot, live up to our moral ideals and to our dreams of perfection . . . The revolt against civilization may be a reaction against the strain of our civilization and its demand for personal responsibility.

Sandall comments: "In Popper's view, what Hitler, Stalin & Co. represented were forms of 'arrested tribalism,' and the more he considered the matter the more he saw a yearning for the past—closed, pre-rational, taboo-ridden, undemocratic, militaristic and fearful of liberty—as equally ubiquitous and malign."

This leads Sandall to question the recent rise of romantic neoprimitivism, which he sees as yet another example of the revolt against openness. Not that this is new. He astutely points out that it seems endemic in civilization. It goes back to antiquity, where there was an "unending revolt of the civilized against civilization" as exemplified by those Athenians who preferred the virtues of the Scythian tribes (that caught Swift's attention) to their own, just as the Rousseauians preferred the American Indian virtues to those of civilized Europe.

Its modern version he sees going hand in hand with the change in use of the word "culture"—from Matthew Arnold's qualitative "the best that has been thought and said and written" (*Culture and Anarchy*, 1869) to the essentially relative anthropological meaning, "way of life"— nonhierarchical, nonjudgmental, pluralistic, and inclusive: all "cultures" were equally beautiful and true. For the neoprimitive mentality this meant that Western industrial capitalist societies could not claim any kind of superior virtue—the problem Morgan and the developmentalists faced, as we saw in the last chapter. In fact, the neoprimitivists reversed the scale of values and asserted the moral superiority of the oppressed "cultures" of the world.

The whole premise of this book has been that the default system of human nature, and hence of human society, is the tribal system; unquestionably Closed. However we change and develop—however Open we become, it is always with us in one form or another. I am therefore, in this scheme, less interested in any kind of choice to be made between forms of society or mentality than in trying to understand the interaction between the tribal default system and the civilized structures we have erected on it or over it. This does not mean that we cannot prefer the Open to the Closed form of society and defend the former against a recursion to the latter. We shall certainly do so. But it does mean that this cannot be done without understanding the nature of the interaction between them and, what is equally important, how we should go about studying this interaction. With this in mind, let us reflect on Popper, tribalism, and the idea of culture, and so come full circle back to the issues that launched this enterprise.

Popper and the Savage Mind

Those of us who were pupils, then colleagues, and, insofar as it was possible, friends of Karl Popper, will be delighted with Sandall's rehabilitation. For the reasons he so eloquently states, current anthropology is not friendly to Popper, sunk as it is in cultural relativism and fashionable neoprimitivism. But then it never was. As a student of both Popper and Raymond Firth in the early 1950s, I was considerably torn. Firth and the social anthropologists taught that Popper's version of "tribal society" in *The Open Society and Its Enemies* was seriously flawed. His views on the "rigidity" of tribalism were themselves, we were told, a sight too rigid. For instance, Popper statements like "Taboos rigidly regulate and dominate all aspects of life . . . The right way is always determined . . . it is determined by taboos, by magical tribal institutions which can never become the objects of critical consideration"—and much more in this vein. Theirs was not a relativist horror of comparing the worth of the two kinds of society; they just thought he had the facts wrong.

Clearly, Firth argued, although Popper might have met a few acculturated Maori during his time in New Zealand, he knew nothing of actual tribal peoples. Firth had lived with the Maori as a Malinowskian "participant observer" and written a book about their economic behavior: *Primitive Economics of the New Zealand Maori*. Firth had shown that their economic behavior was fundamentally "rational": they weighed consequences, made sound investment decisions, calculated returns, and so on, just like their "civilized" counterparts. We were pointed to Bronislaw Malinowski, Firth's mentor only recently gone from the LSE, and his demonstration that the Trobriand Islanders used "science" when lagoon fishing and resorted to "magic" only when faced with the uncertainties of the open sea *(Magic, Science and Religion)*. Even there, magic was only an adjunct to the rational arts of canoe design and navigation. For purposes of an essay on the subject I dredged up Paul Radin's *Primitive Man as a Philosopher* for examples of skeptical questioning by taboo-ridden savages. Popper, it was held, sailed too close to the wind of Lucien Lévy-Bruhl's *La mentalité primitive:* to the notion of the savage lost in a state of prescientific "mystic participation." Indeed, Popper saw mysticism as a characteristic of the Closed Society.

At the same time that Popper was writing *The Open Society* (1945), Claude Lévi-Strauss was struggling with the same problem of "primitive mentality"—as we saw in Chapter 1. Lévi-Strauss opposed Lévy-Bruhl, Freud, and Piaget in rejecting the idea that the thinking (or feeling) of savages was essentially that of children, and asserted the universality of rational thinking. His "elementary structures" (*Les structures élémentaires de la parenté*, 1949) were not elementary because of the simplemindedness of savages. The savage's schemes of classification were based on the same rational (binary) logic as that of modern science. To think otherwise was part of "The Archaic Illusion." Thus, for the social anthropology of the fifties, Popper was reflecting an out-of-date idea of primitive mentality stemming from the social evolutionists of the nineteenth century rather than from modern ethnographic information.

But for me, this rehabilitation of the savage mind seemed to miss Popper's point. He was not talking about different mental types but about different social types: different kinds of society. He didn't doubt that tribal people could act rationally, or that contemporary Western thinking was not to some extent still magical and taboo ridden. But a radical break had occurred in the West in the fifth century BC in Athens, and after that a society different in kind from the tribal became possible.

Popper was decidedly anti-utopian. There will be no utopia; society is always a compromise. But we can nurture the conditions that promote Openness, or "civilization" in the judgmental sense. From the point of view of this book's argument, Openness is something that might or might not develop within "civilization"—or that might develop and then be lost. From the judgmental point of view a civilization cannot be called such unless it has at least some of the features that Popper calls Open. We must note the distinction and press on. In the Closed Society of the tribe, for Popper, the social order was "natural"—part of nature. It was a given, set down like everything else in the ancient "dreamtime" as with the Aborigines, or by the gods or the ancestors. It was familial: the tribe was a family writ large, and family loyalties were the model for morality. It changed, but change was not of its essence. Change was not welcomed; it was actively resisted. The rules and values of the society, which set a life's course, were not the result of rational choice and deliberation, but were the givens of the culture: taboos were the prime example, and we perhaps forget how indeed "taboo ridden" many tribal societies were. This was a world governed by "custom"—which anthropologists used to regard as their subject matter. Within this framework means could be rational but ends were not questioned. Above all, the idea of individual moral responsibility, as opposed to loyalty to kin, clan, and tribe, was absent.

It is easy to criticize Popper's picture by demonstrating the rationality of tribal people, but I think we must view his "Closed" and "Open" societies as Weberian ideal types. Depending on their degree of contact and their stage of social evolution, "tribal" societies might have degrees of Openness. The great civilizations of India and China, for example (which Popper does not discuss), while being absolute theocratic despotisms, did have some Open features. Confucius could travel around China peddling his ideas of good government to the tribal despots, and while he was not very successful, he was not persecuted. Prince Gautama could develop his ideas of personal responsibility for salvation within collectivist Hinduism where caste determined everything. His devotee Ashoka could even try to put Buddhist principles into a political system, but this too fell before the relentless power of caste. Rome under the Republic and during the Pax Romana under Augustus was religiously tolerant to a fault. On the other hand, as Popper readily recognizes, our Western liberal democracies have many Closed features, including, in his view, the English public (i.e., private) schools and men's clubs. He could certainly have added the regimental system in the army, the elaborate conventions of upper-class "society," the ceremonial mummeries of the Houses of Parliament, middle-class conformism, the mass behavior of sports fans, the initiatory absurdities of college fraternities, bureaucratic rigidty, religious and political fundamentalism, and the organization of street gangs, to say nothing of Grateful Dead concerts.

The Open Society must in fact be an ideal that actual societies strive to achieve. No society could be completely Open, determining everything by rational decision, totally skeptical about everything, always looking to be proved wrong rather than seeking to confirm what is thought right. Most of the ends pursued in society at any time will have to be givens—established practices—or there would be no stability. Society would be like a person without habits and dispositions. It would be like the self-conscious centipede that had to think about each leg's movement; it would be paralyzed. But in the society aspiring to be Open, the ends can be challenged and changed by "piecemeal social engineering."

To try to replace the bad old ends by new ends designed to be just as rigidly followed in order to achieve perfection is to fall into the trap of "utopian social engineering." It is to return to the tribalism of the Closed Society. It is for Popper the fatal weakness of doctrinaire socialism, and Marxism in particular, and of all historicist philosophies of history, like those of Hegel, that claim to know the inevitable process of change and therefore to predict the future and act on those predictions. Thus Popper appealed equally to moderate Tories who believed in muddling through, and to Fabian socialists who were for gradual pragmatic reform. He was made a professor by the Fabian LSE and knighted by an admiring Tory government.

The Strain of Civilization

What Popper saw clearly (as Randall points out) was "the strain of civilization" that afflicted any relatively Open society. The Open Society was difficult to achieve. It was not "natural" to us; we had to work devilish hard to make it succeed. Popper agreed with Freud that, as the latter would have put it, the burden of the superego was too great. Popper would have called it the burden of individual moral responsibility. Too many of us too much of the time were only too happy to have some absolutist doctrine, some sacred text, or some charismatic leader take the burden of responsibility from us: to return us to the familial comfort of Closed, tribal society, where it was all decided for us.

Above all there is a fear of the uncertainties of change—particularly rapid change. What is closed in the Closed Society is the future, because it is thought either to eternally repeat the present, or to recycle fixed ages, or to change in completely known and fixed ways. The Closed Society seeks to ignore, deny, and arrest, or to predict and hence totally control, social change. The Open Society accepts the unpredictable reality of change and deals with it. (The roots of this idea were there in Henri Bergson's philosophy, and his "open morality" and "closed morality"—but that is another essay: see *The Search for Society*.)

This contrast was present from the start in the great conflict between democratic Athens (potentially Open but with a heavy burden of Closed features) and tribal Sparta (completely and utterly Closed): the subject of Popper's first volume *(The Spell of Plato)*. Athens had passed consciously from a tribal society to a democratic city-state, which in turn morphed into a maritime empire. (Curiously, Popper, while making much of Solon and Pericles, does not mention the reforms of Cleisthenes, which were critical to the change.) Athens struggled to maintain its democratic system, both against outside opponents and against inside forces. By becoming an empire it threatened its own democracy.

The old order of tribal families, which Cleisthenes had tried to break down, hated democracy and conspired with Sparta, the archetypal closed tribal society, which just as consciously arrested change as Athens had embraced it. Many of the Athenian intellectuals took the pro-Spartan side. Plato, Popper's nemesis, led the intellectual justification for a Spartan-style society in *The Republic* and *The Laws*. Plato's relatives were active in the council of the Thirty Tyrants, who conspired with Sparta and led a reign of terror in Athens.

If all this sounds very contemporary, then Popper has made his point. It is not just the gullible mob and the resentful aristocrats who are ready to betray the Open Society; its own intellectuals are often in the forefront of the stampede. Why, asked Popper, were his intellectual contemporaries so bewitched by Fascism and Communism, just as Plato was by Spartanism? The sinister appeal of the Closed Society to even the best minds haunted Popper. The Western democracies are the most Open societies yet achieved, but they too tend to become, or try to become, empires. Their growing complexity makes harsh demands on our capacity for rationality and individual moral responsibility. The "perennial appeal of tribalism" (my phrase, not Popper's) both to the masses and to the elites, is often overpowering. When things are looking bad for us, we cry out for a savior—a doctrine and a leader—to return us to the unthinking security of tribal society and the tribal mentality.

Max Weber was just as bothered as Popper was by this. But he added an important point. He saw that charismatic leadership had an innate appeal, but he also saw that the growth of giant bureaucracies—indeed, the very bureaucratic principle itself—added a new and dangerous variable to the equation. This was the most "rational" of rational social developments, and yet it had no inherent moral impulse. It could serve a vicious tyranny with the same amoral efficiency as it served a beneficent welfare state. Indeed, it was the perfect instrument for totalitarianism. Popper misses this. The Soviet Union under Stalin, and the Fascist dictatorships, were nightmares of *bureaucracy* as much as nightmares of *tribalism*. Stalin was not, like Hitler, a charismatic madman; he was, like Eichman, the ultimate dull bureaucrat. The tribal elements in these totalitarian societies were the more spectacular (Nuremberg), but the bureaucracy got the totalitarian job done (Politburo). The Soviet system eventually broke down because this form of government became perilously inefficient. The result of the breakdown is not the free enterprise democracy that was our hope, but a resurgence of Russian tribalism.

George Orwell is of course the great fabulist of this new-old phenomenon, and he portrayed dramatically the ruthless mix of tribal and bureaucratic elements in the reign of Big Brother and The Party. (Kafka was its metaphysician.) The Islamic dictatorships, on the other hand (which, as Sandall notes, Popper does not consider), are predominantly tribal, with poorly developed bureaucracies precisely because they are tribal still in mentality. They are societies that have never opened. Most of the mistakes we make with them result from not appreciating this fact, and assuming that if offered the choice they will choose to be good individualistic liberal democracies. We saw what happened when the Athenians offered the model of democracy to Sparta. It was called the Peloponnesian War.

Unnatural Openness

The Open Society and its corollary of liberal democracy, contrary to some modern opinions on the subject, is not the inevitable end product of social evolution. It is not natural to us, and we live constantly on the edge in trying to maintain it. And as Sandall acutely notes, Popper never deals with the paradox that although the use of force is inimical to the ideal Open Society, without that force we cannot defend it against the forces of the Closed Societies—the totalitarianisms—that threaten it. The only recourse, I suppose, is that we should use force sparingly and wisely. One out of two isn't bad.

Sandall mentions Ayaan Hirsi Ali, whom we met in Chapter 3. Her courageous book *Infidel* records in plain and moving prose one person's journey from the inside of the most Closed of tribal societies—clan-dominated Somalia—to the Openness of almost painfully super-open Holland. It is a personal journey that recapitulates the whole development traced by Popper (and most other sociologists of the nineteenth and twentieth centuries) for society as a whole. To those of us who take our Openness, however tarnished, too much for granted, it is a rebuke and a warning. And it illustrates for us our great paradox: how tolerant can an Open Society afford to be of intolerance? In our Open concern with not intruding on "religious freedom" or even with offending "religious sensibilities," are we letting the opponents of the Open Society fester and grow in our midst?

Holland and the rest of Europe are caught in a web of self-delusion on the issue; there is no easy answer. Miss Hirsi Ali is under threat of death from the agents of the Closed Society. A fanatic has already murdered her colleague, filmmaker Theo van Gogh, and the Dutch government has withdrawn her protection outside Holland. Friends of the Open Society, and of the human decency (Orwell's favorite value) on which it must ultimately depend, should rally to her support. This is not an irrelevant footnote. The question of the survival of the Open Society is not simply an issue for academic discussion in journals. It is a life-and-death matter, and we are all burdened with that individual moral responsibility for it that Popper saw as being at its heart.

Perhaps the most serious footnote to Popper's argument is the objection that the distinction he draws is too stark. To say that Fascism and Soviet Communism are relapses into "tribalism" is to miss the point that both had elements of mass-salvation religion about them, elements that, while certainly not Open, were not tribal either. As I have already pointed out, the road from tribal to Open is long and complex, and a major intervening stage is that of the growth of transtribal, transnational religions, like Hinduism, Buddhism, Christianity, and Islam (Judaism remained tribal, with the proviso that it would accept converts). Among these, Roman Christianity and the Islamic Caliphate depended on large and complicated (and celibate) bureaucratic organizations to run their transnational governments, and all needed literate clergy. This was the thin end of the wedge. Despite their mysticism and totalitarianism, therefore, these religions were also the basis for developing education and critical thought.

The route in the West was from magic and mysticism, through metaphysics and scholasticism, to the Renaissance, Reformation, and Enlightenment, to positive science and the modern world. This was a move beyond "tribalism" even though tribal elements remained strong throughout and always exercised their peculiarly human appeal. Thus for me the "Closed" society can have elements that move well beyond the tribal yet are not fully "Open."

When we revert, it is to these elements: the savior, the doctrine, the assurance of meaning, the even greater assurance of salvation—in this world (Fascism and Communism) or in the next (Islam, evangelicalism)—as much as to the raw tribal elements that we turn to in our fear of freedom (*pace* Fromm). Islamic societies are fundamentally tribal and Closed in that sense, but they are also the product of a salvation religion that moves beyond the tribe and seeks to incorporate the world. This is perhaps what Popper misses. The salvation religions can be as decidedly opposed to tribalism as they are to the Open Society itself. The great churches in fact often seek to subvert completely that loyalty to the family and kin on which tribalism depends; they want the individual worshippers to be loyal directly to the church. They rarely succeed entirely, because of the fundamental appeal of tribalism that we have already canvassed.

China has been fighting this battle between kinship and higher (in this case, state) authority over the last century. Here the clan-based Confucian society has been under assault. In traditional Chinese society it supplied members to the emperor's central bureaucracy and these members in turn benefited their clans: it was a mutually supportive system where the state drew on the strengths of tribalism. With the collapse of that society, and its cult of emperor worship, first under the republic then under Communism, the bureaucracy was converted from an instrument of the emperor and tradition to that of the one-party state and "progress." In the process the patrilineal clan system, with its polygamy and ancestor worship, was eventually destroyed, the final blow being the restrictions on reproduction in the one-child family law.

Islam is an interesting and effective balance in which the religion has drawn on the energy of the tribe and clan in its success. But it is not a good formula for producing democratic societies, as we are discovering, any more than is the Chinese model. Thus while I think Popper's "Open vs. Closed" distinction holds, he was perhaps overly influenced by the Athens vs. Sparta contrast in his eagerness to refute Plato. He was therefore perhaps misleading to equate "Closed" totally with "tribal." The Closed Society is more complicated than that, or it would be easier to deal with.

This is therefore the place to note briefly that Popper never meant us to assume that a tribal society was an unreservedly grim place to be. Such societies, when large and warrior dominated, could be truly savage places, but the small ones could be warm and supportive and in many ways very satisfying to their members. The Eskimo, he admits, seem to be a happy people. Thus I have sung the virtues of the "Paleoterrific"—the Old Stone Age societies like those of Lascaux, which Sandall does not want to admit as civilizations—in which he is technically correct (see my *Search for Society*). More-open societies, on the other hand, as Tocqueville noted for America, can be riven with anxiety and uncertainty, with alienation, *anomie,* and *angst.* This was the point about the "burden of civilization." It is why the Closed Society had its powerful attraction for us, even the intellectuals. There was a cost to maintaining an Open system, but it was worth it. The alternative was the modern version of the Closed Society, which was inevitably totalitarian and repressive.

Culture and *Kultur*

The argument between the two meanings of "culture" that Sandall discusses—Mathew Arnold's judgmental version of "high culture" ("the best that has been thought and said and written"), and the anthropological notion of culture as the general lifeways of a people—might also seem like a purely academic matter. But insofar as the distinction affects our behavior in the real world, and it does, it is equally a matter of moral concern. In any case it is central to our current understanding of what is happening in what used to be called "the social sciences," whose methods Popper subjected to such keen scrutiny. It has moved in its meaning from a valuation to a description to a buzzword. Its vulgarization, along with that of the concept of "folk," is part of the surge of neoprimitivism that Sandall deplores and that leaves the door ajar for its own version of the Closed Society.

I might note that back in those balmy intellectual days at the LSE (see my *Participant Observer*), the first essay students had to write in social anthropology was always on the idea of "culture." We read Malinowski's article of that name in the *Encyclopedia of the Social Sciences* and were expected to grasp thoroughly the difference between the Arnoldian and popular idea of culture as high thinking and aesthetics—"playing the piano, reading Byron and watching ballet," as Firth used to put it—and the anthropological notion of culture as the total integrated way of life of a community.

It was usually E. B. Tylor's "enumerative descriptive" definition that was quoted then: "That complex whole which includes . . ." pretty much everything *(Primitive Culture)*. It is a measure of change in our own culture that this emphasis is now reversed and the anthropological meaning now dominates. No one now claims to be "cultured" or to have "cultivated" tastes. It sounds offensively elitist. Students find it hard to imagine a time when this was not true.

The anthropological idea of culture is fundamentally German: *Kultur.* This is a fact largely avoided by anthropologists, with the laudable exception of their finest historian, George Stocking. It would be hard for such an idea to arise in Anglo-Saxon thinking, basically utilitarian, empiricist, and individualist. The German strain—Hegelian, idealist, and collectivist—is much more open to it. It is interesting that the continental Pole, Malinowski, always thought of culture as his subject matter *(A Scientific Theory of Culture),* and thought it should be analyzed in terms of how it answered human needs. In this he was not followed by even his most immediate followers. (I perhaps remain an exception.) They preferred A. R. Radcliffe-Brown *(A Natural Science of Society)* and called themselves "social anthropologists." They saw "society" or "social structure" as their subject matter (essentially following Émile Durkheim). But note the continuing insistence that what they were doing was "science."

In this they took issue with Wilhelm Dilthey (1833–1911) in his absolute and influential separation of *Naturwissenschaften,* the "nature sciences," from *Geisteswissenschaften,* the "spirit sciences." The first searches for causes; its model is physics. The second searches rather for patterns; its model is history. The methods of the one, Dilthey claimed, cannot be applied to the subject matter of the other. This debate runs through anthropology, with the issues of whether anthropology is science or history, and the recent popular upsurge of anthropology as a "humanism" as opposed to a science. The Germans in American anthropology (Boas, Kroeber, Lowie, Sapir, and so on) and their students (Mead, Benedict, Kluckhohn, Linton, and latterly Geertz) tended always to favor the humanistic or historical side against the scientific.

Franz Boas, who taught them all (and who started as a physicist in Germany), had learned profoundly from Dilthey, Humbolt, Wundt, Bastian, and Frobenius and was suffused with their ideas. The non-Germans in America, deriving from Lewis Henry Morgan and his social evolutionism, tended to stick with materialist science, as did Leslie White in *The Science of Culture* and G. P. Murdock in *Social Structure,* or Julian Steward in *Theory of Culture Change,* or Marvin Harris in *Cultural Materialism: The Struggle for a Science of Culture.* But they all shared the same idea of culture, differing only in how to analyze it.

The *Volksgeist*

The idea of *Kultur* in this anthropological sense goes back to Johann Herder (1744–1803). It gets immediately entangled with Herder's other basic notion of the *Volk.* This was the beginning both of German romantic nationalism and of the anthropological concept of culture. Herder distinguished *Volk* (the people) from *Reich* (the state). (The Nazis conflated the two: *"Ein Volk, ein Reich, ein Führer!"*) The state was, for Herder, destructive of the organic spirit *(Geist)* of the people—essentially the unspoiled peasants and rural villagers who enshrined the true, ancient soul of the people, which was lost in the cities.

The *Geist* of each *Volk,* the *Volksgeist,* was unique and produced its distinctive *Kultur.* (See Stocking 1996 for the best history.) This culture, being specific and organic and a *ding-an-sich* (end in itself), could not be judged by the values of other cultures. Dilthey himself was a German romantic nationalist, and his insistence on the autonomy of the human sciences (which gave rise to "hermeneutics") was part and parcel of protecting the uniqueness of the *Geist* of the German *Volk.* Dilthey and Herder were thus attacking the whole Enlightenment project of universal history and universal values, as enshrined in British empiricism, French materialism, and Scottish evolutionism.

The concept of the uniqueness and superiority of the *Kultur* of the *Volk* has an interesting and wayward history. Academically it was reflected in Wundt's *Völkerpsychologie* (folk psychology), Bastian's *Völkergedanke* (folk ideas), and Frobenius's *Kulturkreislehre* (culture area theory). All this was transposed to American anthropology, largely by Boas. But in the wider world it fueled the fires of passionate romantic nationalism throughout Europe in the nineteenth and twentieth centuries. The Brothers Grimm began the collection of "folktales" *(Volkspiel)* that preserved the spirit of the folk. Hans Christian Andersen, Andrew Lang, and Lady Gregory among many others collected "folklore" *(Volkskunde)* from the peasants. Aarne and Thompson produced a massive and definitive study, *The Types of the Folktale.*

"Folk languages" previously ignored or suppressed by the state, began to be revived: Welsh, Irish, Scots Gaelic, Basque, Romansch, Breton, Provençal, Macedonian, Catalonian. The independent Irish government in 1922, as one of its first acts, appointed official "Folklore Collectors" in the Irish-speaking districts. The German language was purified of foreign, particularly Latin, loanwords: producing such wonders as *Kinderwagen* for perambulator, or *Fernsprechmädchen* for telephone operator. And we must not forget, *Volkswagen.* English linguistic nationalists tried to substitute "pushwainling" for perambulator, but it didn't catch on: "pram" won out. In American English the hybrid "baby carriage" prevailed: part Germanic, part Romance, as befits an immigrant nation.

Composers collected "folksongs" *(Volksleider)* and other "folk music" and incorporated them into their nationalistic compositions: Dvořak, Liadov, Kodaly, Borodin, Canteloube, Grieg, Bartok, Vaughan Williams in England, Aaron Copland in the United States. National organizations such as the English Folk Song and Folk Dance Society (of which I was once a member) were organized by Cecil Sharpe and his counterparts in other countries. "Folk Museums" sprang up: Boas started his anthropological life at the Museum für Völkerkünde in Berlin. (Two of my earliest publications were in *Ulster Folklife*—published by the Ulster Folk Museum and the *Journal of American Folklore.*) An American Folk Life Center was established in the Library of Congress. The Lomaxes, John and Alan, began their collection of folksongs for the Smithsonian Institution. "Folk costume" rapidly became "national costume," with the canny Scots textile industry inventing "clan tartans" from scratch to meet the demand.

A huge scholarly effort on philology and mythology got under way—to get the "essential spirit" or "ethos" (the *Geist*) of the folk. "Folk heroes" were discovered and created, and we still use the term (Bruce Springsteen, Superman, Bonnie and Clyde). Norse myths were collected and translated, and Wagner rendered them into a grand musical expression of the Nordic *Kultur* of the Nordic *Volk.* Among other things this nationalist movement helped to import studies of the peasantry wholesale into anthropology, because all this "folk culture" was essentially that of the peasants. (See Robert Redfield, *The Folk Culture of Yucatan.*) This was very useful because tribal, or as they were then called "primitive," societies—the accepted subject matter of the discipline—were vanishing as fast as anthropology was growing.

From Right to Left

But a funny thing happened to the folk concept on the way to modern life. The movement had originally been unabashedly romantic, bourgeois, scholarly, and profoundly nationalistic (the glorification of the nation), and centered on the rural peasantry. But the United States was a young culture with no deep folk traditions—certainly not uniform national ones. Above all it had no ancient peasantry that enshrined the folk values. It tried to invent a folk as it went along, starting with the sturdy New England farmers, moving on to the frontiersmen, taking in the Cajuns and the hill folk of Appalachia, and then the pioneers, and especially the cowboys (totally products of the capitalist beef industry), and even the outlaws.

In some versions it is even the "family farmers" of the Midwest who embody the genuine folk values. (These, like the New England farmers, are a version of the "yeomen" of England, which were that country's folk-substitute for an ancient peasantry.) But this ragbag of candidates emphasized the American problem: if you were going to glorify the folk, who were they? Currently "the folk" has become everyone. Notice how politicians regardless of party address and refer to everyone as "folks." This used to be understood as the folks back home (hence "folksy") but now (listen to President Obama) includes "the folks on Wall Street," "the folks in the Pentagon," "the folks here in Washington," and so on. There was a time when a middle-class audience would have been horrified at being addressed as "folks." Now it is de rigueur, and the rich Republican John McCain desperately tried to attach the proletarian Joe-the-Plumber to his cause as an icon of the folk. This was a counter to Obama (Ivy League president of the Harvard Law Review) winning the battle of folksiness with his own humble-origin (one-of-the-folk) story.

The linking of Sarah Palin and Joe the Plumber as icons of the right was odd enough but points to a strange battle that came to the fore in the sixties between Right and Left to claim the low ground of perfect victim. This battle had always been there with the small-town and rural conservative Christian fundamentalists claiming their place as the true oppressed: the victims of the eggheads and liberal East Coast atheist left-wing intellectuals. What no one of the latter predicted was that this movement of the other folk would actually rise up and take power under the Presidents Bush. It was presumed they were a local anomaly in decline after the Scopes trial. This proved to be a serious miscalculation.

But this universalizing of the folk took time. Sometime in the thirties, in the United States, with the Great Depression and the rise of Fascism and Communism, while remaining romantic, the folk movement turned sharply leftward and became a movement of the urban and rural proletariat, the labor unions, and generally of radicalism and protest. The right-wing nationalism was abandoned and a proletarian universalism substituted. The basic idea was still the superior virtue of the folk, but it was more the folk as in the International Workers of the World than the unique national folk of the unique national culture, although there was that. "This land is your land, this land is my land" attempted to reclaim America for the folk. Labor songs, protest songs, Dixieland, and blues: the folk music of Huddie Ledbetter, Woody Guthrie, Burl Ives, Pete Seeger, and the whole panoply of jazz, soul, country, rock, merging into hip-hop, rap, and all the others.

The theme of only the culture of the proletariat (urban and rural), the downtrodden and the marginal being genuine and virtuous, was revived during and after the Vietnam War with the "counterculture": antiwar, the youth movement, hippies, yippies, and dropouts. Bob Dylan was its songster; Timothy Leary was its guru; Carlos Castaneda was its (phony) ethnographer; Woodstock was its grand orgiastic festival; derivatives of threadbare work clothes were its uniform. But note how easily the whole folk movement after its lurch leftward became hijacked by capitalist consumerism.

Essentially a phenomenon of the U.S. Depression era, it was globalized by the record industry, and by film and television, into a multibillion-dollar commercial enterprise. Elements of the "purity of the folk" continue to have commercial success in the New Age Movement, and the passions for alternative (folk) medicine, organic (read: folk) foods and farming, antiglobalization and anti-IMF movements: all organized and funded, as were the original nationalistic folk movements, by the idealistic urban bourgeoisie.

The purity-of-the-folk doctrine, and its corollary of the superior virtue of the dispossessed and marginal, has many sources, starting with the Sermon on the Mount and continuing through St. Francis of Assisi, Rousseau, Tolstoy and the Narodniki, American populism and yahooism, proletarianism, and the Wobblies. In that London of the 1950s I shared with Popper, young upper-middle-class socialists would routinely go off and try to live working-class lives, because for them only the proletariat was "authentic." They never lasted very long. But within anthropology there is no doubt about the influence of the German nationalist ideas, however strange a twist the leftist lurch gave them.

The Fascism of Culture

We do not have to offer up the history of American "cultural anthropology" from Boas onward to see how it was part and parcel of the folk movement. It adopted its language, its ideas, and its relativist and nativist values wholesale. Sandall tells the story very well. But if American cultural anthropology was a bastard child of German romantic nationalism, so of course was Nazi Fascism, which is its immediate cousin. We could even say its "cousin-german" but the pun might be too archaic.

What they held in common was the idea of the superiority of culture/ *Kultur* over the individual, and the doctrine of the uniqueness of each folk culture, and hence a strict relativism. (Mussolini was perhaps the most eloquent defender of cultural relativism ever.) Where they parted company was in the Nazi insistence on the superiority of the particular culture of a particular race: the *Herrenvolk* (the "noble folk," or "master race" as we translate it). This had always been a part of the German romantic nationalist creed. Boas violently rejected the idea of the racial basis of culture, and certainly of the cultural superiority of any one race or culture, and anthropology generally followed him. But they persisted in their own Germanic cultural determinism, and substituted it for the racial determinism they abhorred.

A. L. Kroeber's "absolute dominance of culture" over the individual, and the whole "culture and personality" movement (an offspring of "national character" studies) and the Sapir-Whorf linguistic determinism of the "language and culture" school, all were children of the German nationalist idea that the *Geist* of the *Volk*, which creates its *Kultur,* is superior to the individual who is shaped by its demands. See Sapir's "Culture, Genuine and Spurious"—pure Herder—or Ruth Benedict's search for the *ethos* of cultures, which was consciously indebted to Oswald Spengler (and Dilthey and Koffka and Worringer and Köhler—see the notes to chapter 3 of *Patterns of Culture*).

In Germany it reached its metaphysical heights in the idealism of Hegel and his followers, which was rendered into materialist form by Marx: the proletariat became the true *Volk* and the bearers of revolution leading to the end settled-state of Communism. In its latest manifestation among anthropologists, it is the doctrine of the "cultural construction" of reality. This is combined with an antiscientism that would have warmed

Dilthey's heart, and is largely a borrowing from muddled European philosophers who seem not to have read Popper.

Contemporary American cultural anthropologists would, if they knew about it, no doubt be horrified by Popper's preference for Open over tribal societies. This offends their basic cultural relativism. But consistency is not their strong point. And it is a great irony, at least to me, that their relativism, their assault on the idea of "truth" (which they invariably put in quotes), comes from the Left. One thing my old-time leftist friends used to preach with passion was that the relativism—and hence the lies—of the capitalists could be countered by an unswerving devotion to the truth (no quotes) about social injustice.

This is why the Fabian Socialists founded the LSE: to collect and analyze those true facts that would force governments to act against inequality and injustice. Alan Sokal, as an old-fashioned American leftist, makes this same observation in *Beyond the Hoax*. The Left academics, he says, took away from the working class the weapon of the truth. But what the anthropologists in fact believe is not the relativism they preach but their own patronizing doctrine of the superiority of the folk. Margaret Mead greatly influenced the trend with her not-too-hidden admiration for the socialization practices of the Samoans. Today, self-described "cultural anthropologists" (the supposed relativists) universally embrace the doctrine of the wickedness of Western capitalism and its evil products, colonialism and globalization. ("Neoliberalism" gets in there too. I think it means laissez-faire capitalism and free trade.)

The Superiority of the Oppressed

In this doctrine, virtue lies not with the "free world" but with the tribes and peasants, the urbanized poor and dispossessed (especially the Palestinians), and the indigenous peoples of the third world, however enamored these might be of the virtues of the Closed Society. The doctrine of multiculturalism asserts the superiority of folk cultures over their host societies, while the "indigenous peoples" movement does the same for "indigenous knowledge" over science. Because it is culture that matters over individuals in this scheme, the result is "identity politics," where one's fate is totally wrapped up in race, gender, class, and ethnicity. The dominance of the interests of these collectivities and their "rights" over the individual is a useful formula for the Closed Society.

This doctrine pervades the whole culture. It is hard to find an independent movie these days in which the superior wisdom and virtue of the marginalized and the oppressed, and even the ignorant and simpleminded, is not the central theme. The book market—via Oprah—is saturated with autobiographies of the lame and the halt and the homosexual. If you have not overcome poverty or a serious disease, survived a brutally abusive family, or triumphed over addiction or homophobia, then forget about publishing your life story. You will be rewarded not because of how well you write but because of how much you have suffered.

Stories of literate and articulate people leading interesting lives are regarded as simply quaint. They belong to that Arnoldian world of "high culture" that multiculturalists see themselves as duty-bound to belittle and bring down. The cultural anthropologists do not see themselves, of course, as attacking the Open Society. They see the result of their activities as greater "equality," as a righting of "injustice," rather than as a dumbing down of culture generally. The cure for inequality, for them, is not to raise up the depressed to participate in high culture, but to invert the Arnoldian hierarchy and make "low culture" the repository of virtue. And if the low cannot be raised, then at least we can raise their self-esteem.

But Sandall is right to link the neoprimitivism of the cultural anthropologists with the treason of the intellectuals that Popper so feared. "Cultural anthropology" today more resembles one of Anthony Wallace's "revitalization movements" than it does an academic discipline. It borrows all the appurtenances of academe—journals, research, footnotes, references, conferences, and the like, but it uses them in the way clever creationists use the same cover: to preach a doctrine. They do not see it this way, of course. They are working for greater inclusiveness and of course "diversity": they want to include more people in the Open Society, but on criteria that are inimical to it.

To this end they passionately support "affirmative action," which again elevates the contingency of skin color over individual worth. Melanin matters more than merit. But they do not want to include more "oppressed" people at the cost of "assimilation." They refuse to equate their Open Society with the high culture of the Western tradition, including its canon and including its science. This involves them in a paradox and no little guilt, because their whole enterprise, and their system of rewards, is derived from that high culture. The further paradox is that by their logic, their own conclusions must be just another "cultural construction" with no claim to authority beyond the boundaries of their community of discourse. (If I may be allowed the indulgence of quoting myself: "If it looks like a duck, and walks like a duck, and quacks like a duck, then it's a cultural construction of a duck"—*The Challenge of Anthropology*.)

Another paradox is that they attack "growth" on the Western economic model as inimical to the survival of indigenous cultures. But the only way to promote the welfare of these cultures (or rather the people in these societies) is through growth, and we have seen that postcolonial governments in the third world cannot manage this, that aid is largely wasted, that socialism always fails, and that the corruption of authoritarian politics leads to a reversion to tribalism. (Watch Kenya, Somalia, Congo, Sudan, Uganda, Zimbabwe . . .) Their only hope lies with the unprejudiced globalizing economy that knows no barriers of race or tribe or nationality, or ethnicity, or religion, or even "gender," but only knows markets and profits. Many of the particularities of culture will disappear in this process, and it will be a bumpy road, but it is the only way to material prosperity for the dispossessed of the world.

I said that most of the fathers of social science, like Morgan, basically agreed that there was universal progress through lower to higher stages of what they called "society." I have listed them so often I will forebear, but they shared Popper's vision of something like the Open Society as the end product. They did not doubt that the shift was for the better. Tylor himself, as we saw, declared anthropology to be a "reformer's science" whose business it was to identify "survivals" of the tribal Closed Society, the better to sweep them away. James Frazer mounted a massive scholarly effort aimed at replacing religion with science. Henry Maine saw the emergence of the idea of individual contract (Open) as an unqualified improvement on the law of status (Closed). Tönnies might have been nostalgic for the security of *Gemeinschaft*, Redfield wistful about the Folk Cultures, and Durkheim might have feared the *anomie* of his state of "organic solidarity"—but they all, led originally by Comte and Spencer, saw the progression as generally upward, and generally a good thing.

Popper's Optimism: Civilization's Hope

Popper was a progressive and an optimist. At the LSE (again) I was secretary of the Rationalist Society, and we invited Popper to be our honorary president for one year, which involved him in giving a presidential address. We had invited Bertrand Russell, but he politely declined. He had not been welcome in leftist intellectual circles after he dared to criticize the USSR in *The Practice and Theory of Bolshevism* in 1920. But Popper accepted and gave us a talk titled "Moral Progress: Confessions of an Optimist"—a piece he later published *(Conjectures and Refutations)*. He saw, as two of his predecessors at the LSE, L. T. Hobhouse *(Morals in Evolution)* and Edward Westermarck *(The Origin and Development of Moral Ideas)*, had seen: that we are as a species moving toward a greater "inclusiveness." We progressively include more and more people, regardless of those irritating distinctions and diacritics, in the circle of those to whom we have moral obligations: to the world as an Open Society. He saw in the United Nations, for example, with all its problems, a struggle toward this ideal.

But he also saw the extreme vulnerability of his Open Society. The continuing existence of "nations" at all was the Closed Society fighting back. (On nationalism and tribalism, see "Nationalism" in my *Conjectures and Confrontations*.) Angst, alienation, and *anomie* dog our civilized footsteps. If I had known then what I learned later, I would have put it to him that human beings were in essence Closed in mentality. They were in that essence no different from the cave-painters of Lascaux. Their brains, forged in the Paleolithic, had not changed. They were evolved to be "by nature" tribal people, although these very brains were capable of so much more. They therefore preferred to live in relatively Closed societies with perhaps experimental Open elements. That is why constitutional monarchies work so well and some of the most Open societies prefer them (Norway, Sweden, Denmark, Holland, Belgium, United Kingdom, and latterly Spain).

It is also part of the secret of the "ancient" universities that they manage a nice balance between Closed elements of tradition and Open elements of scientific and scholarly inquiry. American universities especially have traditionally combined high academic openness with unabashed tribalism in sports, especially football. It is one of the things that make them attractive places to belong to: they allow overly rational individualistic academics to indulge in harmless collective tribal enthusiasm. But this is perhaps a personal prejudice.

Popper probably would not have disagreed (I did discuss this with him later) but he was nostalgic for Socrates and democratic Athens. The Athenians had given us a choice, and we still had to choose between them and Sparta. The whole history of the West was the history of this struggle, to him. And it was now our task to give this choice to the world, even if the world was at heart Spartan not Athenian. The least the intellectuals could do was to remind us of the choice: to advocate Pericles over Plato, Cicero over Caesar, and Mill over Marx; to support the individual over culture, citizenship over ethnicity, and the content of character over the color of skin.

It does not look good for the Open Society right now, but for me at least there is always the memory of Mrs. Popper's Tea Shop and the bright spirit that presided over the scones and strawberry jam, and all the elevated and brilliant talk. That was high culture; Arnold would have approved. He knew that in the same way that civilization requires civility, culture requires cultivation, not just consumption. It requires a cultivated elite, not necessarily an elite of blood, but an elite of intellect—Toynbee's "creative minority"—to nurture and develop the best that has been thought and said and written, and we might add, discovered. This, in a democracy, should come from the universities, which produce for us a democratic elite of merit. But currently the orthodox opinion in the groves of academe denies and degrades that function, and sees diversity as more important than distinction. Civilizations that fail, most often fail from within.

CHAPTER THIRTEEN

The Old Adam and the Last Man

Taming the Savage Mind

F RIEDRICH NIETZSCHE described the Last Man in *Thus Spake Zarathustra* as a creature of "desire and reason" as opposed to the First Man, who was bestial and consumed by the desire for recognition alone. The Last Man *(der letzte Mensch),* the man of modern liberal democratic society, was a "victorious slave" enacting the secular version of the Christian Kingdom of God on Earth. This was a society that put self-preservation first and cultivated physical security and material plenty. Nietzsche's Superman *(Übermensch)* would rise above this and would shed the shackles of conventional morality. But in the meantime we had a society where the weak could control the strong, but one that could become jaded by the experience of history; it could become bored with its own success.

Historia Termina

Francis Fukuyama shares this conclusion in the last section of his *The End of History and the Last Man,* a book firmly in the great tradition of the philosophy of history. He describes the weakness of modern society: "It is the danger that we will be happy on one level, but still *dis*-satisfied on another, and hence ready to drag the world back into history with all its wars, injustices and revolution." But this assumes, as he does, that we left history in the first place. And the history he refers to is of course the blip at the end of human time that passes in an eyeblink of our hourlong film of the human story.

Fukuyama joins the long list of thinkers who, since progressive time was discovered, have sought to predict its end. History may end eventually in the universality of capitalist liberal democracy in this view, but as we see, it will be a bumpy ride. In our terms what he is saying is that the Old Adam—the tribal imagination, or "human nature"—rebels against the egalitarian security of the Last Man, the epitome of civilization. So it does. The weakness of the liberal democratic society according to Fukuyama lies in the universal human need, recognized by Plato, for *thymos*— recognition.

We can from the perspective of this book see it as a profoundly tribal need: however egalitarian the tribe, the need of the warrior or the hunter to receive recognition for his effort in the praise of his fellows is certainly deep. Christopher Boehm has shown how egalitarianism is not the natural state of society but that egalitarian societies are engaged in a constant struggle to stay egalitarian. Boasting was a universal art in the tribal society. I grew up in one where competition was encouraged but overt boasting was in fact discouraged (it was called "putting on side"). However, the art of modest understatement was cultivated to perform the same function: "It was nothing!" (Remember Walter Mitty's Englishman?)

Fukuyama contrasts *megalothymia*, the overwhelming desire for personal recognition ("legacy," as ex-presidents phrase it) with *isothymia*: the passionate desire for absolute equality in recognition (as in the "self-esteem" movement). The success of liberal democracy for him lies in its ability to maximize the latter. Nevertheless, he says, *isothymia* "will quickly run into limits imposed by nature itself." There will always be "thymotic individuals" who will have the urge to excel and the passionate desire to be recognized as superior.

The liberal democratic society of the Last Man is bound together largely by self-interest, but this too runs up against "nature." "In contrast to liberal societies, communities sharing 'languages of good and evil' are more likely to be bound together by a stronger glue than those based merely on self interest." Fukuyama sounds here like Tönnies or Durkheim: he is describing *Gemeinschaft*, the world of mechanical solidarity, of status, of militarism, of the *gens*, of the collectivism of the Closed Society. He is describing the basis of nationalism, of patriotism and at its extreme the jingoism of the nation-tribe and its totems.

The boredom with peace and prosperity, he says, at the beginning of World War I gave rise to enormous upsurges of popular enthusiasm for the war throughout Europe. "Many European publics simply wanted war because they were fed-up with the dullness and lack of community in civilian life." They took to the streets in their millions and rushed to enlist in the national armies. "The exuberance of these crowds reflected the feeling that war meant national unity and citizenship at long last, and an overcoming of the divisions between capitalist and proletariat, Protestant and Catholic, farmer and worker, that characterized civil society." It was, in his words—so reminiscent of Popper's—"a rebellion against middle-class civilization." It was the Drumbeats sounding against the Miracle.

This is a gloomy if honest picture of the children of the Miracle constantly facing the fearsome power of those atavistic tribal motives that their society is supposed to have overcome and rendered obsolete. But it is also a partial picture because the tribal imagination is, as we have been constantly reminded, still with us and still important, however much we might change our institutions in the direction of rational liberalism. And as we have hinted, without the powerful motivations that the tribal mentality provides, we may not have the energy to sustain our novel creations, just as the neocortex cannot function without the urgent emotions of the limbic system and the stereotyped impulses of the brain stem.

Structure and Communitas

Victor Turner, who has perhaps done more than anyone to enhance our understanding of ritual, put this very well when criticizing Morgan's idea that we were, in social evolution, moving to a "higher plane" of brotherhood, equality, democracy, and universal education. Turner says: "It is here that Morgan seemingly succumbs to the error made by such thinkers as Rousseau and Marx: the confusion between *communitas*, which is a dimension of all societies, past and present, and archaic primitive society." We can leave primitive society behind, but *communitas* remains with us (Turner, *The Ritual Process*).

What is Turner's communitas? (He doesn't italicize so henceforth neither shall I.) It is a little like pornography: hard to define but easy to recognize. It is of course "community" but not in the sense of an ongoing social unit. He contrasts it with "structure" in the sense used by the sociologists in "social structure," which is a system of statuses, roles, and offices. But communitas is antistructure: it is rather a *state of social existence* that involves "a relationship between concrete, historical, idiosyncratic individuals" who have a "direct, immediate, and total confrontation of human identities," which involves "a model of society as a homogeneous, unstructured communitas, whose boundaries are ideally coterminous with those of the human species."

It is those spontaneous or liminal states of society where people meet as equal individuals, where the usual structural boundaries are ignored, where there is a sense of transcendence and immersion in humanity. In primitive societies it occurs in certain ritual settings like initiations or communal, often orgiastic, increase ceremonies. In more complex societies it is there in formative religious movements, at the inception of revolutions, or in ecstatic movements like the hippies and the beats, for it is often, at least initially, a spontaneous activity of the marginal and dispossessed. You can see it somewhat in action in Sunday-morning services in black churches and among charismatic sects; it was there perhaps at Grateful Dead concerts, and in things like the Million Man March, the crowds on VE and VJ days, and throughout the civil rights movement and the counterculture movement, with its epitome at Woodstock.

I have personally felt totally spontaneous communitas in such things as the last night of the Proms in London, or the flying of U.S. flags in every yard and from every house in my community immediately after 9/11. I felt it in the crowds of quiet weeping people who left their houses and went out into the London streets, on hearing of the death of President Kennedy, just to be with each other. I felt it in the ecstatic crowd of 40,000 students, faculty, staff, players, townspeople, politicians, boxholders, cheerleaders, and visitors who rushed and filled the football field after Rutgers' seemingly impossible comeback victory over Louisville in 2006, to keep their unbeaten record alive. In these things we were all equals: individuals melding in a joyful or heartbroken mass that knew no boundaries or statuses, no structure. These were spontaneous attempts at absolute *isothymia,* in Fukuyama's terms, often breaking out from the commercial or structured framework that was their setting.

But time, that old and cruel father, is relentless. This "spontaneous communitas" cannot last. It is one of those attempts to get out of time; time is one of the structures that must dissolve and disappear in the eternal present where we prefer to be but cannot stay. We want to prolong the beauty of the communing moment. But the ecstatic condition cannot last, and so if it is to exist in time it must be *routinized*—as Weber said of charisma, which can partake of the same emotions. This is the inherent contradiction of communitas: it is antistructure, but for this pleasurable state to persist, it must develop a structure to which it is in fact antithetical. We see the results in all utopian experiments, including the hippies (who became yuppies) and in the fate of charismatic religions, which become routinized as communes, sects, denominations, and churches.

Turner chooses as an example the order of Franciscans in Europe, which could never resolve the problem of carrying on the communitas message of St. Francis—which was to abandon property and status and embrace egalitarian poverty, while having an organization within the Church that needed both. You cannot exist in a state of "permanent liminality." Similarly in India with the Sahajiya movement of Bengal, there was an attempt to bypass the structure of marriage in a devotion to Shiva and his ecstatic but adulterous relationship with the Gopis. But you cannot have an ongoing society without property and marriage and rights in both, and so "ideological communitas" and its attempt to live outside of time is bound to fail, as the hippies discovered.

It is, however, a "dimension of all societies." It is there in tribal societies but it is not coterminous with them; it is a state of social being not a stage of social evolution. But Turner does not ask why this should be. It may be that the burden of structure is too great—like the strain of civilization—and that we periodically try to escape it; but why the escape to communitas as such? In a little-recognized article "Body, Brain and Culture" written some fourteen years later, just before his death, Turner challenged the anthropological belief in the autonomy of culture and proposed that "our species has distinctive features, genetically inherited, which interact with social conditioning, and set up certain resistances to behavioral modification from without." These features are located in the brain, whose triune structure we have canvassed in Chapter 9 and which is invoked by Turner, along with the specialization of the hemispheres, to explain certain consistent features of trance and ritual.

In this he follows Laughlin and D'Aquili, the originators of "biogenetic structuralism." Trance states, and meditative and mystical experiences, are induced when there is "spillover" between the two hemispheres resulting from the hyperstimulation of one of them. The left is related to "ergotropic" or energy-generating systems, and the right with "trophotropic" or energy-maintaining systems. Trance practitioners, using techniques to stimulate the right-hemisphere/trophotropic system (sonic, rhythmic, visual, photic) reduce the body to an almost baseline homeostasis, which results in the spillover to the left-hemisphere/ergotrophic system and hence trance states. In these the sense of boundaries dissolves and the "trancer" feels a sense of wholeness with all being. It is described by those who experience it as like a prolonged orgasm, and involves the hormone oxytocin, which we saw was involved in sex, suckling, and bonding. Meditation techniques achieve the same result in a quieter form, and drugs can be used to simulate the same effect by a shortcut to ecstasy.

The processes that underlie trance states seem very similar to those encountered in the extremes of communitas, particularly the sense of timelessness and wholeness: the resolution of opposites and paradoxes. Lévi-Strauss taught us that myth and ritual serve to resolve "contradictions"—those between self and other, one and many, life and death, male and female, old and young. The primary feeling involved in both trance and communitas, and in the ritual of both, seems to be the dissolution of the boundaries and the contradictions: the embrace of opposites and impossibilities, as described by d'Aquili and his co-authors in *The Spectrum of Ritual*. The excitation of the hemispheres and the spillover between them, which causes them to fire together rather than alternately, produces "gestalt, timeless, non-verbal experiences," and this is perhaps its secret. It is the escape from language and the categories of language and particularly the categories of time, where we must exist but where we do not want to be. It is to live in the elusive eternal present, forever lost once consciousness and language planted us firmly in the grasp and tyranny of time and the foreknowledge of death: Swinburne's complaint against God.

Turner did not make the connection I have made. Time caught up with him and he died before he could do that. But I discussed this with him briefly and he agreed that the neural processes underlying trance and ritual were there in spontaneous communitas, and that societal stress could stimulate the need for such an escape and so stimulate the same or similar processes in the brains of participants. It is "a dimension of all societies" because all society (or culture) is, as Freud and Popper saw, inherently stressful, *Unbehagen*, and because the response to it is a dimension of the neural system of all humans. It is one place we can go when we need to escape from structure, and we do.

After Turner died, I had to take his place at a conference (on science and religion) where I presented what I summarized in Chapter 9 on brain, memory, and evolution (see *The Search for Society*). But I have had to wait until now to make this point, and to make it inadequately. Turner has much more on ritual, symbolism, play, and archetypes, where he accepts Jung's contention that for man: "The form of the world into which he is born is already inborn in him as a virtual image." So be it. The torch gets passed. It is one way we beat time.

So communitas and structure are dimensions of all societies, not stages in societal development. Turner sees it as a dialectical process in which communitas opposes structure and the outcome is *societas*: "society" as part of a process of continual change. In the boring, micromanaging future *societas* that Fukuyama envisions for us, they will both be there, and we shall need them both. There is a flash of communitas in those huge crowds demanding war and feeling a sense of transcendence in national unity that makes them part of a vital organic whole. But there it is absorbed by nationalistic tribalism, which declares a separation from, and superiority to, humanity as a whole. But the link is there; it was there at Obama's victory speech and the inauguration. It is something that is always with us. It need not be so; we could have evolved differently; the brain could be other than it is. But this is the way it is because this is the way it evolved, and we are stuck with it. The tribal imagination and the civilized imagination are both lodged in the same brain and tap the same resources. We do not leave one behind as we develop.

Styles and Stages

Mary Douglas, another great teacher about ritual thinking, in her *Leviticus as Literature* makes a similar point. She compares the two books of law in the Torah, Leviticus and Deuteronomy. The former is written in a mythopoetic style and is based on analogies; the latter is written in a rational, logical style and depends on deduction and argument. (These correspond, of course, to the distinct functions of the right and left hemispheres of the brain.) The rules of sacrifice in Leviticus are not presented as utilitarian or logical commands, but rather as metaphors and analogies linking, for example, the body, the mountain (Sinai), and the tabernacle. The laws of Deuteronomy, like the moralistic Ten Commandments we saw in Chapter 5, are argued and rationalized. You shall honor your father and your mother *in order to* live a longer life, and so on. The injunctions in the ritualistic ten (from the Book of the Covenant) seem more like Leviticus. You are not told why you should not seethe a kid in its mother's milk. It is simply inappropriate or incongruous; it contradicts the pattern. These are my examples, not hers, but they make a point the reader will recognize.

Most commentators (her main example is Ernst Cassirer) have seen this as evidence of a difference in time between the two, with Leviticus obviously being earlier because of its more "primitive" style. But, she says, there is no evidence of this. What is represented here is a difference in *styles of thinking*, not in *stages of thought*. "Neither mode is more primitive or more evolved than the other, each serves different purposes, the former [Deuteronomy] isolates elements it deconstructs, while the latter [Leviticus] projects whole patterns." She compares this to Suzanne Langer's distinction between "discursive" and "presentational" ways of thinking. Any society is capable of both, but as civilization advances, the rational and deductive mode comes more into play.

There might seem to be a difference between us here in that I argued that the injunctions of the Book of the Covenant were indeed older than their Deuteronomic counterparts, originating in tribal taboos. But she would not disagree. It is just that the writer of Leviticus, using very often the older material, was contemporary with the writer of Deuteronomy, and was not simply archaic but was continuing to use the alternative mode of thinking and writing that remains valid in its sphere. The discursive writer of Deuteronomy would feel it necessary to make some kind of argument about the fate of the unfortunate kid and would rationalize the need to keep it from the maternal milk. Something like, "For the Lord did not create the sustenance of life that it might consume the fruit of its own womb." Clumsy, but you know what I mean. The presentational author of Leviticus would see no such need; he would rather add an analogy: "Neither should the seeds of a plant be roasted in its leaves" or something such. The injunction is not for him part of a logical argument, but part of an aesthetic design.

Douglas quotes Marcel Detienne *(Masters of Truth in Archaic Greece),* who tried to understand why the Greeks became the first to develop "secular, open, enquiring, temporal" thought on any large scale. He calls it "dialogical" thinking as opposed to "analogical." He put it down to the development of a warrior class in Greece that was free from kin ties and forced to be rational and democratic in its conduct of war and military affairs. This is an intriguing idea, but as Douglas points out, it was not that the mythopoetic form was abandoned, far from it. Both forms of dealing with reality are firmly there in our mentalities and will both manifest themselves in, for example the different approaches of art and science, even to our own day (as in the "Two Cultures" of Charles Snow). It is the balance that makes the difference, and that balance, tipped initially by the Greeks, was to be shifted decidedly in Europe.

The Fate of the Turkey

The same distinction is there in Lévi-Strauss's contrast between "concrete science" and "abstract science" that occupied us in Chapter 1. Mankind did not shed the first as it developed the second. They both remain in play and Bacon used the one to lead into the other. The point crops up in unusual places. Nassim Nicholas Taleb (another remarkable son of Lebanon) in *The Black Swan* contrasts two other thought worlds, "Mediocristan" and "Extremistan." He illustrates the first by the parable of the turkey. The turkey is well cared for, fed and nourished for three years, day after day with no variation. The turkey has no reason to think it will ever be otherwise, and if asked, would no doubt predict an indefinite continuance of this blissful state. Then on Thanksgiving Day it is killed; so much for extrapolating from trends. One of my first seminars with Popper (I was there unofficially but he didn't mind) was about social trends and extrapolation. You cannot simply extrapolate, he said, you must know *why* the trend is going the way it is. If we know the turkey is being kept as a pet, then we can perhaps predict its kind treatment will continue. If we know about Thanksgiving Day, our prediction will be very different.

For Taleb, human thinking is dominated by the logic of extrapolation and the normal curve: the world of Mediocristan. This is how we like to think the world works. We expect the world to be tomorrow like it is today, and for things to even out and converge toward the mean, and for large numbers to make things predictable because they will fall along a normal curve. This is true for a large part of nature, but it ignores the probability of the highly improbable. The supreme law of Mediocristan is "When your sample is large, no single instance will significantly change the aggregate or total." The supreme law of Extremistan is "Inequalities are such that one single observation can disproportionately impact the aggregate or the total." As examples: the average height of a thousand humans gathered at random cannot be affected by any one individual, however huge; but if you take the average income of the same thousand, and one of them is Bill Gates, his income would account for 99.9 percent of the total and completely distort the average.

But Taleb suggests we are not mentally equipped to deal with conditions in Extremistan, even though they dominate our lives in the modern world, because *we evolved in Mediocristan*. What is more, conditions there were "as close to utopian equality as reality can spontaneously deliver," while those of Extremistan are "dominated by extreme winner-take-all inequality." We have created the Miracle of the social world of the highly improbable and the inequalities and stresses that characterize it, but we delude ourselves constantly that we are still living in the utopian egalitarian world of the literal mediocre in which we evolved, where nothing any one of us did could much affect the outcome for us all.

Taleb gives us the systems of delusion by which we try to stay mediocre (in the strict sense): we commit the "error of confirmation," as Popper saw, in seeking always to confirm what we know rather than seeking where we might be wrong; we commit "the narrative fallacy" in which we fool ourselves with stories and anecdotes; and the error of "silent history" that Bacon first identified in the *Novum Organum* (chapter 1). The fact that someone prayed and survived is taken as evidence of the power of prayer, ignoring the many who prayed and were not saved. We hear it after every hurricane. The survivor proves nothing except what Goethe recognized as the power of wrong ideas.

Again, we do not shed the one mode of thought as we progress; we rather strive to maintain it and judge and govern the world by it, however inappropriate it might be to our post-Miracle circumstances. Mediocristan reduces our sense of time and the urgent passage of time and the unreliability of the future. It is our natural world, our tribal default system, where we want to be, and we rationalize constantly to keep ourselves there in spirit. We want it both ways: the benefits of the Miracle and Extremistan, and the safety of evolutionary mediocrity. We cannot resist the Drumbeat sounding from Mediocristan, and in social processes like communitas we seek to regain that lost world of utopian egalitarianism, and a sense of the oneness of mankind rather than the drastic division of it into extremes of status or wealth or power.

But as Taleb shows, we seek the same safety at the highest levels of intellectual, political, and economic thinking. The free-market liberal democracies of the Last Man do not keep us safe in Mediocristan. Rather they thrust us further into the world of large improbabilities and lopsided differences: look only at the growing inequality of wealth, at the maldistribution of recognition *(thymia)* despite liberal democracy, at the booms and busts of the market. And we cannot predict the future. That, if nothing else, we should take from Popper, and Taleb does take it.

He puts it this way: "To understand the future to the point of being able to predict it, you need to incorporate elements from this future itself." He gives the example of the Stone Age predictor of the future who would have to have known about the wheel. But if he knew about the wheel, it was not part of the future, it was already present. We are not easily able to conceive of future inventions; if we were, they would already have been invented. We cannot predict the future, says Popper, because we cannot predict technological innovations: we cannot predict change in the conditions of change. Think of predictions of the future by people who did not anticipate the computer.

Rules of Order

So communitas lives with structure, Leviticus with Deuteronomy, presentational thinking with discursive thinking, analogical thought with dialogical thought, concrete science with abstract science, Mediocristan with Extremistan. These are not stages of thought (the "prelogical" to "logical" of Lévy-Bruhl) but modes of thought, the second mode coming to dominate the first over time, but not erasing it. And if they are constant aspects of all societies, it is because they are constant aspects of all human brains. We cannot operate without involving both.

The contrast is there to some extent in the sacred-versus-profane distinction as seen in Durkheim, Mircea Eliade, and Joseph Campbell. If we take Durkheim's definition that the sacred is "things set apart and forbidden," then it works. These things can be infused with the supernatural but they don't need it; they have their own life. The Stars and Stripes is reverenced with or without religious support. Sacred things are "forbidden" in the sense that they cannot be treated casually in a utilitarian or secular fashion; they are "set apart" and they must be reverenced. Nothing that happened to the dead soldier who is the silent hero of the unusual film with Kevin Bacon, *Taking Chance,* was religious. Yet his journey across America to his burial in Montana was a profoundly sacred experience. I have just watched the careful and moving ceremonies in Normandy commemorating the sixty-fifth anniversary of D-Day. (I remember the original well: my father was there on D-2.) Apart from a brief invocation by an army chaplain in military uniform there was no religion, and yet the whole event was soaked in sacredness. These two are "aspects of all societies" and the profane is cradled in the sacred, even in those societies that claim to be the most secular.

The binary contrast keeps cropping up. The poles suggested are not totally isomorphic by any means, but the idea of a polar contrast is persistent. Historically it was there in Nietzsche's contrast of Dionysian and Apollonian (in *The Birth of Tragedy*) that so influenced Ruth Benedict. More recently the medieval historian Daniel Smail, in *On Deep History and the Brain,* introduces us to two different "psychotropic mechanisms"— basically mechanisms that stimulate the production of those mammalian brain chemicals that make us feel good. He calls them *teletropic* and *autotropic* (compare Turner's ergotropic and trophotropic). The first involves altering the moods of others, the second altering one's own moods. The first characterized traditional society with its ranks and hierarchies where ruling elites manipulated moods and the very order of society had a soothing effect on the brain. This shifted in the "long eighteenth century" (1660–1820) with the rapid growth of individualism, to the second or autotropic system in which there was a massive effort by people to alter their own moods by substances obtainable on an increasingly unregulated market. Tobacco, chocolate, coffee, and gin were the original popular forms of autotropic satisfaction. Both mechanisms are there and available, but changing social conditions tip the balance. It is a familiar story. Smail, as we saw in Chapter 1, thinks that in order to understand this shift we should consider "deep history": a history that would include the whole of prehistory and beyond into the history of the hominids and primates, and the formation of the brain.

He could not be more right. We never lose anything in evolution; we constantly reproduce that which produced us. The savage mind lives with the civilized, the Old Adam with the Last Man. The Open Society needs its Closed elements; the autotropic tends to run wild unless constrained by the security of the teletropic. The profane is nurtured by the sacred. Ted Hughes has the two poles of the "mythic" and the "realistic"—two modes that evolve at different rates but can find their unity in ritual drama as in fifth-century BC Athens and Elizabethan/Jacobean England "where the mythic plane itself tilts and pours down the historical cataract." We may be due for another such period, which could help explain the persistence and expansion of ecstatic religion. These opposites then complement each other and they should respect each other, for if they do indeed face the End of History then they will have to fall back on each other to tackle the unpredictable consequences. In the end they are all each other has got.

Francis Fukuyama, with the absolute honesty that is characteristic of his thinking, has come to understand this fully. In *The Great Disruption* he challenges his own conclusions on the End of History, and gives us some slender room for hope. His subtitle tells the story: *Human Nature and the Reconstitution of Social Order.* Though he had seen, in his first book, the Old Adam rebelling against the society of the Last Man, here he sees the disruptions in the inevitable liberal-capitalist-democratic society being repairable and redeemed only by the virtues of the Old Adam. The Miracle succeeded, but at a cost. The cost was, as the early sociologists taught us, the dissolution of social bonds with the growth of individualism and the isolation of the individual. Even so, for Fukuyama's end-of-history thesis, these societies meet Hegel's criteria for the universal extension of *thymia,* recognition, and so there is, at least in the world of ideas, nowhere else to go. But what about the costs?

I was moved when initially thinking about Fukuyama's thesis to ask: Even though the liberal-democratic-capitalist societies may meet Hegel's idealistic criteria, could it be that they have simply become too complex and too expensive to sustain, despite this virtue? Could it be that the authoritarian capitalism of Singapore and China, and the traditionalist and familial capitalism of Japan, offer more viable alternatives? They simplify life at all levels and restrict freedoms we Americans cherish; but they also seem to reduce some of the chaos and hence the costs that inevitably go with such freedoms. There is nothing in Islam that is inherently incompatible with capitalism as such, and it could be that some form of theocratic capitalism might emerge in the Muslim societies. Capitalism emerged from a puritan ethic in the first place; it could happen again. This is a cost–benefit situation, and the costs of unrestricted capitalism could be too great, as we are finding in the latest financial meltdown. If

communism and fascism were not the right answers, and if welfare socialism as in Europe (the "Third Way") staggers and falters under its mountain
of expense, history may look elsewhere before it decides to rest on its thymotic laurels.

Fukuyama understands the problem. He notes that we in the capitalist
West originally expanded individual choice at the expense of social bonds.
The Industrial Revolution forced this development further, and the tight
moralism of the Victorians, under the last gasp of which I was raised, was
the response of society to that challenge. But we have, he argues, recently
gone through an even greater disruption: the displacement of the industrial society by the information society (Daniel Bell's "postindustrial" society). The result is evident in the rise in crime, decline in fertility, collapse
of the family through easy divorce, illegitimacy and cohabitation, and the
general precipitous decline of trust in government and social institutions
generally.

The catalogue is familiar and the causes much debated; he deals with
all this very thoroughly. But what is interesting is Fukuyama's assertion
that there is a reservoir of human action that is not the product of legislation or rational choice or culture or anything but the evolved need of
human organisms to be social: to live in groups according to rules, just as
they speak languages according to rules, both of these tendencies rising
spontaneously. This does not mean we are spontaneously angelic and cooperative, any more than we are cunning and competitive. It does mean
that like our primate ancestors, and those tribal ancestors of the Stone
Age, we are intensely social animals and we need society and we create it
and re-create it to meet our needs.

As Thomas Jefferson and the moral sense school maintained, and as
Darwin himself argued and Henri Bergson repeated, and as James Q. Wilson has recently reaffirmed in *The Moral Sense*, we are social creatures
imbued with a need for morality: not goodness necessarily, but some kind
of normative order in which to exist. Consciousness demands no less, for
without rules we cannot predict each other and we cannot order our lives.
Thus no matter how great the disruptions, we will draw on this reservoir to
repair our societies and produce some kind of rule-driven behavior to govern ourselves, whether in poetry or in society. This is human nature; it is the
way we are.

This is what some of us have been saying for years, in the teeth of
moral relativism (and, for that matter, what Aristotle said 2,500 years
ago). Fukuyama handsomely acknowledges all that, and summarizes the
findings of evolutionary biology in a masterful way. To translate him into
the language of this book, we might say that the Great Disruptions are

the blips at the end of the blip that is history as we conceive it through our chronomyopic lens. They are the results of the convulsions caused by the huge increase in population and rapid technological development in the brief interglacial period in which we are living. Our default system of social behavior has not changed from that of the Upper Paleolithic savage. We are that savage, with all his tribal strengths and weaknesses.

The history that may be going to end is an extension of the millions of years of time in which we evolved. Evolution is history with time for genetic changes to take place. That history will not end and cannot end, unless we are wiped out or wipe ourselves out. Civilization can disrupt itself in many ways and in doing so move our behavior further and further from the Paleolithic baseline (see chapter 10 in *The Search for Society*). But in the end what is there is the savage mind, and in the end that is us, and is both our limit and our hope. We shall never be freed from the tribal imagination as we might be freed from a particular form of economic or political experiment. The result of these experiments in civilization that we call history is still in doubt, and the experiments may well come to an end, but the savage mind is with us forever. The Old Adam will have the Last Word.

The Religion of Humanity

The founder of sociology—the inventor of the Latin-Greek hybrid word itself *(socius-logos)*—was Auguste Comte (1798–1857), and he understood this in a very profound way. Thought for Comte evolved in three stages, from the theological (magical-religious) through the metaphysical to the positive. This last stage of positivism was thinking and action based on hard science, and Comte's vision of the future was that of a social utopia based on humanism and science: the heir to the Elizabethans and the Enlightenment. But he knew not to trust science or humanism *as such* with the handling of a future society. He invented a "Religion of Humanity" complete with its own secular saints (Caesar, Dante, Shakespeare) and its secular calendars and rituals, to handle social order and social cohesion.

In the London of the 1950s that I knew, there was still an active Positivist Church. Harriet Martineau had expanded Comte's influence with her famous rendering of his *Cours de philosophie positive*. A national Positivist Church still exists in Brazil, where Comte's ideas fueled the developing universities and where Lévi-Strauss cut his ethnographic teeth. (The Brazilian flag carries a Portuguese derivation of Comte's posi-

tivist motto: *Ordem e Progresso*—"Order and Progress.") Comte understood, as did Weber and Durkheim, that a purely rational society would
not work. There had to be some framework of belief and ritual that was
unchallengeable and that inspired a reverence for common goals, in order to motivate a collectivity of strangers to behave as if they were close
kin: to hold them together, to produce that *socius,* that bonding which is
the essence of association, of society. The rational *logos* alone would not
do it.

This is what Edmund Burke so intensely understood, and strangely he
shared this conservative understanding with his nemesis Rousseau, who
invented the term "civil religion." Both of them saw this as a necessity of
human nature, although they did not have the time perspective to see
the actual and deep historical context in which that nature was developed. But Rousseau would have been pleased with our conclusion that it
is ultimately the wisdom of the savage mind (noble or ignoble) that we
must trust, if not in the rather quaint form that Comte modeled it, to
give us an anchor in the sea of rational possibilities where we seem to be
floundering.

The trick lies in getting the balance right—as between rational and sectarian activity in science, for example, the sectarian pushing along the rational without overwhelming it. It is there in the balance between the free
rein for the accumulation of wealth in a free-market system, and the redis-
tributive impulse of the tribe, where, to quote the Bantu, "The chief's granary is the granary of the people." Progressive taxation and public welfare
show an understanding of this, as do the Guggenheims, Carnegies, Fords,
and Rockefellers. Perhaps the best example we have unearthed, although
not the only one, is the role of constitutional monarchy in the evolution
and preservation of democracy, especially in ensuring the legitimacy and
continuity of government and the peaceful transfer of power after elections. The monarch provides the fixed center of legitimate authority that is
unchallengeable, and thus leaves the politicians free to be politicians and
vulnerable to challenge.

We saw in Chapter 3 how the American elective monarchy does not
work very well in this respect. The president has to become an unholy
trinity of man, politician, and office. We can despise the man and hate the
politician, but we must revere the office. This can become an impossible
balancing act. For example, if the president fails morally, he can fail politically. Constitutional monarchs (kings and queens with only symbolic
powers), on the other hand, are pretty well immune from this fate. "The
Queen reigns but does not rule." We do not feel responsible for monarchs
because we did not elect them. What is more, because they partake of the

divine ("The king is dead, long live the king") they can behave as badly as the gods have always behaved and still be worshipped.

The old gods (think of Zeus, Aphrodite, Wotan, Krishna, Trickster) were amoral, selfish, scandalous, violent, and adulterous, and their worshippers loved them, just as democratic and republican people love the royal families today. The funeral crowds for Princess Diana (appropriate name) in the London streets, with their massive display of genuine grief and the invented ritual of flower throwing in the path of the hearse, were pure communitas. Puritans and rationalists have never understood this unreasonable, and for our argument tribal, appeal of royalty. Douglas MacArthur understood the appeal of the tribal imagination when he insisted that the Japanese, after their devastating defeat in World War II, be allowed to keep their emperor, who was then incorporated into a constitutional monarchical system that has been an obvious success. The Spanish understood it equally well when, to heal the wounds of their caustic civil war, they restored the monarchy on the death of the dictator Franco. Freely elected socialist governments in Europe live perfectly happily with their hereditary monarchs.

The American substitute perhaps lies in the intensity of civil religion in the United States as a platform for the democratic ideal, as Robert Bellah reminded us. Walk down the Mall in Washington, D.C., and look at the larger-than-life monuments to the Founders and the reverence of the crowds filing by; listen to schoolchildren reciting the pledge of allegiance and retelling the myths of national origin; see the totemic reverence for the remaining copies of the Constitution and the Declaration, and the original Stars and Stripes; watch the crowd at a sports event singing the national anthem and saluting, with solemnity and genuine feeling, that totemic flag; take part in the national rituals of Thanksgiving and of Super Bowl Sunday (which has replaced Easter Sunday as *the* national festival). Be involved in a presidential inauguration or the ceremonies for the nation's warrior dead on Memorial Day vividly captured in the Durkheimian ethnography of W. Lloyd Warner's *Yankee City* series.

Experience these and the deep emotions they can arouse, and Comte's ideas don't seem so quaint after all. Civil religion is the infrastructure of civil society. Even the most atheistic and ruthlessly secular of regimes realize that they need their rituals and ceremonials, their prophets, saints, and heroes, their sacred books and doctrines, their titles and hierarchies and systems of honorific rewards. The gruesome versions of these regimes can frighten us to the point where we reject the whole package; where we see it as nothing but the Closed Society closing in on us with its uniformed thuggery. But then we see the gentle ceremonies of Inauguration Day or the State Opening of Parliament, or a royal wedding or funeral, and are perhaps reassured that there is a benign form that taps the virtues of the tribal and avoids its brutalities; that is patriotic without being jingoistic; that, as President Obama said, will use the power of its influence, not the influence of its power.

Comte wanted, of course, to have all humanity united in his secular religion, and perhaps the United Nations could take time from its practical activities to develop the international equivalent of a civil religion: to become less of a bureaucracy and more of a priesthood. It would be up against the elemental pull of tribal identification that fuels the national versions, but the tribal imagination can always be trusted to fool itself. It wouldn't be the first time: nations themselves fool us into imagining we are large families; the imaginative Family of Man might not be such an impossible idea.

It would have on its side the indisputable advantage of being true. The work of evolutionary geneticists like Luca Cavalli-Sforza *(Genes, People and Languages)* and Spencer Wells *(The Journey of Man)* on human DNA shows us all to be descended from a small band of people in Africa some 60,000 years ago. Perhaps the flag of the United Nations should be based on Cavalli-Sforza's diagram of world genealogy, as in Chapter 4 (Figure 4.1). The Family of Man is no longer a utopian slogan but a genetic fact. But this profane fact needs to be cradled in a sacred Religion of Humanity, as Comte saw in his touching way, if it is to be effective as a symbol of human unity; if it is to help the floundering Last Man tap the oxygenating energies of the Old Adam; to tame but not extinguish the bright flame of the savage mind.

Goethe Redux

We started with Goethe, let us end with him, and because you have been so patient for so long, I shall give you the English first. In book 5, chapter 7, of *Wilhelm Meister's Apprenticeship*, Goethe says, as a prelude to his famous discussion of the reasons for Hamlet's delay, "In the novel as well as in the drama it is human nature and human action that we see" *("Im Roman wie im Drama sehen wir menschlicke Natur und Handlung")*. We have seen how novel and drama, epic and saga, story and verse all search for and reveal that relationship. That is why the unnatural, even petty distinction between the humanities and the sciences that is currently fashionable does not hold. Science looks for the dynamic between nature and action in humanity as passionately as does the artist or dramatist or poet. We are all on the same quest for the same grail, differing only in our methods, not our goals. This is perhaps the hidden, even the unconscious agenda of this book. It emerges from the very motive that drives the quest: the need to make Goethe's connection between human nature and human action, and to make it urgently. There may not be much time.

Epilogue

The Dream-Man

All were at risk, the ripe ones and the runts,
hunted down by that dark shadow-death,
lurking and lunging in the long black nights
on the misty moorlands; no man knows
the place or purpose of these powers from hell.

Beowulf (159–163)

I was a fish-thing   floating shoal-tide seawards
sometimes stranded   trapped in tepid tide-pools
scraping sharp seashells   moving among mollusks
leaving life learning   fragile future fortune
squirming squirting   groveling in gravel
limp lung-sac swelling   flailing finlike fingers
living longer landward   waiting for weak water
amphibious amorphous   mutant of mixed margins

I was a reptile   resting in cold corners
waking with warming   poised perfect predator
moving machinelike   ferns feather fronded
sharp swiftness striking   vulnerable victim
gulping and gorging   deliberate digestion
paragon of patience   sensing sudden stimulus
weaving and waving   meticulous mute mating
deadliest of dancers   complete cold copulation
efficient effective   mindless minus mercy

I was a frightened   furry furtive tree-thing
creeping in canopy   darting in deep darkness
grasping and grooming   constantly companioned
bursting through branches   brilliant brachiation
chirping and chattering   foremost in forest
nursing and nurturing   deadliest of dreamers

powerful and playful   plentiful of paramours
cunning and curious   perpetually puzzling
teasing and tempting   sight of sparse savannah

I was a man-thing   wobbling and wavering
learning long leg-lope   stilt shanks for stalking
fleeing fond forest   fearing fresh fierce-foes
half hunted half hunter   review rich reversal
seeing scenarios   vague vanity envisioned
dreamwork weaves deed-world   thought thrives as thing-like
forms freely fashioned   sound sanctioned symbols
babble of brotherhood   hand heavy hafted
proud preening predator   laughing loud lunging

I was the dream-man   doubting my dark deeds
pursuing perfection   boundlessly building
reaching with reason   limitless lodestars
I was the dream-man   farewell firm forest
fish-free in future   reject rigid reptile
headpiece hurls headlong   pruning past pressure
I was the dream-man   unlimited license
slate safely scoured   willing words waiting
numberless narratives   ready for writing

I am the dream-man   shivering at shadows
senses of serpent   drive dreary dream-world
fearful forest fur-thing   controls archaic action
prideful pack-thing powering   mutinous motivation
sense enslaving symbol   fixing freedom firmly
I am the dream-man   knowing nothing novel
I am the dream-man   natal nightmare neutered
I am the dream-man   buried beneath birthright
I am the dream-man   Do not disturb me

APPENDIX

NOTES AND REFERENCES

ACKNOWLEDGMENTS

INDEX

Appendix

Transitional Time at the Edge of Chaos

I have saved this comment on Lévi-Strauss, kinship, and time for an appendix, because although I think it makes an important point, it is mildly technical and readers have thought it too distracting to introduce in the chapter.

It will have occurred to you, however, thoughtful reader, that the change from cyclical to linear kinship systems and the associated conceptualization of time would not have been an abrupt transition. There must be intermediary stages or phases that reflect the change from "alternating" to "lineal" in the use of kin terms, for example, and indeed there are. Transitional societies do often seem to hover between the two, as shown in Figure A.1.

Here the females alternate in classic alternating fashion, as "grandmother" and "mother," while the males have been amalgamated in unilineal fashion as "grandfather." Sometimes terms used by males and females differ in the ways they represent this transition, female-usage terms often retaining more of the older system.

Claude Lévi-Strauss, in *Structural Anthropology*, where he tried to link genealogy and time, noticed these features for some of the Pueblo Indian groups of the American Southwest, but he did not interpret them there as evidence of transitional systems (see chapter 4, "Linguistics and Anthropology"). Now that you have passed through the time barrier and can tell a transitional system when you see one, it should be interesting and exciting to spot it in Lévi-Strauss's example. For me it is particularly interesting because I started my anthropological life studying the Pueblo Indians, their ritual and kinship systems. These latter were "matrilineal"—for

GM	GF
M	GF
GM	GF
M	GF
GM	GF
M	GF
GM	GF

Figure A.1   Transitional lineal/alternating terms

most purposes relationship was calculated in the female line, the commonest form of kinship reckoning in native North America.

According to Lévi-Strauss

Lévi-Strauss's representation of the "three-dimensional" time scheme of the Hopi Indians of Arizona is shown in Figure A.2. I have redone it to fit our terminology: FZ = father's sister, ZD = sister's daughter, and so on. The *mother's line for a female speaker* (the vertical line in the diagram), he says, uses a time dimension like our own, "progressive and cumulative"—grandmother, mother, sister, daughter, granddaughter, and so forth. However, the *father's mother's line* (horizontal in the diagram), in which all the women are called "father's sister" (FZ), is for him timeless—a kind of "empty time" with no change. In the *mother's line for a male speaker* (inclined) we see there is a classic alternating pattern of sister and niece (Z and ZD). He does not name this form of time, but insists it is a "third dimension" and later uses the term "circular time."

Then as he moves eastward across the Pueblos to Zuni in New Mexico he says he finds a "much reduced" form of the three dimensions, because the Zuni have "a kind of circular framework" with three terms. To quote him directly: "a term that equally means 'grandmother' and 'granddaughter' and then a term for 'mother' and a term for 'daughter'—a woman would call by the same term her grandmother and her granddaughter." Note and move on.

He moves then to the Keresan-speaking Indians of the Rio Grande (and hence into my own area) and finds another "time dimension" that is curiously "flat." The Keres use "self-reciprocal" terms in which the term you call a person who is related to you through someone else is recipro-

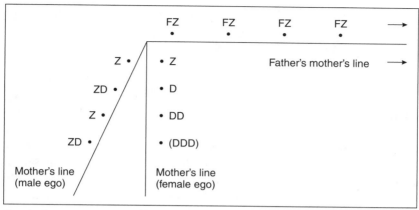

Figure A.2   Hopi time and genealogy (according to Lévi-Strauss)

cated. Thus a man calls his mother's brother *nawa,* and the mother's brother calls his sister's son *nawa* in return (they are related to each other through the mother/sister). There is also a reciprocal term *meme* that we can only translate as "sibling of the opposite sex"—a term lacking in English. As in Zuni the term for "grandparent" is a simple reciprocal: thus I, as a male, call my grandfather *mumu* and he calls me *mumu* back. (My examples, not Lévi-Strauss's; he doesn't give any.) Let us pause on the first two, Hopi and Zuni, and consider what these systems in fact represent.

The reader, now expert in these things, will immediately have seen that what Lévi-Strauss is describing for Zuni is an *alternating generation* series of terms such as we have summarized in Figure 1.1 of Chapter 1. He even calls this a representation of "circular" time. Therefore what he diagrams in the three dimensions of Hopi time is simply a stage in the transformation of an alternating to a lineal system that we have analyzed in Chapter 1.

At least in my analysis, all "Crow-Omaha" systems, like the Hopi, Zuni, and Keres, represent various stages in this transition, and their mix of terminological types clearly shows this. Those Keres "reciprocal terms" that he could only describe as "flat time" are a direct derivative of the older alternating-generation type, surviving into the lineal, as I tried to show in *The Keresan Bridge,* my own contribution to Pueblo studies (and see "The Evolution of Kinship Systems" in *The Challenge of Anthropology*).

Lévi-Strauss, however, does not see this here as a historical problem. He ingeniously tries to show how the ideas of time inherent in the kinship systems are mirrored in the myths of the people—Hopi, Zuni and Keres—and this may be true. But it doesn't get us any further than showing that the ideas, concepts, and categories of a culture have a kind of coherence—or at least that a clever anthropologist can always be trusted to demonstrate such a coherence.

He is absolutely right that the different kinds of terminology reflect different *conceptions of time,* but he does not see this in a developmental context—as systems evolving through time—so he has no logic of change in which to couch these conceptions. He does not see them as reflecting different *stages through time* of changing social structures. In this he mirrors his English counterpart in the study of kinship, A. R. Radcliffe-Brown, who saw these types as simply representing alternative "principles" in the organizing of kinship terms, and roundly denied that they represented evolutionary stages. What then are for Lévi-Strauss and Radcliffe-Brown simply different conceptual schemes, I see as different developmental stages in the transition from cyclical to linear (lineal) systems, with the more recent encapsulating elements of the older.

To be fair to Lévi-Strauss, he had in other places tried magnificently to account in a major way for changes in kinship systems, which he saw as primarily a shift in forms of marital exchange: the exchange of wives between groups (*The Elementary Structures of Kinship,* especially chapter 28). Thus, in what we have called the alternating system, the form of exchange is usually "restricted." This means simply that any two kinship groups (families, lineages, clans, moieties) simply swap spouses directly on the model A $\leftrightarrow$ B (as we shall see in Chapters 3, 6, and 11). This direct exchange system eventually gives way to "generalized" exchange, in which A gives wives to B but has to take wives from a third group, on the model A $\rightarrow$ B $\rightarrow$ C $\rightarrow$ A.

Thus what we have called transitional systems would represent for him compromises between the two forms of marriage. This would happen when increasing population density meant that more and more groups had to be integrated in a way not possible with the simple direct system. In other words, when hunting and gathering societies start to settle, to cultivate and domesticate, and to grow in numbers and complexity, they cannot continue with their simple cyclical pattern. They have to "open up" and accommodate this new complexity, and with it a new complexity in their view of time.

This is important because changed perceptions of time are reflections, as we have seen, of changing social conditions. People are forced to view the world differently as they adapt to these changing conditions, and their view of the nature of the passage of time, and the very nature of time itself, will always reflect these. But the point of Chapter 1 has been to posit the hypothesis that all the recent changes in time perception are involved in a struggle with the basic temporal module fashioned in the environment of evolutionary adaptedness.

Readers familiar with chaos and complexity theory will perhaps see an echo of it in my insistence that the "mixed" systems are "transitional." It might be too much to say that all such "Crow-Omaha" systems exist on "the edge of chaos," as the complexity theorists like to call it. (See the Notes and References for some books that have influenced me on this.) But consider: the cyclical systems lasted in a stable equilibrium for as long as there had been language and the classification of kin. Because this must have been one of the original functions of language, they are as old as speech, which is to say anywhere from a few hundred thousand to over a million years old. One of their main features was that in the exchange of wives that characterized them, the wife had been a specified cousin, as we saw in some cases called "grandmother." (We saw this again in Chapter 11.)

In a very short evolutionary time—the Neolithic—this equilibrium broke down and what we had were the essentially unstable and constantly varying "lineal" systems that we have described. So of Lévi-Strauss's "elementary structures" the lineal one was in evolutionary time relatively brief, unstable, and very recent. As society changed ever more rapidly, it gave way to what he calls, prophetically, "complex systems." These were kinship systems like our own in which the wife is not a prescribed cousin but is theoretically any female available, the actual one being determined by probability (proximity, class, religion, and so on). Thus the sequence:

long phase of stability →
    short chaotic transition phase →
        emergent period of complexity

seems to fit the pattern. It would make the "Crow-Omaha" phase an edge-of-chaos phenomenon: a period when chaos and order come into a state of balance that propels the system into a relatively sudden change, like the origin of life itself. The next great edge-of-chaos period was when the forces of the Reformation, the Renaissance, nationalism, and science propelled us into the age of the Miracle. This may only be an analogy, but we now know (Chapter 13) that analogical thinking is one of the Drumbeats that we do well to heed.

Notes and References

Book references are to the edition actually used. With translations I have tried also to give the original. If I used the original edition in a foreign language, I have also given an English translation.

Prologue

The extracts from the poem by C. Day Lewis, "In Me Two Worlds," are taken from his *Selected Poems* (Harmondsworth: Penguin, 1951). This was one of the original Penguins, number 17 of the "Penguin Poets," and so part of the paperback revolution. My copy is yellow and frail, but in those days, when books were precious things, I bound it carefully in brown paper and so, brittle and faded, it clings to life. Lewis was obviously an upper-class Englishman of the interwar years, since he pronounced "ancestor" to rhyme with "war" in a way that would not happen today in England, but in the United States, where the postvocalic *r* is common, it rhymes quite naturally.

Some readers have been curious about my singling out "digressions." I borrow this, as so much else, from Jonathan Swift, in this case *A Tale of a Tub* (1704), which has my favorite: "A Digression in Praise of Digressions." Swift, ever the anthropologist, refers there to the custom of the Scythians, as described by Herodotus, who "blew up the privvies of their mares that they might yield the more milk." He finds this to be an apt metaphor for the practices of Modern Wits. We shall meet the Scythians again in Chapter 12.

A Digression on Inspiration.   Sources of scientific information are one thing; sources of imaginative inspiration are another. There is a long list of writers whose ideas and stories have stirred up my imagination in this direction from the days when Darwin was only a name to me. It starts with Jonathan Swift, then to Emily

Brontë, Edgar Allen Poe, Thomas Hardy, and Robert Louis Stevenson. H. Rider Haggard and Edgar Rice Burroughs get in there early. It is massively affected by H. G. Wells and William Golding and pushed along by Herman Melville, D. H. Lawrence, T. E. Lawrence, Franz Kafka, Joseph Conrad, Aldous Huxley, George Orwell, Vercors, Anthony Burgess, Walter Miller, John Wyndham, Doris Lessing, Mario Puzo, Frank Herbert, and Kurt Vonnegut Jr.—who was for many years an amusing and sympathetic correspondent (as were Golding and Lessing). Here I must stop the list and let the readers ponder it and add their own examples. I shall only add Rudyard Kipling, who knew that the real war between civilization and the tribes was not fought at Isklandwana or Little Big Horn, but inside our own skulls, in our own imaginations—the most dangerous battlefield on earth.

References
Ardrey, Robert. 1961. *African Genesis*. London: Collins.
Barash, David. 1979. *The Whisperings Within: Evolution and the Origins of Human Nature*. New York: Harper and Row.
———. 1986. *The Hare and the Tortoise: The Conflict between Culture and Biology in Human Affairs*. New York: Viking Press.
Barkow, Jerome H., Leda Cosmides, and John Tooby. 1992. *The Adapted Mind: Evolutionary Psychology and the Generation of Culture*. New York: Oxford University Press.
Bear, Greg. 1997. *Slant*. New York: Tor Books.
Bloom, Howard. 2010. *The Genius of the Beast: A Radical Re-Vision of Capitalism*. New York: Prometheus Books.
Bowlby, John. 1969. *Attachment and Loss,* vol. 1: *Attachment*. London: Hogarth Press and the Institute of Psycho-analysis. (International Psycho-analytical Library, no. 79.)
Carroll, Joseph. 1995. *Evolution and Literary Theory*. Columbia: University of Missouri Press.
Eaton, S. Boyd, Marjorie Shostak, and Melvin Konner. 1988. *The Paleolithic Prescription: A Program of Diet and Exercise and a Design for Living*. New York: Harper and Row.
Fox, Robin. 1959. "Therapeutic Rituals and Social Structure in Cochiti Pueblo." *Human Relations* (Tavistock Institute) 13, no. 4: 291–303. Reprinted as "Witches, Clans and Curing," in Ari Kiev, ed., *Magic, Faith and Healing: Studies in Primitive Psychiatry Today*. Glencoe, IL: Free Press, 1965.
———. 1996. "Sociobiology." In Adam Kuper and Jessica Kuper, eds., *The Social Science Encyclopedia,* 2nd ed. London: Routledge.
Fox, Robin, and Lionel Tiger. 1966. "The Zoological Perspective in Social Science." *Man: The Journal of the Royal Anthropological Institute,* n.s., 1, no. 1: 75–81.
Freud, Sigmund. 1963. *Civilization and Its Discontents*. Trans. J. Strachey. Intro. Louis Menand. New York: W. W. Norton. Originally published as *Unbehagen in der Kultur*. Vienna: Internationaler Psychoanalytischer Verlag, 1930.

Gellner, Ernest. 1988. *Plough, Sword and Book: The Structure of Human History.* Chicago: University of Chicago Press.

Gibbon, Edward. 1909 [1776–1788]. *The History of the Decline and Fall of the Roman Empire.* 7 vols. London: Methuen.

Hamburg, David. 1962. "Relevance of Recent Evolutionary Changes to Human Stress Biology." In Sherwood L. Washburn, ed., *Social Life of Early Man.* London: Methuen.

Horowtiz, David. 2006. *The Professors: The 101 Most Dangerous Professors in America.* Washington, DC: Regnery.

Hughes, Ted. 1992. *Shakespeare and the Goddess of Complete Being.* New York: Farrar, Straus and Giroux.

Huxley, Julian. 1942. *Evolution: The Modern Synthesis.* London: Allen and Unwin.

Jay, Antony. 1971. *Corporation Man: Who He Is, What He Does, Why His Ancient Tribal Impulses Dominate the Life of the Modern Corporation.* New York: Random House.

———. 1990. "Understanding Laughter." *Proceedings of the Royal Institution* 62: 99–113.

———. 2009. *A New Great Reform Act.* London: Center for Policy Studies.

Kahneman, Daniel, Paul Slovic, and Amos Tversky. 1982. *Judgment under Uncertainty.* Cambridge: Cambridge University Press.

Konner, Melvin J. 1982. *The Tangled Wing: Biological Constraints on the Human Spirit.* New York: Holt, Rinehart and Winston.

———. 2010. *The Evolution of Childhood: Relationships, Emotion, Mind.* Cambridge, MA: Belknap Press of Harvard University Press.

Lévi-Strauss, Claude. 1963. *Totemism.* Trans. Rodney Needham. Boston: Beacon Press. Originally published as *Le totémisme aujourd'hui.* Paris: Presses Universitaires de France, 1962.

———. 1966. *The Savage Mind.* Chicago: Chicago University Press. Originally published as *La pensée sauvage.* Paris: Plon, 1962.

McGuire, Michael, and Alfonso Troisi. 1998. *Darwinian Psychiatry.* Oxford: Oxford University Press.

McNeill, William H. 1976. *Plagues and Peoples.* New York: Anchor Books.

Merton, Robert, 1949. *Social Theory and Social Structure.* New York: Free Press.

Mills, C. Wright. 1959. *The Sociological Imagination.* Oxford: Oxford University Press.

Monod, Jacques. 1970. *Chance and Necessity: An Essay on the Natural Philosophy of Modern Biology.* Trans. Austryn Wainhouse. New York: Viking. Originally published as *L'hasard et la necessité.* Paris: Éditions du Seuil, 1970.

Morris, Desmond. 1969. *The Human Zoo.* London: Jonathan Cape.

Russell, Bertrand. 1935. *Sceptical Essays.* London: Allen and Unwin.

Tiger, Lionel. 1969. *Men in Groups.* London: Thomas Nelson.

———. 1979. *Optimism: The Biology of Hope.* New York: Simon and Schuster.

———. 1987. *The Manufacture of Evil: Ethics, Evolution and the Industrial System.* New York: Harper and Row.

———. 1999. *The Decline of Males.* New York: Golden Books.

Tiger, Lionel, and Robin Fox. 1971. *The Imperial Animal.* New York: Holt, Rinehart and Winston.

Toynbee, Arnold J. 1946. *A Study of History.* Abridgement of vols. 1–6 by D. C. Somervell. Oxford: Geoffrey Cumberlege, Oxford University Press (for the Royal Institute of International Affairs).

Trevathan, Wenda R. 2010. *Ancient Bodies, Modern Lives: How Evolution Has Shaped Women's Health.* Oxford: Oxford University Press.

Trevathan, Wenda R., James J. McKenna, and Euclid O. Smith. 1999. *Evolutionary Medicine.* Oxford: Oxford University Press.

Trivers, Robert. 2002. *Natural Selection and Social Theory.* Oxford: Oxford University Press.

Warner, W. Lloyd. 1937. *A Black Civilization: A Social Study of an Australian Tribe.* New York: Harper and Brothers.

Wells, H. G. 1951 [1920]. *The Outline of History: Being a Plain History of Life and Mankind.* Revised by Raymond Postgate. London: Cassell.

Wilson, E. O. 1975. *Sociobiology: The New Synthesis.* Cambridge, MA: Harvard University Press.

Wrangham, Richard. 2009. *Catching Fire: How Cooking Made Us Human.* New York: Basic Books.

Books by the Author Mentioned in the Text

Biosocial Anthropology (contributor and editor). London: Malaby Press, 1975.

The Challenge of Anthropology: Old Encounters and New Excursions. New Brunswick, NJ: Transaction, 1994.

Conjectures and Confrontations: Science, Evolution, Social Concern. New Brunswick, NJ: Transaction, 1997.

Encounter with Anthropology. New York: Harcourt Brace Jovanovich, 1973.

The Imperial Animal (with Lionel Tiger). New York: Holt, Rinehart and Winston, 1971.

The Keresan Bridge: A Problem in Pueblo Ethnology. London: Athlone; New York: Humantities, 1967.

Kinship and Marriage: An Anthropological Perspective. Baltimore: Penguin, 1967. 2nd ed., Cambridge: Cambridge University Press, 1983.

Neonate Cognition (contributor and editor with Jacques Mehler). Hillsdale, NJ: Erlbaum, 1985.

Participant Observer: Memoir of a Transatlantic Life. New Brunswick, NJ: Transaction, 2006.

The Passionate Mind: Sources of Destruction and Creativity. New Brunswick, NJ: Transaction, 2000.

The Red Lamp of Incest: An Enquiry into the Origins of Mind and Society. Notre Dame, IN: University of Notre Dame Press, 1983. Originally published New York: E. P. Dutton, 1980.

Reproduction and Succession: Studies in Anthropology, Law and Society. New Brunswick, NJ: Transaction, 1993.

The Search for Society: Quest for a Biosocial Science and Morality. New Brunswick, NJ: Rutgers University Press, 1989.

The Tory Islanders: A People of the Celtic Fringe. Notre Dame, IN: University of Notre Dame Press, 1983. Originally published New York: Cambridge University Press, 1978.

1. Time out of Mind

This chapter uses some material from my short article that suggested its title: "Time out of Mind: Anthropological Reflections on Temporality," *Kronoscope: Journal for the Study of Time* 1, nos. 1–2 (2001): 129–137. J. T. Fraser, the founder of the International Society for the Study of Time, urged me to write this and helped me formulate the idea.

I also benefited from the graduate seminar I ran for several years with Dieter Steklis at Rutgers titled "The Anthropology of Consciousness" and from conversations in the early 1970s with the late Julian Jaynes at Princeton about the ideas he would publish as *The Origin of Consciousness in the Breakdown of the Bicameral Mind* (Boston: Houghton Mifflin, 1976). Julian did not have a very sympathetic audience among orthodox psychologists, so he used me as a sounding board. Although I often disagreed with him, I received a first-class free education that I draw on to this day. The third party in these talks was the psychologist Stevan Harnad, and I must thank him for introducing me to, among many things, the ongoing debate on categorical thinking.

The best reference for the cyclical and organic theories of history remains Sorokin. For some of the other social theorists, see the volume by Turner, Beeghley, and Powers. William James on time is in *The Principles of Psychology*, vol. 2, chap. 15, "The Perception of Time." A good introduction to chronobiology is Dunlap, Loros, and DeCoursey.

References

Aveni, Anthony F. 2001. "Time, Number, and History in the Maya World." *Kronoscope* 1, nos. 1–2: 29–61.

Campbell, Joseph. 1962. *The Masks of God: Oriental Mythology*. New York: Viking Press.

Douglas, Mary. 2007. *Thinking in Circles: An Essay on Ring Composition*. New Haven: Yale University Press.

Dunlap, Jay C., Jennifer J. Loros, and Patricia J. DeCoursey, eds. 2004. *Chronobiology: Biological Timekeeping*. Sunderland, MA: Sinauer Associates.

Durkheim, Émile, and Marcel Mauss. 1963. *Primitive Classification*. Trans. Rodney Needham. Chicago: University of Chicago Press. Originally published as "De quelques formes primitives de classification: Contributions à l'étude des représentations collectives." *Année Sociologique* (Paris) 6 (1903): 1–72.

Eggan, Fred. 1934. "The Maya Kinship System and Cross-Cousin Marriage." *American Anthropologist* 36: 188–202. Reprinted in *Essays in Social Anthropology and Ethnology*. Chicago: University of Chicago Press, 1975.

Fisher, H. A. L. 1935. *A History of Europe*. London: Eyre and Spottiswoode.

Fowler, Thomas, ed. 1889. *Bacon's Novum Organum*. Oxford: Clarendon Press. (Latin original.)

Fox, Robin. 1967. *The Keresan Bridge: A Problem in Pueblo Ethnology*. London: Malaby Press.

———. 1994. "The Evolution of Kinship Systems and the Crow-Omaha Question." In *The Challenge of Anthropology*. New Brunswick, NJ: Transaction.

Fraser, J. T. 1999. *Time, Conflict and Human Values*. Urbana: University of Illinois Press.

Fukuyama, Francis. 1992. *The End of History and the Last Man*. New York: Free Press.

Gellner, Ernest. 1988. *Plough, Sword and Book: The Structure of Human History*. Chicago: University of Chicago Press.

Hesse, Hermann. 1969 [1943]. *The Glass Bead Game*. Trans. Richard and Clara Winston. New York: Holt, Rinehart and Winston.

Hume, David, 1817 [1739]. *A Treatise of Human Nature*. 2 vols. London: J. M. Dent and Sons.

James, William. 1890. *The Principles of Psychology*. New York: Henry Holt.

Jesperson, Otto. 1924. *The Philosophy of Grammar*. Chicago: University of Chicago Press.

Konner, Melvin, 2010. *The Evolution of Childhood: Relationships, Emotion, Mind*. Cambridge, MA: Belknap Press of Harvard University Press.

Lévi-Strauss, Claude. 1949. *Les structures élémentaires de la parenté*. Paris: Presses Universitaires de France. Published in English as *The Elementary Structures of Kinship,* trans. J. H. Bell, J. R. von Sturmer, and Rodney Needham, ed. Boston: Beacon Press, 1969.

———. 1963. *Totemism*. Trans. Rodney Needham. Boston: Beacon Press. Originally published as *Le totémisme aujourd'hui*. Paris: Presses Universitaires de France, 1962.

———. 1966. *The Savage Mind*. Chicago: Chicago University Press. (Translator not given.) Originally published as *La pensée sauvage*. Paris: Plon, 1962.

———. 1967. *The Scope of Anthropology*. London: Cape Editions.

Lévy-Bruhl, Lucien. 1922. *La mentalité primitive*. Paris: Presses Universitaires de France.

Macey, Samuel L. 1987. *The Patriarchs of Time: Dualism in Saturn-Chronus, Father Time, the Watchmaker God, and Father Christmas*. Athens: University of Georgia Press.

Marshack, Alexander. 1971. *The Roots of Civilization: The Cognitive Beginnings of Man's First Art, Symbol, and Notation*. New York: McGraw-Hill.

Middleton, Christopher, ed. 1994. *Goethe: The Collected Works*, vol. 1: *Selected Poems*. Princeton: Princeton University Press.

Morgan, L. H. 1877. *Ancient Society, or Researches in the Lines of Human Progress from Savagery through Barbarism to Civilization.* New York: Henry Holt.

Radcliffe-Brown, A. R. 1952. *Structure and Function in Primitive Society.* London: Cohen and West.

Russell, Bertrand. 1945. *A History of Western Philosophy.* New York: Simon and Schuster.

Smail, Daniel Lord. 2008. *On Deep History and the Brain.* Berkeley: University of California Press.

Sorokin, Pitirim. 1952. *Social Philosophies of an Age of Crisis.* London: A. and C. Black.

Toynbee, Arnold. 1908 [1884]. *Lectures on the Industrial Revolution of the Eighteenth Century in England.* London: Longmans, Green.

Turner, Jonathan, Leonard Beeghley, and Charles H. Powers. 2006. *The Emergence of Sociological Theory.* 6th ed. Stamford, CT: Cengage Learning.

Tylor, E. B. 1871. *Primitive Culture: Researches into the Development of Mythology, Philosophy, Religion, Language, Art and Custom.* Vol. 2. London: John Murray.

Weber, Max. 1930. *The Protestant Ethic and the Spirit of Capitalism.* Trans. Talcott Parsons. London: Allen and Unwin; New York: Charles Scribner's Sons. Originally published as "Die protestantische Ethik und der Geist des Kapitalismus." *Archiv fur Socialwissenschaft und Socialpolitik* 20–21 (1904–1905).

2. The Human in Human Rights

This chapter is based on the article "Human Nature and Human Rights," *The National Interest* 62 (Winter 2000/2001): 77–86. Owen Harries, who was then editor, asked me to write it and was a great support at that time, as he was over many years. The debate in the pages of *The National Interest* that ensued, with Francis Fukuyama and William F. Schultz (director of Amnesty International), along with commentaries by John Bolton, Owen Harries, Roger Pilon, and Irving Kristol, is collected as part 4 of R. James Woolsey, ed., *The National Interest in International Law and Order* (New Brunswick, NJ: Transaction, 2003). This volume reproduces my article "Human Rights and Foreign Policy," *The National Interest* 68 (Summer 2002): 118–121, which is largely a response to Schultz.

The original article was abbreviated and published in *Harper's*, April 2001, 19–26. Many people responded, and I am grateful for all their comments and suggestions. Also let me thank Frank Fukuyama, for even though we have obviously disagreed on some issues (as in this chapter), he has always been both an inspiration to me and a valued critic and commentator.

References
Still the best general introduction to kin selection, inclusive fitness, and so on, is:

Dawkins, Richard. 1976. *The Selfish Gene.* Oxford: Oxford University Press.

See also:

Hamilton, W. D. 1996/2001. *The Narrow Roads of Geneland.* 2 vols. Oxford: Oxford University Press.

But see the criticisms of individual selection theory in:

Wilson, E. O. 2008. "One Giant Leap: How Insects Achieved Altruism and Colonial Life." *BioScience* 58, no. 1: 17–25.

On parental investment and cheating:

Trivers, Robert. 1985. *Social Evolution.* Menlo Park, CA: Benjamin/Cummings.
———. 2002. *Natural Selection and Social Theory.* Oxford: Oxford University Press.

On the ubiquity of polygamy, see Fox (1993) below.

Benchley, Robert. 1949. *Chips off the Old Benchley.* New York: Harper and Brothers.
Bradley, F. H. 1876. "My Station and Its Duties." In *Ethical Studies.* Oxford: Clarendon Press.
Donnelly, Jack. 1989. *Universal Human Rights in Theory and Practice.* Ithaca, NY: Cornell University Press.
Fox, Robin. 1989. "Inhuman Nature and Unnatural Rights." In *The Search for Society: Quest for a Biosocial Science and Morality.* New Brunswick, NJ: Rutgers University Press. First version published in *Encounter* 58, no. 4 (1982).
———. 1993. "The Case of the Polygamous Policeman." In *Reproduction and Succession: Studies in Anthropology, Law and Society.* New Brunswick, NJ: Transaction.
Moynihan, Daniel Patrick (with Suzanne Weaver). 1978. *A Dangerous Place.* New York: Little, Brown.
Rawls, John. 1971. *A Theory of Justice.* Cambridge, MA: Belknap Press of Harvard University Press.
Wrangham, Richard, and Dale Peterson. 1996. *Demonic Males: Apes and the Origins of Human Violence.* Boston: Houghton Mifflin.

3. The Kindness of Strangers

This chapter is a much-expanded version of an article of the same name: "The Kindness of Strangers," *Society* 44, no. 6 (September/October 2007): 164–170, and is used here with kind permission of Springer Science and Business Media. Irving Louis Horowitz suggested I write it even though he knew we might disagree—but that is his way: the way of a great editor. After an abbreviated version was reprinted in *Harper's,* November 2007, 19–26, I received a large number of e-mails and letters with many astute observations, and a few pointed criticisms. I cannot mention all those who wrote, but I thank them and have incorporated quite a few of their suggestions. Philip Salzman, Don Beck, James Katz, and Linda Stone have been particularly helpful.

I have not been to Iraq, although I have many contacts who have and who know the state of things there (and in Iran). I have been to Israel, Lebanon, and Jordan. I have an extended family of in-laws in Lebanon, and my daughter and grandsons speak fluent Arabic, of which I have picked up a little, and I have become interested in classical Arabic poetry—see Chapter 9.

A good history of Iraq is Charles Tripp, *A History of Iraq*, 2nd ed. (Cambridge: Cambridge University Press, 2002). If this chapter seems too bleak an assessment of the consequences of tribalism, see David Pryce-Jones, *The Closed Circle: An Interpretation of the Arabs* (New York: Harper and Row, 1989). The best recent work (there are so many) is perhaps Adeed Dawisha, *Iraq: A Political History from Independence to Occupation* (Princeton: Princeton University Press, 2009).

References

Ajami, Fouad. 1998. *The Dream Palace of the Arabs: A Generation's Odyssey.* New York: Pantheon.

———. 2006. *The Foreigner's Gift: The Americans, the Arabs, and the Iraqis in Iraq.* New York: Free Press.

Bellow, Adam. 2003. *In Praise of Nepotism: A Natural History.* New York: Doubleday.

Fukuyama, Francis. 1995. *Trust: The Social Virtues and the Creation of Prosperity.* New York: Free Press.

Gellner, Ernest. 1981. *Muslim Society.* Cambridge: Cambridge University Press.

———. 1994. *Conditions of Liberty: Civil Society and Its Rivals.* New York: Viking Penguin.

Hermann, Arthur. 2008. *Gandhi and Churchill: The Epic Rivalry That Destroyed an Empire and Forged Our Age.* New York: Bantam Books.

Hirsi Ali, Ayaan. 2007. *Infidel.* New York: Free Press.

Huntington, Samuel. 1996. *The Clash of Civilizations and the Remaking of the World Order.* New York: Simon and Schuster.

Ibn Khaldûn. 1967 [1377]. *The Muqaddima: An Introduction to History.* Abridged ed. Trans. Franz Rosenthal. London: Routledge and Kegan Paul.

Ikenberry, G. John, Thomas J. Knock, Anne-Marie Slaughter, and Tony Smith. 2009. *The Crisis of American Foreign Policy: Wilsonianism in the Twenty-first Century.* Princeton, NJ: Princeton University Press.

King, Diane E., and Linda Stone. 2010. "Lineal Masculinity: Gendered Memory within Patriliny." *American Ethnologist* 37, no. 2: 323–336.

Krader, L. 1976. *Dialectic of Civil Society.* Assen: Van Gorcum.

Macfarlane, Alan. 1978. *The Origins of English Individualism: The Family, Property and Social Transition.* Oxford: Blackwell.

———. 2002. *The Making of the Modern World: Visions from the West and East.* London: Palgrave.

Obama, Barack. 2006. *The Audacity of Hope: Thoughts on Reclaiming the American Dream.* New York: Crown.
Salzman, Philip Carl. 2008. *Culture and Conflict in the Middle East.* New York: Humanity Books.
Tierney, John. 2003. "Iraqi Family Ties Complicate American Efforts for Change." *New York Times,* September 28, 2003.

4. Sects and Evolution

This chapter is based on "Sects and Evolution," *Society* 41, no. 6 (2004): 36–46, and is used here with kind permission of Springer Science and Business Media. The original version was a plenary address to the Evolution and Human Behavior Society annual conference at Rutgers in 2002 (thanks to Lee Cronk). This will explain the context of some of the comments on "academic sects" in the last section. Ed Wilson offered useful information and comment on recent developments in the theory of group selection, one of the many things on which we have seen eye to eye over the years.

The "Prince Tudor" theory holds that the works attributed to "William Shakespeare" were largely written by Edward de Vere, 17th Earl of Oxford (a theory with which I have some sympathy—Fox 2009, 2010a, 2010b). It goes on to assert that Henry Wriothesley, Earl of Southampton, to whom the long poems (*Venus and Adonis* and *The Rape of Lucrece*) are dedicated, was de Vere's natural son by Queen Elizabeth (about which I have some doubts). It also holds that Wriothesley was the "fair youth" of the *Sonnets,* for which a case can be made (Wittemore 2005). Some enthusiasts believe de Vere was the natural son of Elizabeth, and there they lose me completely. A new sect has not yet grown, but the seeds are planted.

Details of sects in the major religions can be found in any of the encyclopedias or handbooks of religion, or the histories of particular religions. My desk references are the *Encyclopaedia of Religion and Ethics,* ed. James Hastings (New York: Charles Scribner's Sons, 1908–), and *The Encyclopedia of Religion,* ed. Mircea Eliade (New York: Macmillan, 1987). The best general discussion I know of regarding the phenomenon of dispersion in evolution is in Howard Bloom's *The Global Brain,* chap. 10, on "diversity generators" and "creative bickering." I take this chance to thank Howard ("the man who invented the sixties") for his ongoing help and encouragement.

References
Anton, Susan C., Aziz Facroel, and Zaim Yahdi. 2001. "Plio-Pleistocene Homo: Patterns and Determinants of Dispersal." In Phillip Tobias et al., eds., *Humanity from African Naissance to Coming Millennia.* Florence: Firenze University Press.
Bateson, P. P. G., ed. 1983. *Mate Choice.* Cambridge: Cambridge University Press.
Beer, M. 1921. *A History of British Socialism.* 2 vols. London: National Labour Press/G. Bell and Sons.

Bischof, Norbert. 1975. "Comparative Ethology of Incest Avoidance." In Robin Fox, ed., *Biosocial Anthropology*. London: Malaby Press.

Bloom, Howard. 2000. *The Global Brain: The Evolution of the Mass Mind from the Big Bang to the 21st Century*. New York: John Wiley.

———. 2010. *The Genius of the Beast: A Radical Re-Vision of Capitalism*. New York: Prometheus Books.

Carr-Saunders, Alexander M. 1922. *The Population Problem: A Study in Human Evolution*. Oxford: Oxford University Press.

Chagnon, Napoleon. 1968. *Yanomamo: The Fierce People*. New York: Holt, Rinehart and Winston.

———. 1979. "Male Competition, Favoring Close Kin, and Village Fissioning among the Yanomamo Indians." In Napoleon A. Chagnon and William J. Irons, eds., *Evolutionary Biology and Human Social Behavior: An Anthropological Perspective*. North Scituate, MA: Duxbury Press.

Cross, Whitney. 1950. *The Burned-over District: The Social and Intellectual History of Enthusiastic Religion in Western New York, 1800–1850*. Ithaca, NY: Cornell University Press.

Dunbar, Robin. 1992. "Neo-Cortex Size as a Constraint on Group Size in Primates." *Journal of Human Evolution* 20: 469–493.

———. 1993. "Co-evolution of Neo-Cortical Size, Group Size and Language in Humans." *Behavioral and Brain Sciences* 16, no. 4: 681–735.

———. 1998. *Grooming, Gossip and the Evolution of Language*. Cambridge, MA: Harvard University Press.

Ellis, Joseph J. 2000. *Founding Brothers: The Revolutionary Generation*. New York: Alfred Knopf.

Engels, Friedrich. 1957 [1894]. "On the History of Early Christianity." In *K. Marx and F. Engels on Religion*. Moscow: Foreign Languages Publishing House.

Eysenck, Hans J. 1954. *The Psychology of Politics*. London: Routledge and Kegan Paul.

Fox, Robin. 1967. *Kinship and Marriage: An Anthropological Perspective*. Harmondsworth: Penguin. 2nd ed., Cambridge: Cambridge University Press, 1983.

———. 2009. "Shakespeare, Oxford and the Grammar School Question." *The Oxfordian* 11: 113–136.

———. 2010a. "Why Is There No *History of King Henry VII*?" *The Shakespeare-Oxford Newsletter* 46, no. 2: 1–4.

———. 2010b. "A Matter of Pronunciation: Shakespeare, Oxford and the Petty School Question." *The Oxfordian* 12: 18–36.

Franks, Thomas. 2004. *What's the Matter with Kansas?* New York: Metropolitan Books, Henry Holt and Company.

Gaunt, William. 1943. *The Pre-Raphaelite Dream*. London: Reprint Society.

Ibn Khaldûn. 1967 [1377]. *The Muqaddimah: An Introduction to History*. Trans. from the Arabic by Franz Rosenthal. Abridged and ed. N. J. Dawood. London: Routledge and Kegan Paul/Secker and Warburg.

Jay, Antony. 1990. "Understanding Laughter." *Proceedings of the Royal Institution* 62: 99–113.

Kuhn, Thomas. 1962. *The Structure of Scientific Revolutions.* Chicago: University of Chicago Press.

Mead, Frank S. 1985. *Handbook of Denominations in the United States.* 8th ed. Revised by Samuel S. Hill. Nashville: Abingdon Press.

Sahlins, M. D. 1961. "The Segmentary Lineage: An Organization of Predatory Expansion." *American Anthropologist* 63: 322–345.

Sitwell, Edith. 1932. *Bath.* London: Faber and Faber.

Stone, Linda, Paul F. Lurquin, and L. Luca Cavalli-Sforza. 2007. *Genes, Culture and Human Evolution.* Oxford: Blackwell.

Trilling, Lionel. 1965. *Beyond Culture.* New York: Harcourt Brace Jovanovich.

Trivers, Robert. 1985. *Social Evolution.* Menlo Park, CA: Benjamin/Cummings.

Weber, Max. 1947. *The Theory of Social and Economic Organization.* Trans. A. M. Henderson and Talcott Parsons. Glencoe, IL: Free Press.

Williamson, M. 1996. *Biological Invasions.* New York: Chapman and Hall.

Wilson, David S., and Elliott Sober. 1994. "Reintroducing Group Selection to the Human Behavioral Sciences." *Behavioral and Brain Sciences* 14: 585–654.

Wilson, David S., and Edward O. Wilson. 2007. "Re-thinking the Theoretical Foundation of Sociobiology." *Quarterly Review of Biology* 82, no. 4: 327–348.

———. 2008. "Evolution 'for the Good of the Group.'" *American Scientist* 96: 380–389.

World Christian Encyclopedia, 2nd ed. 2001. Ed. David B. Barrett et al. New York: Oxford University Press.

Wright, Sewall. 1984. *Evolution and the Genetics of Populations.* 4 vols. Chicago: Chicago University Press.

Wynne-Edwards, V. C. 1962. *Animal Dispersion in Relation to Social Behaviour.* Edinburgh: Oliver and Boyd.

5. Which Ten Commandments?

The original, shorter version of this chapter appeared as "Which Ten Commandments?" *Society* 43, no. 1 (January/February 2006): 8–11, and is used here with kind permission of Springer Science and Business Media. I thank Fred Turner amd Steven Grosby for their help, and David Oestreicher for introducing me to the work of his old teacher Cyrus Gordon.

To forestall tedious argument, let me say that I have no particular stand on the specifics of the "JEDP" controversy on the authorship of the Pentateuch. But either we must accept that Moses/God was self-contradictory or we must admit that there were *at least* two versions of Exodus, a "folkloristic" and a "priestly," brought together in a later editing, in order to produce the anomaly discussed here.

A Digression on Destruction and Recreation.   The destruction and recreation of the world were there at the heart of Nordic mythology. The great event would be Ragnarok, as told in the tenth-century *Poetic Edda.*

An axe-age, a sword-age, shields will be gashed:
With a wind-age and a wolf-age the world is wrecked,
Wrenched and wracked by wars for three winters.
Fathers will slay sons; brothers drown in brother's blood.
Mothers will leave their men and seduce their own sons,
Brothers will bed with sisters. So the end will begin.

(after Crossley-Holland 1980)

After this lapse into total human disorder, in a vast cataclysm the gods and their enemies, principally the Giants, will fight, and the whole earth be destroyed. But the world tree Yggdrasill will survive Ragnarok, and hiding in it are the two humans Lif and Lifthrasir, who will breed a new race of humans.

There will be life and new life, life everywhere on earth.
That was the end; this is the beginning.

The old corrupt order has to be destroyed and a new beginning made: destruction and renewal. The creators cannot get it right the first time; it has to be done over.

As told by Ovid in his *Metamorphoses,* book 1 (completed in about AD 7), Jove has already contended with the revolt of the Giants, thus echoing the brief reference in Genesis 6:4 and its expansion in the apocryphal *Book of Enoch.* Jove then calls a council of the gods. He reports that as a result of his sojourn among men he is disgusted with the impiety of mankind, and calls on the winds and Neptune to destroy the world with a great flood. In the end he spares only Deucalion and his wife, Pyrrha, who repopulate the earth, on the enigmatic advice of the goddess Themis, by throwing stones (the "bones" of their mother earth) over their shoulders, which stones then turn into men and women. The rest of creation is restored by the action of the sun on the mud: "vapor umidus omnes res creat" (1:432–433).

This account is part of the local East Mediterranean/Near East flood motif, as in Gilgamesh, perhaps reflecting a real catastrophe with the dramatic opening of the Dardanelles. But at the other end of the world, in the *Popol Vuh,* the sacred book of the Maya, the gods try three times to make human beings, and end up destroying all three experiments. On the fourth attempt they finally manage to create a creature that can "walk, talk, speak and pray." It is interesting (at least to an evolutionary anthropologist) that their third attempt—the men made of wood—is not destroyed completely, but the inadequate humans are turned into the ancestors of the monkeys (Tedlock 1996)! And of course in Maya cosmology, as in the Hindu, the world has been created and destroyed several times. According to the Mayan calendar, the next destruction is due in 2012.

References

Barth, Frederick. 1981. "A General Perspective on Nomad-Sedentary Relations in the Middle East." In *Process and Form in Social Life.* London: Routledge and Kegan Paul.

Crossley-Holland, Kevin. 1980. *The Norse Myths.* New York: Pantheon Books.

Douglas, Mary. 1966. *Purity and Danger.* London: Routledge and Kegan Paul.

Frazer, James. 1922. *The Golden Bough.* Abridged ed. London: Macmillan.

———. 1923. *Folklore in the Old Testament: Studies in Comparative Religion, Legend and Law.* Abridged ed. New York: Tudor.

Gordon, Cyrus. 1977. "Poetic Legends and Myths from Ugarit." In *Berytus: Archaeological Studies,* vol. 25. Beirut: American University.

———. 1997. *The Bible and the Ancient Near East.* New York: W. W. Norton.

Grosby, Steven. 2002. *Biblical Ideas of Nationality: Ancient and Modern.* Winona Lake, IN: Eisenbrauns.

Ibn Khaldûn. 1967 [1377]. *The Muqaddimah: An Introduction to History.* Trans. from the Arabic by Franz Rosenthal. Abridged and ed. N. J. Dawood. London: Routledge and Kegan Paul / Secker and Warburg.

Maimonides, Moses. 1963. *The Guide of the Perplexed.* Trans. Schlomo Pines. 2 vols. Chicago: Chicago University Press.

Ovid (Publius Ovidius Naso). 1984. *Metamorphoses.* 2nd ed. Trans. Frank Justus Miller. Revised trans. G. P. Goold. Loeb Classical Library. Cambridge, MA: Harvard University Press.

Smith, W. Robertson. 1956 [1889]. *The Religion of the Semites.* New York: Meridian Library.

Tedlock, Dennis, trans. 1996. *Popol Vuh: The Mayan Book of the Dawn of Life.* New York: Touchstone.

Thompson, Thomas L. 1999. *Mythic Past: Biblical Archaeology and the Myth of Israel.* New York: Basic Books.

6. Incest and In-Laws

This and the next chapter are derived from a Byrne Family Freshman Seminar, "Forbidden Partners: The Incest Taboo in Fact and Fantasy," at Rutgers in 2008–2009. I should like to thank the students in this lively seminar for their interest, help, and very useful suggestions.

Where I have used literary texts that appear in numerous popular editions, I have not cited a source. I have arranged the references by subheading for convenience.

Genesis of the Taboo

Fox, Robin (J. R.). 1962. "Sibling Incest." *British Journal of Sociology* 13: 128–150.

———. 1983. *The Red Lamp of Incest: An Enquiry into the Origins of Mind and Society.* Notre Dame, IN: University of Notre Dame Press. Originally published New York: E. P. Dutton, 1980.

———. 1994. "The Evolution of Incest Inhibition." In *The Challenge of Anthropology: Old Encounters and New Excursions.* New Brunswick, NJ: Transaction.

For an excellent account with up-to-date references:

Turner, Jonathan, and Alexandra Maryanski. 2005. *Incest: Origins of the Taboo.* Boulder, CO: Paradigm.

Kindred and Affinity
A brilliant recent account of incest avoidance, in-laws, and social origins is:

Chapais, Bernard. 2008. *Primeval Kinship: How Pair-Bonding Gave Birth to Human Society.* Cambridge, MA: Harvard University Press.

Intra-genome conflict over inbreeding:

Burt, Austin, and Robert Trivers. 2006. *Genes in Conflict: The Biology of Selfish Genetic Elements.* Cambridge, MA: Belknap Press of Harvard University Press.

The Ancient World
Charles, R. H., trans. 1917. *The Book of Jubilees.* London: Society for Promoting Christian Knowledge. (There are numerous other editions.)
Frazer, James. 1922. *The Golden Bough: A Study in Magic and Religion.* Abridged ed. London: Macmillan.
Friedrich, Paul. 1978. *The Meaning of Aphrodite.* Chicago: University of Chicago Press.

Ovid, text:

Ovid (Publius Ovidius Naso). 1984. *Metamorphoses.* 2nd ed. Bks. 9–15. Trans. Frank Justus Miller. Revised trans. G. P. Goold. Loeb Classical Library. Cambridge, MA: Harvard University Press.

Latin originals from Ovid:

Esse quidem laesi poterat tibi pectoris index
et color et macies et vultus et umida saepe
lumina nec causa suspira mota patenti
et crebri amplexus, et quae, si forte notasti
oscula sentiri non esse sororia possent. (Bk. IX, 535–539)

Sic lacrimis consumpta suis Phoebeia Byblis
vertitur in fontem, qui nunc quoque vallibus illes
nomen habet dominae, nigraque sub illice manat. (Bk. IX, 663–665)

Myrrha datis nimium gaudet consultaque, qualem
optet habere virum, "similem tibi" dixit; at ille
non intellectam vocem conlaudet et "esto
tam pia semper" ait. Pietatis nomine dicto
demissit vultus sceleris sibi conscia virgo. (Bk. X, 363–367)

Accipit obsceno genitor sua viscera lecto
Virgineosque metus levat hortarturque timentem.
Forsitan aetatis quoque nomine "filia" dixit,
Dixit et illa "pater," sceleri ne nomina desint. (Bk. X, 465–468)

Sophocles, text:

Storr, F., ed. and trans. 1912. *Sophocles,* vol. 1 *(Oedipus the King, Oedipus at Colonus, Antigone).* Loeb Classical Library. Cambridge, MA: Harvard University Press.

On the two lineages in Thebes:

Fox, Robin. 1993. "The Virgin and the Godfather: Kinship Law versus State Law in Greek Tragedy and After." In *Reproduction and Succession.* New Brunswick, NJ: Transaction.

The Westermarck Effect and FBD marriage:

Walter, Alex, and Steven Buyske. 2003. "The Westermarck Effect and Early Childhood Co-Socialization: Sex Differences in Inbreeding Avoidance." *British Journal of Developmental Psychology* 21: 353–365.

The Middle Ages
Archibald, Elizabeth. 2001. *Incest and the Medieval Imagination.* Oxford: Oxford University Press.
Bradley, Marion Zimmer. 1982. *The Mists of Avalon.* New York: Alfred A. Knopf.
Jones, Ernest, 1949. *Hamlet and Oedipus.* London: Hogarth.
Malory, Thomas. N.d. *The Noble and Joyous History of King Arthur (Morte D'Arthur: The First Nine Books); The Book of Marvellous Adventures and Other Books of the Morte D'Arthur (Morte D'Arthur: The Last Twelve Books).* Ed. Ernest Rhys. London: Walter Scott.
"The Story of the Volsungs and Niblungs." 1910. Trans. William Morris and Eiríkr Magnússon. In Charles Eliot, ed., *Epic and Saga.* Harvard Classics, vol. 49. New York: P. F. Collier and Son.

The Renaissance
Contrasting views of the "repressed incest" in Lear:

McCabe, Richard A. 1993. *Incest, Drama and Nature's Law, 1550–1700.* Cambridge: Cambridge University Press.
Nordlund, Marcus. 2007. *Shakespeare and the Nature of Love: Literature, Culture, Evolution.* Evanston, IL: Northwestern University Press.

7. Forbidden Partners

The Romantics

A Digression on William Blake: William Blake, The Mental Traveller *(ca. 1803).* Blake was a harsh critic of the materialism of the new age, but it is not easy to place him within Romanticism, so I will treat him as a digression, knowing that for Swift the digressions were of the essence. Blake's *Prophetic Books* have more than a hint of incest in the propagation of the descendants of Albion (foreshadowing Byron's *Cain*), but his most graphic assault on materialism is in his strange *The Mental Traveller.* Here a conscious version of Miltonic myth uses parent–child incest as a metaphor for some kind of self-perpetuating hopelessness. I prevaricate here because Blake is always gnomic while being savagely graphic. His "mental traveller" is a kind of time-traveling alien observer who lands in the world "of women and of men"—our world. He (It) watches the birth of children:

> And if the babe is born a Boy
> He's given to a Woman Old,
> Who nails him down upon a rock,
> Catches his shrieks in cups of gold.

She tortures him and feeds vampire-like on his shrieks and cries: "and she grows young as he grows old."

> Till he becomes a bleeding youth,
> And she becomes a Virgin bright;
> Then he rends up his Manacles
> And binds her down for his delight.

Then, its seems, he gets older, she gets younger, and "from the fire on the hearth" springs forth as a little female babe. The imagery is murky here, but the aging man "to allay his freezing age" takes the young girl into his arms:

> The honey of her infant lips,
> The bread and wine of her sweet smile,
> The wild game of her roving eye,
> Does him to infancy beguile;

> For as he eats and drinks he grows
> Younger and younger every day . . .

> Till he becomes a wayward Babe,
> And she becomes a Woman Old . . .

And the whole cycle begins again as she nails him down upon the rock, "And all is done as I have told." The whole poem has an effect like a metaphysical blow to the head, and is perhaps better read when mildly stoned. It may be unclassifiable, but it is terrifying, and must be recognized. Better than the extended comments of scholars perhaps is the running commentary on the poem in Joyce Carey's *The Horse's Mouth*. The trickster antihero, Gully Jimson, sees it as Blake's reflections on the tragedy of the artist, hence himself: as good an interpretation as any. But the incest imagery is overpowering and poetically condensed, compared to the wordy and melodramatic tales to follow.

On the incest theme in nineteenth- and twentieth-century art and literature:

Twitchell, James. 1987. *Forbidden Partners: The Incest Taboo in Modern Culture*. New York: Columbia University Press.

See also:

Chateaubriand, Francois-René de. 1964. *Atala/René*. Chronology and preface by Pierre Reboul. Paris: Garnier-Flammarion.
Shelley, Percy Bysshe. 1970. *The Cenci*. Ed. Roland A. Duerkin. Indianapolis: Bobbs-Merrill.
Twitchell, James. 1985. *Dreadful Pleasures: An Anatomy of Modern Horror*. New York: Oxford University Press.

The Victorians
A Digression on Thomas Hardy: Thomas Hardy, Jude the Obscure, *1895.* Let us recall the often-overlooked case of Thomas Hardy's last novel, which has a telling reference to Shelley and the attachment of siblings. The central pair of the novel is Jude Fawley, the stonemason with ambitions to be a scholar, and his "cousin" Sue Bridehead, the emancipated and freethinking new woman. As far as I can make out, she is his first cousin once removed: the aunt who raised Jude refers to Sue as her "great niece." Jude marries the earthy Annabella, who leaves him, while Sue marries the schoolteacher Roger Phillotson and eventually leaves *him,* having refused to sleep with him. Sue has serious inhibitions about sex, while Jude is all for it. Jude and Sue then get together, having recognized each other as soul mates. They finally, after a period of chastity, have children and acquire Jude's son ("Little Father Time") by Annabella. They do not marry, on principle, and are spurned by society and descend into poverty. In the depths of their despair the son kills his siblings and hangs himself, Sue becomes morbidly religious and goes back to Roger, while Annabella reclaims the ailing Jude, who dies in her bed after walking miles in the rain for one last interview with his soul mate, Sue.

The interesting thing for our present argument is the tortured but passionate relationship, alternating between chastity and lust, between the first cousins, Sue and Jude, and the consequent running conflict with the "legitimate" spouses, Annabella and Roger. The cousin relationship is overtly considered to border on the unnatural, and when asked to describe it, Roger Phillotson denounces it angrily as "Shelleyan." Because we have seen what Shelley wrought in *The Revolt of Islam,* we can appreciate the schoolmaster's sarcasm. Jude and Sue are indeed a kind of Shelleyan sibling pair who do not live by the world's standards and are doomed therefore to suffer in classic tragic fashion. Sue has four miscarriages before her living children are killed.

The classic essay on *Wuthering Heights* that raised the incest issue is:

Solomon, Eric. 1959. "The Incest Theme in Wuthering Heights." *Nineteenth Century Fiction* 14 (June).

The remarkable essay by "C. P. S." on *Wuthering Heights* is found in the rare out-of-print volume:

Willis, Irene Cooper. 1967. *The Authorship of Wuthering Heights.* Bound with C. P. S., *The Structure of Wuthering Heights.* London: Dawsons of Pall Mall.

On cousin marriage among the Victorians:

Kuper, Adam. 2009. *Incest and Influence: The Private Life of Bourgeois England.* Cambridge, MA: Harvard University Press.

The Moderns
Daly, M., and M. Wilson. 1996. "Violence against Stepchildren." *Current Directions in Psychological Science* 5, no. 3: 77–81.
———. 1997. The *Truth about Cinderella: A Darwinian View of Parental Love.* New Haven: Yale University Press.
Herman, Judith. 2000. *Father–Daughter Incest.* Cambridge, MA: Harvard University Press.
Hopkins, Keith, 1980. "Brother–Sister Marriage in Roman Egypt." *Comparative Studies in Society and History* 22: 304–354.
Sprigge, Elizabeth. 1973. *The Life of Ivy Compton-Burnett.* New York: George Braziller.

On Nabokov specifically, but excellent on the sibling incest theme:

Johnson, D. Barton. 1986. "The Labyrinth of Incest in Nabokov's Ada." *Comparative Literature* 38, no. 3 (Summer): 224–255.

8. In the Company of Men

This chapter is based on "Male Bonding in the Epics and Romances," in Jonathan Gottschall and David Sloan Wilson, eds., *The Literary Animal: Evolution and the Nature of Narrative* (Evanston, IL: Northwestern University Press, 2005). Both editors, along with Lionel Tiger, Robert Trivers, and Frederick Turner, offered much useful help. Gottschall's outstanding *The Rape of Troy* has great bearing on the theme. See my review essay "Demonic Males and Missing Daughters," *Evolutionary Psychology* 6, no. 3 (2008): 432–435. Thomas Kinsella's translations of the *Táin* are used by kind and generous permission of the author. Translations from the *Iliad* are my own.

References: Texts
Gilgamesh: A New Rendering in English Verse. 1992. By David Ferry. New York: Farrar, Straus and Giroux.
The Táin. 1969. Translated from the Irish Epic *Táin Bó Cualinge* by Thomas Kinsella. London: Oxford University Press (in association with The Dolmen Press, Dublin).
Ancient Irish Tales. 1969. Ed. T. P. Cross and C. H. Slover. Dublin: Allen Figgis. Originally published New York: Henry Holt, 1936.
Epic and Saga: Beowulf, The Song of Roland, The Destruction of Dá Derga's Hostel, The Story of the Volsungs and Niblungs. 1938. Ed. Charles W. Eliot. Harvard Classics. New York: P. F. Collier. (The *Beowulf* translation by Francis Gummere is used in this chapter.)
Homer. *The Iliad.* 1974. Trans. Robert Fitzgerald. Oxford: Oxford University Press.
Homer. *The Iliad.* 1990. Trans. Robert Fagles. New York: Viking.
Homer. *The Iliad.* 1999. Trans. A. T. Murray. Revised trans. by William F. Wyatt. Loeb Classical Library. Cambridge, MA: Harvard University Press.
La Chanson de Roland. 1982. Trans. Joseph Bédier. Paris: Union Générale d'Éditions. Originally published 1922.
Malory, Thomas, N.d. *The Noble and Joyous History of King Arthur (Morte D'Arthur: The First Nine Books); The Book of Marvellous Adventures and Other Books of the Morte D'Arthur (Morte D'Arthur: The Last Twelve Books).* Ed. Ernest Rhys. London: Walter Scott.
The Song of Roland. 1957. Trans. Dorothy L. Sayers. Harmondsworth: Penguin.
Volsunga Saga: The Story of the Volsungs and Niblungs, with certain songs from the Elder Edda. N.d. Trans. from the Icelandic by Eríckr Magnússon and William Morris. Ed. H. Halliday Sparling. London: Walter Scott. Originally published 1888. (Note: This is the same translation that appears in *Epic and Saga* above.)

Other References
Fisher, Helen. 2004. *Why We Love: The Nature and Chemistry of Romantic Love.* New York: Henry Holt.
Fox, Robin. 1983. *The Red Lamp of Incest: An Enquiry into the Origins of Mind and Society.* Notre Dame, IN: University of Notre Dame Press, 1983. Originally published New York: E. P. Dutton, 1980.
———. 1993. "Sisters' Sons and Monkeys' Uncles: Six Theories in Search of an Avunculate." In *Reproduction and Succession: Studies in Anthropology, Law and Society.* New Brunswick, NJ: Transaction.

———. 1997. "Sexual Conflict and Epic Narrative." In *Conjectures and Confrontations: Science, Evolution, Social Concern.* New Brunswick, NJ: Transaction.

Gottschall, Jonathan. 2008. *The Rape of Troy: Evolution, Violence and the World of Homer.* Cambridge: Cambridge University Press.

Hamill, John. 2005. "Shakespeare's Sexuality and How It Affects the Authorship Issue." *The Oxfordian* 8: 25–59.

Hope Moncrieff, A. R. 1978. *Romance and Legend of Chivalry.* New York: Bell.

Singh, Nagendra Kumar. 1997. *Divine Prostitution.* Delhi: A. P. H. Publishing Corporation.

Tiger, Lionel. 1968. *Men in Groups.* London: Thomas Nelson.

Trivers, Robert S. 1971. "The Evolution of Reciprocal Altruism." *Quarterly Review of Biology* 46 (March): 35–57.

———. 1972. "Parental Investment and Sexual Selection." In Bernard Campbell, ed., *Sexual Selection and the Descent of Man.* Chicago: Aldine.

Veyne, Paul. 1982. "L'homosexualité à Rome." In *Sexualités occidentales,* ed. Phillipe Ariès, Michel Foucault, and André Béjin. Special issue, *Communications* 35. Paris: Éditions du Seuil.

9. Playing by the Rules

This chapter is a much enlarged version of "Playing by the Rules: Sound and Sense in Swinburne and the Rhyming Poets," *Philosophy and Literature* 32, no. 2 (October 2008): 17–40.

Frederick Turner, Dennis Dutton, Mansour Ajami, and Michael Egan made valuable suggestions, as did the late Richard Moore (see his *The Rule That Liberates*). Jonathan Bate's essay on Swinburne is one of the most appreciative in recent years. The poem "Donne in His Coffin" is reproduced by kind permission of the author, Frederick Turner, who inspires everything I write about the arts and humanities. The thin-paper two-volume edition of Swinburne that I carry around is *Swinburne's Collected Poetical Works* (New York: Harper and Brothers, n.d.). This is the edition I quote from in this chapter.

A Digression on Mayan Poetics. The neural "line," while reflected in written poetry, is, as the authors say, an acoustical phenomenon, and so it is characteristic of oral poetry too. They cite such collections as J. Rothenburg's *Technicians of the Sacred* (New York: Doubleday-Anchor, 1968), which have numerous examples from ancient and preliterate societies of metered verse. From my own experience with Native Americans, I cannot tell, because all "verse" was sung, and song imposes its own rhythmical rules, which are related to, but different from, those of metered verse. However, such verse in preliterate or ancient society, whether sung, chanted, or spoken, is not rhymed. A good place to look for the transition of oral to written verse is among the Maya, who developed a high literate culture in Middle America completely spontaneously, and wrote down their own oral traditions. In his translation of the Mayan *Popol Vuh,* Dennis Tedlock includes these lines of Mayan epic verse as a dedication (the end quote is a glottal stop):

> Are k'u wa'nu tak'alib'al, nu presenta
> Chikiwach ri nantat, comon vhuchkajawib'
> Much'ulik ulew, much' ulik poqlaj, much'ulik baq.

I don't know what they mean (they are recognizably Amerind), but that is a good test. Because there might be different vowel lengths, it is hard to be certain, but if you read each line phonetically, giving each vowel equal weight (as is usual with Amerind), the lines all sound metrically the same. There are 12–14 syllables, with the repetitions in the last line adding metric weight, like the "nor" repetitions in the last line of the Swinburne sonnet. Tedlock also lays out some Mayan examples of different poetic forms using a stanza of five- and four-syllable lines more typical of lyric verse. The "neural line" here would be the typical full fourteen or fifteen syllables, broken into three units like a haiku.

k'a katz'ininoq	now it still ripples
k'a kachamamoq	now it still murmurs
katz'inonik	ripples
k'a kasilanik	it still sighs
k'a kalolinik	it still hums
katalona putch	and it is empty

Tedlock (as sensitive and skilled an interpreter as you could get) describes this piece as "dense with alliteration and assonance," which it so obviously is. It invokes "the sounds of a primordial world that consists only of a flat sea and an empty sky." Its patterns "run below the level of syntax"—that is, they are metrical. But it also seems to me to rhyme, with the *-oq* and *-ik* endings. In any case it is clearly verse as carefully contrived as the most exquisite haiku:

> The sea ripples and
> murmurs, still it sighs and hums,
> still it is empty.

We saw that rhyme, with the elaboration of metrical forms, was something that came with the high literate and intellectual civilizations in the West and Asia. The Maya were this for the ancient Americas. It is worth pondering.

A Digression on Dame Edith.   Dame Edith loved the hissing "s" sounds of the little serpents, but she was rather given to liking this device. She supported Alexander Pope against Robert Graves on the matter. Graves thought Pope "lost control" of his "s" sounds in the famous lines on Sporus in *An Epistle to Dr Arbuthnot.* And the following is only the half of it:

Let *Sporus* tremble. What? That thing of silk,
Sporus that mere white curd of asses milk?
Satire or sense alike can *Sporus* feel?
Who breaks a butterfly upon a wheel?
In puns, or politics, or tales, or lies,
Of spite, or smut, or rhymes, or blasphemies.
His wit all see-saw between *that* and *this,*
Now high, now low, now master up, now miss,
And he himself one vile Antithesis.

Dame Edith thought, to the contrary, that all the hissing actually finessed the sense of acid disgust for the bisexual, "amphibious thing"—Lord Hervey. ("Now trips a Lady and now struts a Lord.")

A Digression on Edna Millay.   For me the poet who most resembles Swinburne in the subtle use of the death/breath motif and the vivid sense of mortality is Edna St. Vincent Millay (1892–1950):

Love cannot fill the thickened lung with breath,
Nor clean the blood, nor set the fractured bone;
Yet many a man is making friends with death
Even as I speak, for lack of love alone.
(Fatal Interview, XXX)

Academic critics, like our faux-Ivy lady, usually condescend to Edna and treat her sonnets as mere extensions of romantic dime novels. They are so wrong. She was smart, witty, masochistic in love, and elegantly thanatophobic. Swinburne would have liked and recognized her:

O race of Adam, blench not lest you find
In the sun's bubbling bowl anonymous death,
Or lost in whistling space without a mind
To monstrous Nothing yield your little breath
    You shall achieve destruction where you stand
    In intimate conflict, at your brother's hand.
(Epitaph for the Race of Man, V)

This is pure Swinburne—remember his "bubbling bitterness of life and death"? But it both equals and exceeds his cynicism, while the sharp-edged "lost in whistling space without a mind" is all hers, with a nod to the master's sibilants.

A Digression on Basque Rhyme.   Basque is not an Indo-European language and has always been something of a mystery. But for that reason it provides an interesting control. I know a little about it because I supervised a doctoral thesis on the Basque region. Also, the great Basque poet Gabriel Aresti was evidently reading *Kinship and Marriage* on his deathbed, the better to understand the kin-loyalties of his people, and his friend, the anthropologist Joseba Zulaika, sent me a bilingual (Spanish-Basque) copy of his poems. Spoken now only in a small area of northern Spain and southern France, it was spoken widely in Western Europe before the coming of the Indo-European speakers—Celts, Latins, Franks, Visigoths, and so on. It has no obvious connections, although Berber and Pictish have been suggested. It bears some resemblance to Caucasian tongues like Chechnyan, but there is no positive identification. Fortunately it is written in Roman characters, and these are faithfully phonetic. The earliest preserved Basque ballads, like the Ballad of Karloman *(Altabiskarco Cantua),* which we mentioned in Chapter 8, either did or did not use rhyme. Rhyming is easy in Euskaria, and in the earliest known poem *(Leloaren Cantua)* it seems very like some of the Arabic rhyming schemes in which the same rhyme makes the end of all the (four-line) stanzas:

eloa/Zanzoa/vizcayocoa/
molsoa/leusoac/daughogoa/surboa/pochoa . . .

By the fifteenth century the Basques were producing written poetry. The first poet to be published was Bernat (Bernard) Etxepare in 1545. Here is one stanza that shows the rich use of rhyme in Basque (*x* is "ch"):

Hire potak, baziakiat, bertze gauza nahi dik,
Anderea, atzi zira nihaurk erran geberik.
Bada utzi ahal bainentzak ni holakoz ixilic.
Horein gaitz alraden gero, eginen dut bertzerik:

Your kiss, I know demands something else,
Lady, you have guessed even before I spoke.
Then stop saying such things to me.
As you are so shrewish, I shall do something else.

(Trans. Toni Strubell)

The previous stanza had used the *-ik* rhyme throughout, just like the little Mayan verse. So this non-Indo-European, non-Semitic language rapidly took on the conventions of rhyme that the Arabs had transmitted to Europe. Anyone interested in Basque poetry should look at the book Joseba Zulaika edited with Samuel Armistead (below). A good Web source is www.basquepoetry.net, from which the above translation was taken.

References

Ajami, Mansour. 1990. "Death Transformed: A Counter Reading of Crucifixion (Ibn Al-Anbārī's Elegy on the Vizier Ibn Baqiyya)." In *Journal of Arabic Literature* (Leiden: E. J. Brill) 21, pt. 1: 1–13.

Armistead, Samuel G., and Joseba Zulaika. 2005. *Voicing the Moment: Improvised Oral Poetry and the Basque Tradition.* Reno: Center for Basque Studies, University of Nevada.

Bailey, H. Kent. 1987. *Human Paleopsychology: Applications to Aggression and Pathological Processes.* Hillsdale, NJ: Lawrence Erlbaum.

Bate, Jonathan. 2009. "A Century after Swinburne." *Times Literary Supplement* (London), July 8.

Corkery, Daniel. 1956. *The Hidden Ireland.* Dublin: M. H. Gill and Son.

Crick, Francis, and Graeme Mitchison. 1983. "The Function of Dream Sleep." *Nature* 304: 111–114.

Denes, Marcel. 1993. *Vico, Metaphor and the Origin of Language.* Bloomington: Indiana University Press.

Feirstein, Frederick. 1981. *Manhattan Carnival.* Woodstock, VT: Countryman Press.

Fox, Kate. 1999. *The Racing Tribe: Watching the Horsewatchers.* London: Metro Books.

———. 2004. *Watching the English: The Hidden Rules of English Behaviour.* London: Hodder and Stoughton.

Fox, Robin. 1983. "The Matter of Mind." In *The Red Lamp of Incest: An Enquiry into the Origins of Mind and Society.* Notre Dame, IN: University of Notre Dame Press. Originally published New York: E. P. Dutton, 1980.

———. 1989. "Brain, Dreams, Memory, Evolution and Social Categories." In *The Search for Society: Quest for a Biosocial Science and Morality.* New Brunswick, NJ: Rutgers University Press.

———. 2001. *The Passionate Mind.* New Brunswick, NJ: Transaction.

———. 2007. "Life Is Too Short." www.expansivepoetryonline.com/journal.

Havelock, Eric. 1963. *Preface to Plato.* Cambridge, MA: Harvard University Press.

Henderson, Phillip. 1974. *Swinburne: Portrait of a Poet.* New York: Macmillan.

Herz, Robert. 1960. *Death and the Right Hand.* Trans. Rodney Needham and Claudia Needham. London: Cohen and West. Originally published as "La pre-éminence de la main droite: Étude sur la polarité religieuse." *Revue Philosophique* 68 (1909): 553–580.

Ingalls, Daniel H. H. 1968. *Sanskrit Poetry.* Cambridge, MA: Belknap Press of Harvard University Press.

Levitin, Daniel J. 2006. *This Is Your Brain on Music: The Science of a Human Obsession.* London: Penguin.

MacLean, Paul. 1990. *The Triune Brain in Evolution: Role in Paleocerebral Functions.* New York: Springer.

Millay, Edna St. Vincent. 1988. *Collected Sonnets.* Revised, expanded ed. New York: HarperCollins.

Moore, Richard. 1994. *The Rule That Liberates.* Vermillion: University of South Dakota Press.

Opie, Iona, and Peter Opie. 1959. *The Lore and Language of Schoolchildren.* Oxford: Oxford University Press.

Piaget, Jean. 1965. *The Moral Judgment of the Child*. New York: Free Press.

Pinsky, Robert. 1994. *The Inferno of Dante: A New Verse Translation*. New York: Farrar, Straus and Giroux.

Shors, T. J. 2001. "Inescapable Stress Rapidly Induces and Persistently Enhances Memory Formation in the Male Rat." *Neurobiology of Learning and Memory* 75: 10–29.

———. 2002. "Opposite Effects of Stressful Experience on Memory in Males versus Females." *Dialogues in Clinical Neuroscience* 4: 193–198.

Sitwell, Edith. 1960. *Swinburne: A Selection*. London: Weidenfeld and Nicholson.

Turner, Frederick, and Ernst Pöppel. 1983. "The Neural Lyre: Poetic Meter, the Brain and Time." *Poetry* (August): 277–309. Reprinted in Frederick Turner, *Natural Classicism* (Charlottesville: University Press of Virginia, 1992) and in Frederick Feirstein, ed., *Expansive Poetry: Essays on the New Narrative and the New Formalism* (Santa Cruz, CA: Story Line Press, 1989).

Welby, T. Earle. 1926. *A Study of Swinburne*. New York: George H. Doran.

Winson, Jonathan. 1985. *Brain and Psyche: The Biology of the Unconscious*. New York: Anchor Press.

10. Seafood and Civilization

References on the Calusa can be found in Fox (1994), from which the current description is drawn. I draw also on my own ongoing experience of research in southwest Florida, and I would like to thank the members of the Randell Research Center (Florida Museum of Natural History) on Pine Island for their help, and also Rutgers for several useful grants-in-aid. The lively meetings of the Southwest Florida Archaeological Association were an opportunity to discuss these ideas and trade information.

The most recent work on the Calusa is MacMahon and Marquardt (2004), with references up to that date. The classic work on the Potlatch is Codere (1950), which followed Boas closely. See the later work of Suttles for a more critical view. I have made several visits to the Northwest Coast, but although I got to Mexico and Colombia, erratic health has prevented me from visiting Peru. It is on my list.

William Marquardt, Bonnie Mackay, Fran Mascia-Lees, and the members of the Chair's Breakfast Seminar of the Rutgers Anthropology Department all made helpful criticisms and contributions, as did the members of my undergraduate seminar "Explanation in Anthropology."

References on Göbekli Tepe, apart from a few popular articles, are in German and hard to come by. There is, however, a very good Wikipedia entry, translated from the German. This is the best place to start. I first heard of it through a DVD of the eye-opening (and eye-delighting) BBC/KCET program with Nigel Spivey: *How Art Made the World* (2005–2006). I thank my wife, Lin, for dragging me away from the computer and making me watch.

References

Boas, Franz. 1897. *The Social Organization and Secret Societies of the Kwakiutl Indians, Based on Personal Observations and Notes Made by George Hunt.* U.S. National Museum Report for 1895, 311–738. Washington, DC.

————. 1921. *Ethnology of the Kwakiutl.* 2 vols. Thirty-fifth Annual Report of the Bureau of American Ethnology. Washington, DC.

Benedict, Ruth. 1934. *Patterns of Culture.* Boston: Houghton Mifflin.

Codere, Helen. 1950. *Fighting with Property: A Study of Kwakiutl Potlatching and Warfare.* Monographs of the American Ethnological Society, No. 18. New York: Augustin.

Diamond, Jared. 1997. *Guns, Germs and Steel: The Fate of Human Societies.* New York: W. W. Norton.

Drucker, Philip. 1955. *Indians of the Northwest Coast.* New York: McGraw-Hill.

Durkheim, Émile. 1933. *The Division of Labour in Society.* Trans. G. Simpson. New York: Macmillan. Originally published as *De la division du travail social: Étude sur l'organisation des sociétés supérieures.* Paris: Alcan, 1893.

Fox, Robin. 1994. "The Origins of Social Complexity." In *The Challenge of Anthropology.* New Brunswick, NJ: Transaction.

Haywood, John. 2005. *Historical Atlas of Ancient Civilizations.* London: Penguin.

MacMahon, Darcie A., and William H. Marquardt. 2004. *The Calusa and Their Legacy: South Florida People and Their Environments.* Gainesville: University Press of Florida.

Mann, Charles C. 2003. "Cotton (or Anchovies) and Maize: Tales of Two Civilizations, Part 1." In *1491: New Revelations of the Americas before Columbus.* New York: Alfred A. Knopf.

Mauss, Marcel. 1954. *The Gift: Forms and Functions of Exchange in Archaic Societies.* Trans. I. Cunnison. London: Cohen and West. Originally published as "Essai sur le don: Formes et raisons de l'échange dans les sociétés archaïque." *Année Sociologique,* n.s., 1 (1925): 30–186.

Morgan, L. H. 1877. *Ancient Society, or Researches in the Lines of Human Progress from Savagery through Barbarism to Civilization.* New York: Henry Holt.

Moseley, Michael E. 1975. *The Maritime Foundations of Andean Civilization.* Menlo Park, CA: Cummings.

————. 1992. *The Incas and Their Ancestors: The Archaeology of Peru.* New York: Thames and Hudson. Revised ed. 2001.

Rick, Torben C., and Jon M. Erlandson. 2009. "Coastal Exploitation: How Did Ancient Hunter-Gatherers Influence Coastal Environments?" *Science* 325, no. 5943: 952–953.

Sandweiss, Daniel H., Ruth Shady Solis, Michael E. Moseley, David K. Keefer, and Charles R. Ortloff. 2009. "Environmental Change and Economic Development in Coastal Peru between 5,800 and 2,600 Years Ago." *Proceedings of the National Academy of Sciences* 106: 1359–1363.

Solis, Ruth Shady, Jonathan Haas, and Winifred Creamer. 2001. "Dating Caral, a Preceramic Site in the Supe Valley." *Science* 292, no. 5517: 723–726.

Steward, Julian. 1963. "Development of Complex Societies: Cultural Causality and Law—A Trial Formulation of the Development of Early Civilizations." In *Theory of Culture Change*. Urbana: University of Illinois Press. Originally published 1955.

Stringer, Chris. 2006. *Homo Britannicus: The Incredible Story of Human Life in Britain*. London: Penguin.

Suttles, Wayne. 1960. "Affinal Ties, Subsistence, and Prestige among the Coast Salish." *American Anthropologist* 62: 452–463.

Veblen, Thorstein. 1973. *Theory of the Leisure Class*. Introduction by C. Wright Mills and J. K. Galbraith. Boston: Houghton Mifflin. Originally published 1899.

Wittfogel, Karl. 1957. *Oriental Despotism: A Study of Total Power*. New Haven: Yale University Press.

11. The Route to Civilization

This chapter draws on material from "Lewis Henry Morgan and the Reason for Anthropology," which appeared in a reprint of Morgan's *Ancient Society* (New Brunswick, NJ: Transaction, 2000), used here by permission of the publisher. I thank Alan Macfarlane, the late Per Hage, Nick Allen, Robert Grumet, and the members of the graduate proseminar in anthropology I taught with Jack Harris at Rutgers.

A Digression on Tetradic Theory. Per Hage brought to my attention the brilliant work of Nick Allen of Oxford University. His theory of "tetradic kinship" and the "big bang" eruption of kinship systems is close to my own thinking and to chaos and complexity theory (my observation, not his) but is not well enough known having been largely published in a local journal. We both think there are four basic terms (with an indicator for sex), but his reduction is more logical. It does not need the reciprocal grandparent term. He completely, for me, demonstrates that all other kinship systems are derived from the rupture of the logically most primitive tetradic system. Figure N.1 is his diagram of that system, which I present here simply to tempt readers to explore it further.

Those who have followed thus far will easily see the logic of the system as Allen diagrams it. It is fundamentally the "four section" system described in Chapter 11. They will see, among other things, that the cycling of alternate generations that I described in Chapter 1 (Figure 1.2) can be represented by only two generations. This means that small bands of early humans could have been held together as a "kinship society" with the use of only four terms (corresponding to the four "sections") embracing the whole society (perhaps the "linguistic tribe") and one simple rule of marriage (sister or daughter exchange). It can't get more elementary than that, and it makes far more sense as the Ur-system than assuming some com-

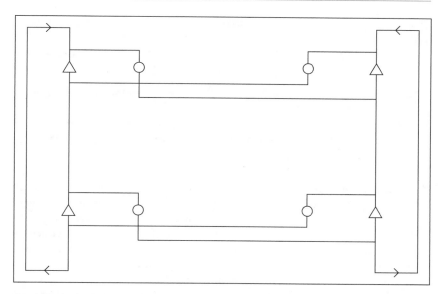

Figure N.1   Nick Allen's tetradic system

plex calculation of genealogical relationships among hominids who had probably only just developed language itself. It requires no such calculation; all relatives would fall into one of the four categories of kin. Following are some references.

Allen, N. J. 1982. "A Dance of Relatives." *Journal of the Anthropological Society of Oxford* 13, no. 2: 139–146.

———. 1986. "Tetradic Theory: An Approach to Kinship." *Journal of the Anthropological Society of Oxford.* 17, no. 2: 97–109.

———. 1989. "Assimilation of Alternate Generations." *Journal of the Anthropological Society of Oxford* 20, no. 1: 45–55.

———. 1989. "The Evolution of Kinship Terminologies." *Lingua* 77: 173–185.

———. 2008. "Tetradic Theory and the Origin of Human Kinship Systems." In N. J. Allen, Hilary Callan, Robin Dunbar, and Wendy James, eds., *Early Human Kinship: From Sex to Social Reproduction.* Malden, MA: Blackwell.

Unfortunately, as we have seen in this chapter, most anthropologists have abandoned this foundational topic of their discipline. But there are signs of a revival, and even a revival of interest in the evolution of kinship systems. The 2008 book Allen co-edited shows a welcome return to these issues of origin and evolution. Bernard Chapais's *Primeval Kinship* (2008), mentioned in Chapter 6, which integrates my approach and that of Lévi-Strauss, is a massive step in the right direction, as was the whole life career of Per Hage. Per improved my understanding of the evolution of kinship systems beyond measure. His premature death was an incommensurable loss to his friends and to anthropology. Let this be a small dedication to his memory. See his account of Maya kinship, referenced below, which revived interest in Eggan's reconstruction mentioned in Chapter 1. The forthcoming memorial volume for him (Milicic and Jones) has an encouraging subtitle.

Hage, Per. 2003. "The Ancient Maya Kinship System." *Journal of Anthropological Research* 59: 5–21.

Milicic, Boja, and Doug Jones, eds. Forthcoming. *Kinship, Language and Prehistory: Per Hage and the Renaissance in Kinship Studies.* Salt Lake City: University of Utah Press.

A Digression on David Schneider.   The swing away from kinship was heavily influenced by David Schneider as part of his rearguard action against the damaging criticisms from Rodney Needham of Schneider's (and George Homans's) misinterpretation of Lévi-Strauss (see my account of this quarrel, its principles and principals, in *Participant Observer*). Schneider could not accept that he was wrong on the issue of cross-cousin marriage, but because he clearly was, the only tactic open to him was to question the category of "kinship" itself. His tactic was to take the criticism leveled against Morgan, regarding the lack of fit between kinship terminology and biological relatedness, and make this into a case for abandoning the concept of "kinship" altogether. This was greeted with relief and enthusiasm by the hordes of analytically challenged baby boomers flooding into anthropology.

"Kinship" according to Dave (who was something of a trickster and was probably playing a cruel joke on anthropology) is an ethnocentric invention based on European notions of bilateral relatedness anyway. Obviously I disagree with him, but this is not the place to deal with Schneider at length, simply to notice the influence of his ideas on the current refusal to deal with kinship systems as we have traditionally understood them (Schneider 1984). Today most of so-called kinship studies, and a lot of current "cultural anthropology," are products of David Schneider's rearguard action and his intellectual scorched-earth policy.

References
The works of the classical authors mentioned in the text are all available in standard editions. I have not provided references for every author whose work is mentioned. Such comprehensive histories as Voget's (1975) give them all. The following are the works of Morgan cited in the text, other specific items cited, and works on Morgan and the historical background of Victorian anthropology.

Morgan's Works
1843. "Mind or Instinct: An Enquiry concerning the Manifestations of Mind in the Lower Animals." *Knickerbocker* (November and December): 414–420, 507–515.

1851. *League of the Ho-de-nau-sau-nee or Iroquois.* Rochester: Sage and Brother.

1868. *The American Beaver and His Works.* Philadelphia: Lippincott.

1871. *Systems of Consanguinity and Affinity of the Human Family.* Smithsonian Institution, Contributions to Knowledge, vol. 17. Washington, DC: Government Printing Office.

1877. *Ancient Society, or Researches in the Lines of Human Progress from Savagery through Barbarism to Civilization.* New York: Henry Holt.

Other References

Bachofen, J. J. 1861. *Das Mutterrecht.* Stuttgart: Kriese und Haffman.

Boas, Franz. 1896. "The Limitations of the Comparative Method of Anthropology." *Science* 4: 901–908.

Burrow, J. W. 1966. *Evolution and Society: A Study in Victorian Social Theory.* Cambridge: Cambridge University Press; Chicago: Aldine.

Carneiro, R. L. 2003. *Evolutionism in Cultural Anthropology.* Boulder, CO: Westview Press.

Durkheim, Émile, 1915. *The Elementary Forms of the Religious Life.* Trans. Joseph Ward Swain. London: George Allen and Unwin. Originally published as *Les formes élémentaires de la vie religieuse.* Paris: Alcan, 1912.

Eggan, Fred. 1949. *The Social Organization of the Western Pueblos.* Chicago: University of Chicago Press.

———. 1966. "Lewis H. Morgan and the Study of Social Organization." In *The American Indian.* Chicago: Aldine.

Fortes, Meyer. 1969. "Morgan: The Founding Father." In *Kinship and the Social Order.* Chicago: Aldine.

Fox, Robin. 1967. *Kinship and Marriage.* London: Penguin. 2nd ed., New York: Cambridge University Press, 1983.

———. 1994. "The Evolution of Kinship Systems and the Crow-Omaha Question." In *The Challenge of Anthropology.* New Brunswick, NJ: Transaction.

Frazer, James. 1910. *Totemism and Exogamy: A Treatise on Certain Early Forms of Superstition and Society.* London: Macmillan.

Freud, Sigmund. 1952. *Totem and Taboo.* Trans. James Strachey. New York: W. W. Norton. Originally published as *Totem und Tabu.* Vienna: Hugo Heller, 1913.

Goldenweiser, Alexander. 1946. *Anthropology: An Introduction to Primitive Culture.* New York: F. S. Crofts.

Hofstadter, Richard. 1944. *Social Darwinism in American Thought.* Philadelphia: University of Pennsylvania Press.

Krader, Lawrence, ed. 1972. *The Ethnological Notebooks of Karl Marx.* Assen: Van Gorcum.

Kroeber, A. L. 1917. *Zuni Kin and Clan.* Anthropological Papers of the American Museum of Natural History, vol. 18, pt. 2.

Kuper, Adam. 1999. *Culture: The Anthropologists' Account.* Cambridge, MA: Harvard University Press.

Leacock, Eleanor. 1963. Introduction. In L. H. Morgan, *Ancient Society*. Glouces-ter, MA: Peter Smith.

Lévi-Strauss, Claude. 1949. *Les structures élementaires de la parenté*. Paris: Presses Universitaires de France.

Lubbock, John. 1865. *Pre-historic Times: As Illustrated by Ancient Remains, and the Manners and Customs of Modern Savages*. London: Williams and Norgate.

Maine, Henry. 1861. *Ancient Law: Its Connection to the Early History of Society and Its Relation to Modern Ideas*. London: John Murray.

Murdock, G. P. 1949. *Social Structure*. New York: Macmillan.

Reseck, Carl. 1960. *Lewis Henry Morgan: American Scholar*. Chicago: University of Chicago Press.

Schneider, David. 1984. *A Critique of the Study of Kinship*. Ann Arbor: University of Michigan Press.

Stern, Bernard J. 1967. *Lewis Henry Morgan: Social Evolutionist*. New York: Russell and Russell.

Stocking, George W. 1987. *Victorian Anthropology*. New York: Free Press.

Tylor, Edward B. 1871. *Primitive Culture*. London: John Murray.

———. 1878. *Researches into the Early History of Mankind and the Develop-ment of Civilization*. Boston: Eastes and Lauriat.

Voget, Fred. W. 1975. *A History of Ethnology*. New York: Holt, Rinehart and Winston.

White, Leslie A. 1949. *The Science of Culture*. New York: Farrar, Straus.

12. Open Societies and Closed Minds

This chapter is based on "Open Societies and Closed Minds," *Society* 45, no. 3 (May/June 2008), which was a contribution to a symposium on Roger Sandall's *The Culture Cult* and is used here with kind permission of Springer Science and Business Media.

I am grateful to Roger Sandall in particular for comments and help. He sug-gested the subheadings. Note that I dedicated *Conjectures and Confrontations* to Sir Karl Popper and Sir Raymond Firth.

Works of Karl Popper

1934. *The Logic of Scientific Discovery*. London: Hutchinson; New York: Basic Books, 1957. Originally published as *Logik der Forschung*. Vienna: Julius Springer.

1945. *The Open Society and Its Enemies*, vol. 1: *The Spell of Plato*. London: George Routledge and Sons.

1945. *The Open Society and Its Enemies*, vol. 2: *The High Tide of Prophecy: Hegel, Marx and the Aftermath*. London: George Routledge and Sons.

1947. *The Poverty of Historicism*. London: Routledge and Kegan Paul; Boston: Beacon Press.

1963. *Conjectures and Refutations: The Growth of Scientific Knowledge*. London: Routledge and Kegan Paul.

1972. *Objective Knowledge: An Evolutionary Approach*. Oxford: Clarendon Press.

On Popper's work, see:

Schlipp, Paul Arthur, ed. 1974. *The Philosophy of Karl Popper*. 2 vols. Library of Living Philosophers, vol. 14. La Salle, IL: Open Court.

Other References
Again, where a reference is generic—to the totality of an author's work—a specific citation is not given here.

Aarne, A., and S. Thompson. 1961. *The Types of the Folktale*. Helsinki: Suamalainen Tiedeakatemia Academia Scientarum Fennica.

Arnold, Matthew. 1932 [1869]. *Culture and Anarchy*. Ed. J. Dover Wilson. Cambridge: Cambridge University Press.

Benedict, Ruth. 1934. *Patterns of Culture*. Boston: Houghton Mifflin.

Berlin, Isaiah. 1976. *Vico and Herder: Two Studies in the History of Ideas*. New York: Viking Press.

Feuer, Lewis. 1963. *The Scientific Intellectual: The Psychological and Sociological Origins of Modern Science*. New York: Basic Books.

Firth, Raymond. 1929. *Primitive Economics of the New Zealand Maori*. London: Routledge.

Freud, Sigmund. 1952. *Totem and Taboo*. Trans. J. Strachey. New York: W. W. Norton. Originally published as *Totem und Tabu*. Vienna: Hugo Heller, 1913.

Fromm, Eric. 1941. *The Fear of Freedom*. London: Routledge.

Harris, Marvin. 1979. *Cultural Materialism: The Struggle for a Science of Culture*. New York: Random House.

Hobhouse, L. T. 1906. *Morals in Evolution: A Study in Comparative Ethics*. 2 vols. London: Chapman and Hall.

Kroeber, A. L. 1952. *The Nature of Culture*. Chicago: University of Chicago Press.

Lévi-Strauss, Claude. 1949. *Les structures élémentaires de la parenté*. Paris: Presses Universitaires de France.

Lévy-Bruhl, Lucien. 1922. *La mentalité primitive*. Paris: Presses Universitaires de France.

Malinowski, Bronislaw. 1944. *A Scientific Theory of Culture*. Chapel Hill: University of North Carolina Press.

———. 1958. *Magic, Science and Religion, and Other Essays*. Glencoe, IL: Free Press.

Murdock, George P. 1949. *Social Structure*. New York: Macmillan.

Radcliffe-Brown, A. R. 1957. *A Natural Science of Society*. Glencoe, IL: Free Press/Falcon's Wing Press.

Radin, Paul. 1927. *Primitive Man as a Philosopher*. New York: Dover.

Redfield, Robert. 1941. *The Folk Culture of Yucatan*. Chicago: University of Chicago Press.

Russell, Bertrand. 1920. *The Practice and Theory of Bolshevism*. London: Allen and Unwin.

Sandall, Roger. 2001. *The Culture Cult: Designer Tribalism and Other Essays*. Boulder, CO: Westview Press.

Sapir, Edward. 1924. "Culture, Genuine and Spurious." *American Journal of Sociology* 29: 401–429.

Sokal, Alan. 2008. *Beyond the Hoax: Science, Philosophy and Culture*. Oxford: Oxford University Press.

Spengler, Oswald. 1991. *The Decline of the West*. Ed. Arthur Helps and Helmut Werner. Trans. Charles F. Atkinson. New York: Oxford University Press. Originally published as *Der Untergang des Abendlandes*. Munich: C. H. Becksche, 1918–1923.

Steward, Julian. 1963. *Theory of Culture Change: The Methodology of Multilinear Evolution*. Urbana: University of Illinois Press.

Stocking, George. 1996. *Volksgeist as Method and Ethic: Ethnography and the German Anthropological Tradition*. Madison: University of Wisconsin Press.

Tocqueville, Alexis de. 1966 [1835–1840]. *Democracy in America*. Trans. George Lawrence. New York: Harper and Row.

Tylor, E. B. 1871. *Primitive Culture*. London: John Murray.

Westermarck, Edward. 1924. *The Origin and Development of Moral Ideas*. 2 vols. London: Macmillan.

White, Leslie. 1949. *The Science of Culture*. New York: Grove Press.

13. The Old Adam and the Last Man

I should like to thank Kathleen Faraone for helpful observations on the sacred–profane dichotomy. Perhaps this chapter can also be my small memorial to Victor Turner and Mary Douglas for all they have meant to me.

Readers might want to look at the work of Don Beck and the Spiral Dynamics movement, based on the thought of the psychologist Clare W. Graves. With its strain of futuristic utopianism and transcendental uplift, it is perhaps too rich fare for the academy. But in its vertical view of society and its literally colorful attempt to present the stages of social development and show how the past stages remain operative in the present (in both individuals and societies) and how this helps to explain current sociocultural differences, there is much that is close to the spirit of what I am saying. See how they describe Iraq, for example. The best way to access their work is perhaps to start online with www.spiraldynamics.net.

References
Bellah, Robert. 1992. *Broken Covenant: American Civil Religion in a Time of Trial*. Chicago: University of Chicago Press.

Boehm, Christopher. 1999. *Hierarchy in the Forest: The Evolution of Egalitarian Behavior.* Cambridge, MA: Harvard University Press.

Cavalli-Sforza, L. L. 2000. *Genes, Peoples and Languages.* Trans. Mark Seielstad. New York: North Point Press.

Comte, Auguste. 1860 [1830–1842]. *Cours de la philosophie positive.* 3rd. ed. Paris: J. B. Baillière et Fils.

D'Aquili, Eugene D. 1993. "The Myth-Ritual Complex: A Biogenetic Structural Analysis." In James B. Ashbrook, ed., *Brain, Culture and the Human Spirit: Essays from an Emerging Evolutionary Perspective.* Lanham, MD: University Press of America.

D'Aquili, Eugene D., Charles D. Laughlin, and John McManus, eds. 1979. *The Spectrum of Ritual: A Biogenetic Structural Analysis.* New York: Columbia University Press.

Detienne, Marcel. 1996. *Masters of Truth in Archaic Greece.* Trans. Janet Lloyd. New York: Zone Books. Originally published as *Les maîtres de la vérité dans la Grèce archaïque.* Paris: Maspero, 1967.

Douglas, Mary. 1999. *Leviticus as Literature.* Oxford: Oxford University Press.

Fukuyama, Francis. 1992. *The End of History and the Last Man.* New York: Free Press.

———. 1999. *The Great Disruption: Human Nature and the Reconstitution of Social Order.* New York: Free Press.

Laughlin, Charles D., and Eugene G. D'Aquili. 1974. *Biogenetic Structuralism.* New York: Columbia University Press.

Martineau, Harriet. 1896 [1853]. *The Positive Philosophy of Auguste Comte.* New York: George Bell and Sons.

Nietzsche, Friedrich. 1909. *Thus Spake Zarathustra: A Book for All and None.* Trans. Thomas Common. Vol. 4 of *The Complete Works of Friedrich Nietzsche,* ed. Oscar Levy. Edinburgh: T. N. Foulis. Originally published as *Also sprach Zarathustra.* Cheminitz: Ernst Schmeitzner, 1883.

———. 1927. *The Birth of Tragedy from the Spirit of Music.* Trans. Clifton Fadiman. In *The Philosophy of Nietzsche.* New York: Modern Library. Originally published as *Die Geburt der Tragödie as dem Geiste der Musik.* Leipzig: E. W. Fritzsch, 1872.

Smail, Daniel Lord. 2008. *On Deep History and the Brain.* Berkeley: University of California Press.

Taleb, Nassim Nicholas. 2007. *The Black Swan: The Impact of the Highly Improbable.* New York: Random House.

Turner, Victor. 1969. *The Ritual Process: Structure and Anti-Structure.* Chicago: Aldine.

———. 1974. *Drama, Fields and Metaphors.* Ithaca, NY: Cornell University Press.

———. 1983. "Body, Brain, and Culture." *Zygon* 18, no. 3 (September): 221–245. Reprinted in James B. Ashbrook, ed., *Brain, Culture and the Human Spirit: Essays from an Emerging Evolutionary Perspective.* Lanham, MD: University Press of America, 1993.

Warner, W. Lloyd. 1959. *The Living and the Dead: A Study in the Symbolic Life of Americans.* Yankee City Series, vol. 5. New Haven: Yale University Press.

Wells, Spencer. 2002. *The Journey of Man.* Princeton: Princeton University Press.

Wilson, James Q. 1993. *The Moral Sense.* New York: Free Press.

Epilogue

With some changes, "The Dream-Man" is from *The Passionate Mind* (New Brunswick, NJ: Transaction, 2000) and is used here by permission of the publisher. The late Ashley Montagu, having noted the Anglo-Saxon alliterative device, said there in his foreword: "His dream-man is surely Beowulf contemplating Grendel. The human hero looks into himself and sees reflected the reptilian-amphibian thing he is trying to exterminate, but which is part of him—which is part of us all." In deference to my friend's opinion, and in his memory, I have included as an epigraph my own paraphrase of a Beowulf fragment. It is best to read the poem aloud, with four strong stresses (or drumbeats) to each line: "Í wăs ă físh-thĭng flóatĭng shŏal-tĭde séawărds . . ." There should be a crescendo up to the penultimate verse, then a diminuendo until the last line is hissed.

Appendix

Works by Claude Lévi-Strauss

1949. *Les structures élémentaires de la parenté.* Paris: Presses Universitaires de France. Published in English as *The Elementary Structures of Kinship.* Trans. James H. Bell, J. R. von Sturmer, and Rodney Needham. Boston: Beacon Press, 1960.

1963. *Structural Anthropology.* Trans. Claire Jacobson and Brooke Grundfest Schoepfe. New York: Basic Books. Originally published as *Anthropologie structurale.* Paris: Plon, 1958.

On Chaos and Complexity

Argyros, Alexander A. 1991. *A Blessed Rage for Order: Deconstruction, Evolution and Chaos.* Ann Arbor: University of Michigan Press.

Gleick, James, 1987. *Chaos: Making a New Science.* New York: Viking Press.

Kaufman, Stuart. 1993. *The Origins of Order: Self-Organization and Selection in Evolution.* New York: Oxford University Press.

Rescher, Nicholas. 1998. *Complexity: A Philosophical Overview.* New Brunswick, NJ: Transaction.

Acknowledgments

People who helped with individual chapters are recognized in the notes to those chapters. The list of people who have in general inspired and supported me with counsel and friendship is too long to print here. They are acknowledged in these pages and it will be obvious who they are. Some of those to whom I have most reason to be grateful have passed from us: a grim consequence of advancing age. They are remembered in previous books, and here and there in the pages of this one, and of course in its dedication.

Roger Sandall (who figures mightily in Chapter 12) read the manuscript, and I am truly grateful for his wise and witty observations. Bernard Chapais and Stephen Faraone also courageously read the whole manuscript and made valuable suggestions and corrections. I have followed them where I could, always to my advantage. Where I remain stubbornly wrong, it is entirely my own fault. I did take out, on their sound advice, a chapter on the education of "Shakespeare" and the making of the modern world. While relevant to the theme of the Miracle, it somewhat overloaded the text. Should time and temper forge a second chance, it may acquire its own ISBN. In the meantime readers can look at the references in the notes to Chapter 4 and get a flavor of it.

At Harvard University Press I would like to thank Anne Zarrella for all her patience and wisdom through the book's sometimes frustrating evolution. Thanks are due also to Hana Hsu, and to John Donohue and Wendy Nelson as editors, who combined professional high standards with a generous tolerance for eccentricity. Very special thanks to Michael Fisher, who supported the project from an idea to a book and who became a part of it, haikus and all. Let me thank Rutgers University for unfailing support, especially Vice-President Phillip Furmanski and the staff of the Office of Academic Affairs. Also thanks to the faculty and staff of the Department of Anthropology (my home for forty-three years), to everyone at the Center for Human Evolutionary Studies, to Michael Siegel of the Geography department for the maps, and of course to the Scarlet Knights.

Let me add a special thanks to Michael Egan, a friend from my Shakespeare world, who is a constant guide to everything I touch in the humanities and who is editing a Festschrift for me, tentatively titled *The Last Anthropologist* (Edward Mellen Press, 2011).

As always, thanks to *mia famiglia allargata:* my gentle wife, Lin, and her family; my three daughters—Kate, Ellie, and Anne—who continue to amaze me; my now five grandsons; my sons-in-law and their families; and my English cousins and their families in turn. This lively network of consanguinity and affinity teaches me to appreciate the supportive side of tribalism. My newest grandson, Alexander Anthony Fox Maag, was born in the year of Claude Lévi-Strauss's one-hundredth birthday. I am sure this is auspicious. Finally, my warmest thanks again to my friends, the Sandpipers of Sanibel Island, Florida, especially to Charles Reina (who monumentalized DNA) and his ancient racing catboat converted to a gaff-rigged sloop, the *Lunar-C*. They keep me afloat.

Index

Note: page numbers in *italics* indicate figures and maps.

Academic sects, 108–113

Ada, or Ardor: A Family Chronicle (Nabokov), 189–191, *190*

Adapted Mind, The (Tooby and Cosmides), 5

Afghanistan, 80

Africa, 70, 338

Age of Reason, incest in literature of, 165–168

Agriculture. *See* Seafood, growth of social complexity and

Ajami, Fouad, 55, 58, 61–62, 68, 72–73, 74, 80

Ajami, Mansour, 239

Alice Doane's Appeal (Hawthorne), 184

Allen, Nick J., 396–397

Al-Malaki. *See* Malaki, al-

Al-Qaeda. *See* Qaeda, al-

Al-Sadr. *See* Sadar, Muqtadar al-

Alternating-generation kinship, 19–21, *20, 26*

American Beaver and His Works, The (Morgan), 284

American exceptionalism, 30, *59*

Anasazi, 264–265

Ancient Bodies, Modern Lives (Trevathan), 9

Ancient Society (Morgan), 28, 263, 285, 297, 311

Ancient world, incest in literature of, 138–145

Animal dispersion, sects and, 88–93

Anthropology, 282–318; Australian Aborigines, 301–306, *302, 304, 305;* comparative method and development hypothesis, 286–287, 291–292; kinship studies, 296–300, 306–308; Marx, Engels, and Morgan, 312–313; moral advancement question, 288–289; Morgan and, 282–285, 313–315; relation of progress to race and assimilation, 289–291, 294; social development hypothesis, 285–288, 291–296, 315–318; transformation from gentile to political society, 308–312; uniformitarianism assumption, 292–296

Anton, Susan, 92

Antz (film), 45–46

Apocalyptic religions, 25, 29

Aquinas, St. Thomas, 240

Ardrey, Robert, 4

Aresti, Gabriel, 392

Arnold, Matthew, 329

Ashton, John, 97

Aspero (city), 275–277

Atala (Chateaubriand), 29, 168, 169

Atalanta in Calydon (Swinburne), 229–230, 236, 245–246, 248–249, 250

Athens. *See* Greece

Attachment and Loss (Bowlby), 4

Attenborough, Richard, 225

Audacity of Hope, The (Obama), 70
Austen, Jane, 176–177
Australian Aborigines, 13–14, 21, 93, 285, 292–293; marriage classes and, 301–306, *302, 304, 305*
Aztecs, 309

Bachofen, J. J., 296, 308
Bacon, Francis, 37–38, 349
Barak (root), and cousin marriage, 143, *144,* 145
Barash, David, 7
Barth, Frederick, 122–123
Basque rhyme, 391–392
Bate, Jonathan, 252
Bateson, Patrick, 89
Bawden, David, 104
Bear, Greg, 10
Beck, Don, 377
Beer, M., 87
Bell, Daniel, 353
Bellow, Adam, 61
Benchley, Robert, 52
Benedict, Ruth, 265, 268, 351
Beowulf, 199, 205–207, 359
Bergson, Henri, 325, 353
Bible: incest taboo, 139–142; styles of thinking and stages of thought, 347–348. *See also* Creation story; Ten Commandments
Bible and the Ancient Near East, The (Gordon), 123
"Birth of the Seven Gods, The" (Ugarit story), 121
Bischof, Norbert, 89
Black Civilization, A (Warner), 13–14
Black Swan, The (Taleb), 348–350
Blake, William, 163, 385
Bloom, Howard, 88, 378
Boas, Franz, 265, 331, 335
"Body, Brain and Culture" (V. Turner), 345
Boehm, Christopher, 342
Book of Jubilees, 142–143, 172, 173, 191
Book of the Covenant: styles of thinking and stages of thought, 347–348; Ten Commandments, 119–120, 123, 127
Boorman, John, 157
Bowlby, John, 4, 10–11
Bradley, F. H., 45
Bradley, Marion Zimmer, 157
Brain: evolution and structure of, 226–228; trance states and, 345–346

Brazil, 354–355
Bremer, Paul, 72
Brontë, Emily, 177–179, *179,* 181, 191
Brothers and Sisters (Compton-Burnett), 186–188, *187*
Brother–sister incest taboo, 134–135
Brown, Dan, 225
Buddhism, sects in, 100
Burke, Edmund, 355
Burt, Austin, 131
Bush, George H. W., 72
Bush, George W., 59, 73, 75
Byblis, story of, 149–150, 151–152, 170
Byron, George Gordon, Lord, 170–173, 181, 183

Cain: A Mystery (Byron), 172–173
Calusa Indians of southwest Florida, seafood and growth of social complexity and, 261, 269–273, *270, 280*
Camelot. See *Morte D'Arthur, Le*
Campbell, Joseph, 19, 24
Capitalism. *See* Miracle, the
Caral (city), 275–277
Carey, Joyce, 386
Carmina Burana, 240
Carr-Saunders, Alexander, 90, 92
Carter administration, 53
Castle of Otranto (Walpole), 181
Catching Fire: How Cooking Made Us Human (Wrangham), 9
Cavalli-Sforza, Luca, 95, 357
Cenci, The (P. B. Shelley), 173–175, 193
Chagnon, Napoleon, 93, 94
Chanson de Roland, 215–218, *216,* 255
Chaos and complexity theory, 367
Chateaubriand, François-René de, 29, 168–170, 181
Chiasmus, 27
Childe, Gordon, 262
China, 23, 32, 52, 65, 328–329
Christianity: Biblical creation and recreation theme, 125–126; Engels on Socialism and, 84–87; sects in, 103–108
Christie, Agatha, 185
Chronobiology, 26–27
Chronomyopia, 16–18
Chronovores, 9–10
Churchill, Winston, 56, 166
Civilization, use of term, 14
Civilization and Its Discontents (Freud), 39, 320
Civil religion, 354–357

Classical world, incest in literature of, 146–152
Clinton administration, 41–42, 46
Closed Societies. *See* Open Societies
Closing the Ring (film), 225
Codere, Helen, 269
Cohen, Leonard, 254
Communism, 29, 320–321, 324–325, 328, 335. *See also* Marx, Karl
Communitas, structure and, 343–347
"Comparative Ethology of Incest Avoidance" (Bischof), 89
Comparative method, anthropology's development hypothesis and, 286–287, 291–292
"Complaint of Lisa, The" (Swinburne), 231–232
Compton-Burnett, Ivy, 186–188, *187*
Comte, Auguste, 28, 285, 286, 338, 354–357
Conditions of Liberty (Gellner), 81–82
Confucianism, 32
Constitutional monarchy, 60, 165, 320, 355–356
Cool (ahistorical) social structures, 19–24, 25–26
Corkery, Daniel, 241
Corman, Roger, 184
Corporation Man (Jay), 6
Cousins, marriage of, 62–69, *63, 64,* 131, 134–136, *135,* 143, 191–195, 268
Coward, Noel, 253
Creation story, 23–24, 124–125, 142–143, 380–381
Crick, Francis, 244
Crossley-Holland, Kevin, 381
Crow-Omaha systems, 307–308, 365–367
Culture, 26; cultural relativism and superiority of oppressed, 335–338; human rights, 50–51; *Kultur* and, 329–331. *See also* Folk culture
Culture and Conflict in the Middle East (Salzman), 55, 77
Culture Cult, The (Sandall), 320
Curb Your Enthusiasm (television program), 257
Cyclical time, 18–21, *18, 20,* 25, 30

Dante Alighieri, 247–248, 255
D'Aquili, Eugene D., 345, 346
Darwin, Charles, 39, 90, 283, 286, 296, 353
David, Larry, 257

Da Vinci Code, The (Brown), 225
Day Lewis, C., 1, 15, 255, 369
Death and the Right Hand (Hertz), 236
"Death Be Not Proud" (Donne), 232, 258
Defoe, Daniel, 166–167
Democracy, 55–82; motivations for spreading, 57–60; as overcoming, not product of, human nature, 60–62; prospects for foreign promotion of, 70–71; reluctance to accept "stranger's gift" and prospects for, 55–57; trust of strangers in, 62–69; U.S. invasion of Iraq and, 55, 57–62, 67–69, 71–81; West's historical progress toward, 69–70
Detienne, Marcel, 348
Deuteronomy, styles of thinking and stages of thought, 347–348
Development hypothesis, comparative method and, 286–287, 291–292
Diamond, Jared, 262–264
Diffusion coefficient (D), in mammals, 92
"Diffusionists," in anthropology, 291–292
Dilthey, Wilhelm, 330–331
Disabling female. *See* Male bonding
Dispersion, aversion and incest taboo's origins, 128–133
Division of Labour in Society, The (Durkheim), 262
Donne, John, 232–233, 258
"Donne in His Coffin" (F. Turner), 258–259
Donnelly, Jack, 52
Don Quixote (Cervantes), 215
Douglas, Mary, 27, 121–122, 123, 347–348
Dracula (Stoker), 181–185
"Dream-Man, The" (R. Fox), 359–360
Dream Palace of the Arabs, The (F. Ajami), 74
Dreams, rhyme and, 242–244
Duchess of Malfi, The (Webster), 161
Dumont, Louis, 66
Dunbar, Robin, 94, 95, 112
Dune (Herbert), 194
Durkheim, Émile, 66, 262, 330, 338; sacred versus profane, 350–351; social development hypothesis, 285, 289, 293, 310

Eddas, 152, 218, 219
Eggan, Fred, 24, 315
Egypt, 75

Elections: human rights and history of, 60; in Iraq, 71–72, 74, 76; voluntary ceding of power after, 60–61

Elegy on the Vizier Ibn Baqiyya (Ibn al-Anbārī), 239

Elementary Forms of the Religious Life, The (Durkheim), 293

Eliot, George, 180–181, 184, 283

Emigration, sects and dispersion, 91–92

Enchantress of Florence, The (Rushdie), 194

Ending time, 25–28

End of History and the Last Man, The (Fukuyama), 341–343

Endogamy ("marriage in"), 64, 68, 143

Engels, Friedrich, 29, 84–87, 97, 108, 109, 285, 312–313

England, 60, 66, 70

Environment of evolutionary adaptedness (EEA), 4–5, 8–9, 197

Epic and Saga (Gummere), 206

Epigenesis, 11

Erlandson, Jon M., 267, 280–281

Evolutionary medicine, 5

Evolution of Childhood, The (Konner), 11, 19

Excalibur (film), 157

Exogamy ("marriage out"), 64, 68, 133

Eysenck, Hans, 101–102, 104

Fall of the House of Usher, The (Poe), 184–185

Faraone, Stephen, 136

Fascism, 320–321, 324–325, 328, 335

Father–Daughter Incest (Herman), 193

Father–daughter incest taboo, 133–134

Father's brother's daughter marriage, 62–63, *63*, 145, 192

"Faustine" (Swinburne), 255

Ferry, David, 199

Feuer, Lewis, 320

Fielding, Henry, 167–168

Firth, Raymond, 322

Fisher, H. A. L., 25

Fisher, Helen, 222

Fishing, prejudice against, in evolution of social complexity, 263. *See also* Seafood, growth of social complexity and

Fison, Lorimer, 301, 304

Fitzgerald, Edward, 240

Flickering Lights (film), 225

Florida. *See* Calusa Indians of southwest Florida

Folk culture, 331–333; cultural relativism, multiculturalism, and superiority of oppressed, 335–338; leftward movement of, 333–335. *See also Volksgeist*

Folklore in the Old Testament (Frazer), 119–120

Forbidden Partners: The Incest Taboo in Modern Culture (Twitchell), 176

Ford, John, 161–162

Foreigner's Gift, The (F. Ajami), 55

Foreign policy, human rights and national interest and, 51–54. *See also* Democracy

"Forsaken Garden, A" (Swinburne), 246

Fostering, 202, 223

Four Feathers, The (film), 225

Fox, Kate, 256

France, 62, 65, 70

Frankenstein (M. Shelley), 182

Franks, Thomas, 104

Fraser, J. T., 27, 373

Frazer, James, 28, 35, 119–120, 296, 338

Free-trade advocates, democracy and, 58–59

Freud, Sigmund, 39–40, 97, 243, 320, 323, 325; *Hamlet* and, 159–160; incest taboo and Oedipus complex, 146–147; incest taboo's origins and, 129, 132–133

Friedrich, Paul, 139

Fukuyama, Francis, 16, 65, 341–343, 346, 352–354, 375

Gandhi, Mohandas Karamchand, 56, 71, 257

Gaunt, William, 86

Gellner, Ernest, 31–32, 75, 81–82

Genes in Conflict (Burt and Trivers), 131

Genesis, Lot and incest taboo, 139–141

Genetic drift, 89

Genius of the Beast, The (Bloom), 88

Germany, 66, 70

Ghana, 70

Gift, The (Mauss), 265

Gilbert, W. S., 235

Gilgamesh, story of, 199–201

Göbekli Tepe ("Navel Hill"), 278–279, 281, 394

Godfather, The (Puzo), 65, 225

Godwin, William, 181

Goethe, Johann Wolfgang von, 16, 183, 357–358

Golden Bough, The (Frazer), 120
Golding, William, 185–186, 369
Gordon, Cyrus, 121, 123, 124, 125
Great Disruption, The (Fukuyama), 352
Great Expectations (Dickens), 244
Greece, 309–311, 313, 325–326, 327, 339
Grosby, Steven, 123
Group selection, 90–91
Gummere, Francis, 206
Guns, Germs, and Steel (Diamond), 262–264

Hage, Per, 397
Hamburg, David, 5
Hamilton, William, 90, 110
Hamlet (Shakespeare), 158–160, 183
Handbook of Denominations in the United States (F. S. Mead and Hill), 103, 105
Hardy, Thomas, 386
Hare and the Tortoise, The (Barash), 7
Harnad, Stevan, 373
Harries, Owen, 375
Harris, Jack, 33
Havelock, Eric, 242
Hawthorne, Nathaniel, 184
Haywood, John, 262, 265
Hebrews. *See* Jews and Judaism; Ten Commandments
Hegel, G. W. F., 25, 286, 330, 335, 352
Herbert, Frank, 194, 369
Herder, Johann, 331
Herman, Judith, 193
Herr Vogt (Marx), 85
Hertz, Robert, 236
Hidden Ireland, The (Corkery), 241
High-trust societies, 66
Hill, Samuel S., 103, 105
Hinduism, sects in, 99–100
Hirsi Ali, Ayaan, 80–81, 327
Historical Atlas of Ancient Civilization (Haywood), 262
History of British Socialism, A (Beer), 87
History of Europe, A (H. A. L. Fisher), 25
Hobhouse, L. T., 286, 289, 338
Homo Britannicus (Stringer), 281
Homosexuality, male bonding and question of, 221–223
Hopi Indians, 36, 364–365, *365*
Horse's Mouth, The (Carey), 386
Hot (historical) social structures, 24–25, 29

"Hounds of Spring, The" (Swinburne), 246–247, 255
Hughes, Ted, 244, 352
Human rights, 41–54; culture and, 50–51; foreign policy and national interest, 51–54; natural selection and reproductive struggle, 46–49; political rights, inclusive fitness, and surrender of power of revenge, 42–46
Human sects: dispersion and, 92–97; personality types and, 101–103; religious, 97–101, 103–108
"Human zoo," 6
Hume, David, 27
Hunt, Leigh and Shelley, 181
Hussein, Saddam, 58, 68, 73
Huxley, Julian, 5
"Hymn to Persephone" (Swinburne), 230

Ibn al-Anbārī, 239
Ibn Khaldûn, 77, 84, 114, 123
Iliad, The (Homer), 199, 207–210, 223, 242
Imperial Animal, The (Tiger and R. Fox), 11
"I'm Your Man" (Cohen), 254
Incest: animal dispersion and reproduction, 89; aversion, dispersion, and taboo's origins, 128–133; kindred, affinity and, 133–136. *See also* Incest, in literature
Incest, in literature, 136–138, 191–195; in Age of Reason, 165–168; in ancient world, 138–145; in classical world, 146–152; in Middle Ages, 152–158; in modern era, 183–195; in Renaissance, 158–164; in Romantic era, 168–176, 191; in Victorian era, 176–183
Inclusive fitness, 43–45, 51
India, 56, 70, 71
Individual selection, 90–91
Inferno (Dante), 247–248, 255
Infidel (Hirsi Ali), 80–81, 327
Ingalls, Daniel, 239
In Praise of Nepotism (Bellow), 61
Inspector Lewis (television program), 194
"Intercession" (Swinburne), 233–234
Iran, 75, 76–77, 81
Iraq, 55; expectations of democracy in short time, 61–62; motivations for U.S. invasion of, 57–60; respect for kinship and prospects for democracy, 62, 67–69, 81; tribalism and prospects for democracy, 71–81

Iroquois, Morgan and, 283–285, 299–300, 307–308, 309
Irruption, sects and, 91–92, 105–108
Isis and Osiris myth, incest and, 138–139
Islam, 79, 84, 98–99, 326–327, 328, 329, 352
Italy, 65, 70. *See also* Rome

Jainism, 24, 32
James, William, 26
Japan, 66
Jay, Antony, 6, 94
Jaynes, Julian, 373
"JEDP" controversy, 380
Jefferson, Thomas, 101, 103, 353
Jensen, Anders Thomas, 225
Jesperson, Otto, 18, 21
Jesus Christ Superstar (Lloyd Webber), 225
Jews and Judaism: Bible as record of transformation from tribe to nation, 114–115; law and marriage, 145; sects, 99. *See also* Ten Commandments
Jones, Ernest, 158, 160
Jude the Obscure (Hardy), 386
Jung, Carl, 346

Kenya, 70
Keresan-speaking Indians, 307, 364–365
Khayyám, Omar, 239–240
Khulman, George, 84
Kindly Ones, The (Little), 194
Kinsella, Thomas, 203
Kinship: affinity and, 133–136; kinship atom, 134–135, *134;* kinship structures, 19–24, *20, 26;* kinship studies, 296–308, 314–315; respect for and prospects for democracy, 62, 67–69, 81
Kinship and Marriage (R. Fox), 312, 315–316
Knickerbocker magazine, 284
Konner, Melvin J., 7–8, 11, 19
Korea, 65
Kroeber, A. L., 307, 335
Kuhn, Thomas, 108
Kultur, 329–331
Kurds, 71
Kuwait, 52

"Lament for Art O'Leary" (anonymous), 241
Langer, Suzanne, 347
Language groups, human dispersion and sects, 93–95, *96*

Last Man and First Man, 341–358; civil religion, 354–357; communitas and structure, 343–347; contrasted, 342; end of history and, 341–343; human nature and human action, 357–358; rules of order, 350–354; social trends and extrapolation, 348–350; styles of thinking and stages of thought, 347–348
Latin America, 70
Laughlin, Charles D., 345
Law of the Neural Line, 237–238
Lawrence of Arabia (film), 68, 78
Leacock, Eleanor, 292
League of the Ho-de-no-sau-nee or Iroquois, The (Morgan), 283, 285, 309
Lebanon, 73
Lebor na hUidre, 202
Lectures on the Industrial Revolution (Toynbee), 32
Lehrer, Tom, 253
Lévi-Strauss, Claude, 1–2, 10, 67, 128, 323, 345, 348; kinship, 134, 314–315; time, 19, 24, 26, 34–35, 36, 363
Leviticus, styles of thinking and stages of thought, 347–348
Leviticus as Literature (Douglas), 347–348
Levitin, Daniel, 241
Lévy-Bruhl, Lucien, 35, 323
Liberal democratic society. *See* Last Man and First Man
"Life Is Too Short" (R. Fox), 228
Linear time, 21–24, *22*
Linguistics, 282, 288, 316
Little, Jonathan, 194
Lloyd Webber, Andrew, 194
Longevity. *See* Chronovores
Lore and Language of Schoolchildren, The (Opie and Opie), 253
Lot and daughters, incest taboo and, 139–141
Low-trust societies, 65–66
Lubbock, John, 287–288, 290, 299

Macey, Samuel, 32
Macfarlane, Alan, 66
Magnússon, Eiríkr, 152
Maimonides, 120–121
Maine, Henry, 66, 285, 296, 310, 338
Making of the Modern World, The (Macfarlane), 66
Malaki, al-, government in Iraq, 69, 74, 75
Male bonding, 196–197; enduring nature of, 225; questions of homosexuality,

221–223; tension with heterosexual bonding, 197–199, 223–224. *See also* Male bonding, in literature

Male bonding, in literature: *Beowulf,* 199, 205–207; *Chanson de Roland,* 215–218, 216; Gilgamesh story, 199–201; the *Iliad,* 199, 207–210, 223; *Le Morte D'Arthur,* 199, 210–215, 211, 213, 223; *Táin Bó Cualinge,* 202–205; *The Volsunga Saga,* 199, 218–221, 219, 223, 224

Malinowski, Bronislaw, 322, 330

Malory, Sir Thomas, 156–158, 156, 199, 210–215, 211, 213, 223

Manfred (Byron), 170–172

Mansfield Park (Austen), 176–177

Manufacture of Evil, The (Tiger), 6, 12

Man Who Would Be King, The (film), 225

Marriage: Australian Aborigines, 301–306, 302, 304, 305; freedom of choice and "human rights," 47–48; kinship studies and growth from promiscuity to, 296–300; "marriage in" (endogamy), 64, 68, 143; "marriage out" (exogamy), 64, 68, 133. *See also* Cousins, marriage of

Martineau, Harriet, 354

Marx, Karl, 31, 66, 85, 285; Morgan's work and, 28, 29, 309, 312–313

Masks of God: Oriental Mythology, The (Campbell), 24

Master and Commander (O'Brian), 225

Matilda (M. Shelley), 181

Mauss, Marcel, 265

Mayans, 24; cosmology 381; poetics, 389–390

McLennan, John, 299, 308

Mead, Frank S., 103, 105

Mead, Margaret, 336

Melville, Herman, 184

Men in Groups (Tiger), 197, 198

Mental Traveller, The (Blake) 385

Metamorphoses (Ovid), 148–152, 193, 381

Middle Ages, incest in literature of, 152–158

Millay, Edna St. Vincent, 391

Mill on the Floss, The (Eliot), 180–181, 184, 283

Milton, John, 162–164

Miracle, the: cost of, 352; origin of term, 2; time and, 31–34. *See also* Last Man and First Man

Mists of Avalon, The (film), 157

Mitchison, Graeme, 244

Modern era, incest in literature of, 183–195

Modern Synthesis, The (Huxley), 5

Moieties, 35; marriage classes and, 301–306, 302, 304, 305

Moll Flanders (Defoe), 166–167

Moncrieff, Hope, 215, 216

Monetary credit, societal trust and, 65–66

Monod, Jacques, 11

Monogamy, 49

Montagu, Ashley, 404

Moral development, anthropology and question of, 288–289

Moral Sense, The (J. Q. Wilson), 353

Morgan, Lewis Henry, 66, 275, 280, 331, 343; background, influence, and legacy of, 282–285, 313–315; kinship studies, 296–300, 306–308; kinship studies and Australian Aborigines, 301–306; Marx and, 28, 29, 309, 312–313; relation of progress to race and assimilation, 290–291; social development hypothesis, 263, 285–288, 291–292, 294–296, 315–318; transformation from gentile to political society, 308–312

Morris, Desmond, 6

Morris, William, 86, 152

Morte D'Arthur, Le (Malory): incest, 156–158, 156; male bonding, 199, 210–215, 211, 213, 223

Moseley, Michael, 265

Moynihan, Daniel Patrick, 53–54

Multiculturalism, superiority of oppressed and, 335–338

Multi-level selection (MLS), 91

Munday, Anthony, 215

Muqaddimah, The (Ibn Khaldûn), 123

Murdock, G. P., 314–315

Murdock, Iris, 185

Music, verse and, 245–246

Mutterrecht, Das (Bachofen), 296

Myrrha, story of, 150–152

Myth, contemplation of time and, 18, 19

Nabara, The (Lewis), 255

Nabokov, Vladimir, 189–191, 190

National Institute for Health and Clinical Excellence (NICE), 10

Natural selection, human rights and reproductive struggle, 46–49

Needham, Rodney, 398

Neolithic Paradox, 36, 260

Nepotism, 48–49, 70
New Great Reform Act, A (Jay), 6
New Oxford Annotated Bible, 127
New World: A Proclamation of the Kingdom of the Spirit on Earth, The (Khulman), 84
Nietzsche, Friedrich, 341, 351
Nigeria, 70
Norte Chico of Peru, seafood and growth of social complexity and, 261, 273–278, 274, 280
Northwest coast of America tribes, seafood and growth of social complexity, 261, 265–269, 266, 280
Novel environment hypothesis (NEH), 4
Novum Organum (Bacon), 37, 349

Obama, Barack, 70, 333, 357
O'Brian, Patrick, 225
Oedipus Rex (Sophocles), 146–148, 148, 155, 194
Okeechobee, Lake, ceremonial mounds around, 271–272
On Deep History and the Brain (Smail), 31, 351
"On the Sands" (Swinburne), 250
Open Societies, 319–340; cultural relativism, multiculturalism, and superiority of oppressed, 335–338; culture and *Kultur,* 329–331; fragility of, 320–322; leftward movement of folk culture, 333–335; Popper and tribalism, 322–325, 329, 336; uncertainty and appeal of Closed Society, 325–329; universities' role and, 339–340; *Volksgeist,* 331–333
Open Society and Its Enemies, The (Popper), 322
Opie, Iona and Peter, 253
Optimum number, theory of, 90
Orwell, George, 30, 326
Ovid (Publius Oviduis Naso), 148–152, 193, 381
Owen, Robert, 87
Owen, Wilfred, 255

Pacific Northwest. *See* Northwest coast of America tribes
Pakistan, 75
Pane Lingua (Aquinas), 240
Paradise Lost (Milton), 162–164
Parker, Eli (Hasanoanda), 284–285
Parsinia (Byron), 183

Parsons, Talcott, 67
Patience (Gilbert), 235
Patriarchs of Time, The (Macey), 32
Patterns of Culture (Benedict), 265
Pavlov, Ivan, 101–102
Peregrinus Proteus, 84
Perfectibility, time and rise from savagery and, 28–31
Peru. *See* Norte Chico of Peru
Petraeus, David, 62, 76
Phantom of the Opera, The (Lloyd Webber), 194
Phèdre (Racine), 183
Philosophy of Grammar, The (Jesperson), 18
Piaget, Jean, 256, 323
Pierre: Or the Ambiguities (Melville), 184
Pinsky, Robert, 248, 255
Planck, Max, 108, 113
Plato, 326
Poe, Edgar Allen, 181, 184–185
Poetic Edda, 381
Polanyi, Karl, 67
Political rights, human rights, inclusive fitness, and surrender of power of revenge, 42–46
Polygamy/polyandry, right to, 49
Polynesia, 23
Popol Vuh, 381, 390
Pöppel, Ernst, 237, 238, 257
Popper, Karl, 30, 39, 66; narrative fallacy and, 349, 350; Open versus Closed Societies, 320–321, 338–339; science and error, 319–320; tribalism and Open Society, 322–325, 329, 336; uncertainty and appeal of Closed Society, 325–329
Positivist Church, 354
Potlatch, 265, 268–269
Pottery: of Calusa, 271–272: Morgan and, 275
Power, voluntary ceding of, after elections, 60–61
Pre-Raphaelite Dream, The (Morris), 86
Presidential system, 60–61, 355
Primitive Culture (Tylor), 28
Primitive Economics of the New Zealand Maori (Firth), 322
Primogeniture, 69
"Prince Tudor" theory, 378
Principles of Psychology, The (James), 26
Procreation, right to, 49

Progressive and cumulative time, 24–25
Protestant Ethic and the Spirit of Capitalism, The (Weber), 32
Protestantism: the Miracle and, 32, 36–37; sects in, 105
Psychology of Politics, The (Eysenck), 101–102
Pueblo Indians, 36, 307–308, 363–364, 365
Purity and Danger (Douglas), 121–122
Puzo, Mario, 65

Qaeda, al-, in Iraq, 73–74, 75–76

Race, relationship of progress to, 289–291, 294
Racine, 183
Racing Tribe, The (K. Fox), 256
Radcliffe-Brown, A. R., 330, 366
Ragnarok, 380–381
Reciprocal altruism, 95, 223
Redfield, Robert, 66, 310, 338
Renaissance, incest in literature of, 158–164
Renan, Ernst, 84
René (Chateaubriand), 168–170
Reproduction: animal dispersion and sects, 89; human rights and natural selection, 46–49
Researches into the Early History of Mankind and the Development of Civilization (Tylor), 287
Revenge, power of, surrendered to state, 43–45, 79
Revolt of Islam, The (P. B. Shelley), 175–176
Rhyme, 226–259; brain structure and evolution, 226–228; death, breath, and Swinburne, 228–237; dreams, memory, and, 242–244; importance of rules to, 255–258; Law of the Neural Line and, 237–238; meter and rhyme in history, 238–242; music of verse, 245–246; rules and comic verse, 252–255; sound, sense, and rhyme, 248–252; translation issues, 246–248
Rick, Torben C., 267, 280–281
Ring composition, 27–28
Ring des Nibelungen, Der (Wagner), 152–153, 154–156, *155*
Rivers, W. H. R., 314
Roman Catholic Church, sects in, 103–105
Romantic era, incest in literature of, 168–176, 191

Rome, 309–311, 313
Rousseau, Jean-Jacques, 29, 355
Rubaiyat (Khayyám), 239–240
Rule of 150, 93, 94, 95
Rushdie, Salman, 194
Russell, Bertrand, 38
Russia, 70

Sadr, Muqtadar al-, 76
Sahlins, Marshall, 94
Salomé (Wilde), 182–183
Salzman, Philip, 55, 77–78, 79, 81
Sandall, Roger, 320–321, 327, 329–330, 335, 337
Sanderson, Judith E., 127
Sanskrit Poetry (Ingalls), 239
Savage, use of term, 14
Savage Mind, The (Lévi-Strauss), 1–2, 10, 34–35
Savagery: perfectibility, time, and rise from, 28–31; Popper and Open Society, 322–325
Sayers, Dorothy L., 217–218
Schneider, David, 398
Science: error and, 319–320; sects and, 108–113
Science of Culture, The (White), 314–315
Scientific time, 36–40
Scope of Anthropology, The (Lévi-Strauss), 19
Scorpion God, The (Golding), 185–186
Seafood, growth of social complexity and, 260–281; Calusa Indians of Southwest Florida, 261, 269–273, *270*, 280; correlates of emergence of civilization, 261–265; Göbekli Tepe and, 278–279, 281; Norte Chico of Peru, 261, 273–278, *274*, 280; Northwest coast of America tribes, 261, 265–269, *266*, 280
Sects and sectarianism, 83–113; academic and scientific sects, 108–113; animal dispersion, 88–93; Christianity and Socialism, 84–88; human dispersion, 92–97; human sects, personality types and, 101–103; human sects, religious, 97–101, 103–108
Secular time, the Miracle and, 31–34
Seinfeld (television program), 256–257
Serial monogamy, 49
Severed Head, A (Murdoch), 185
Shakespeare, William, 158–160, 183
Shelley, Mary, 181, 182

Shelley, Percy Bysshe, 173–176, 181, 193
Shia tribes, 72–74, 76
Shinto, sects in, 101
Sister exchange, 134–136, *135*
Sitwell, Edith, 97, 235; on Alexander Pope, 390
Slant (Bear), 10
Sleeping Murder (Christie), 185
Smail, Daniel, 31, 351
Smith, J. E., 87
Smith, W. Robertson, 120
Snow, Charles, 191
Social contract, 43–45
Social Darwinism, 3, 28, 287
Social development hypothesis, in anthropology, 263, 285–288, 291–296, 315–318
"Social evolutionism," 286
Socialism, Engels on Christianity and, 84–87
Social Life in the Reign of Queen Anne (Ashton), 97
Social Organization of the Western Pueblos, The (Eggan), 315
Social Structure (G. P. Murdock), 314–315
Sociology, anthropology's development hypothesis and, 285–288
Sokal, Alan, 336
Somalia, 23, 80–81, 327
Sophocles, 146–148, 155, 194
South Africa, 70
Southey, Robert, 215
Sparta, 325–326, 327, 339
Spencer, Herbert, 28, 31, 58, 66, 283–284, 285, 310, 338
Spiral Dynamics movement, 402
Steklis, Dieter, 373
Steward, Julian, 262, 263, 265
Stocking, George, 330
Stoker, Bram, 181–185
Strangers: democracy and trust of, 62–69; reluctance to accept gifts from, 55–57; slowness of extension of rights to, 41
Strangers and Brothers (Snow), 191
Stringer, Chris, 280, 281
Structural Anthropology (Lévi-Strauss), 363
Structure of Scientific Revolution, The (Kuhn), 108
Structures élémentaires de la parenté, Les (Lévi-Strauss), 314–315
Study of Swinburne (Welby), 251
Sumner, William Graham, 67

Sunni tribes, 71, 74, 75
Swift, Jonathan, 97, 369
Swinburne, Algernon Charles, 254, 255, 257; death rhymes and, 228–237; music of verse of, 245–246; sound, sense, and rhyme of, 248–252
Switzerland, 60
Syndicalism, 87
Systems of Consanguinity and Affinity of the Human Family (Morgan), 285, 297

Taboos. *See* Ten Commandments
Táin Bó Cualinge, 202–205, 242
Taleb, Nassim Nicholas, 348–350
Tale of a Tub, A (Swift), 369
Tamar and Amnon incest taboo, 141–142
Taoism, sects in, 101
Technicians of the Sacred (Rothenburg), 389
Tedlock, Dennis, 381, 390
Ten Commandments, 114–127; anthropological explanations of taboos in, 120–122; Book of the Covenant and, 119–120, 123, 127; creation and recreation theme, 124–126; in current law and life, 126–127; familiar version, 115–116; moralistic versus ritualistic versions, 116–120; origins of Hebrews and, 123–124
Tense, time and, 18, *18,* 27
Tetradic theory, 308, 396
Theory of Culture Change (Steward), 262, 263, 265
Theory of the Leisure Class (Veblen), 265
Thinking in Circles (Douglas), 27
This Is Your Brain on Music (Levitin), 241
Thomas, Edward, 252
Thus Spake Zarathustra (Nietzsche), 341
Tierney, John, 62
Tiger, Lionel, 6, 11, 12, 197, 198, 221
Time, notions of causality and, 16–40; chronomyopia, 16–18; communitas, 344; cyclical time, 15, 18–21, *18, 20,* 30; ending time, 25–28; fundamentals of logical thinking, 34–36; linear time, 21–24, *22;* the Miracle and secular time, 31–34; perfectibility and rise from savagery, 28–31; progressive and cumulative time, 24–25; scientific time, 36–40; transitional time, 363–367, *364, 365*

'Tis Pity She's a Whore (Ford), 161–162
Tocqueville, Alexis de, 257, 329
Tom Jones (Fielding), 167–168
Tönnies, Ferdinand, 66, 67, 289, 310, 338
Totemism (Lévi-Strauss), 10, 35
Toynbee, Arnold, 32, 340
Trance states, 345–346
Transitional time, 363–367, *364, 365*
Translation, rhyme and, 246–248
Trevathan, Wenda, 9
Tribal, use of term, 15
Trivers, Robert, 131, 198, 223
Trust (Fukuyama), 65
Turner, Fred, 237, 238, 257, 258, 389
Turner, Victor, 343–347, 402
Twitchell, James, 176, 181
Tylor, Edward B., 28, 35; social development and anthropology, 285, 287, 290, 295, 330, 338

Uniformitarianism, anthropology and assumption of, 292–296
United Nations, 53–54, 357
United States, 60
Universal Human Rights in Theory and Practice (Donnelly), 52
Universities, Open versus Closed Societies and, 339–340
Usher, Archbishop, 23

Veblen, Thorstein, 265, 268
Veyne, Paul, 222
Victorian era, incest in literature of, 176–183
Volksgeist, 331–333
Volsunga Saga, The: incest, 152–156, *153, 155,* 191; male bonding, 199, 218–221, *219,* 223, 224
Voting rights. *See* Elections

Wagner, Richard, 152–153, 154–156, *155,* 199, 218–221, *219,* 223, 224
Wallace, Alfred Russel, 94
Walpole, Horace, 181
Walter, Alex, 145
Warner, W. Lloyd, 13–14
Warrior epics. *See* Male bonding
Watching the English (K. Fox), 256
Weber, Max, 31–32, 37, 67, 88, 310, 326
Webster, John, 161
Welby, T. Earle, 251
Wells, Spencer, 357–358
Westermarck, Edward, 130–132, 145, 286, 289, 296, 338
Whisperings Within, The (Barash), 7
White, Leslie, 314–315
Wilde, Oscar, 182–183
Wilhelm Meisters Lehrjahre (Goethe), 183
Wilson, Edward O., 12
Wilson, James Q., 353
Winson, Jonathan, 242, 243
Wittfogel, Karl, 264
Wordsworth, William and Mary, 181
Wrangham, Richard, 9
Wright, Sewall, 89
Wuthering Heights (Brontë), 177–179, *179,* 191
Wynne-Edwards, V. C., 90, 91

Yanomamo: The Fierce People (Chagnon), *93,* 94
Yeats, W. B., 254
Yellow Book of Lecan, The, 202
Yugoslavia, 52

Zulaika, Joseba, 392
Zuni, 36, 307, *364–365*
Zuni Kin and Clan (Kroeber), 307